'Can't you just leave the past buried, it won't hurt anyone then?'

'Mum, it's already hurt people. It's hurt you and me and Nan, all of us . . .'

In 1982 Sally Morgan travelled back to her grandmother's birthplace. What started out as a tentative search for information about her family, turned into an overwhelming emotional and spiritual pilgrimage. Sally Morgan and her family were confronted with their own suppressed history, and with fundamental questions about their identity.

My Place begins with Sally Morgan tracing the experiences of her own life, growing up in suburban Perth in the fifties and sixties. Through the memories and images of her childhood and adolescence, vague hints and echoes begin to emerge, hidden knowledge is uncovered, and a fascinating story unfolds – a mystery of identity, complete with clues and suggested solutions.

Sally Morgan's *My Place* is a deeply moving account of a search for truth, into which a whole family is gradually drawn; finally freeing the tongues of the author's mother and grandmother, allowing them to tell their own stories.

My Place is a powerful autobiography of three generations, by a writer with the gift for language of a born story-teller. Sally Morgan has produced a beautifully crafted book; at once a work of great humour, humanity, poignancy and courage.

. . . as compelling and as impossible to put down as a detective story . . . it is deeply informed with life and truth – Nancy Keesing.

. . . compulsive reading . . . richly colloquial and often very funny – Elizabeth Riddell.

Sally Morgan was born in Perth, Western Australia, in 1951 and grew up in suburban Manning. She completed a Bachelor of Arts degree at The University of Western Australia in 1974, majoring in Psychology. She also has post-graduate diplomas from the Western Australian Institute of Technology (now Curtin University of Technology) in both Counselling Psychology and Computing and Library Studies. She is married with three children.

As well as writing, Sally Morgan is also establishing a reputation as an artist. She has works in numerous private collections and in the Australian National Gallery, Canberra, and the Dobell Foundation Collection. *My Place* was her first book, and upon publication it immediately achieved best-seller status. Her second book, *Wanamurraganya,* was published to wide acclaim in 1989.

Cover painting by Sally Morgan (Photographed by Victor France).

My Place

Sally Morgan.

My Place

SALLY MORGAN

FREMANTLE ARTS CENTRE PRESS

First published 1987 by
FREMANTLE ARTS CENTRE PRESS
193 South Terrace (P.O. Box 320), South Fremantle
Western Australia, 6162.

*Reprinted 1987 (three times). Mass paperback edition published
February 1988. Reprinted 1988 (four times). 1989 (four times).
1990 (three times). 1991 (twice), 1992 (twice), 1993.*

Consultant Editor B.R. Coffey.
Designed by Susan-Eve Barrow Ellvey.

Typeset in 11/11 pt Clearface by Typestyle, Perth, Western Australia
and printed by McPherson's Printing Group, Victoria.

National Library of Australia
Cataloguing-in-publication data

Morgan, Sally, 1951-
   My Place.

   ISBN 0 949206 31 8.

   1. Morgan, Sally, 1951-. 2. Aborigines, Australian —
   Biography. 3. Aborigines, Australian — Women — Biography.
   4. Aborigines, Australian — Social life and customs. I. Title.

994'.0049915

To My Family

How deprived we would have been
if we had been willing
to let things stay as they were.
We would have survived,
but not as a whole people.
We would never have known
our place.

ACKNOWLEDGEMENTS

The author wishes to acknowledge the Aboriginal Arts Board of the Australia Council and the Australian Institute of Aboriginal Studies for their financial assistance with the preparation of this book.

Some of the personal names included in this book have been changed, or only first names have been included, to protect the privacy of those concerned.

The Fremantle Arts Centre Press creative writing programme is assisted by the Literature Board of the Australia Council, the Australian Federal Government's arts funding and advisory body.

Fremantle Arts Centre Press receives financial assistance from the Western Australian Department for the Arts.

CONTENTS

Chapter One

THE HOSPITAL

The hospital again, and the echo of my reluctant feet through the long, empty corridors. I hated hospitals and hospital smells. I hated the bare boards that gleamed with newly applied polish, the dust-free window-sills, and the flashes of shiny chrome that snatched my distorted shape as we hurried past. I was a grubby five-year-old in an alien environment.

Sometimes, I hated Dad for being sick and Mum for making me visit him. Mum only occasionally brought my younger sister and brother, Jill and Billy. I was always in the jockey's seat. My presence ensured no arguments. Mum was sick of arguments, sick and tired.

I sighed in anticipation as we reached the end of the final corridor. The Doors were waiting for me again. Big, chunky doors with thick glass insets in the top. They swung on heavy brass hinges, and when I pushed in, I imagined they were pushing out. If it weren't for Mum's added weight, which was considerable, I'd have gone sprawling every time.

The Doors were covered in green linoleum. The linoleum had a swirl of white and the pattern reminded me of one of Mum's special rainbow cakes. She made them a cream colour with a swirl of pink and chocolate. I thought they were magic. There was no magic in The Doors, I knew what was behind them.

Now and then, I would give an awkward jump and try to peer through the glass and into the ward. Even though I was tall for my age, I never quite made it. All I accomplished was bruises to my knobbly knees and smudged finger-marks on the bottom of the glass.

Sometimes, I pretended Dad wasn't really sick. I imagined that I'd walk through The Doors and he'd be smiling at me. 'Of course I'm not sick', he'd say. 'Come and sit on my lap and talk to me.' And Mum would be there, laughing, and all of us would be happy. That was why I used to leap up and try and look through the glass. I always hoped that, magically, the view would change.

Our entry into the ward never failed to be a major event. The men there had few visitors. We were as important as the Red Cross lady who came around selling lollies and magazines.

'Well, *look* who's here', they called.

'I think she's gotten taller, what do ya reckon, Tom?'

'Fancy seeing you again, little girl.' I knew they weren't really surprised to see me; it was just a game they played.

After such an enthusiastic welcome, Mum would try and prompt me to talk. 'Say hello, darling', she encouraged, as she gave me a quick dig in the back. My silences were embarrassing to Mum. She usually covered up for me by telling everyone I was shy. Actually, I was more scared than shy. I felt if I said anything at all, I'd just fall apart. There'd be me, in pieces on the floor. I was full of secret fears.

The men on the ward didn't give up easily. They continued their banter in the hope of winning me over.

'Come on sweetie, come over here and talk to me', one old man coaxed as he held out a Fantail toffee. My feet were glued to the floor. I couldn't have moved even if I'd wanted to. This man reminded me of a ghost. His close-cropped hair stood straight up, like short, white strands of toothbrush nylon. His right leg was missing below the knee, and his loose skin reminded me of a plucked chicken. He tried to encourage me closer by leaning forward and holding out two Fantails. I waited for him to fall out of bed; I was sure he would if he leant any further.

I kept telling myself he wasn't really a ghost, just an Old Soldier. Mum had confided that all these men were Old Soldiers. She lowered her voice when she told me, as though it was important. She had a fondness for them I didn't understand. I often wondered why Old Soldiers were so special. All of these men were missing arms or legs. Dad was the only one who was all there.

I tried not to look directly at any of them; I knew it was rude to stare. Once, I sat puzzling over a pair of wooden crutches for ages and Mum had been annoyed. I was trying to imagine what it would be like being lopsided. Could I get by with only one of my monkey legs or arms? That's what I called them. They weren't hairy, but they were long and skinny and I didn't like them.

I found it hard to comprehend that you could have so many parts missing and still live.

The Old Soldier rocked back on his pillow and I sneaked a quick glance at Dad. He was standing in his usual spot, by the side of his bed. He never came forward to greet us or called out like the other men did, and yet we belonged to him. His dressing-gown hung so loosely around his lanky body that he reminded me of the wire coat-hangers Mum had hanging in the hall cupboard. Just a frame, that was Dad. The heart had gone out of him years ago.

Once Mum finished having a little talk and joke with the men, we moved over to Dad's bed and then out onto the hospital verandah.

The verandahs were the nicest place to sit; there were tables and chairs and you could look over the garden. Unfortunately, it took only a few minutes for the chairs to become uncomfortable. They were iron-framed, and tacked onto the seat and across the back were single jarrah slats painted all colours of the rainbow. When I was really bored, I entertained myself by mentally rearranging the colours so they harmonised.

As Mum and Dad talked, I sniffed the air. It was a clear, blue spring day. I could smell the damp grass and feel the coolness of the breeze. It was such an optimistically beautiful day I felt like crying. Spring was always an emotional experience for me. It was for Nan, too. Only yesterday, she'd awakened me early to view her latest discovery. I had been in a deep sleep, but somehow her voice penetrated my dreams.

'Sally . . . wake up . . .' Even as I dreamt, I wondered where that voice was coming from. It was faint, yet persistent, like the glow of a torch on a misty night. I didn't want to wake up. I burrowed deeper under the mound of coats and blankets piled on top of me. In my dream, they were heavy and lacking in warmth. I wrapped my hands around my feet in an attempt to warm them. Sometimes, I thought coldness and thinness went together, because I was both.

Every night I'd call out, '*Mum* . . . I'm cold'. And then, to speed her up, '*Mum . . . I'm freezing!!*'.

'Sally, you can't possibly be.' It was often her third trip to my bedside. She'd lift up the coat I'd pulled over my head and say, 'If I put any more on you, you'll suffocate. The others don't want all these coats on them.' I shared a bed with my brother Billy and my sister Jill. They never felt the cold.

I'd crane my head over the moulting fox-fur collar that trimmed one of the coats and retort, 'I'd rather suffocate than freeze!'.

Nan had only to add, 'It's a terrible thing to be cold, Glad', for Mum to acquiesce and pull out the older, heavier coats hanging in the hall cupboard.

Now, sitting on the hospital verandah, I smiled as I remembered the way Nan had rocked my sleepy body back and forth, in an attempt to wake me up. It took a few minutes, but I finally came up for air and murmured dopily, 'What is it? It's so early, Nan, do ya have to wake me so early?'

'Ssh, be quiet, you'll wake the others. Don't you remember, I said I'd wake you early so you could hear the bullfrog again, and the bird?'

The bullfrog and the bird, how could I have forgotten. For the whole week Dad had been in hospital, she'd talked of nothing else.

Nan encouraged me out by peeling back the layers on top of me. I lay temporarily in a tight, curled ball. The underneath of me was warm, but, with all my coats and rugs removed, the top of me was rapidly chilling. With sudden decision, I leapt from my bed and shivered my body into an old red jumper. Then, barefoot, I followed Nan out onto the back verandah.

'Sit still on the steps', she told me. 'And be very quiet.' I was used to such warnings. I knew you never heard anything special unless you were very quiet. I rubbed my feet together for warmth and tried to shrug the rest of me into my misshapen red jumper. I pulled my hands up inside my sleeves, wrapped my arms around my legs, and waited.

The early morning was Nan's favourite time of the day, when she always made some new discovery in the garden. A fat bobtail goanna, snake tracks, crickets with unusual feelers, myriads of creatures who had, for their own unique reasons, chosen our particular yard to reside in.

I wanted spring to last for ever, but it never did. Summer would come soon and the grass would yellow and harden, even the carefully nurtured hospital grass wouldn't look as green. And the giant nasturtiums that crowded along our side fence and under our lemon tree would disappear. I wouldn't hunt for fairies any more, and Nan wouldn't wake me so early or so often.

I'd heard the bullfrog yesterday, it was one of Nan's favourite creatures. She dug up a smaller, motley brown frog as well, and, after I inspected it, she buried it back safe in the earth. I shivered as an early morning breeze suddenly gusted up between my bare legs. I expected the bullfrog to be out again this morning. I gazed at the patch of dark earth where I'd last seen him. He'll come out any minute, I thought.

I felt excited, but it wasn't the thought of the bullfrog that excited me. This morning, I was waiting for the bird call. Nan called it her special bird, nobody had heard it but her. This morning, I was going to hear it, too.

'Broak, Broak!' The noise startled me. I smiled. That was the old bullfrog telling us he was broke again. I looked up at the sky, it was a cool, hazy blue with the promise of coming warmth.

Still no bird. I squirmed impatiently. Nan poked her stick in the dirt and said, 'It'll be here soon'. She spoke with certainty.

Suddenly, the yard filled with a high trilling sound. My eyes searched the trees. I couldn't see that bird, but his call was there. The music stopped as abruptly as it had begun.

Nan smiled at me, 'Did you hear him? Did you hear the bird call?'

'I heard him, Nan', I whispered in awe.

What a magical moment it had been. I sighed. I was with Dad now, there was no room for magic in hospitals. I pressed my teeth together and, resting my chin on my chest, I peered back at Mum and Dad. They both seemed nervous. I wondered how long I'd been day-dreaming. Mum reached over and patted Dad's arm.

'How are you feeling, dear?' She was always interested in how he was feeling.

'How do ya bloody well think!' It was a stupid question, he never got any better.

Pelican shoulders, I thought, as I watched him hunch forward in his chair. The tops of his shoulders poked up just like a pelican's. I wondered if mine were the same. I craned my head to look. Yep. Pretty much the same; my elbows were pointy, too. Dad and I had a lot in common.

Dad's fingers began to curl and uncurl around the arms of his chair. He had slim hands for a man. I remembered someone saying once, 'Your father's a clever lad'. Was that where I got my ability to draw from? I'd never seen Dad draw or paint, but I'd seen a letter he'd written once, it was beautiful. I knew he'd have trouble writing anything now, his hands never stopped shaking. Sometimes, I even had to light his cigarettes for him.

My gaze moved from his hands, up the long length of his arms, to his face. It dawned on me then that he'd lost more weight, and the realisation set my heart beating quickly. Dad caught my gaze; he was paler and the hollows under his cheek-bones were more defined. Only the familiar hazel eyes were the same, confused, wet, and watching me.

'I'm making you something', he said nervously. 'I'll go and get it.' He disappeared into the ward and returned a few minutes later with a small, blue, leather shoulder-bag. There was maroon thonging all the way around, except for the last part of the strap, which wasn't quite finished. As he laid it quietly in my lap, Mum said brightly, 'Isn't Daddy clever to make that for you?'. I stared at the bag. Mum interrupted my thoughts with, 'Don't you like it?'.

I was trapped. I mumbled a reluctant yes, and let my gaze slip from the bag to the large expanse of green grass nearby. I wanted to run and fling myself on the grass. I wanted to bury my face so Dad couldn't see. I wanted to shout, *'No!* I don't think Daddy's clever. *Anyone* could have made this bag. *He* doesn't think it's clever, either!'

By the time I turned back, Mum and Dad were both looking off into the distance.

'Can we go now, Mummy?' I started guiltily. Had I really said that? My eyes widened as I waited for their reaction. Then I noticed that they weren't even looking at me, they were both staring at the grass. I breathed a slow, undetectable sigh of relief. The last time I had voiced that question out loud, Mum had been cross and embarrassed, Dad silent. He was silent now. Such sad, sad eyes.

The visitors bell rang unexpectedly. I wanted to leap up. Instead, I forced myself to sit still. I knew Mum wouldn't like it if I appeared too eager. Finally, Mum rose, and while she gave Dad a cheery goodbye, I slowly prised myself from my chair. The backs of my legs must have looked like a crosswalk, I could feel the indentations the hard slats had made in my skin.

As we walked into the ward, the men called out.

'What? Leaving already?'

15

'You weren't here for long, little girl.'

The Old Soldier with the Fantail smiled. He still held the lollies in his hand. They all made a great show of waving goodbye, and just as we passed through The Doors and into the empty corridor, a voice called, 'We'll be waiting for you next time, little girl'.

Strong, cool air blew through the window all the way home in the bus. I kept thinking, can a person be wrinkled inside? I had never heard adults talk about such a thing, but that's how I felt, as though my insides needed ironing. I pushed my face into the wind and felt it roar up my nostrils and down into my throat. With cold ruthlessness, it sought out and captured my reluctant inside wrinkles, and flung them onto the passing road. I closed my eyes, relaxed and breathed out. And then, in a flash, I saw Dad's face. Those sad, silent eyes. I hadn't fooled him. He'd known what I'd been thinking.

Dad came home for a while a couple of weeks after that, and then, in the following January, 1957, Mum turned up on the doorstep with another baby. Her fourth. I was really cross with her. She showed me the white bundle and said, 'Isn't that a wonderful birthday present, Sally, to have your own little brother born on the same day as you?'. I was disgusted. Fancy getting that for your birthday. And I couldn't understand Dad's attitude at all. He actually seemed pleased David had arrived!

Chapter Two

THE FACTORY

Mum chattered cheerfully as she led me down the bitumen path, through the main entrance to the grey weatherboard and asbestos buildings. One look and I was convinced that, like The Hospital, it was a place dedicated to taking the spirit out of life.

After touring the toilets, we sat down on the bottom step of the verandah. I was certain Mum would never leave me in such a dreadful place, so I sat patiently, waiting for her to take me home.

'Have you got your sandwich?' she asked nervously when she realised I was staring at her.

'Yeah.'

'And a clean hankie?'

I nodded.

'What about your toilet-bag?'

'I've got it.'

'Oh.' Mum paused. Then, looking off into the distance, she said brightly, 'I'm sure you're going to love it here.'

Alarm bells. I knew that tone of voice, it was the one she always used whenever she spoke about Dad getting better. I knew there was no hope.

'You're gunna leave me here, aren't ya?'

Mum smiled guiltily. 'You'll love it here. Look at all the kids the same age as you. You'll make friends. All children have to go to school someday. You're growing up.'

'So what?'

'So, when you turn six, you have to go to school, that's the law. I couldn't keep you home even if I wanted to. Now don't be silly, Sally, I'll stay with you till the bell goes.'

'What bell?'

'Oh . . . they ring a bell when it's time for you to line up to go into your class. And later on, they ring a bell when it's time for you to leave.'

'So I'm gunna spend all day listenin' for bells?'

17

'Sally', Mum reasoned in an exasperated kind of way, 'don't be like that. You'll learn here, and they'll teach you how to add up. You love stories, don't you? They'll tell you stories.'

Just then, a tall, middle-aged lady, with hair the colour and shape of macaroni, emerged from the first class-room in the block.

'May I have your attention please?' she said loudly. Everyone immediately stopped talking. 'My name is Miss Glazberg.'

From my vantage point on the bottom step, I peered up slowly at her long, thick legs and under her full skirt. Mum tapped me on the shoulder and made me turn around. She thought I was curious about far too many things.

'The bell will be going shortly', the tall lady informed the mothers, 'and when that happens I want you to instruct your children to line up in a straight line on the bitumen playground. I hope you heard that too, children, I will be checking to see who is the straightest. And I would appreciate it if the mothers would all move off quickly and quietly after the children have lined up. That way, I will have plenty of time to settle them down and get to know them.'

I glared at Mum.

'I'll come with you to the line', she whispered.

The bell rang suddenly, loudly, terrifyingly. I clutched Mum's arm.

Slowly, she led me to where the other children were beginning to gather. She removed my hands from her arm but I grabbed onto the skirt of her dress. Some of the other mothers began moving off as instructed, waving as they went. One little boy in front of me started to cry. Suddenly, I wanted to cry, too.

'Come now, we can't have this', said Miss Glazberg as she freed Mum's dress from my clutches. I kept my eyes down and grabbed onto another part of Mum.

'I have to go now, dear', Mum said desperately.

Miss Glazberg wrenched my fingers from around Mum's thigh and said, 'Say goodbye to your mother'. It was too late, Mum had turned and fled to the safety of the verandah.

'Mum', I called as she mounted the last wooden step, *'Mum!'*.

She turned quickly and waved, falling badly on the top step as she did so. I had no sympathy for her wounded ankle, or for the tears in her eyes.

'Mum!' I screamed as she hobbled off. *'Come back!'*

Despite the urgings of Miss Glazberg to follow the rest of the children inside, I stood firmly rooted to the bitumen playground, screaming and clutching for security my spotted, plastic toilet-bag and a Vegemite sandwich.

By the beginning of second term at school, I had learnt to read, and was the best reader in my class. Reading opened up new horizons for me, but it also created a hunger that school couldn't satisfy. Miss Glazberg

18

could see no reason for me to have a new book when the rest of the children in my class were still struggling with the old one. Every day, I endured the same old adventures of Nip and Fluff, and every day, I found my eyes drawn to the back of the class where a small library was kept.

I pestered Mum so much about my reading that she finally dug up the courage to ask my teacher if I could have a new book. It was very brave of her. I felt quite proud, I knew she hated approaching my teacher about anything.

'I'm sorry, darling', Mum told me that night, 'your teacher said you'll be getting a new book in Grade Two'.

There weren't many books at our house, but there were plenty of old newspapers, and I started trying to read those. One day, I found Dad's plumbing manuals in a box in the laundry. I could work out some of the pictures, but the words were too difficult.

Towards the end of second term, Miss Glazberg told us there was going to be a night when all the parents came to school and looked at our work. Then, instead of our usual sheets of butcher's paper, she passed out clean, white rectangles that were flat on one side and shiny on the other. I gazed in awe at my paper, it was beautiful, and crying out for a beautiful picture.

'Now children, I want you all to do your very best. It has to be a picture of your mother and your father, and only the very best ones will be chosen for display on Parents' Night.'

There was no doubt in my mind that mine would be one of the chosen few. With great concentration and determination, I pored over my page, crayoning and detailing my parents. I kept my arm over my work so no one could copy. Suddenly, a hand tapped my shoulder and Miss Glazberg said, 'Let me see yours, Sally'. I sat back in my chair.

'Ooh, goodness me!' she muttered as she patted her heart. 'Oh, my goodness me. On no, dear, not like that. Definitely not like that!'

Before I could stop her, she picked up my page and walked quickly to her desk. I watched in dismay as my big-bosomed, large-nippled mother and well equipped father disappeared with a scrunch into her personal bin. I was hurt and embarrassed, the children around me snickered. It hadn't occurred to me you were meant to draw them with clothes on.

By the beginning of third term, I had developed an active dislike of school. I was bored and lonely. Even though the other children talked to me, I found it difficult to respond.

Dad didn't seem to be very interested in my schooling, either. He never asked me how I was going or whether I had any problems. In fact, the closest contact Dad had with my education was a brutal encounter with my black print pencil.

I was sitting on our old velvet lounge, sharpening the pencil for school, and, just when I decided I was satisfied with its razor-sharp tip, Dad strolled in and bent down to sit on the arm of my chair. Without thinking, I stood my pencil pointy-end upwards and watched as blue buttocks descended. On contact, Dad leapt up in pain and swore loudly. As he swung around, I waited for him to belt me. To my utter surprise, all he could manage to do was splutter, 'Go to your room!'.

'Why on earth did you do it, Sally?' Mum asked as she escorted me down the passage that led from the lounge-room to the bedroom I shared with Jill and Billy. I didn't really know. Curiosity about cause and effect, I guess.

I was allowed certain privileges now I was at school. The best one was being allowed to stay up later than the others and share Dad's tea. He loved seafood. He had a drinking mate with a boat, and if there was a good catch, crayfish came our way. Fleshy, white crayfish and tomato dipped in vinegar, that was Dad's favourite meal. At first, I hated the taste of vinegar, but I gradually grew accustomed to it. I was careful not to eat a lot, I knew how much Dad enjoyed crays. It was a happy time then, crays and tomato, Dad and me.

I knew some of Dad's tastes were a legacy of the war. That particular one from the time Italian partisans had sheltered him from the Germans. I knew all about the war. Dad had told me about his friends Guiseppe and Maria, and their daughter Edmea. He'd taught me to sing the Communist anthem in Italian. I thought I was very clever being able to sing in another language.

We had some good times, then. Some nights, Dad would hide chocolates in the deep pockets of his overalls and we were allowed to fish them out. Sometimes, he'd laugh and joke, and when he swore, we knew he didn't really mean it.

Dad slipped in and out of our lives. He was often in hospital for periods of a few days to a month or so, and the longest he was at home at one time was about three months; usually, it was a lot less. When he first came home from hospital, he would be so doped up with drugs he wasn't able to communicate much. Then, he would seem to be all right for a while, but would rapidly deteriorate. He stayed in his room, drinking heavily, and didn't mix with us at all. And soon, he was back in hospital again.

Dad was a plumber by trade, but, when he was at home, he was often out of work. Every time he returned from hospital, he had to try and find another job. Mum provided the only steady income, with various part-time jobs, mostly cleaning.

When Dad was happy, I wished he'd never change. I wanted him to be like that for ever, but there was always the war. Just when things seemed to be looking up, it would intrude and overwhelm us. The war had never ended for Dad. He lived with it day and night. It was a strange thing, because he'd told me how important it was to be free, and I knew that Australia was a free country, but Dad wasn't free. There were things in his head that wouldn't go away. Sometimes, I had the impression that if he could have got up and run away from himself, he would have.

Part of the reason I was so unhappy at school was probably because I was worrying about what was happening at home. Sometimes, I was so tired I just wanted to lay my head on my desk and sleep. I only slept well at night when Dad was in hospital; there were no arguments, then.

I kept a vigil when Mum and Dad argued, so did Nan. I made a secret pact with myself. Awake, I was my parents' guardian angel; asleep, my power was gone. I was worried that, one night, something terrible might happen and I wouldn't be awake to stop it. I was convinced I was all that lay between them, and a terrible chasm.

Some nights, I'd try and understand what they were arguing about, but, after a while, their voices became indistinguishable from one another, merging into angry abandonment. It was then I resorted to my pillow. I pulled it down tightly over my head and tried to drown out the noise.

I was grateful Dad didn't belt Mum. Although, one night, he did push her and she fell. I'd been allowed to stay up late that night, and was squatting on the kitchen floor and peering around the door jamb to see what had happened. Mum just lay in a crumpled heap. I wondered why she didn't get up. I peered up at Dad, he was so tall he seemed to go on for ever. He ran his hand back through his hair, looked down at me, and groaned. Swearing under his breath, he pushed roughly past Nan and staggered out to his room on the back verandah. I felt sorry for Dad. He hated himself.

Nan hurried into the hall and hovered over Mum. As she helped her up, she made sympathetic noises. Not words, just noises. I guess that's how I remember Nan all those early years — hovering, waiting for something to happen.

I sat on the kitchen floor a few minutes longer, then I crept quietly into Mum's room. I pressed my back up against the cool plaster wall, and watched as Nan made a great show of tucking in the rugs around her. Nan's eyes were frightened, and her full bottom lip poked out and down. I often saw it like that. Otherwise, she wasn't one to show much emotion.

I tried to think of something to say that would make things all right, but my lips were glued together. Finally, Nan said, 'If you haven't got anything to say, go to bed!' I fled.

Chapter Three

I'M IN THE ARMY NOW

The task of enrolling another member of our family in school the following year fell once again to Mum. I was pleased Jill was starting school, I felt sure I would not be so lonely with her there.

As we joined the small groups of children and parents walking to school that morning, I watched Jill curiously. She seemed neither excited nor daunted by the prospect of being away from home. I put her calmness down to ignorance, and felt sure that, once our walk led us within sight of school, Jill would break down.

'Hasn't the school got a lovely garden, Jilly?' Mum commented as we rounded the last corner and approached the entrance.

'Yeah, we've got roses like that.'

I narrowed my eyes and looked at her, not a tear in sight. Oh well, I thought, wait till it's time for Mum to leave, then it'll be on.

Mum deposited me at the door of my new class, then, taking Jill's hand, she said, 'Come on, I'll show you the toilets'.

'Are you coming, Sally?' Jill asked.

'Naah, saw 'em last year. Ask Mum to show ya the boys' toilets, I've never been in there.'

'Don't be stupid, Sally, Jilly doesn't want to see the boys' toilets.'

'Yes I do!'

I watched as, a few minutes later, Jill emerged from her tour of the toilets.

'What do I do now?' she asked as she trotted up the verandah to me.

'Aah, ya have to wait for the bell. That's your class down there. Go and sit with Mum on the step, she'll be with you till the bell goes, but she won't be here all day.'

'Okay.' I scanned her face. Poor kid, I thought, it hasn't sunk in yet.

Jill walked back and plopped down on the verandah step. I watched as Mum smiled at her in exactly the same way she'd smiled at me the previous year. Jill grinned back. Mum had actually convinced her she was going to like school. She was so gullible, sometimes.

Within a few minutes, the bell was ringing loudly. Mum waved and began moving off. I was shocked when Jill calmly took her place in the queue that was forming at the front of her class.

Just before Mum disappeared completely from sight, I saw her cast an anxious glance towards the Grade One line. Now, Jill, now! I thought. It was the perfect moment. For some reason, Jill sensed my interest, and turned and waved happily to me. I groaned in despair. She was obviously dumber than I'd suspected. 'Mum's going now!' I called out, but she was too busy chatting to the boy in front of her to reply.

I watched with a mixture of envy and surprise as she continued talking to the other children. They were all strangers to her, and yet she seemed to fit in, somehow. I knew then that, when it came to school, Jill and I would never agree.

My day-dreaming was suddenly interrupted by a deep, grumbly voice calling, 'You girl, you with the long plaits, come here and pay attention'. I felt so embarrassed. I'd been so busy watching Jill that I'd failed to notice my class-mates had also formed a line.

My new teacher began slowly walking down the line, carefully inspecting each of her forty charges. 'Don't slouch. Stomach in, chest out, chin up!' She tapped my chin lightly with her wooden ruler. I attempted to follow her instructions, but found myself leaning so far backwards, I nearly fell over.

We moved quietly into class and the presence of each one of us was duly recorded in the roll book. When that was finished, our teacher drew herself up to her full flat-chested height of five foot eleven inches and said, 'I . . . am Miss Roberts'. Apart from her pause after the word 'I', she spoke quickly and very, very clearly.

'Now children, I . . . am going to hand out some reading books. You will all remain as quiet as mice while I'm doing this. Then we will check to make sure you have all brought the things you were supposed to bring.'

I smiled to myself, it wasn't going to be so terrible after all, my new book was on its way.

I waited expectantly as Miss Roberts walked first down one row and then another. By the time she finally reached my desk, I was practically brimming over with excitement. She placed my book on my desk, and I couldn't help groaning out loud. It seemed that Dick, Dora, Nip and Fluff had somehow managed to graduate to Grade Two.

In a way, I felt sorry for them. None of them lived near a swamp, and there was no mention of wild birds, snakes or goannas. All they ever did was visit the toy shop and play ball with Nip. I resigned myself to another year of boredom.

There was no comparison between Miss Roberts and my Grade One teacher. If Mum had felt awkward about approaching Miss Glazberg, she was positively terrified when it came to Miss Roberts.

'Has Miss Roberts ever been in the army, Mum?' I asked her one afternoon.

'What a strange question, whatever makes you ask that?'

'Well, sometimes she acts like a man.'

'When?'

'When we line up for school. She won't let us in the class unless we're all straight and stiff. She pokes you in the stomach and says, "Stomach in, chest out, eyes forward". Dad told me they do that to you in the army.'

Mum laughed, it was obvious she thought I was exaggerating again. However, the following week, she confided to me over tea that it seemed Miss Roberts had, indeed, been in the women's army. One of the cleaners at the school had told her. I found this information very interesting. Dad often talked about the army. He'd been too much of a non-conformist to take naturally to army life. Now, I understood how he felt. I didn't like being told what to do, either.

From then on, whenever I marched into class, I would silently sing an old army ditty Dad had taught me.

> *I'm in the army now*
> *I went to milk a cow*
> *the cow let-off and I took off*
> *I'm out of the army now!*

Jill, Billy and I loved rude songs. We often marched around the yard singing that one. Billy beat on his old tin drum and Jill and I pretended to blow army trumpets. I could play reveille, too. By placing a piece of paper tightly over a comb and blowing on it, I could produce a high pitched, farty sort of sound that I could then manipulate into a recognisable tune. I learnt to play many tunes on the comb, but reveille was my favourite.

Towards the end of first term, I had an encounter with Miss Roberts that wiped out any confidence I might have had for the rest of the year.

Our school seats comprised a heavy metal frame, with jarrah slats spaced across the seat and back. This proved unfortunate for me, because one day, after what seemed hours of holding my arm in the air trying to attract Miss Roberts' attention, I was unable to avoid wetting myself.

Miss Roberts had been intent on marking our latest tests and had failed to notice my desperately flailing arm. But one of the clean, shiny-haired, no-cavity girls next to me began to chant quietly, 'You've wet ya pa-ants, you've wet ya pa-ants!'.

'I have not', I denied hotly, 'it's just water under my chair'.

'Oh yeah, well then, how come you've dumped all those hankies on it?' She had me there.

By this time, most of the surrounding children were starting to giggle.

24

Miss Roberts raised her horn-rimmed eyes and said firmly, '*Quiet* please!'. She stared at us a few seconds longer, obviously waiting for her eagle-like gaze to have its usual effect. When the last giggle was giggled, she pushed back her solid wooden chair, breathed deeply and said: 'I . . . have an announcement to make'.

We were very impressed with Miss Roberts' use of the word 'I'. For the whole term, I had been convinced Miss Roberts was even more important than the headmistress.

'I . . . have finished marking your test papers.' There was complete silence after this statement. Under Miss Roberts' reign, our weekly tests had assumed great importance. We all waited anxiously to hear who had missed the mark this time.

'I . . . must commend you all on your efforts. All, except Rrrodney.' She always rolled her R's when she said Rodney. You'd think he was her favourite with the amount of attention she gave him. In fact, the opposite was true, Rodney could do nothing right.

'Rrrodney', she continued, 'how many times have *I* told you bottom is spelt b-o-t-t-o-m *not* b-u-m!'.

Rodney grinned, and we all snickered, but were instantly checked by Miss Roberts' look of disgust. She disliked anything even slightly earthy. I had a grudging admiration for Rodney. He'd been spelling bottom like that for three weeks now. He was my kind of person.

'Now', she said, in a way that made us all straighten up and give full attention, 'where is Sally, hmmmn?'. Resting her chin on her neck, she peered around the class in an attempt to locate my non-descript brown face amongst a sea of forty knowing smiles. 'Oh, there you are, dear.' I had been cowering behind the girl in front of me, with my hands stuffed between my legs in an attempt to prevent further trickles.

'Sally has, for the *first* time this year, managed to complete her test correctly. In fact, this week she is the only one to have done so.' Pausing, she allowed time for the greatness of my achievement to sink in. Everyone knew what was coming next, and, mistaking the smothered raspberries and giggles for eagerness, she said: 'Well, come on Sally. Come out to the front and hold up your book. I . . . can tell the class is anxious to see your work.'

Miss Roberts waited patiently as I rose carefully to my feet. I hurriedly twisted the wet part of my dress around as far as I could, holding it tightly bunched in my left hand. With my knees locked together, and my left elbow jutting out at an unusual angle behind my back, I jerked spasmodically forward. Fortunately, Miss Roberts was gazing in amazement at my test book, and so was not confronted with the sight of my contorted body.

'I . . . want you to hold it up to the class so they can all see it. Look how eager they are to see a test that has scored one hundred per cent!'

Clutching my book in my right hand, I leant as far from Miss Roberts as possible, lest she smell my condition.

My misshapen body must have alerted her to the fact that something was wrong, because she snapped impatiently, 'Hold the book with two hands! And put your dress down, we are not interested in seeing your pants!'

A wave of giggling swept over the class. As I patted down the full skirt of my blue cotton dress, Miss Roberts' large, sensitive nostrils flared violently, and she snorted in disgust.

Grasping me by the elbow, she hauled me back to my desk and, pointing to the offending puddle, demanded, 'And *where* have all those handkerchiefs come from?'. Flinging back the lid of my desk, she shrieked: 'Oh no! There are more in here!'. I felt so embarrassed. It was obvious she didn't know what to attack first, my pile of dirty handkerchiefs nestled near my overflowing jar of pencil shavings, my collection of hardened orange peel, or my old apple core turned brown and on the brink of mould.

Shaking her head in disbelief, she muttered, 'You dirty, dirty girl'. She dragged me back to the front of the class and shoved me out the door.

'Out you go, you are not to enter this class again. You sit out there and dry off!'

I sat alone and wet on the hard jarrah bench.

My attitude towards school took an even more rapid downhill turn after that incident. I felt different from the other children in my class. They were the spick-and-span brigade, and I, the grubby offender.

Chapter Four

DRINKING MEN

Things at home weren't getting any better, either. Dad was drinking more than he was eating, he was very thin.

He had stopped even trying to get work, and was in hospital more than he was at home. Gone were the days when he used to bring fluffy baby chickens home for us to play with. There was a time when he couldn't go past a pet shop window without buying half a dozen little chickens for us. He still lived in his favourite blue overalls, but he never hid tiny Nestles milk chocolates in the deep pockets any more. He only hid himself, now. When he was home, he never came out of his room. The only thing he seemed interested in was the pub.

Our local pub was called the Raffles; it was situated on the banks of the Swan River, and had a Mediterranean outlook. Dad was popular at the Raffles. There was a huge group of returned soldiers who drank there. It was like a club. Give Dad a few beers down the Raffles with his mates and he was soon in another world. He forgot about us and Mum, and became one of the boys.

We kids often went to the pub with Dad. While he enjoyed himself in the bar, we sat, bored and forgotten, in the car.

Summer was worst. Dad always wound the windows up and locked what doors were lockable in case anyone should try to steal us. He forbade us ever to get out the car. These precautions meant that on hot summer's nights, we nearly suffocated.

One summer's evening, I could stand it no longer, Dad had been gone for ages, and I'd given up all hope of him returning with some bags of potato chips. Somehow, the sweet, clean smell of the Swan River managed to penetrate our glass and metal confines. Like the wisp of a cloud on a misty night, it floated around my shoulders and head, beckoning me to come.

'Let's go play down the river', I said suddenly. 'Dad's not going to bring us any chips. He won't notice we've gone.'

'We're supposed to stay in the car', Jill said as she eyed me doubtfully. Two terms at school and she was a real stickler for convention.

'Look Jill, there's no use hanging around, hoping he'll turn up with something. He's forgotten about us again. I'm going whether you come or not.'

The thought of a paddle was too much for Billy, who leapt out with me. Jill followed, reluctantly. We wound our way quickly through the crowded car-park and down to the sandy foreshore. We splashed and laughed and built sand-castles decorated with bits of seaweed and stick.

Just as we were constructing an elaborate moat, a tall figure loomed above the beach.

'What the bloody hell are you kids doing down here. I told you to stay in the car.' Dad advanced menacingly, and we froze.

Suddenly, I yelled, 'Well what did ya expect us to do, sit in the car all night? You've been gone for ages *and* ya didn't give us any chips!' I stopped abruptly, my mouth wide open. Where had my sudden bravery come from? I often had vehement thoughts, but I generally kept them to myself. Now I'd done it.

Fortunately, Dad was as surprised as me. He stopped and stood looking down at us. His gaze took in three haphazard sand-castles, and the beginning of an elaborate irrigation system. Without another word, he ushered us quietly to the car and took us home.

The following night, I stayed home with Mum. I'd decided the chances of procuring a packet of chips were too slim. Billy and Jill insisted on going with Dad. 'They'll be in for another boring time', I told Mum as we waved them goodbye.

Dad was home early that night. He was furious. Apparently, Jill had become so bored she'd gone hunting for Dad in the public bar. Someone had put her up on the counter and said, 'All right, who owns this one?'. It was so unlike Jill and, in Dad's eyes, an unforgivable sin. The pub was his domain. He felt she'd shown him up in front of his mates.

My father's brothers were great drinkers, too, and proud of it. The only one who seemed different was Uncle John; he was a lot younger than Dad, and we kids quite liked him. He always had a joke with us and never drank as much as the others.

Even apart from our relations, we seemed surrounded by drinking men. There wasn't one of Dad's mates who was a teetotaller. I was always amazed at how much a good man could drink. In fact, drinking seemed to be the main hobby of everyone we mixed with. Dad's mates, mostly ex-servicemen, didn't tend to bring their wives to our place. But the few women who were included could generally hold their own when it came to drink.

I remember only one occasion when Grandpa actually came to our house to help out in a practical way. There were some tall gums that grew close to the house and Dad wanted them chopped down. He said they were a fire hazard. Grandpa volunteered to help him. I sat on the back steps of the verandah and watched as they both climbed high into the trees. I was sorry to see the gums go. They were tall and beautiful and I'd seen maggies nesting in them.

'Righto, Pop', Dad called as he positioned his saw. 'You get that branch on your side and I'll tackle this one here.'

'Righto, Bill.' Grandpa was sweating like a pig and hadn't had a drink for at least half an hour.

'Jeez, I could do with a cold one, Bill', he muttered as he sawed away.

Suddenly, there was a crack and then a splitting noise, followed by a scream. Grandpa, and the branch he was sitting on, crashed to the ground. Dad dropped his own saw and climbed down, shouting, 'Not the branch ya sitting on, ya stupid bastard!'.

For the rest of the afternoon, Dad worked alone. Grandpa sat inside, recuperating and drinking beer. By the time Dad drove him home, he was too drunk to feel any pain.

Dad's family often came to our place for Christmas lunch. Actually, I always found the two days before Christmas more exciting. Mum and Nan cooked cakes and puddings, gave the house a real good clean, and prepared the stuffing for the chickens. I was really excited, because we only ate chicken once a year, and I loved it.

On the twenty-fourth of December, Dad would stride to the chook shed, armed with the axe. He always looked really determined, and I would sit and think that maybe this year he'd do it. About ten minutes would pass, and then he'd stride back again, with a clean axe and no chooks. War had spoilt him for killing anything. He'd walk past me and hand the axe to Nan, who'd be patiently waiting on the back verandah. 'Jeez, I can't do it Dais, you'll have to.'

It wasn't a task Nan relished. She had a special relationship with the birds and chooks we kept, but she knew we were too poor to be able to consider her finer feelings. Within a few minutes, she'd be back with two limp chooks and a bloody axe. 'Come on Sal, time to gut.'

She'd spread newspaper over an old table we had on the back verandah, and we'd set to work. I liked pulling out the feathers, because I was keen to collect those. Jill would walk past and eye us both in disgust. Sometimes, to scare her, I'd thrust a bloodied arm in her direction, and she'd scream and run inside to Mum.

'Aah, she's got no guts.'

'Well these chooks have, you get on with your work and leave poor Jilly alone!'

One Christmas, Grandpa told us all about the history of his family. 'Aah, yes', he sighed as he downed another cold one, 'the Milroy men have always been great gamblers and drinkers'.

I watched curiously as he brushed a tear from his eye. Give Grandpa a few beers and he'd cry over anything.

'In the early days, we were quite well off. Had a business in Albany, coffee palace it was. By jeez, you could make a few bob then with all the bastards that were comin' into the country. As soon as the sailing ships docked, all the owners of boarding-houses, pubs, you name it, would rush down to the harbour to try and capture the trade."Come to my place", one of them would call. "A free drink with every feed and a lolly for the little-uns", another might shout. "Double helpings of pud to all the men. Anything you want, we got!" Aah, the company was rough and ready, but business was booming. They all made a fortune, every last one. All except your great grandfather, he never got past the pub half-way down the main street!'

I suppose it's not surprising that I developed a keen interest in drinking and smoking at a young age. I was adept at rolling Dad's cigarettes and then passing them to him to light. I could pour a glass of beer with no head on it in a few seconds. Dad encouraged me to sip from his glass, Mum protested in vain. If she complained about the same thing too often, Dad would go out of his way to annoy her. He was a rebellious man.

Fortunately, it wasn't long before the taste of beer sickened me. I thought it tasted just the way I imagined urine to taste. And the fact that I heard some of Dad's mates refer to it as 'The Piss' only deepened my impression. I decided that that was one tradition I wasn't going to maintain.

The day Uncle Frank entered our lives, I felt I'd found a kindred spirit. He just blew in out of nowhere one day and Dad was very pleased to see him.

'Oh God', Mum groaned as she eyed the brown paper bag tucked snugly under Frank's muscly arm. 'That's all Bill needs, more grog.'

I could tell by the gleam in Dad's eye that, contrary to Mum's opinion, he thought it was exactly what he needed. Mum gave them both The Silent Treatment. She was sick of us mixing with drinking men.

'You kids go out the back and play', she commanded as Dad and Frank plonked themselves on the front porch. 'He's got the most dreadful language', Mum whispered to Nan, 'I don't want the children hearing talk like that'.

My ears instantly pricked up. What dreadful language?

'Out you go, Sally', Mum repeated.

'Okay, okay, I'm going', I sighed as I nipped down the back verandah steps. It took only a few seconds for me to run around to the front of the house, where I happily joined the drinking men on the porch.

Within a few minutes, Frank had me totally fascinated. He used so many words I'd never heard before, and they all sounded exciting. I'd have given anything to be able to talk like Frank.

'Young lady', said Frank as he drained his glass, 'do ya know this bastard saved my life during the war?'.

'Jeez, give it a rest, Frank', Dad groaned.

I leaned forward, eagerly, in the hope that Frank would continue.

Suddenly, Mum popped her head around the front door. 'Sally, you come inside right now!' I gave her a grin and turned back to face Frank. 'Sally', she whispered in a more determined way, 'come inside'.

Dad hated it when Mum began whispering from the doorway. He knew she kept her voice down because of the neighbours, so he said loudly, 'She's all bloody right!'. Dad didn't give a damn what the neighbours thought. Mum admitted defeat and disappeared back behind the door.

'Aah, yes, your father's a silly bastard, doesn't like me telling this story. I'm gunna tell you!' Frank pointed his brown, calloused finger towards me.

'We were both poor bastards stuck on a POW transport bound for the camps, Italian job she was, when *Boom!,* a bloody Pommy sub got us right up the Mediterranean! Jesus bloody Christ, I'll never forget that one. Anyhow, we stayed afloat and beached on the Greek coast. I couldn't move, I was wounded in the chest. I thought I'd cashed in me chips. Then ya know what happened?'

'No, what?' I whispered.

'This son-of-a-bitch', he jerked his thumb towards Dad, 'heaved me over his shoulder, dragged me up to the top deck and got me to shore. Christ-All-Bloody-Mighty, I was no lightweight then, either. I made bloody sure I got a look at his face before I passed out. I wasn't going to forget a bastard like that in a hurry.' Frank threw back his tight, curly head and roared laughing.

'Jeez, Frank', Dad said, 'you were so bloody I thought you were dead already!'.

That made them both laugh. I thought they were very tough. Why was I cursed with being a girl?

Frank visited regularly after that. I loved to hear him talk about all the crazy things that happened down on the Fremantle docks. He was always bringing us around something that had happened to drop out of a crate. I decided all his muscles must be due to all the crates he lifted. He was always talking about lifting crates. He had the biggest, brownest belly I'd ever seen. It was as tight as a drum, I'm sure you could have played a tune on it.

One day, I said to Mum, 'How come Frank's got such a big stomach, is it all the work he does on the wharf?'.

Mum laughed. 'Dunno about work, more likely it's all the food he eats, and the way he washes it down with jugs of beer.'

I grew quite fond of Uncle Frank, but I never demonstrated my affection. Kissing Uncle Frank would have been like kissing a barnacle, he had a lot of rough edges.

Like Frank, Dad was the kind of man who enjoyed defying the odds. I think it gave him a sense of power he didn't normally have.

31

I'll never forget when, in September that year, he took us on a picnic to Roleystone. It was the only picnic I remember him taking us on. When he wasn't in hospital, he was rarely in a fit state to drive far, even if he wanted to.

All year, Mum had been promising us that Dad would take us on a picnic. We'd spent the May holidays playing down the swamp and visiting Dad in hospital. Now, we were half-way through the August holidays and we'd given up all hope of the picnic ever eventuating. So we were very surprised when, one sunny Saturday morning, Dad said, 'Right, we're off to the hills'.

We had an old 1948 Ford van by then. The Studebaker we had had for years was up on blocks in the drive; it was another one of those things Dad hadn't gotten around to fixing. The van had been a gift from one of Dad's old employers. When Dad was sober, he was a good worker, and it had been given to him in appreciation of a job well done.

The van had no back doors, just a big open back. The roof was padded with kapok, and soft, fluffy pieces poked through the torn lining.

In summer, the van was great, because it let in the breeze, but in winter, the roof acted like a sponge, soaking up the rain and depositing lumps of soggy kapok into our laps. While we shouted our complaints from the back, Mum sat, dry as a bone, in the cab, giggling away.

She'd confided to me once that she'd learned to laugh over difficult situations early in life, but I found this philosophy no comfort when it came to smelly, wet kapok.

The roads around Roleystone were narrow, steep and winding, and going for a picnic to the hills was no tame, family outing, it was a real adventure.

Once we'd eaten our camp pie sandwiches and stuffed down the cake Mum had cooked, we all ran, screaming, into the bush. We spent hours collecting stones, insects, rocks and wildflowers. We knew that, when we returned home, Nan would ask us what we'd found. She loved the bush, and always made us hand over any of our treasures that she thought could have special significance.

Too soon, Mum began shouting for us to return to the car. We played a bit longer, but when we heard Dad tooting the horn, we knew he meant business.

Billy, Jill and I leapt in the back, while Mum took her usual place in the front, holding our baby brother David on her lap.

It wasn't too long before we began to realise what a difficult task Dad had trying to manoeuvre the van around on a tiny section of bitumen. He had a rough gravel track ahead of him, a cliff face on one side and a deep bush valley on the other. We all hung on tightly as he backed towards the edge of the bitumen and closer to the valley.

In sudden terror, we pressed as close to the cab as we could. With no back doors to hold us in, we feared that one sudden brake from

Dad and we'd be catapulted into oblivion.

To our horror, Dad failed to brake at all. Instead, he continued to back closer and closer to the precipice. The wheels may have been on safe ground, but we felt practically airborne. Worse than that, the back of the van now sloped down, making it even more difficult for us to hold on. We began to scream.

'Shut up, you bloody kids!' Dad roared as he poked his head out the side window. He edged a few inches more and we screamed louder.

'For God's sake, Bill, *stop!* We're going over the edge', Mum shrieked as she clasped his shoulder. She was scared of heights. Her obvious panic incited us to greater efforts. We squashed our faces against the small window that separated the front cab from the back and, without taking a breath, we screamed as loud and as long as we could.

'Bill, *please.*'

'Listen, Glad, you bloody stupid woman, I *know* what I'm doing!'

'Bill, *stop!* You can kill yourself if you want to, but you're not going to bloody kill the rest of us!'

By this time, Dad had had enough. He pulled on the hand-brake and shouted, 'Get out, the bloody lot of you!'.

We eagerly clambered to safety and stood in a nearby gully. We watched helplessly as Dad continued with what, we were sure, would be a death plunge. The back wheels rolled off the bitumen and spun on the loose gravel. There was a sudden roar of the engine as the van leapt forward and Dad neatly executed an awkward turn. With a look of smug satisfaction, he told us to get in.

Mum was quiet all the way home. Dad whistled.

Chapter Five

PRETENDING

Nineteen fifty-nine, and another Milroy began school. Billy's initial reaction was similar to mine, he hated it. Every morning when we set off for school, Billy lagged behind, sobbing. How he managed to walk straight and not trip over always puzzled me, because while his body was trudging in the direction of school, his face was turned backwards towards our house.

He knew that Mum would be watching us from behind the curtains, and, if he looked really upset, she might weaken and call him back. Some days, he began his sobbing ritual so early that by the time we left, his face was red and puffy, his nose snotty and snorting. These occasions were generally too much for Mum, who only let him get as far as our letter-box before calling him back.

Billy's unhappiness at school never spilled over into recess and lunchtime. He was the kind of boy other boys looked up to, so he was never short of a pal. Billy was the image of Dad and, when it came to mateship, exactly like him.

Nan had a soft spot for Billy, too. She supported him in his dislike of school. 'Let him have the day off, Glad', she pleaded when Billy began his crying routine, 'the child's not well'.

To Billy's credit, he didn't look well. I attempted to copy his mournful look several times, but to no avail. After a few pathetic attempts, it became obvious that what worked for Billy would not work for me. I had to resort to more deceitful means.

I found that a light spattering of talcum powder, rubbed first into my hands and then patted lightly over my face, worked wonderfully well.

'I feel really sick in the stomach, Nan', I groaned as she gazed at my pale face. 'I think I'm gunna vomit.' Nan grabbed an empty saucepan and bent me over it. After emitting a few strangled noises, I straightened up and said, 'It's no use, it's gone down again'.

'Go and lie down', Nan instructed, 'I'll send your mother in'.

Within a few minutes, Mum was standing by my bedside, looking extremely sceptical. 'Sally . . . are you *really* sick?'

Nan always interrupted, 'Course she's sick, Glad, look at the child's face'.

'I'm not puttin' it on, Mum, honest. I feel real crook. Maybe I'll be better by lunch-time, Nan can send me to school then.'

'Don't be stupid, Sally', Nan countered, rising to the bait, 'you can't go to school, you'll pass out'.

'All right', Mum relented, 'you can stay home, but don't eat anything and stay in bed'.

Jill wandered in after Mum and Nan had left and said, 'You're rotten. You're not really sick, are you?'

'Course I am! Go away, you're makin' me feel sick. *Mu-um,* tell Jill to go away, she's makin' me feel worse.'

'You come out of there, Jilly. You let Sally sleep.' Jill gave me a disgusted look and walked off.

Once Jill and Billy had left for school, and Mum had left for her part-time job in Boans' Floral Department, I called out to Nan, 'I'm feelin' a bit better, Nan. Do ya think I could eat something?'

Nan pottered in, with her old tea-towel slung over her shoulder, and said, 'Oooh, you still look white, Sally. I don't think you eat enough, your mother can't expect you to get better if you're not going to eat. You stay there and I'll bring in some toast and a hot cup of tea.'

After six or so rounds of toast and jam and a couple of mugs of tea, I said to Nan, 'Gee, it's stuffy in here, Nan'.

'Yes, it is, go and sit outside, there's nothin' like a bit of fresh air when you're sick in the stomach.'

Nan only spoke to me after that to tell me when lunch was ready. I spent the rest of the day outdoors, playing all my usual games and climbing trees.

I was sitting on the back verandah step, inspecting the cache of small rocks I'd collected, when Mum returned home from her day at work.

'How's Sally?'

'Hmmph, she's all right', Nan grumbled. And then, with a giggle, she added, 'Been sittin' in that tree all day'.

Mum wandered out. 'Another miraculous recovery, eh Sal?'

'Yeah, dunno what it was, Mum, but I hope I don't get it again.'

'Don't hope too much'.

Apart from learning different ways to feign illness, there wasn't much to school that year. All my lessons seemed unrelated to real life. I often wondered how my teacher could be so interested in the sums I got wrong, and so disinterested in the games I played outside school, and whether Dad was home from hospital or not.

The best thing about school was that Grades Two and Three shared the same room, so this meant I saw more of Jill and we sat near one

35

another.

One afternoon, our teacher asked if there were any children in the class who could sing in a foreign language. Four children immediately raised their hands, Jill and I included. At the teacher's instruction, the first two kids got up and sang 'Frere Jacques' one after the other. Then it was Jill's and my turn. We were both very shy and embarrassed and walked to the front with our eyes down.

We linked arms and then, swaying energetically back and forth, loudly sang 'The Internationale' in Italian.

Mrs White was as stunned as the rest of our class at our sudden show of theatrical talent. We usually shunned any form of public display. 'Lovely, girls', she finally said, 'lovely'.

Dad was in hospital at the time so we were unable to tell him how we'd performed, but we knew that he would have been proud of us.

Whenever Dad was in hospital, Mum and Nan went out of their way to make home a nice place for us. We were allowed to stay up late, and we didn't have to worry about keeping quiet. It was much more relaxed.

Sometimes, Mum even scraped together enough money to shout Jill, Billy and me to the local outdoor theatre.

The theatre fascinated us. We loved the gaily striped canvas seats, the large spotlights and the huge white screen. It was such a magical place, we even felt excited during intermission.

But one of the best nights we had there was the time Mum provided the entertainment.

After we paid our threepence entry fee, we walked up and down, searching for four empty seats. Mum reckoned we'd be lucky to find any, because they always sold more tickets than they had seats. We were fortunate, Billy's keen eyes spotted four beauties.

'Over there, Mum', he shouted. 'Look over there.'

Mum looked in the direction he was pointing and sighed: they were in the middle row of the centre block, and almost impossible to get at. The rows of seats were so narrowly spaced it was difficult to walk between them, even when they were vacant. Only a fool, or someone very brave, would consider trying to claim them when all the surrounding seats were full, and, when one of our party happened to be a woman who was eight months pregnant . . .

'There must be somewhere else', Mum said helplessly as she glanced around the overflowing theatre.

'There's not, Mum', I said matter-of-factly. 'If we want to sit together, it'll have to be those.'

As we struggled over the various arms and legs jutting in our path, Mum kept apologising, 'I'm sorry, I'm awfully sorry. Please excuse me . . .' By the time we reached the empty seats, Mum was blushing and exhausted.

Darkness descended and we all grinned when we heard Mum breathe out. She responded by giving us a no-nonsense look that said shut up and watch the picture!

It was half-way through a new item on the Queen Mother that Mum disappeared. There was a sudden rip, followed by an urgent gurgling noise. All we could see was her desperately flailing arms and legs.

Fumbling in the dark, we managed to grasp her hands and tried the old heave-ho, but to no avail. A sympathetic chap in front leaned over the hard metal railing that separated each row and gave us a hand. As he pulled, we pushed Mum's feet towards the ground in the hope that it would give her more leverage. Instead, our fake grunts and groans sent her into a fit of giggles, which was no help at all.

The newsreel rolled on, but the Queen Mum's final wave was totally ignored. A lady kindly went to fetch the manager, and returned with the bouncer as well. When they reached Mum, she was a quivering, giggling mass and we were near hysteria.

By the end of the newsreel, Mum was free. Embarrassed, but free. She was supplied with a hard metal chair to sit on, and a small bottle of lime cool drink by way of compensation. Mum consoled herself with the fact that at least it hadn't been necessary to turn on the lights.

It was early in Grade Three that I developed my infallible Look At The Lunch method for telling which part of Manning my class-mates came from. I knew I came from the rough-and-tumble part, where there were teenage gangs called Bodgies and Widgies, and where hardly anyone looked after their garden. There was another part of Manning that, before I'd started school, I had been unaware of. The residents there preferred to call it Como. The houses were similar, only in better condition. The gardens were neat and tidy, and I'd heard there was carpet on the floors.

Children from Como always had totally different lunches to children from Manning. They had pieces of salad, chopped up and sealed in plastic containers. Their cake was wrapped neatly in grease-proof paper, and they had real cordial in a proper flask. There was a kid in our class whose parents were so wealthy that they gave him bacon sandwiches for lunch.

By contrast, kids from Manning drank from the water fountain and carried sticky jam sandwiches in brown paper bags.

Nan normally made our sandwiches for school. She made them very neatly, and, sometimes, she even cut the crusts off. I was convinced that made our sandwiches special. There were occasions when Mum took over the sandwich-making. Her lunches stand out in my mind as beacons of social embarrassment. With a few deft strokes, she could carve from an unsuspecting loaf the most unusual slabs of bread. These would then be glued together with thick chunks of hardened butter and globules of jam or Vegemite. Both, if she forgot to clean the knife between sandwiches. We always felt relieved when, once again, Nan

37

assumed the sandwich-making role.

In April that year, my youngest sister, Helen, was born. I found myself taking an interest in her because at least she had the good sense not to be born on my birthday. There were five of us now; I wondered how many more kids Mum was going to try and squeeze into the house. Someone at school had told me that babies were found under cabbage leaves. I was glad we never grew cabbages.

Each year, our house seemed to get smaller. In my room, we had two single beds lashed together with a bit of rope and a big, double kapok mattress plonked on top. Jill, Billy and I slept in there, sometimes David too, and, more often than not, Nan as well. I loved that mattress. Whenever I lay on it, I imagined I was sinking into a bed of feathers, just like a fairy princess.

The kids at school were amazed to hear that I shared a bed with my brother and sister. I never told them about the times we'd squeezed five in that bed. All my class-mates had their own beds, some of them even had their own rooms. I considered them disadvantaged. I couldn't explain the happy feeling of warm security I felt when we all snuggled in together.

Also, I found some of their attitudes to their brothers and sisters hard to understand. They didn't seem to really like one another, and you never caught them together at school. We were just the opposite. Billy, Jill and I always spoke in the playground and we often walked home together, too. We felt our family was the most important thing in the world. One of the girls in my class said, accusingly, one day, 'Aah, you lot stick like glue'. You're right, I thought, we do.

The kids at school had also begun asking us what country we came from. This puzzled me because, up until then, I'd thought we were the same as them. If we insisted that we came from Australia, they'd reply, 'Yeah, but what about ya parents, bet they didn't come from Australia'.

One day, I tackled Mum about it as she washed the dishes.

'What do you mean, "Where do we come from?" '

'I mean, what country. The kids at school want to know what country we come from. They reckon we're not Aussies. Are we Aussies, Mum?'

Mum was silent. Nan grunted in a cross sort of way, then got up from the table and walked outside.

'Come on, Mum, what are we?'

'What do the kids at school say?'

'Anything. Italian, Greek, Indian.'

'Tell them you're Indian.'

I got really excited, then. 'Are we really? Indian!' It sounded so exotic. 'When did we come here?' I added.

'A long time ago', Mum replied. 'Now, no more questions. You just tell them you're Indian.'

It was good to finally have an answer and it satisfied our playmates. They could quite believe we were Indian, they just didn't want us pretending we were Aussies when we weren't.

Chapter Six

ONLY A DREAM

By the time I was eight-and-a-half, an ambulance parked out the front of our house was a neighbourhood tradition. It would come belting down our street with the siren blaring on and off, and halt abruptly at our front gate. The ambulance officers knew just how to manage Dad, they were very firm, but gentle. Usually, Dad teetered out awkwardly by himself, with the officers on either side offering only token support. Other times, as when his left lung collapsed, he went out on a grey-blanketed stretcher.

Jill, Billy and I accepted his comings and goings with the innocent selfishness of children. We never doubted he'd be back.

Dad hated being in hospital, he reckoned the head shrinkers didn't have a clue. He got sick of being sedated. It was supposed to help him, but it never did.

I heard him telling Mum about how he'd woken up in hospital one night, screaming. He thought he'd been captured again. There was dirt in his mouth and a rifle butt in his back. He tried to get up, but he couldn't move. Next thing he knew, the night sister was flicking a torch in his eyes and saying, 'All tangled up again are we, Mr Milroy? It's only a dream, you know. No need to upset yourself.'

Dad laughed when he told Mum what the sister had said. Only a dream, I thought. I was just a kid, and I knew it wasn't a dream.

When Dad got really bad, and Mum and Nan feared the worst, our only way out was a midnight flit to Aunty Grace's house. Other nights, the five of us were shut up in one room, and, sometimes, Mum put Helen and David, the babies of the family, to bed in the back of the van. I was so envious. I complained strongly to Mum, 'It's not fair! They have all the adventures. Why can't I sleep in the van?'

'Oh, don't be silly, Sally, you don't understand.' She was right. I never realised that if we had to leave the house suddenly, the babies would be the most difficult to wake up.

Aunty Grace was a civilian widow who lived at the back of us. Nan had knocked out six pickets in the back fence so we could easily run

40

from our yard to hers.

It often puzzled me that we only needed a sanctuary at night. I associated Dad's bad fits with the darkness and never realised that, by dusk, he'd be so tanked up with booze and drugs as to be just about completely irrational.

Many times, we were quietly woken in the dark and bundled off to Grace's house.

'Sally . . . wake up. Get out of bed, but be very quiet.'

'Aw, not again, Nan.' It had been a bad two weeks.

'Your mother's waiting in the yard, you go out there while I wake Billy and Jill.'

I walked quickly through the kitchen, scuttled across the verandah and into the shadows, where Mum was standing with the babies.

Mum was rocking Helen to stop her from crying and David was leaning against her legs, half asleep. I shook his shoulder. 'Not yet, wake up, we'll be going soon.' Nan shuffled down the steps with Billy and Jill, and we were on our way.

'No talking, you kids', Mum said, 'and stay close'.

We followed the line of shadows to the rear of our yard. Just as we neared the gap in the back picket fence, Dad flung open the door of his sleepout and staggered onto the verandah, yelling abuse.

Oh no, I thought, he knows we're leaving, he's gunna come and get us! We all crouched down and hid behind some bushes. 'Stay low and be very quiet', Mum whispered. I prayed Helen wouldn't cry. I hardly breathed. I was sure Dad would hear me if I did. I would feel terrible if my breathing led him to where we were all hiding. I remembered all the stories Dad had told me about the camps he'd been in. Horse's Head Soup. They'd had Horse's Head Soup, fur and all. The men fought over the eye because it was the only bit of meat. I was shivering, I didn't know whether it was from nerves or cold. I remembered then that the Germans had stripped Dad naked and forced him to stand for hours in the snow. His feet were always cold, that must be why.

My heart was pounding. I suddenly understood what it had been like for Dad and his friends; they'd felt just the way I was feeling now. Alone, and very, very frightened.

For some reason, Dad stopped yelling and swearing; he peered out into the darkness of the yard, and then he turned and shuffled back to his room.

'Now, kids', Mum said. We didn't need to be told twice. With unusual speed, Billy, Jill and I darted through the gap to safety.

Within seconds, we were all grouped around Grace's wood stove, cooking toast and waiting for our cup of tea. I felt safe, now. Had I really been so terrified only a moment ago? It was a different world.

We never stayed at Aunty Grace's long, just until Dad was back on an even keel. Prior to our return, I would be sent to negotiate with him. 'He'll listen to you', they said. I don't think he ever did.

41

After my mother had bedded my brothers and sisters down on the floor of Grace's lounge, Nan walked me to the gap in the picket fence. After that, I was on my own. One night, I told Nan I didn't want to go, but she replied, 'You must, there's no one else'.

If I was really worried, she stood in the gap and watched me until I reached the back verandah. She didn't have to stand there long, fear of the dark usually made my progress pretty rapid.

My father's room was the sleepout, and his light burnt all hours. I think he disliked the dark as much as me.

Our house seemed particularly menacing. It was surrounded by all kinds of eerie shadows, and I wondered if I'd find something horrible when I got there. I didn't, there was only Dad sitting on his hard, narrow bed, surrounded by empties. He always knew when I had come, quietly opening his bedroom door when he heard the creak on the back verandah.

I took up my usual position on the end of his bed and dangled my feet back and forth. The grey blanket I sat on was rough, and I plucked at it nervously.

Dad sat with his shoulders hunched. His hair, greased with Californian Poppy, curled forward, one persistent lock drooping over his brow and partly obscuring three deep parallel wrinkles. They weren't a sign of age, he had a clear sort of face apart from them. They reminded me of marks left in damp dirt after Nan had dug her spade in.

It was on the tip of my tongue to ask, who dug your wrinkles, Dad? I knew it would make him cry. When Dad smiled, his eyes crinkled at the corners. It was nice. He wasn't smiling now, just waiting.

'Dad, we'll all come back if you'll be good', I stated matter-of-factly. I'd inherited none of Mum's natural diplomacy, but I sensed that Dad hated being alone, so I started from there. He responded with his usual brief, wry smile, and then gave me his usual answer, 'I'll let you all come back as long as your grandmother doesn't'. He had a thing about Nanna.

'You know we won't come back without her, Dad', I said firmly. We both knew Mum would never agree. How would she cope with him on her own? And anyway, where would Nan go?

Dad ran his hand through his hair. It was a characteristic gesture; he was thinking. Reaching behind his back and down the side of his bed, he pulled out three unopened packets of potato chips. Slowly, he placed them one by one in my lap. I could feel the pointed corner of one pack sticking through the cotton of my thin summer dress and into my thigh. Suddenly my mouth was full of water.

'You can have them all', he said quietly, 'if . . . you stay with me'.

Dad looked at me and I looked at the chips. They were a rare treat. I swallowed the water in my mouth and reluctantly handed them back. We both understood it was a bribe. I was surprised Dad was trying to bribe me, I knew that he knew it was wrong.

42

'I always thought you liked your mother better than me.' He didn't really mean it, it was just another ploy to get me to stay. Deep down, he understood my decision. Reaching up, he opened the door and I walked out onto the verandah. Click! went the lock and I was alone.

I walked towards the outside door and stopped. Maybe if I waited for a while, he would call me back. Maybe he would say, 'Here, Sally, have some chips, anyway'. There was no harm in waiting. I squatted on the bare verandah, time seemed to pass so slowly. I shuddered, the air was getting cooler and damper.

Some sixth sense must have told him I was still there, because his bedroom door suddenly opened and light streamed out, illuminating my small hunched figure. Towering over me, Dad yelled, 'What the bloody hell do you think you're doing here, GET GOING!', and he pointed in the direction of Aunty Grace's house.

I shot down the three back steps and sped along the track that cut through our grass. With unexpected nimbleness, I leapt through the gap in the back picket fence and, in no time at all, arrived panting at the door of Aunty Grace's laundry.

Mum and Nan always questioned me in detail about what Dad said. It was never any different, he always said the same thing. They'd nod their heads seriously, as though everything I said was of great importance.

Once I'd finished telling them what he'd said, they'd then ask me how he seemed. I found that a difficult question to answer, because Dad was more aggressive towards them than he was towards me.

Eventually, I'd go to bed, and the following day, we generally returned home. I guess Dad slept it off.

There was only one occasion when Dad intruded into our sanctuary. We were sitting in Grace's kitchen, eating chip sandwiches, when he appeared unexpectedly in the doorway. No one had heard him come, he could move quietly when he wanted to.

We were all stunned. No one was sure what was going to happen. For some reason, Dad didn't seem to know what to do, either. He looked at all of us in a desperate kind of way, then he fixed his gaze on Mum. I heard him mumble something indistinct, but Mum didn't reply. She just stood there, holding the teapot. It was like she was frozen. I think it was her lack of response that forced him to turn to me.

'All right, Sally, which one of us do you love the most? Choose which one of us you want to live with, your mother or me.'

I was as shocked as Mum. I wanted to shout, 'Don't do this to me, I'm only a kid!', but nothing came out. I had trouble getting my mouth to work in those days.

Dad stayed a few seconds longer, then, in a resigned tone, he muttered, 'I knew you'd choose her', and left as quickly as he'd come.

That night, I found myself feeling sorry for Dad. He was so lost.

I blamed myself for being too young.

Chapter Seven

A CHANGE

It was half-way through the second term of my fourth year at school that I suddenly discovered a friend. Our teacher began reading stories about Winnie the Pooh every Wednesday. From then on, I was never sick on Wednesdays. In a way, discovering Pooh was my salvation. He made me feel more normal. I suppose I saw something of myself in him.

Pooh lived in a world of his own and he believed in magic, the same as me. He wasn't particularly good at anything, but everyone loved him, anyway. I was fascinated by the way he could make an adventure out of anything, even tracks in the snow. And while Pooh was obsessed with honey, I was obsessed with drawing.

When I couldn't find any paper or pencils, I would fish small pieces of charcoal from the fire, and tear strips off the paperbark tree in our yard, and draw on that. I drew in the sand, on the footpath, the road, even on the walls when Mum wasn't looking. One day, a neighbour gave me a batch of oil paints left over from a stint in prison. I felt like a real artist.

My drawings were very personal. I hated anyone watching me draw. I didn't even like people seeing my drawings when they were finished. I drew for myself, not anyone else. One day, Mum asked me why I always drew sad things. I hadn't realised until then that my drawings were sad. I was shocked to see my feelings glaring up at me from the page. I became even more secretive about anything I drew after that.

Dad never took any interest in my drawings, he was completely enveloped in his own world. He never went to the pub now, we were too poor to be able to afford the petrol. There was never any money for toys, clothes, furniture, barely enough for food, but always plenty for Dad's beer. Everything valuable had been hocked.

One day, Dad was so desperate he raided our money-boxes. I'll never forget our dismay when Jill and I found our little tin money-boxes had been opened with a can-opener and all our hard-won threepenny

bits removed. What was even more upsetting was that he'd opened
them at the bottom, and then placed them back on the shelf as though
they'd never been tampered with. We kept putting our money in and
he kept taking it out. 'Who knows how long we've been supplying
him!' I complained to Mum. I felt really hurt; if Dad had asked me,
I'd have given him the contents, willingly.

As usual, Mum saw the funny side of things.

'How can you think it's funny?' I demanded. 'It was a rotten trick!'

'Can't you see the funny side? It was such a childish thing to do.'

I knew what she meant, but I didn't think it was funny. He was
just like a child, sometimes, he never mended anything around the
house, or took any responsibility. I felt very disappointed in him.

Dad hated being poor, and I could forgive him for that, because
I hated it myself. He loved the luxuries working-class people couldn't
afford. If he had been able to, he would have given us anything. Instead,
his craving for beer and his illness left us with nothing. I knew that
Mum and Dad had had dreams once. It wasn't supposed to have turned
out like this.

That year, Dad's love of luxuries really broke our budget, but it also
gave us the status of being the first family in our street to have television.

As he carried it in, an awkward-looking square on four pointy legs,
and tried to manoeuvre it through the front door, we all rushed at
him excitedly. 'Get out the bloody way, you kids', he yelled as he staggered
into the hall. Televisions were heavy in those days. A few more lunges
and the hallowed object was finally set down next to the power point
in the lounge-room.

We lined up in awe behind Dad, waiting for our first glimpse of
this modern-day miracle. We were disappointed. All we saw was white
flecks darting across a grey screen, all we heard was a buzzing noise.
While Mum pressed the power point, Dad fiddled with the knob marked
vertical hold. It was only after they'd both banged the set several times
that Dad realised the rental people had forgotten to leave the aerial.

We all went racing out the front, hoping the ute that had delivered
our television set was still parked in the drive. 'Jesus Bloody Christ!'
Dad swore as he gazed up the long length of empty road. I shrugged
my shoulders in disappointment and went inside.

The aerial arrived the following day, but it never made the difference
I imagined it would. Grey, human-like figures became discernible and
their conversations with one another audible, but they didn't impress
me. I had the feeling they weren't quite sure of whatever it was they
were supposed to be doing.

In July, we had a surprise visit. We were all playing happily outside
when Mum called us in. There was an urgency in her voice. What's
going on, I thought. We don't do midnight flits during the day. I peeped
into Dad's room on the way through. He was lying down, reading an

old paper.

When we reached the hall, I stopped dead in my tracks. Mum grinned at me and said, 'Well, say hello, these are your cousins'. As usual, my mouth had difficulty working. The small group of dark children stared at me. They seemed shy, too. I felt such an idiot.

Just then, a very tall, dark man walked down and patted me on the head. He had the biggest smile I'd ever seen. 'This is Arthur', Mum said proudly, 'he's Nanna's brother'. I stared at him in shock. I didn't know she had a brother.

Arthur returned to the lounge-room and us kids all sat on the floor, giggling behind our hands and staring at one another. Mum slipped into the kitchen to make a cup of tea. I glimpsed her going into Dad's room. Then she returned, finished off the tea and dug out some biscuits. I helped pass them around.

Mum said, very brightly, to Arthur, 'He's asleep. Perhaps he'll wake up before you leave.' I knew she was lying, but I didn't understand why. Sleep never came easily to Dad.

After a while, they all left. I was surprised to hear Arthur speak English. I thought maybe he could speak English and Indian, whereas the kids probably only spoke Indian.

I don't remember ever seeing them again while I was a child, but the image of their smiling faces lodged deep in my memory. I often wondered about them. I wanted them to teach me Indian. I never said anything to Mum. I knew, instinctively, that if I asked about them, she wouldn't tell me anything.

Dad seemed to be getting sicker and sicker. By the time September came around, he had been in hospital more than he'd been home. At least he managed to return for Jill's birthday towards the end of September.

Mum asked a special favour of him that day. She wanted him to stay in his room while the party was on. It was the first party Jill had ever asked her friends to, and Mum didn't want Dad to spoil it by walking around, drunk. To my surprise, he actually agreed.

It was half-way through a round of Queenie, Queenie, Who's Got The Ball that Dad appeared, a bottle and glass in his right hand. I watched as he casually seated himself on the front porch and poured a glass of beer. After a couple of drinks, he began to call out and make comments about the game we were playing. Mum suddenly appeared behind him in the hall and began to whisper crossly, 'Bill, come inside, you're making a fool of yourself, the neighbours will hear you'. As Mum's whispers became more urgent, so Dad refilled his glass more often, he delighted in taking the mickey out of Mum.

One morning a few weeks later, Dad emerged from his room early, we were just finishing breakfast. All the previous week, he'd been in hospital, so we were surprised by the cheery look on his face. Nan

47

hovered near the table, intent on hurrying us along. She knew we'd seize on any pretext to miss school.

'Come on, you kids, you'll be late', she grumbled when she noticed our eating had slowed to a halt.

'Aw, let them stay home, Dais', Dad said. 'I'll look after them.' Had I heard right? I froze half-way through my last slice of toast and jam, it wasn't like Dad to interfere with anything to do with us. I'd heard him call Nan Dais before. It was his way of charming her.

Nan was as surprised as me. She flicked her dirty tea-towel towards us and muttered in her grumpiest voice, 'They have to go to school, Bill, they can't stay home'. I sensed that she was unsure of herself, and beneath her lowered lashes, she eyed Dad shrewdly.

'Well, let little Billy stay then, Dais', Dad coaxed. I smiled, he'd called her Dais again, how could she resist?

'All right', Nan relented, 'just Billy. Now, off you girls go!'

Billy waved at us smugly. Jill and I grumbled as we dressed. Nan had always favoured the boys in our family, and now Dad was doing the same.

By lunch-time, we'd forgotten all about Billy. Jill and I had been taken off normal classwork to help paint curtains for the school's Parents' Night, which was held at the end of each year. We were half-way through drawing a black swan family, when the headmaster came down and told us we could go home early. We were puzzled, but very pleased to be leaving before the other kids.

Nan wasn't happy when she saw us shuffling up the footpath.

'What are you kids doing here? They were supposed to keep you late at school.'

We just shrugged our shoulders, neither Jill nor I had the faintest idea what she was talking about.

'Go outside and play', Nan ordered grumpily.

Jill immediately raced out the back to play with Billy, but I decided I'd like something to eat first. I was just coming out of the kitchen with a Vegemite sandwich half-stuffed in my mouth when the familiar sound of an ambulance siren drew me to the front door. Nan stood impatiently on the porch, she had her hand over her mouth. When she saw me, she turned crossly and said, 'I told you to go out the back and play!'.

Two ambulance men hurried up the path. A stretcher case, I noted, as they walked briskly through. In a few minutes, they returned, and I watched as they carried Dad carefully, but quickly, down our faded red footpath. This time, I couldn't see his face.

Billy, Jill and David pushed up behind me, followed by Mrs Mainwaring, our neighbour. Before I knew it, she'd ushered us into the lounge-room and told us to all sit down, as she had something important to say. It was then that I noticed Mum squashed in the old cane chair in the corner of the room. Nan hovered beside her, stuffing men's handkerchiefs into her hand. It occurred to me she already had more than enough.

'What are ya crying for, Mum?' I asked, puzzled. Whenever he'd gone before, she hadn't cried. Dad was like a boomerang. Mum continued to sniffle. I tried to reassure her by saying confidently, 'He always comes back', at which, she broke down completely and hid her face in a striped grey handkerchief.

'Please sit down, Sally', said Mrs Mainwaring, 'I have something to tell you all'. I obeyed instantly. She was a nice middle-aged lady and we were a little in awe of her. Her home was very neat.

'Now . . .', she continued. 'I have some bad news for you all.' She paused and took a deep breath.

'He's dead, isn't he?' I was sure I said it out loud, but I couldn't have, because everyone ignored me.

'He's dead, isn't he?' I repeated, but still no response. My heart was pounding. Mrs Mainwaring's lips were moving, but I couldn't hear a word. He was dead. I knew it, Dad was gone.

'Now children, I want you all to go to your rooms.' Somehow, this sentence managed to penetrate my numbed brain. I looked around at my brothers and sisters, no one was moving. I craned my neck to look at Mum, she was avoiding my gaze. We all looked blank, what were we going to do in our rooms?

Mrs Mainwaring finally pulled each one of us up and ushered us out. As I closed the bedroom door, Jill said, 'What are we s'posed to do?'.

I was shocked, it wasn't like her not to know what the right thing was. With the superior confidence of a nine-year-old, I flung myself stomach-down on the bed and said, 'I s'pose we'd better cry'.

We cried for what seemed a long time, when our bedroom door slowly opened and the freckled face of Billy peered around.

'I'm going outside, who wants to come and play?'

'You horrible boy', I growled, 'don't you know he's dead?!'. After all, he'd been with Dad all day. Billy vanished.

'He doesn't understand', Jill defended him as usual. 'He doesn't know what he's s'posed to do.'

We lay on our beds a few moments longer. I began to count the fly specks on the ceiling.

'Sally . . . do ya think . . . we could . . . go outside and play now?' Jill asked, hesitantly.

'You're as bad as Billy.'

'Well at least I cried. That wasn't easy, you know.' Jill put her head under her arm. I watched her silently.

'Oh, come on then', I relented. And leaping up, we joined Billy in the yard.

Chapter Eight

FAMILY AND FRIENDS

I felt very strongly about families sticking together. So strongly, in fact, that I had a secret meeting with my brothers and sisters; for some reason, I was frightened we would be put in an orphanage. I'd read about things like that happening and I was determined it wouldn't happen to us. We all pledged to run away together if it looked like happening.

But we needn't have worried. A couple of weeks after Dad had died, Mum informed us all that Billy was now the man of the house. This came as a great surprise to me, because Billy was only six years old.

But Billy took Mum's Man Of The House thing very seriously. For example, whenever anything broke down, he insisted that it was his job to fix it. But, whenever Billy fixed anything, Mum ended up having to pay out money. So much so that when he accidentally locked himself in the toilet, she felt like leaving him there.

'I'm sure he'll grow up to be a great inventor, one day', Mum said after she let him out. 'He's so interested in the way things go together.' I just grinned and listed the clock, the toaster, Dad's old watch and David's clockwork train that were all now in pieces. Mum laughed, 'Well, he has to practise on something'.

Whenever one of us mentioned Dad's death, Mum would say, 'Never mind, Billy's the Man Of The House now. He'll look after us, won't you Billy?' It was an old-fashioned thought, Billy was the eldest son. I think Mum meant to reassure us with her statements, but she only confused us. We wondered if Billy had special powers we didn't know about.

A few months after Dad's death, Mum found out the contents of the Coroner's Report. The verdict was suicide. Mum was very upset. She had told us all that the war had killed Dad. She'd fixed it into our minds that Dad's death was due to something called War Causes.

In a way, the coroner did our family a favour. He attributed Dad's suicide to the after-effects of war, and that meant there were no problems with Mum obtaining a war pension. It was regular money at a time when we needed it.

The suicide verdict never worried me a great deal. Though, I guess like Mum, it made me feel guilty and a little responsible. I knew there was nothing any of us could do to bring Dad back, and, to a large extent, that was a relief.

Fear had suddenly vanished from our lives. There were no more midnight flits to Aunty Grace's house, no more hospitals, no more ambulances. We were on our own, but peace had returned. I was still afraid of the dark, but I didn't burrow under my pillow any more.

Dad's death crystallised many things for me. I decided that, when I grew up, I would never drink or marry a man who drank. The smell of alcohol, especially beer, had the power to make me sick. I also decided that I would never be poor. It wasn't that I was ashamed of what we had, or the way we lived, it was just that there were things I longed for that I knew only money could buy. Like art paper and paints, piano lessons, a pink nylon dress and bacon sandwiches.

It had also made me very choosy about different men who seemed keen to befriend our family. There was one local chap who was always keen to take us on outings, but I knew he was only interested in Mum, not us. I'd heard about men like him, they play up to the mother and get rid of the kids on the sly. That was the only time in my life when I wanted to be a witch. I'd have loved to turn him into a frog.

Mum growled at me several times for being so rude to him. This made me really mad, because I felt she couldn't see through him and I could. I decided another secret meeting was necessary.

My brothers and sisters were shocked when I told them what our neighbour was really like. We all agreed that he had to go. And go he did. We told Mum, quite bluntly, that if this chap continued to persist, we would run away. Helen and David began to cry then, because they suddenly realised that when you run away, you leave the mother behind. When Mum finally calmed them down, I made her promise faithfully never to marry again. She agreed to this quite happily and it certainly was a weight off our minds.

We saw very little of Dad's brothers during those early months. One uncle gave Mum what he thought was good advice. 'Glad', he said, 'a good-looking woman like you, in your position, there's only one thing ya can do. Find a bloke and live with him. If ya lucky, he might take the kids as well.' Another uncle turned up a few weeks later and drove off in our only asset, the 1948 Ford van. He reasoned that as Mum didn't have her driver's licence, she wouldn't be needing it.

Mum was pretty down after that. It wasn't like her. She didn't know how to assert herself, she was too confused. 'Men', she told us cynically, 'they're useless, no good for anything!'.

If it hadn't been for Uncle Frank, we probably would have gone along with Mum's theory. Mind you, she wasn't too pleased when he showed up. She was sick of drinking men.

'G'day, Glad', he said when she answered the front door, 'just brought this around for ya. How ya goin', kids?', he grinned as we appeared behind Mum in the doorway. 'Well, better get goin'. See ya later, kids. We'll have to go out one day, 'bye Glad.' Mum smiled and closed the door.

'What you got there?' Nan said as she poked in the box. 'Chicken, eh? And vegetables. Who gave you that?'

'It was Uncle Frank, Nan', I said, 'do ya think we could have it tonight, do ya?'.

I couldn't believe it was real chicken, such a luxury. I don't think Mum could believe it, either. Frank, of all people — she'd thought he was just another boozer.

To our surprise, Frank came around the following weeks with the same thing. Then, Mum found out that the Raffles Hotel was holding a weekly lottery. The prize was always a box of fruit and vegetables and a fresh chicken, and the winner was always Uncle Frank. His lucky run was to continue for over twelve months.

Frank gave us more than just a helping hand. He introduced his wife to Mum and they became good friends. Aunty Lorna had a little car and she took us for picnics in the bush. She always packed a delicious lunch.

Frank encouraged Mum to have driving lessons. He was a bit of a mechanic in his spare time. He said he'd fix the van up for Mum. For some reason, my uncle had returned it. Mum said she'd heard that other blokes had made comments to him.

Pretty soon, Mum got her licence, then she and Lorna took it in turns to drive to the hills. We were still poor, but Nan was good at making a little bit go a long way. And, as far as us kids were concerned, it was more than we'd ever had.

Now that Mum had her driver's licence, she also began to make regular visits to Grandma and Grandpa's house. I think she was hoping they'd take an interest in us kids, but it didn't really work out like that. The only one of us they were really keen on was Billy, and that was only because he was the image of Dad. Grandpa always liked to have Billy close to him, but the rest of us were relegated to the backyard. Our cousins were allowed inside, but we had to stay outside.

Being outdoors at their place wasn't much fun. There was no bush near Grandma and Grandpa's, and no old bikes or toys. We spent our time sitting on an old log and brushing our fingers through the sandy dirt, exposing and collecting the small, brownish pebbles that lay just below the surface.

Other times, we amused ourselves by hiding behind a large bush and pretending we were in prehistoric times. When we tired of playing dinosaurs, we resorted to endless rounds of Simon Says. Finally, Mum would come out with a tray of drinks and a piece of cake for each of us. After that, we knew it was time to go home.

It wasn't that our grandparents disliked us. In fact, they always treated us kindly, in their own way. After all, half of us belonged to Dad. It was the other half they were worried about.

It took only a few months for our regular visits to cease. Sometimes, we bumped into Grandpa in town; Mum was always taking us window-shopping. Grandpa would cry when he saw Billy. I remember once he actually tried to apologise to Mum for Grandma's attitude. 'What can I do, Glad. Ya know what she's like.' Mum just shrugged her shoulders. When we said goodbye, Grandpa would mop his eyes in a resigned kind of way. He always spoke nicely to us, but Grandma ruled the roost.

Fortunately for us, Mum somehow managed to hang on to the television after Dad died. There were many other things we needed in our house far more desperately, but the TV did more for us than warm clothes or extra beds ever could. It gave us a way out.

We got into the habit of making up rough beds on the floor of the lounge-room. Mum stoked up the fire, and, snuggled beneath our coats and rugs, we became enraptured in movies of the twenties, thirties and forties.

Apart from romantic musicals, the Nelson Eddie and Jeannette Macdonald variety, we were very fond of war movies. Mum often said, 'Your father fought there', or, 'I remember your father telling me about that place'. It made the pictures seem more important than they really were. Sometimes, one of the actors would look like Dad, and I'd try and pretend it was him, living out an earlier part of his life on the screen. It never worked for long, the glamorous heroism portrayed in the movies seemed far removed from what I'd heard Dad describe.

When television finished for the evening, Mum made us all hot cups of sweet tea and toast with jam or Vegemite. We stoked up the fire again and swapped yarns and stories until the early hours of the morning. Sometimes, we had a singalong — those went on for hours. We only stopped when we were asleep or too hoarse to sing any more.

I'll never forget those evenings, the open fire, Mum and Nan, all of us laughing and joking. I felt very secure, then. I knew it was us against the world, but I also knew that, as long as I had my family, I'd make it.

I had little idea of how hard that first year was for Mum and Nan. Mum was thirty-one when Dad died, and she had five of us to rear. I was nine years old, while Helen, the youngest, was only eighteen months old.

Mum didn't like leaving us, but she knew that if we were ever to get ahead, she would have to work.

That was one thing you could say about Mum, she wasn't afraid

53

to work She had always kept some money coming in all the years Dad was sick, with some part-time work, but now she increased her load and took on whatever jobs were going. It was difficult to find full-time employment, so she accepted numerous part-time positions, most of which only lasted a few weeks.

Mum had a old friend, Lois, who helped out financially. Lois was an older lady who we didn't see much of, but she had befriended Mum in Mum's teenage years and, having no children of her own, considered her a daughter. She'd never liked Dad, but wasn't one to bear a grudge.

I remember, at one stage, we were really desperate. Mum and Nan kept talking in whispers. They decided to write a letter to Alice Drake-Brockman in Sydney to see if her family could lend us some money. They were really disappointed when the reply came; it said that they were broke, too, and couldn't lend us anything. Nan was very bitter. She said she didn't care that they were bankrupt, they owed her. I didn't know what she was talking about.

Besides good old Uncle Frank and Lois, the other saviour of our family at this time was Legacy. All fatherless families of returned soldiers were assigned a Legatee. Legatees were generally gentlemen of good community standing who had a soft spot for children, and, while the system was only as good as the particular Legatee you got, we were very fortunate. Ours proved to be a kindly, older man with only one child of his own. His name was Mr Wilson, but we affectionately shortened it to Mr Willie.

Mr Willie got into the habit of taking us to the beach, and on picnics and barbecues. He had what we considered a really flash car, and we always felt very special when we rode in it.

Mr Willie told us he would be taking us to all the Legacy outings, and he also informed us that we would all have to take part in the Anzac Day march once a year.

'Why do we have to march?' I asked him one day.

'Because your father was a soldier. All children who belong to soldiers have to march. People need to be reminded of the legacy the war has left. And anyway, your father was a brave man, you should march to honour him.'

I wasn't keen to remind people of the war, but I couldn't fault his argument about Dad.

Chapter Nine

WILDLIFE

In no time at all, our house became inundated with pets. Cats, dogs, budgies, rabbits and, of course, the chickens — any stray creature found a home with us. When our cat population hit thirteen, Mum decided it was too much and found homes for half of them. Then, my white rabbit escaped, one of the dogs was run over, and another cat went wild.

The dog we lost had been an old and treasured member of the family. I decided we needed another dog to replace him, so I persuaded Mum to look around some local pet shops.

'We won't buy one, Mum', I confided, 'we'll just look'.

'No more animals, Sally.'

'I know, Mum, I know, but can't we look?'

'All right. It'll be an outing for you kids.'

A pet shop nearby had six kelpie-cross pups, all of them adorable. We all huddled around their cage in awe as they licked our fingers and looked at us appealingly.

'That one', I said to Mum, as I eyed the largest pup. 'We'll take that one, Mum.'

'I'm not buying a dog, Sally. I've hardly got enough money to feed what we've got without adding to it.'

'That one's older than the others', interrupted the shopkeeper. 'No one seems to want him.' It was the best thing he could have said.

'You see, Mum, no one wants him. What'll become of him if we don't buy him?'

'I'm not buying him.'

'Can I take him out of the cage and hold him, Mum, it might be the only cuddle he ever gets.'

'Good idea, little lady', said the storekeeper enthusiastically as he opened the cage.

I lifted the pup out, he was gangly and awkward. 'Isn't he beautiful.' I held him up to Mum.

'Oh my God, look at the size of his paws, they're huge.'

'I'm sure his mother was only a corgi', said the shopkeeper quickly.

'More like an Alsatian. No, Sally, not now I've seen his feet. He'll be a big boy when he's fully grown.'

'But Mum, we've never had a big dog.'

'Please, Mum', pleaded my brothers and sisters.

'We-ll', Mum sighed as the pup gave her a lick.

'Be a good guard dog, Mum', said Billy.

'I'll let you have him for half price', coaxed the storekeeper.

'Oh, all right', Mum groaned, 'we'll take him.'

'A real bargain, Mum', I smiled.

We named the pup Blackie, because he was mostly black. A few weeks later, we renamed him Widdles, because of a tendency he had that we didn't seem to be able to train him out of.

One night, Mum complained about this new name. 'I feel silly calling out Widdles when I want him to come for his tea, the neighbours are all laughing.' So, while we all continued calling him Widdles, from then on, whenever Mum wanted him, she shouted out, 'Here Widdees, here boy'. The neighbours still laughed, but, in Mum's mind, it made some sort of difference.

The only pets we weren't allowed to keep were wild ones. Goannas, tadpoles, frogs, gilgies* and insects all had to be returned alive and well to their natural habitat. Nan influenced us greatly when it came to our attitudes to the wildlife around us.

Our lives revolved around her, now, she kept the home fires burning while Mum worked three part-time jobs, two with a florist and one cleaning. Nan did the cooking, the cleaning, the washing, the ironing and the mending, as well as chopping all our wood and looking after the garden. The kitchen had become her own personal domain, and she disliked us kids intruding. 'You kids get out of my kitchen', she'd yell as she flicked a tea-towel towards us. Even when we offered to help, she scolded us and sent us outside to play.

Nan fostered our interest in the local wildlife by showing great concern for any new creature we brought home from the swamp. Frogs and goannas seemed to be her favourites.

One afternoon, I discovered a big, fat bobtail goanna curled up under a bit of rusty tin that leant against the wall of our chook shed.

'Jill, come quick, look what I've found.' We both lay, stomach-down, in the dirt and stared into its glassy eyes for ages.

When Nan found us, she said, 'What are you kids up to?'. According to her, we were always up to something.

'It's a goanna, Nan. Bobtail, and a beauty. Look.'

'Oooh he's fat', Nan exclaimed. 'Now you kids leave him there. He can live there if he wants. Don't you go hurtin' him.'

---

* *gilgies* — a small fresh-water crayfish. (Known in most parts of Australia as *yabbies*.)

'Course we're not gunna hurt him', I said indignantly. Nan would never forgive us if she thought we'd been deliberately unkind to wild creatures.

'Can we feed him, Nan?' I asked.

'No need to, he'll find his own tucker.'

I thought that was a bit mean. I decided I'd like to tame that goanna, so that night after tea, I crept out with an old bit of stale cake. I slid it under the tin, and then, in a quiet voice, I let the goanna know who had put it there. After all, I didn't want him palling up with someone who hadn't even gone to the trouble of feeding him.

The next morning, my friend had disappeared. Nan came over to check on him and found me squatting in the sand with a puzzled expression on my face.

'That goanna still there?'

'Naah, he's gone. Where do ya reckon he's gone? I wanted him for a pet.'

'I bet he's hiding further back, he doesn't want us to see him. Look out, I'll move the tin along a bit.' I slid back in the dirt and Nan slowly moved the tin. No goanna.

'How did this get here?' Nan asked. In her hand was the stale bit of yellow cake I'd put there the night before.

'Thought he might be hungry', I replied guiltily.

'Told you he could get his own tucker. You've scared him off, now.'

Nan explained to me that it wasn't the right kind of food for a goanna.

I just nodded. I was convinced he'd had a nibble of Mum's cake and crawled away to die. I felt awful, it was a terrible thing to have the poisoning of a goanna on your conscience.

The highlight of 1961 occurred when I was walking home late one afternoon and happened to hear an urgent call coming from the bush nearby. I stopped dead in my tracks and listened intently. There it was again, a frantic Cheep! Cheep! I walked carefully into the bush until I came to a small clearing; there, at the base of a tall, white gum tree, was a tiny baby mudlark. I stepped back and looked up at the branches high above me. Amongst the moving leaves, I could just glimpse the dark outline of a small nest. I knew there was no chance of returning him up there, it was far too high, and, even if I did, the mother might smell human on her baby and kick him out. I'd heard of animals doing that, birds might be the same. There was only one thing I could do, take him home.

When Mum saw the bulge in the pocket of my dress, she sighed, 'Oh no, what have you got in there?'.

I showed her the bird. 'I'm going to call him Muddy', I said optimistically. I knew Mum was fed up with me bringing home strays.

'No more pets, Sally. I told you, no more pets. You kids bring them home and I'm the one that ends up feeding them.'

'But he's only a baby. I promise I'll look after him.'

'What have you got there?' Nan said as she entered the fray.

'It's a baby mudlark, Nan, fell out of a tree. Mum wants to kick it out.'

'Sally, I do not!'

'Then you'll let me keep it?'

'Oh...all right, but you have to look after it. I'm not having anything to do with it.'

'Aah, ya better with dogs, anyway.' Mum had a natural rapport with dogs.

'You know, Sally, there might be something wrong with that bird. I've heard of mothers getting rid of babies for that reason. He might not live, he's very small.'

'Hmmph, he'll be all right', said Nan, 'bit of food, make sure he's warm at night, that's all he needs'. Nan loved birds, no one was allowed to say a word against her bantam hens, and even when her favourite pink and grey galah bit off half the top of Jill's finger, it was Jill's fault, not cocky's.

I devised my own method of feeding Muddy. I simply placed a small piece of meat on the end of my finger and then stuck my finger down his throat. The technique seemed to suit him, because in no time at all, he'd grown into a fine, healthy bird. I was his mother and he was my pal, and while our greatest adventure together was no more than running errands to the corner shop, in my mind, we experienced far more exciting escapades. About that time, I was into reading Famous Five books, and Muddy fulfilled the role of Timmy, George's dog.

At night, Mud slept on a chair in my room. Jill didn't like him much.

'Don't put him next to my bed, he might poop on me, and if I'm asleep, I won't be able to wipe it off.' She flung herself under the rugs, leaving me to study her lumpy figure in resentment.

I wonder if I could make him poop on her, I thought. I glanced at Mud, he was perched in his usual place, his feet entwined around the narrow rung across the chair back next to my bed. Better not encourage him, I decided, Mum would never forgive me. Still, I could always claim it was an accident. With that thought, I yawned and snuggled down. 'Night Mud', I whispered. He stared back, his eyes and beak intense. I often wished birds could talk. I was considering trying to teach Mud some sign language. My eyes grew heavy and gradually closed. I smiled. Mud raised his left claw twice. Yes! Twice for yes and once for no! I knew he could do it. That night, I dreamt of all the tricks I would teach him. What a show that would be, Mud and me, stars!

The next morning, I awoke to silence, I yawned and stretched. Normally, Muddy's shrill, hungry calls disturbed my sleep; this morning, there were none. I glanced at his chair, Mud was hanging upside down.

58

I half smiled. What's he doing, I thought. Must be a new trick.

'Birds just don't do tricks like that, dear', Mum explained to me later.

I felt terrible that Mud had hung stiffly upside down, not because he was concentrating, but because rigor mortis had set in.

He joined a host of past pets buried under the fig tree in the far corner of our yard. I felt that some of my own personal status died with him. Now, when I ran errands to the corner shop, no one commented on the wild mudlark perched precariously on my shoulder. There was just me, a scrawny, pigtailed kid wearing grubby clothes and a sulky look. Adventures, even in your imagination, were no fun on your own.

The swamp behind our place had become an important place for me. It was now part of me, part of what I was as a person. When I was in the swamp, I lost all track of time. I wallowed in the small, muddish brown creek that meandered through on its way to join the Canning River. I caught gilgies by hanging over an old stormwater drain and wriggling my fingers in the water. As soon as the gilgies latched on, it required only a quick flick of the wrist to land them, gasping, on the bank. I imagined myself as an adventurer, always curious to know what was around the next bend, or behind the clump of taller gums that I glimpsed in the distance.

I loved to think of the swamp as a very wild place. Every summer, our neighbours caught at least three or four large dugites and tiger snakes. It was strange, because, in all my forays into the bush, I never encountered any. Of course, I sensed they were about, but as long as I stayed out of their way, they seemed happy to stay out of mine.

Jill and I had many fun times down there. And we were always carting home some new find to show Nan. Once she'd inspected our prizes and we'd discussed what they were and how they lived, she'd make us return them to the swamp.

But there was no need to visit the swamp during winter, because our backyard invariably flooded with water teeming with tadpoles and small fish. Normally, the water rose to just above our ankles, but after a really good rain, it would get as high as half-way up our lower legs. Such days were greeted with squeals of delight as we splashed boisterously about, squeezing our toes into the muddy bottom and flicking up sand at one another.

'We don't need a swimming pool, do we, Mum?' I laughed as I splashed towards her.

'No, not only have we got water, but fish as well!'

Nan had a less optimistic nature, especially during winter. Her view of the physical world was a deeply personal one. And when she wasn't outside chopping wood or raking leaves, she was observing the weather. Her concern with atmospheric conditions was based on a rather pessimistic view of the frequency of natural disasters. Even though she avidly listened to weather reports on the radio, she never put her complete faith in any meteorologist's opinion. Nan knew their predictions weren't as reliable as her own.

Daily, she checked the sky, the clouds, the wind, and, on particularly still days, the reactions of our animals. Sometimes, she would sit up half the night, checking on the movement of a particular star, or pondering the meaning of a new colour she'd seen in the sky at sunset.

On rare occasions, Mum was called in for consultation. It always amused me to see them standing at the end of our footpath, arms raised upwards, as if in supplication — Nan pointing out various dubious cumulus formations, and Mum nodding and muttering, 'Yes, yes. I see what you mean.' Then, they would both test the wind direction with a wet finger. Nan's catch-phrase at such times was, 'You never know, Glad. You just never know what the weather could bring.'

Since Dad had died, Nan had developed various emergency routines to cope with what she considered likely natural disasters. For earthquakes, she instructed us to run onto the oval opposite our house, avoiding the electric light poles as we went. If we were unfortunate enough to have the earth open up in front of us, we had to jump as high as we could, and hope that by the time we came back down, the earth had closed up again.

While the threat of a major quake was considered extremely remote by the rest of our neighbourhood, Nan had convinced us that it was one of the hazards of daily living. I used to have nightmares where I'd picture myself running onto the oval in my pyjamas as electric light poles crashed and thundered around me.

Besides earthquakes, Nan feared storms the most. Lightning and thunder, her old favourites, never failed to trigger her panic button. Tearing through the house like a whirlwind, she swept us up in her arms and deposited us in a jumbled heap in the hall. Then she raced to the back verandah and dragged in a box of firewood. Hurrying back, she thrust a large, splintery piece of wood into each pair of reluctant hands, with the cryptic instruction, 'Don't you kids let go of those or you'll get electrocuted'.

We were so frightened we didn't dare move. While we sat, panic-stricken, on the floor, Nan hurried from room to room, switching off lights and throwing sheets over mirrors, crockery, cutlery, the bath and even the kitchen sink. Once this was done, she dashed to the meter-box and pulled out all the fuses.

In Nan's mind, lightning and electricity were one and the same, both dangerous and totally untrustworthy. She removed the fuses because it meant the electricity, inspired by the raging storm, couldn't escape and harm us. She threw sheets and blankets over anything shiny, because it was common knowledge that there was nothing lightning loved better than a shiny surface.

If we were lucky, the storm soon passed, but there were occasions when we sat on the floor all afternoon, clutching our chunks of firewood.

'Can't we get up now?'

'You just sit still', Nan said tersely, glowering over us as she guarded the door to the kitchen in case one of us should make a bid for freedom. 'You kids don't know what storms are. I've seen them up North. Terrible, terrible things. People have been killed.'

When Mum returned from work, we would still be sitting there, our limbs numb with cold.

'Oh get up, you kids', Mum said in exasperation as she threw Nan a disgusted look. 'God Nanna, I bet you've had them there all day, they must be frozen stiff.'

'Better cold than dead.'

Mum replaced the fuses and lit the fire and Nan stormed off to her room in a fit of rage. She considered Mum was totally ignorant when it came to child safety.

'Stupid old bugger', Mum muttered as she made us some toast.

By the time tea-time came around, Nan had cooled down. She would emerge, grumpily, from her room and begin to peel potatoes, the whole time complaining about the weather in a low-pitched monotone. We knew then everything was back to normal.

Chapter Ten

CURE-ALLS

We didn't know about Mum's secret weapon. Apparently, she'd given up trying to control us and placed us in the hands of God, instead.

I guess Mum had always been quite religious in her own way, but it only became really obvious to us as we grew older, and after Dad died. She had occasionally gone to a church meeting when I was younger, but Dad was not very positive towards such things and that would have discouraged it. Basically, I suppose, religion and the spiritual were private and personal with Mum.

She supplemented her prayers by taking us to every religious meeting imaginable. That was one thing you could say about Mum, she wasn't biased when it came to religion. We attended the Roman Catholic, Baptist, Anglican, Church of Christ and Seventh Day Adventist churches.

Our favourites were the Seventh Day Adventists. One of our neighbours, Mrs Brown, was an SDA, and every second weekend, she entertained the local children with films. We didn't mind the films, even though the content never varied. Nearly every film was about the devil.

One night, hundreds of fluffy, white angels appeared on the screen, they were all smiling and floating on large, golden clouds. Unfortunately, the sound-track that accompanied these visions of holiness gave the impression of a raging storm. Through the whooshes of wind and crashes of thunder came the sound of heavy footsteps and evil, raucous laughter. We all burst into giggles. Mrs Brown flicked on the lights and began fiddling with the machine at her side.

'There, I think that's got it, lights please.'

This time, the devil appeared. He was predominantly black, except for a red face, and two small, red horns. His long, dark cape billowed around him like a bulging thunder-cloud. Lightning flashed, sharp and yellow, across the screen, illuminating his awesome visage. The rain clouds above shook, heaved and burst forth, but the rain turned to hissing steam when it reached the devil, who kept shooting bright, red flames from his large pitchfork.

If it hadn't been for the sound-track, we would have been terrified. He was the most frightening creature we'd ever seen. However, each time he threw back his horny red head and laughed a presumably wicked laugh, the only sound we heard was that of rushing heavenly voices singing Alleluia, Praise the Lord!

Jill took all our religious instruction seriously, and there was nothing she feared more than the devil. One day as we sat in our backyard, creating elaborate tunnels out of wet sand, a narrow white bone, about the width of a finger, suddenly appeared, pointing upwards.

'Jill', I shouted, 'it's the devil's finger! He's come to get you!' Jill took one look and ran, screaming, inside.

A few minutes later, Mum came stomping out, she was furious. Jill kept trying to get away, but Mum held her firmly and tried to drag her closer to the devil's finger. 'Sally, you sod of a kid, tell Jill it's not really the devil!'

I looked down at the knobbly white bone in front of me, and then, slowly, I looked at Jill.

'It is', she cried, 'it is', and, with a desperate heave, she wrenched herself from Mum's grasp and ran inside. Mum pulled the bone out of the ground, then she looked at me and burst out laughing. It was the closest she'd ever come to belting me.

Every evening before we went to bed, Mum liked us to recite the Lord's Prayer. Jill had a wonderful memory. She could read a large page of writing and then recite it word for word. We all thought she was very clever. After Mum listened to Jill's prayer, she came and sat on the end of my bed to coax me to say mine.

Usually, I hid my head under the covers and pretended I was asleep, but she would pull back the rugs and say, 'It's your turn now, Sally'.

'I never say the Lord's Prayer. I can't see the point, Mum.'

Mum sighed and said, 'Well, perhaps you'll feel like saying it tomorrow night'. Then, she tucked me in and turned out the light. The bathroom was just near our room and the light there burned all night. I was too scared to sleep in total darkness.

'You're horrible, Sally', Jill whispered after Mum had left. 'Every Sunday, they ask me why you won't come to Sunday School. What am I s'posed to say? I can't keep telling them you're sick.'

'Aw, I don't care what you say. It's none of their business.'

'That's the trouble with you, you just don't care what other people think. You're the only kid in Sunday School who doesn't get a book at the end of the year because you haven't gone enough. You make me 'shamed.'

'Aw, shut up and go to sleep', I muttered as I rolled the other way. I knew I'd hurt her feelings, I could hear her sniffling under the rugs. It was years before I learnt what compromise meant.

When Mum wasn't praying for the benefit of my health and well-being, she was taking me to the doctor. I used to feel very frustrated with my weak body. If I could have, I would have disowned it.

During one visit, the doctor told Mum, 'You're living in the worst possible place for this child. Isn't there any way you can move? She won't get any better unless you do.' I looked hopefully at Mum, I'd always wanted to travel. Mum just shook her head and said, 'I have to stay where I am.'

She was quite cynical about his advice. On the way home, she said, 'I'm a widow with five kids, where does he think I can move to?'.

'Don't worry, Mum', I said confidently, 'I'll survive'.

'I pray you will', she sighed. And pray she did. I never saw her praying, but I knew if there were a competition, Mum would be the best prayer in the neighbourhood.

Almost a year to the day after Dad died, I contracted rheumatic fever. Many times on the way to school, I had to stop and hold my chest until the pain had passed. Mum rushed me to the local doctor twice, but he maintained that I was merely suffering from growing pains. I had no idea that getting taller could be such agony.

Night-times were the worst. I curled myself up into a tight little ball and willed the pain to go away. I hurt too much to cry. Nan tried to help me as much as she could. I could tell by the look on her face and the sympathetic noises she made that she was worried about me. She admonished me for sleeping in such a peculiar position and then, gently, she straightened out my arms and legs, encouraging me to sleep more normally.

She spent hours wrapping wet towels and torn-off strips of sheeting around my limbs, all the time reassuring me that the pain would soon disappear. I remember a couple of nights, when I was particularly bad, she just ran her hands slowly down the full length of my body, not touching me, but saying, 'You'll be all right, I won't let anything happen to you'.

As soon as the bandages and towels had dried, she slowly unwound them and then went and wet them again. 'You're very hot, Sally', she said, 'it's not good for a child to be that hot'. By the time I finally fell asleep, I felt as stiff as a cardboard doll. When I awoke the following morning, the pain had generally gone, but not for long. I learnt a valuable lesson from being that sick, I learnt I was strong inside. I had to be to survive. My illness eventually subsided without any medical treatment.

Nan had many beliefs to do with health that she passed on to us. For one thing, she was obsessed with healthy bowels. So was Mum, but whether this was because of Nan's influence or because she'd reached the same beliefs herself from her lengthy sessions in the toilet was hard to tell.

Nan worried about people who stayed in the toilet too long. If Mum took longer than ten minutes, Nan manifested her concern by knocking on the toilet door and calling, 'Glad . . . are you in there?'. Mum invariably replied, 'Of course I am, you stupid old woman'.

'Now don't get nasty with me, Glad', Nan responded. 'You always get nasty with me when you're in the toilet. I just wanted to make sure you were all right.'

'What the bloody hell do you think's going to happen to me in here?'

'You could faint, Glad. I'll never forget old Mrs Caulfield, she fainted in the toilet. It was hours before her daughter found her. You're lucky you've got someone to check on you, Glad. Glad . . . are you still in there?'

By this time, Mum was so annoyed that she flushed the toilet violently and emerged, ready to berate Nan. Nan's sense of timing was perfect; when she heard the chain being pulled, she walked quickly to her room and locked herself in.

I later realised that the time Mum spent in the toilet was her only chance for peace and quiet. With five children in the house, where else could she go?

Both Mum and Nan convinced us that a lot of illness was caused by constipation. We were quite happy to go along with their views in theory, but when their obsession began to extend to us in the form of regular doses of castor oil, Laxettes and what we crudely termed 'glycerine sticks', we balked. Our co-operation became more and more difficult to obtain, and Mum finally decided that the hassle in first discovering our separate hiding places and then literally dragging us from them wasn't worth the satisfaction she got when we all lined up for the toilet.

In a sense, Mum and Nan weren't health fanatics so much as sickness fanatics. They took great pleasure in reading of the discovery of diseases with unknown causes. They were particularly interested in tropical medicine, reasoning that as Australia was in cooee of the equator, anything could come wafting down.

While Mum and Nan's interest in exotic diseases may have added a little excitement to their daily grind, it added only fear to ours. Our views concerning common childhood illnesses were a trifle unbalanced. We were convinced that leprosy and the bubonic plague abounded in our piece of suburbia, and when we caught measles and chicken pox, we wondered what they would lead to. Illness was a great mystery to us, we didn't know what caused it or how to cure it, and Nan's gloomy hints added nothing to our already tenuous sense of security.

It was Nan who first brought out the sceptic in me. I was suspicious of outsiders, especially those in authority. Nan convinced me that most people were untrustworthy, especially doctors. For years, she had been talking about the Old Cures, the ones they used in the early days. I knew the Old Cures were the best.

One of Nan's great cure-alls was pepper. Any gashes were stuffed full with pepper and then tightly bound with strips torn from an old, white sheet. She also believed that eating a tin of beetroot would replace the blood you lost. While we exhibited various higgledy-piggledy scars on our arms and legs, the result of wounds stitched at Hollywood Repatriation Hospital, Nan had none. Her skin always healed soft and whole.

But there were two of Nan's health measures that I found difficult to accept. The first concerned Enos. She regularly dosed herself with Enos because she was convinced it helped oxygenate the blood. 'You try it, Sally', she said to me one day. 'It makes your blood clean and your head clear.' I did take a mouthful, but, to me, the taste was so foul I immediately spat it out.

The second measure involved kerosene. Nan maintained it was wonderful for removing aches and pains and for generally keeping your body in tiptop condition. When I was suffering from rheumatic fever, Nan begged me to let her rub my arms and legs with it. I steadfastly refused, I hated the smell. Nan was so conscientious about her twice daily kerosene rubs we feared that, combined with her chain-smoking, a sudden blaze might one day be the cause of her death.

Nan's interest in health was not restricted to the human population.

One hot Saturday afternoon, when I was stretched out on an itchy blue towel, soaking up the sun, it slowly dawned on my numbed senses that Nan's restless movements around the yard had ceased. Curiosity overcame lethargy, and, peering under my sweaty armpit, I took a quick glance around to see where she was.

I observed her, standing very still, close to the smallest gum tree in our backyard. Using the back of her knuckles, she tapped on the trunk twice, and then once with her stick. Then, she inclined her head towards the trunk as though listening for something. After a lengthy pause, she seemed satisfied, and, giving the earth a quick prod with her stick, she moved on to the paperbark further down.

'Nan', I called out, 'what on earth are you doing?'

She started in surprise. I had been quiet for so long it was obvious she'd forgotten I was there. She waved her stick at me in a threatening manner and said crossly, 'I'm not doing anything, you go back to sleep!'.

'Come on, Nan, I saw you tapping on that tree, what were you doing?'

She jabbed her stick in the sand, turned to me and said, 'You can't be trusted any more, Sally. I can't walk round my own backyard without one of you kids spying on me.'

'You know I wasn't spying. I just happened to see what you were doing, that's all. Now, are you going to tell me or not?'

She could see I wasn't going to give up without a fight, so she said quickly, 'All right, I was just checking on them to make sure they were all right, that's all. Now, no more questions, I got work to do!'

66

'Okay', I sighed as I burrowed my head down into my towel once again.

I hadn't comprehended her answer at all. What on earth did she mean, making sure they were all right? I puzzled over her words for a few seconds and then dismissed them. There was so much about Nan I didn't understand.

Chapter Eleven

GETTING AHEAD

Mum was offered a job as a cleaner at our school at the beginning of the year I started Grade Six. The hours were perfect, because they fitted in with the two other part-time jobs she was doing. But she didn't accept the job straight away. First, she got us all together and asked if we would mind her taking it.

'What on earth are you talking about, Mum?' I said.

'Well, I don't want to take the job if you children would mind. I thought you might worry about what your friends would think.'

Without hesitation, I replied, 'We wouldn't mind, Mum, we'd really like it because we'd see more of you'.

Mum smiled at me. She knew how naive I was, that I didn't realise being a school cleaner carried with it very little status.

We helped after school, wiping down the boards, emptying the bins and sweeping the floors. I enjoyed the boards the most, mainly because it gave me access to the chalk. Before wiping them down, I would scrawl rude comments about school across the whole length of the wall. It gave me a great sense of power.

With more money coming in, Mum took to indulging us whenever she could. This indulgence took the form of unlimited lollies and fruit, rather than new clothes, toys or books. She'd managed to take us all to the Royal Show the year before, and this year, she told us that, because of her new job, we would really do it in style.

Like the year before, our first port of call at the show was our uncle's stall. He ran one of the amusement centres in sideshow alley, and we thought it was such a magical place. While we looked at the machines, Mum chattered on to Uncle, discussing one triviality after another. Even when Uncle excused himself on the pretext of fixing one of his money-grabbing machines, Mum followed, mentioning the weather or some person they both knew, but whom she hadn't seen for years. Eventually, Uncle fished out five ten-bob notes and told us all to run along. Mum could be boring when it suited her.

We bought show-bags crammed with Smarties, Cherry Ripes, Samboy

Potato Chips and Violet Crumble Bars, we weren't interested in the educational ones. Mum insisted on buying Nan a Mills and Ware suitcase filled with biscuits. Nan loved it. She ate all the biscuits and then used the suitcase to store things in.

One of our show-bags had had a large packet of marshmallows in it and Mum came up with the super idea of toasting them over the fire. Just like the Famous Five. We were all terribly excited about this, we loved anything new.

While Mum stoked up the fire, we all gathered sticks from the garden. I cleaned down my stick as best I could and then hurriedly shoved a marshmallow on the end and placed it close to the coals. It immediately smoked and went black. Everyone laughed. Jill insisted on having a turn then, but the same thing happened. Finally, Mum squeezed between us, her stick adorned with blobs of pink and white, one marshmallow for each of us.

We waited patiently. Mum'll be able to do it, we thought. She can do anything when she sets her mind to it. Seconds passed. We all leapt up in fright when she let out a sudden shriek.

'Arrgh! Stupid bloody thing!' Dropping her stick, she jumped up, holding her hand. The bottom pink marshmallow, being closest to the coals, had melted quicker than the others and slid down the short length of remaining stick and onto her hand. It was hot and sticky, and clung as Mum tried to remove it by stretching it from one hand to the other.

We all choked. It was a compromise between coughing and laughing. Mum's pantomime had us in stitches, but the stick she'd dropped had fallen into the fire, and the remaining marshmallows were smoking vigorously. Carefully, I reached over and flicked her stick from the fire with my own. It lay on the floor-boards, blackened and sticky. Mum retreated to the kitchen, she needed a knife to scrape the marshmallow off.

Fifteen minutes later, she returned with a tray laden with tea, toast and jam, and sardines. Soon, we were all laughing and joking as we normally did on a Sunday night.

For Nan, Mum's extra job meant she had more work to do around the house, but it also meant a twice yearly bottle of brandy and a reasonable amount to bet on the TAB. Sometimes, Nan let us pick a horse, too, and she would get the lady next door to put a bet on for us as well. We had a rule in our house when it came to backing horses: never back the same horse as Nan, they never came in. Before any of us picked out our horses, we asked Nan which ones she fancied. It narrowed the field down considerably.

Besides the TAB, Nan loved lottery tickets. Both she and Mum were convinced that, one day, our family would come into a lot of money. It was a poor-man's dream, but we believed it. The dream became such a reality in my mind that I often thought, well, it doesn't matter if

I don't get a job when I'm grown up, we'll probably have won the lotteries by then. Billy thought the same. Jill was the only one among us who seemed keen to work at anything.

Having more money also meant that Nan could really indulge in chain-smoking. In fact, she took to smoking so consistently that the front of her hair changed colour. While the rest of her frizzy mop was a light grey, the front was nicotine yellow. When we pointed it out to her, she was quite pleased. 'It's better than hair dye', she chuckled as she looked in the mirror, 'now if only I could get it to go round the back as well . . .'.

We came to consider Nan's cigarettes as an extension of her anatomy. She had mastered the skill of being able to talk and smoke at the same time. It seemed it didn't matter what Nan did, her cigarette would remain glued to the corner of her mouth as securely as that part of her lip.

And she had the longest ash in the neighbourhood. I always waited expectantly for it to fall off. I was sure that with one more puff, it would disintegrate and burn yet another hole in her cardigan. Four puffs later, it was still there. While smoking, and the cough she was developing with it, were now an integral part of her personality, there were two important occasions when she didn't smoke.

The first was at night when she was in bed. For a long time, one of her greatest pleasures had been to lie in bed at night and enjoy a leisurely puff. However, one night she'd set fire to her mattress, and Mum, seeing the smoke, had rushed in and thrown a kettle of water over her. Nan hated getting wet, so she gave up her night-time fag.

The other occasion was during summer when the dry bush surrounding the swamp would ignite into a raging bushfire. She never smoked while the fire was still burning. She felt it added to the heat.

Bushfires were a real threat to our house in those days. As billowing clouds of black smoke engulfed the neighbourhood, the firemen came knocking at each door with the message: 'Look luv, if the wind doesn't change soon, you'll have to evacuate'.

Nan always responded with: 'We're not leavin', this is the only home we got'. If the men tried to argue with her, she pointed to her garden hose and said, 'You're not the only ones with water, you know'.

Their usual response to that was to try and explain to Nan how easily the flames could leap from roof to roof. Nan countered this by giving them a tour of our yard just to show them how many hoses she had. For some reason, six strategically placed garden hoses meant little to the firemen. 'Listen, luv', they reasoned, 'if that wind doesn't change, the flames'll be in next door's and then they'll be in your place and you'll all go up in smoke. You got five kids here, too, can't someone have them for the day?'

'We got no one', Nan would reply grumpily. 'Anyway, they're all right, I've wet them down.' It was true, we were dripping wet. Any hint of a fire in the swamp and Nan would line us all up and squirt us down with the hose. Then it was the chooks', cats', dogs' and budgies' turn.

Sometimes, Mum thought Nan's precautions were a little premature. 'God, Nan, have you wet them down already?' she'd complain. 'No one's even called the Fire Brigade yet!' Nan always narrowed her eyes and looked at Mum as though she couldn't believe how stupid she was. When Mum turned to go inside, she'd squirt her with the hose.

Nan kept great stores of men's handkerchiefs in case of fire. She would wet them and then plaster them over our heads and faces. It made it easier to breathe when the ash rained down.

Fortunately for us, the wind did always change, and somehow we survived the heat and the ash and the billowing smoke. It was only when the fire in the swamp was completely out that Nan would relax and light up another cigarette.

Grade Six in primary school wasn't a bad year for me. Jill and I were often taken off normal classwork to help paint and design special things for the school. Also, I liked my teacher. He was firm, but very kind, and he got on well with Mum. He'd broken his nose as a child, so he was an unusual-looking man. I was impressed with the way he joked about his nose and never let its odd shape worry him. He always used to point out to the accident-prone ones in our class how they would end up if they didn't stop doing silly things.

I was unexpectedly made president of the Red Cross Club that year. Part of my job was instructing younger children in road safety. There was also a paper test that they sat for in their lunch hour. If they passed, I was allowed to award them a Safety First Certificate. Jill sat for the test and went home crying to Mum because I failed her. You were only allowed to make two errors and she, uncharacteristically, had made three.

Mum was furious. She maintained I should have passed Jill simply because we were related. Jill sat the test the following week and passed. I breathed a sigh of relief. I wasn't sure how long I could hold out against Mum's Blood's Thicker Than Water routine.

They had a Safety First Week at school that year and several members of parliament were invited to attend. Being president of the Red Cross Club, I was to have the honour of showing them over the class displays.

That Friday, just before the bell rang for home time, our teacher warned us again to be careful over the weekend and not to have any accidents. Unfortunately, our class was accident-prone. There was a small nucleus of children who were always missing the bus for swimming, skinning their knees on the playground, and jamming their fingers in the sliding door. We all glanced guiltily at one another, each of us wondering who was going to be stupid enough to muff it.

I was extra careful that weekend, but, on Sunday, Billy teased me

71

once too often. I decided to teach him a lesson. Around and around the house we ran, Billy's howls of laughter slowly changing to cries of trepidation as I gained on him. As we rounded the corner of the house for the fourth time, Billy decided he needed Mum's protection. He leapt onto the front porch, flung open the door and darted inside, slamming the door in my face as he went. I was running so fast I was unable to stop myself from going into it. Unfortunately for me, the entire door, except for the jarrah frame, was made of bubbled glass. I went straight through and landed with a thud against the inside wall. I screamed when I looked down at my arm. There was a large slice of skin missing, and a long, pulsating blue vein was protruding.

Mum came running. She took one look at the multitude of tiny cuts all over my body, then focused on the gash in my arm and shrieked, 'Oh, my God!'. Wrapping my arm in a towel, she drove straight to Hollywood Hospital. Well, as straight as she could in her condition, shock was beginning to set in. On arrival, they placed us both on stretchers and, while they stitched me up, Mum revived. A cup of tea and two Milk Arrowroot biscuits later and she was her old self.

On Monday, I arrived at school with a large, white sling, an armful of stitches and a guilty conscience. My teacher eyed me in dismay. I conducted the tour of the Safety Displays anyway, trying to walk discreetly, with the injured part of my body turned away from our Very Important Guests. I think they found my efforts amusing.

By the time Guy Fawkes night came around that year, we had a huge amount of fireworks stockpiled in the laundry, so it was only fitting that we build an extra large bonfire as well. It took us all day. We gathered everything that was burnable and dumped it in a heap in the yard. We even raided the swamp for dry wood.

Mum was very impressed with our efforts, so we gave her the honour of lighting it. With great ceremony, she set fire to a long length of rolled newspaper, which she then pressed firmly into our huge mound. Instead of being rewarded with the usual sudden vrroom, as the fire took hold, there was only a small hissing sound. Even the fire on Mum's newspaper extinguished.

We all began complaining and arguing about what had gone wrong. Finally, Mum told us all to be quiet and she inspected our creation very closely.

'Nanna!' she growled, ominously, as she turned around, 'what have you done?'.

We all turned to look at Nan. As usual, she was standing by with her faithful garden hose. She chuckled guiltily and wiggled the hose at us.

That was the last straw for Mum. 'How could you have wet down the kids' bonfire after they worked so hard all day? So help me I'll never buy you another hose as long as you live!'

Nan defiantly squirted a bit more water on the bonfire. 'You've got no sense Glad. You know how bad those fires were last summer.'

'What?' Mum gasped in astonishment. 'You mean those bloody bushfires? That was over eight months ago. What's that got to do with the kids' bonfire?'

As they continued to argue, I sighed and dropped down on the grass. I don't know why Mum even bothered to try to reason with her. After years of living with Nan, she should have realised that there didn't necessarily have to be a direct connection between any two natural events for Nan to feel she was doing the right thing by protecting us from possible danger. The evening was a real fizzog.

That Christmas, Mum's old friend Lois gave her a dog. It was a tiny, pedigree terrier. When Billy first heard we were getting another dog, he was keen for it to be his. He'd always liked dogs, and had a hankering for one that belonged solely to him. He was sick of family pets. However, when he saw the size of it, he changed his mind. I mean, what self-respecting eight-year-old boy would want to be seen with a dog that size yapping at his heels.

But Jill loved our new dog and her affection was returned. Tiger, as she named him, soon answered only to her. Tiger used to yap viciously from our bedroom window-sill every morning at anything that moved. I complained to Mum one morning that she never let him outside. It wasn't a healthy way for a dog to live. Mum said she was afraid he might get run over or bite someone. I howled with laughter.

But, because of my complaint and the fact that Tiger spent his time tearing around the house, destroying anything he could sink his fangs into, Mum relented. Tiger was given his freedom and then proceeded to attack the cat next door. By the time Mum managed to catch him, she was worn to a frazzle. I got The Silent Treatment.

We were certainly glad that Widdles wasn't fierce. He'd grown into a beautiful big dog and could have really hurt someone if that was his nature. With absolutely no encouragement on our part, he'd trained himself to do many helpful things around the house, like bringing in the paper, and generally tidying up the place. He shared his food and bed with our black and white cat and had never been in trouble in his life, until now.

Tiger decided that he liked his freedom, so as soon as Mum opened the front door early in the morning, he darted swiftly between her legs and tore onto the oval opposite. There was a large group of neighbourhood dogs who were in the habit of taking an early morning stroll and Tiger loved to nip behind each one and sink his sharp little fangs into their back legs. Within minutes, the pack would be in a frenzy and Mum would dispatch faithful old Widdles to the rescue. He would bark his authority over the pack and then pick Tiger up by the scruff of the neck and carry him home.

It was a wonderful partnership, but one destined for an early end.

One afternoon, Mum broke the sad news to Jill that Tiger had passed on. Jill naturally assumed that one of the bigger dogs from the pack had finally got its revenge. Mum found it difficult to keep a straight face as she explained how Tiger had single-handedly attacked the number 37 bus. It was a fitting end.

With all the extra jobs Mum kept digging up, the money was really rolling in. At least, that's how it seemed to us. For one thing, we now had access to ridiculous quantities of food, especially during winter. We arrived home from school, soaked to the skin, dumped our bags in the hall and then made straight for the wood stove in the kitchen, where we set our smelly shoes and socks to dry on the open door of the oven. I always managed to squeeze the closest to the fire, and, when Nan wasn't looking, I poked my bare feet inside the oven, a practice that invariably led to chilblains.

'Eat! Eat!' Nan commanded as she placed huge chunks of jam tart and mince pie before us. 'You kids got to eat. I know what it's like to be hungry, it's a terrible thing.'

We never thought much about the way Nan carried on over food, much less considered the possibility that she might have known hard times. We had no conception of what it was like to have a really empty stomach; even when Dad was alive, there'd always been something to fill up on. Nan had cooked rabbit a lot and she was good at making damper. Now, we had food aplenty, and Nan was giving us the impression that going without food for any length of time wasn't normal. While she thought she was doing the right thing by squeezing in as many meals as possible in one day, it would lead to eating habits later in life that were difficult to break.

We learnt not only to eat in quantity, but quickly as well. It was a matter of expediency. The child who finished its dinner last often had part of its dessert pinched, or missed out on the extra baked potatoes browning in the oven.

Our conversations were never regulated, either. When we spoke, we all spoke at once, and whoever had the loudest voice or the funniest story dominated the table, even if his or her mouth was full of potato.

There was nothing we loved better than huddling around the wood stove on cold afternoons, swapping stories. An open fire was always at the centre of our family gatherings. If it wasn't inside, it was out in the yard. And if it wasn't the wood stove in the kitchen, it was in the red-brick fireplace in the lounge-room. There was something about an open fire that drew us all together. We felt very secure in front of an open fire.

Countless times, after Nan had woken me early to show me something special in the garden, she said, 'Come inside, we'll light the fire'. I screwed up newspaper and Nan pushed the kindling in on top and then passed me the matches. I lit it just the way she'd shown me, striking the match away from my body. Sometimes, if the wood was green or a bit damp, we helped it along with a dash of kero.

Once the fire was lit, Nan passed me the toasting fork. It had been hand-made out of two bits of wire twined together. There were three sharp prongs and a long handle with a loop on the end so you could hang it on a nail next to the stove. The nail had fallen out a couple of years ago and had never been replaced, so we tended to keep it lying around on top of the oven. I thought of it as the devil's pitchfork.

I stabbed a piece of sliced white bread across the prongs and poked it towards the flames. Having singed one side, I quickly turned it over and singed the other. It couldn't really be called toast, because it was soft in the middle, but on cold mornings, it did just as well. It was hot, topped with melted butter and lashings of jam, and it soon warmed an empty tummy. By the time the kettle had boiled, we'd eaten at least six slices.

Pretty soon, my four brothers and sisters wandered out and demanded breakfast. 'What's for brekky?' Jill slurred as she eyed me gulping the last sweet, sticky remnants of tea in my mug. 'S'pose you've eaten all the toast.'

'Get a move on, Sally', Nan muttered. 'You get dressed for school and let Jilly cook the toast now.' I was always reluctant to leave the warmth of the fire. I slowly eased myself off the small, white stool and let Jill take my place. I knew she hated cooking toast, so I took my time.

She was a puzzle to me, she didn't like gutting chickens or chopping wood, either, and she kept her clothes neat and tidy. She had a natural sense of order.

Chapter Twelve

TRIUMPHS AND FAILURES

Grade Seven was a mixture of triumphs and failures. It was also the year my brother David began primary school.

David was a quiet, gentle little boy with lots of imagination. Unfortunately for him, he was landed with a teacher who was a middle-aged spinster. She was stern and unyielding. David was easily flustered, especially when he was trying to do the right thing; consequently, he was continually in trouble over minor details like lost rubbers, books, drawings and pencils. It wasn't, of course, entirely David's fault, our home was so disorganised it was difficult to find even large items, let alone the small things he was supposed to keep in his school case.

By far the greatest trauma David experienced was the intermittent loss of his black print pencil. He seemed to spend most of his first year at school crying over it. And we knew that whenever he burst into tears at home, the first words to come from his wobbly mouth would be 'Black Print Pencil!'.

Mum was disgusted at the hard attitude his teacher seemed to be taking towards him. She bought David a couple of extra black print pencils as back-ups. However, David lived more in his imagination than in reality at that stage, and he was so absent-minded that he soon lost track of those as well.

I lost count of the number of times he ran from the lower end of our primary school to the upper end, where Jill and I had to console him over his latest disaster. Invariably, it was the dreaded Black Print Pencil.

In that last year at primary school, I developed an allergy to chalk. On one of my many trips to the doctor, Mum had naively enquired, 'Do you think it's the chalk, doctor? She seems to get an attack of hay fever every time she goes near the blackboard.'

I was amazed that, by now, Mum hadn't twigged to the fact that I was allergic to school, not chalk. To my even greater amusement, the doctor prevaricated; he was filling in for our family doctor and it was his first year out of the hospital. He'd néver heard of it happening, but then, anything was possible.

The chalk allergy proved a wonderful bonus. I no longer lingered over breakfast or dragged my feet reluctantly down the footpath when it was time to leave for school. Instead, I walked cheerfully off, secure in the knowledge that, by mid-morning, I would be on my way home again. I usually managed to leave school and arrive in Manning Road just as Mum drove past in the old Vanguard on her way home from an early morning stint at her latest job, cleaning the doctor's surgery. If I was late, she'd park the car on the corner and wait for me.

Recognition came at the beginning of third term, when I won the coveted Dick Cleaver Award for Citizenship. The whole school voted, and, for some reason, I won. I wondered who Jill had bribed, she had a lot of influence in the lower grades.

My prize was a choice of any book available from the bookshops. When our headmaster, Mr Buddee, asked me what I had in mind, I replied, without hesitation, 'A book of fairy tales please'. I think he was rather taken aback, because he told me to go away and think about it for a few days.

I stuck to my choice, even though my class teacher tried to talk me into something more suitable. My class-mates thought I was potty, too, they didn't understand. I knew fairy tales were the stuff dreams were made of. And I loved dreams.

Mr Buddee announced to the school assembly one morning that our end-of-the-year extravaganza was going to be the biggest we'd ever had. We were all excited, especially when we heard there were going to be dancing and play-acting as well as singing and exhibitions of our work. He was a very creative man. Under his administration, parents had seen progressively bigger and brighter displays of children and their work.

I was convinced that, because of my inability to co-ordinate my limbs, I wouldn't be chosen for anything, and I desperately wanted to participate in one of the dances. So my glee knew no bounds when my teacher informed me that I was to be in the Dance of the Black Swans, as well as the Maypole. Jill was also very excited, because she was chosen for the Dance of the Leaves.

In no time at all, it seemed, the big night was upon us. At the sound of two piano rolls, thirty pairs of black, painted swan feet swept onto the bitumen playground. We all held our heads stiffly and our arms and legs flowed in unison, gliding as a swan might across a lake. A host of adoring Mums and Dads, all of whom thought their particular daughter a budding Margot Fonteyn, watched proudly. All, of course, except my Mum. She cherished many illusions, but, fortunately for me, that wasn't one of them.

With the sound of the applause for the Black Swan Dance still ringing in my ears, I waited with bated breath to participate in the Maypole. My over-confidence was to be my undoing. Half-way through the second time round the Maypole, I suddenly realised that my red ribbon was pulling on the other girls, and that the girl who was normally ahead of me was now two girls behind. I couldn't understand what had happened. Hadn't I woven an intricate pattern in a graceful and gentle manner? I looked up and, to my dismay, realised that I had woven an intricate pattern, so intricate no one had been able to follow it. The hushed whispers from the audience were not from admiration but embarrassment.

Dropping my tightly held red ribbon, I pushed past the other girls and fled. I could still hear the music playing as I hid in shame behind one of the darkened class-rooms. I crouched as low as I could and prayed the earth would open and swallow me up so I wouldn't have to face my class-mates.

The music finally ended, and, as I pressed against the hard, outer wall of the class-rooms, I heard Mrs Oldfield, our Maypole teacher, thunder past, growling, 'Where is that girl?'. I was stricken with terror. Mrs Oldfield was a big woman, even the boys in the school were scared of her. If you had a choice between the cane and Mrs Oldfield, you always chose the cane. There was no comparison.

After about half an hour of hiding in terror, Mum found me. 'Don't be silly, Sally', she scolded as she looked down at my huddled form, and, after bundling me into the car, we drove home in silence. Jill held her sides and stared out the window all the way. Mum had forbidden her to laugh.

It was during that final year at primary school that I noticed that whenever we brought our friends home to play after school, Nan would disappear.

'How come Nan nicks off when our friends are here?' I asked Jill one day.

'Dunno.'

'Why's she started doing it now, she never did it before, did she?'

'She's been doin' it for years.'

'I never noticed.'

'You never notice anything!'

Later that day, I asked Mum the same question and she put it down to Nan's old age. This wasn't news to me; in my mind, Nan had always been old. I couldn't imagine her actually getting older, though. She was the sort of person that would stay the same age for ever.

One day, I walked into the kitchen with one of my friends and Nan was there, making a cup of tea. She was furious with me. After my friend had left, she said, 'You're not to keep bringin' people inside, Sally. You got no shame. We don't want them to see how we live.'

'Why not?'

'People talk, you know, we don't want people talkin' about us. You dunno what they might say!'

'Okay, Nan', I agreed. It wasn't often I had friends after school, I wasn't pally with a lot of kids.

Towards the end of the year, our class was given a batch of IQ tests. We were told that they were a sure way of measuring our intelligence. The tests would indicate at which level we would be placed the following year in high school.

There were only two streams in high school: the Professional stream, which generally included at least two maths and one science subject, and was aimed at entrance to university or other colleges of advanced education; and the Commercial stream, which meant you took shorthand and typing and left school at fifteen. On the basis of the tests, it was recommended that I be placed in the Commercial stream.

Mr Buddee took a personal interest in my case. He couldn't understand how I could do so well in school, despite all my illnesses, and yet so badly on the IQ tests.

One morning, he called Mum in for an interview and explained to her the difficulty he was having in getting me placed in the Professional stream. By the time I was ushered into the office, Mum was sitting next to Mr Buddee with a dumbfounded look on her face. She'd never heard of IQ tests before, and I think she thought they'd discovered I was mentally retarded. Perhaps she even thought it might explain some of my past behaviour.

Mr Buddee asked me if I had been ill on the day of the tests. He also asked if there was anything I would like to say about them.

I felt incredibly stupid. I wanted to explain my feelings, but whenever anyone questioned me directly about anything, I automatically clammed up.

We had been given one test after another. There were pages of complicated drawings and numerous questions about farmers and their produce. It wasn't long before I came to regard Farmer Jones and his three sons, with their two bushels of wheat, five bags of navel oranges and three ton of granny smiths, as cretins. When I wasn't day-dreaming, I simply marked each multiple choice question a,b,c simultaneously.

That night, I pestered Mum to tell me what Mr Buddee had said. At first, she refused, but, after some pestering, she finally explained what it all meant. I was deeply offended by the fact that I had been labelled dumb by the stupid, boring test. Yet, at the same time, I was excited by the prospect that I would be allowed to leave school at fifteen. Mum wasn't having a bar of it. She was determined that, by hook or by crook, I would go on to tertiary studies.

'But Mum, the only place I want to study is at that famous art school in Paris. If I can't do that, I don't care what I do.'

Mum was aghast. She protested that she wasn't made of money. 'Wouldn't you miss your family?' she added as an afterthought.

'Naah', I retorted, 'I'd be too busy painting'.

Poor Mum. She had a heart like a sponge and the most flexible will in the neighbourhood. I gave her the run-around for years. She deserved better.

Chapter Thirteen

GROWING UP

At school, we had been warned over and over about strangers. The police had visited nearly every year to give talks and show films, and Mum had always stressed the importance of refusing lifts from anyone we didn't know, especially if they offered you lollies. What no one ever warned us about were friends or relations.

The summer vacation following my final year in primary school was spent with some elderly friends of Dad's. We called them Uncle and Aunty.

Aunty was a pleasant, white-haired old soul who wore the kind of glasses that glittered in the dark. Uncle wasn't so nice. I disliked him on sight. He was short, with corrugated hair, a beetroot-shaped nose and a ruddy face. He was a boozer and very friendly to Jill and I, often patting us on the head or shoulder.

One day, he told us about some beautiful jewellery that he kept in his tool-shed, which was hidden behind some tall trees at the rear of the yard. It was a Blue Bird necklace and bracelet. That jewellery was all the rage then, so we were quite happy to go with him to the shed.

As promised, he showed us his treasure, but then he climbed up and tucked it away on a shelf too high for us to reach.

I tugged at Jill's arm. 'C'mon, let's go', I whispered. It was obvious we weren't going to get anything out of him. Jill wouldn't move. Her eyes were glued to the shelf where he'd hidden the jewellery.

'Don't go yet, girls', he coaxed, 'I've got other things to show'.

'Listen', I said urgently, 'I can hear Mum calling us for lunch'. I grabbed Jill's arm and we both raced out of the shed and back towards the house. I hadn't liked the way he was looking at us.

He certainly was persistent. He took to following Jill and me around whenever Mum wasn't on the scene. One day, he did some fast talking and convinced us that, if we came to his shed, he'd actually give us the jewellery.

When we reached the shed, he climbed up on the bench and retrieved the necklace and bracelet. Then he showed them to us once again, but instead of giving them to us as promised, he quickly placed them in his tool-box, closed the lid, and sat on it.

'You said you were going to give them to us', I said suspiciously.

'In time', he smiled. 'In time.' Uncle's teeth and fingers were discoloured from a lifetime of smoking. His teeth were the same colour as the small, brownish pebbles we'd dug up at Grandma's house. His fingers were so stained they reminded me of barbecue sausages. He began to talk softly to both of us about what nice girls we were. I felt very nervous.

'Jill, I think we should go', I said as I edged her towards the door. Just then, we heard Billy shout from another part of the garden, 'Ji-ill, Ji-ill, come and find me. I'm hiding.' Jill and Billy were good mates. She ran off immediately, forgetting all about the jewellery.

I turned to follow, but Uncle grabbed my arm. 'You stay with me', he said. 'You can have the necklace. I might even give you the bracelet as well.' I backed up against the wall. Uncle moved closer and tried to put his hand down my pants. I shoved him away, he fell over and landed on his tool-box. Serves him right, I thought. I dashed off. He never got within cooee of me after that. I warned Jill never to go up to his shed again.

I was frightened for her, yet I couldn't explain what I was frightened of. She disregarded my warning. On two occasions, I caught her plodding along silently after Uncle. I caught up with her and distracted her with something else.

It was a reversal of roles for us. Jill had always been physically stronger than me and was always fighting my battles. Now, it was my turn to look out for her.

That summer signalled the start of my growing up. I was very self-conscious, none of my body seemed to be in proportion. I had long legs, long arms and the bit in between was flat and skinny.

I think what I disliked most about myself, though, was the lack of pigmentation in certain patches of skin around my neck and shoulders. I always buttoned my shirts right up to the collar. If the top button happened to be missing, I pulled my collar close in around my neck and held it there with a large safety-pin.

Mum must have noticed how self-conscious I was, because she took me to see a skin specialist, who said there was nothing he could do and referred me to a cosmetician.

The cosmetician gave me different coloured batches of make-up to mix together so I could conceal my patches.

After all the trouble Mum had gone to, I didn't have the courage to tell her I had no intention of ever using the make-up. Actually, I was mad at her. It was one thing for me to stick a safety-pin in my collar, but quite another for her to drag me around to specialists, exhibiting me to the world. At the first opportunity, I wrapped my make-up in newspaper and threw it in the bin. It was a symbolic gesture. I decided that, from then on, I would bare that part of my body, and if people were repulsed, that was their problem, not mine. It was the first time my lower neck had seen the light of day for years.

Apart from my appearance, over those holidays, my main worry was high school. I kept wishing it didn't exist. For a time, I had very romantic notions about running away to join a circus. I would climb up into the small gum tree in our backyard and sit there for hours, day-dreaming about circus life. But the circus never came and, in February 1964, I started high school.

I felt terribly old-fashioned. I still had two long plaits dangling down my back. All the other girls had short hair, and they were much more mature than me. There were about twelve hundred students at our school. I felt lost and intimidated.

As we all waited silently in line that first day, I kept wondering what stream they were going to put me in, Commercial or Professional. We'd been told there were going to be four Professional classes, denoted by the letters A to D. Only the exceptionally brainy students were permitted in the A class, everyone else was slotted into the other classes, according to their varying degrees of intelligence. I sat glumly as the teachers read through first the A list, the B and C. By the time they got to the bottom of the D list, my name still hadn't been mentioned. My hopes began to rise. Suddenly, another man, who I later found out was the principal, came over and joined our group. After a brief conversation with one of the teachers, he called out, 'Is there a Sally Milroy here?'.

I slowly raised my hand.

'You're in D group, too, off you go.' I didn't know whether I wanted to laugh or cry. I hated school, yet, at the same time, I didn't want people thinking I was the sort of kid who didn't have a brain in her head.

Mum was ecstatic when I arrived home. Apparently, Mr Buddee had rung her and told her he'd fixed things up. She greeted me excitedly with, 'Maybe you'll become a vet'. That was the next best thing to being a doctor.

'I've gone off animals, Mum', I replied sarcastically.

'A doctor, then?' Mum said hopefully.

'Don't like 'em.'

'Well, anything Sally, anything. You've got too much talent to waste.'

'Look, Mum', I said, 'can I have something to eat? I'm starving.'

'Jam tart in here', Nan called from the kitchen. 'Leave the child alone, Glad. She's got to eat.'

Mum was rather deflated. I think she expected me to be as excited as she was. As I sat munching a huge piece of jam tart, I found myself feeling a little sorry for her. She had five kids and she seemed to be pinning her hopes on me, the worst one. Jill would be the one to achieve something, not me. I sighed and cut myself another slice. I consoled myself with the thought that there were four kids in our family younger than me, at least one of them must have a good chance of becoming a doctor, especially if Mum kept pushing. I didn't like to think of all of us ending up as failures.

Early in the school year, I made friends with a girl called Steph. She lived seven blocks away from us, in the part they called Como, so we took to visiting each other on weekends. I was fascinated by Steph's family, they were very neat and tidy. I loved Steph's bedroom, it was decorated mainly in lilac and it reminded me of something straight off a Hollywood film set. Surprisingly, Steph was equally fascinated by my home. She loved the free and easy atmosphere, and the tall stories and jokes.

But I think my intense admiration for Steph's room caused me to become somewhat dissatisfied. I suddenly realised there was a whole world beyond what I knew. It was frightening. Sometimes when Steph's parents talked to me, my mind went blank. I always seemed to say the wrong thing, so, for fear of offending them, I began saying nothing at all, which was even worse. Steph's dog Tina had more social graces than me.

That year, Mr Willie took us to the usual Legacy march. It was our fourth since Dad had died and I still disliked them. When I told kids at school I'd be marching for Legacy, they all killed themselves laughing. 'Talk about daggy', one of them muttered. I desperately wanted to be like them, but I just didn't seem to be made of the right stuff.

Even my attempt at a new hairdo failed. Mum had been adamant in her refusal to allow me to go to the hairdresser, so, in desperation, I simply chopped my two plaits off, leaving two stubby, half-plaited wads of hair. Mum was so embarrassed when she saw what I'd done that she took me up the road to the local lady who did hairdressing from home. Her efforts weren't much better than mine, but at least my hair was now even. Nan was the only one who had anything good to say. "Minds me of the old days, seein' you like that, Sally', she said chirpily, 'that's what they call a basin cut'.

I tried everything I could to get out of marching that year, but when Mum found she couldn't talk me into it, she enlisted the help of Mr Willie. I could never resist his Your Father Was A Brave Man routine.

As a reward for my eventual capitulation, Mum said I could wear Dad's big medals, while Bill wore the miniatures. Jill sported a couple of medals of somebody's from World War One.

Mr Willie gave us a special treat that year, morning tea in his office at the top of the AMP building. It was the tallest building in Perth in those days and we were anxious to see the view.

As it turned out, we were more impressed with Mr Willie's office than the view. It was spacious, with soft carpet and a rather imposing desk, but what fascinated us most of all was his little fridge. To begin with, when you opened the door, it lit up. Ours never did. It was packed with cool drink and cake, and we were amazed to discover that it was for his use only. None of us said anything, but we all looked at each other as if to say, so this is how wealthy people live, you all have your own personal fridge.

It was towards the middle of that year that Nan and I had our first major row. I arrived home from school one day with the facts from a science lesson freshly imprinted in my brain, and proceeded to inform Nan that when it came to eradicating germs, onions were totally useless.

For years, she had been using freshly chopped onions to sterilise our house and it was the first time I'd ever openly criticised any of her theories concerning our health.

Nan was cross, she said high school had gone to my head and then she accused me of being as silly as my mother. I pointed out that none of my friends ever got sick and they lived without the stink of moulding onions. Nan retaliated by asserting that, one day, they'd probably all fall down dead and then they'd wish they'd known about onions.

That was the last straw. I walked into my room, flung back the curtains and collected up all the onion quarters that sat neatly along my bedroom window-sill. I hesitated at picking up two of them. They were slightly mouldy and they looked at me as if to say, remove us and you'll get a deadly disease, just like your Grandmother says! I grasped them courageously with my bare hands and flung them dramatically in the kitchen bin. 'No more onions', I told Nan quietly, but firmly.

I was trying to be rational about the whole thing. After all, I was studying science. By the time Mum arrived home, we were at it again. Nan knew just how to provoke me. I must have been under the influence to throw away her onions, she said. Had I been sneaking her brandy? Didn't I realise that I was putting the lives of my brothers and sisters at risk? How else could we maintain a germ-free environment?

Mum just stood and watched us in amazement. Nan began to explain what it was all about. I stormed back into my room and screamed, 'I don't care what you say, Mum, no onions. Steph's room doesn't stink the way mine does.'

Mum came and stood in the doorway of my bedroom and eyed me sympathetically. Nan came up behind her and held up a fistful of freshly cut onions, just to annoy me. 'Here they come, Sally', she growled, 'I'm bringing them in!'.

'MUM!' I screamed.

'Well, perhaps you should leave it for now, Nan', Mum suggested, tactfully. 'Put those ones in the bathroom.'

For the next few days, my room remained onion-free. But then one day, as I lay on my bed, a strong oniony smell came wafting through. I checked my window-sill, nothing there. Suddenly, out of the corner of my eye, I saw a small, curved, white object jutting over the top of my wardrobe. I grabbed the broom from the kitchen and knocked them down.

I ranted and raved at Nan over this latest intrusion, but she just chuckled and continued to puff on her cigarette.

The following week, she resorted to tucking the onions in the same drawer in which I kept my underpants. Even Mum thought that was funny. 'You wait until she tucks onions in your corsets', I grumbled, 'then you won't be laughing'.

'Keep your voice down, Sally', Mum said, horrified. 'She might hear you. Don't go giving her any more ideas!'

Our battle remained unresolved for the next few weeks, until Nan discovered a product called Medic, which had a very strong, hospital-type odour. It came in a small, blue spray can and was specifically for use with people suffering from colds and flu.

'What a marvellous clean smell that has, Glad', Nan commented as Mum sprayed a small amount in the kitchen.

'I thought you might like it', Mum smiled. 'That's why I bought it, you know what that smoker's cough of yours is like. This will help you breathe.'

'Aah, that's good, Glad', said Nan as she inhaled deeply. 'I can feel it clearing my lungs.' Nan thumped her chest with her fist. 'By gee, I feel good now, that's a good medicine. Smells like it's got some of the old cures in it, it's not often you get a medicine like that these days.'

From then on, my room smelled of Medic. My clothes and my rugs smelled of Medic. Nan sprayed Medic down the toilet and in the bathroom. The whole house smelled of Medic. I disliked the smell, but I wouldn't have dared utter one word of criticism. Medic was better than onions.

By the time I turned fourteen and was in second year high school, I was becoming more and more aware that I was different to the other kids at school. I had little in common with the girls in my class. Even Steph was changing. She no longer raced me to the top of the tree in her yard and she thought my frequent absences from school were something to be ashamed of.

Jill was in high school now and, as I expected, was having no difficulty at all in fitting in. Sometimes, I desperately wished I could be more like her. Everything seemed to be so hard for me. Even little Helen had taken to school like a duck to water. She began primary school that year.

'Maybe she'll be the doctor then', I said sarcastically.

'Yes, perhaps you're right', Mum replied thoughtfully. 'I'm sure you'll all do well, once you set your minds to it.'

'Yeah, but setting your mind to it, that's the hard part.'

'You could do anything, if you really wanted to.'

'But that's just it, Mum, I don't want to.'

When I looked at other people, I realised how abnormal I was, or at least, that's how I felt. None of my brothers and sisters seemed to be tormented by the things that tormented me. I really felt as though I just couldn't understand the world any more. It was horrible being a teenager.

Part of the reason why I hated school was the regimentation. I hated routine. I wanted to do something exciting and different all the time. I really couldn't see the point in learning about subjects I wasn't interested in. I had no long-term goals and my only short-term one was to leave school as soon as I could.

I found that the only way to cope was to truant as much as possible. Being away from school gave me time to think and relieved the pressure. I always felt better inside after I truanted.

I was starting to become an expert in ways to miss school. One way was to deliberately miss the school bus that pulled up in front of our local library. I would walk to the stop with Jill, then, when she was talking to her friends, I would nick off and hide behind the library building. After the bus had pulled in, collected its passengers and left, I would reappear and walk happily home. My excuse to Mum was that the bus was too crowded to fit me on. For some reason, she either believed me or just accepted it.

But one morning, Jill decided she and her friends would truant also. I wasn't keen to help. There were too many of them and they'd never done it before. However, Jill was eager for me to show everyone the ropes, so I agreed.

Five of us hid behind the library that morning, and when the bus pulled in, we all had a chuckle. However, our smiling faces soon changed to dismay when, instead of driving off, the bus remained parked at our stop. We were soon joined by an older girl, who had walked up to where we were hiding and said crossly, 'You might as well come out. The driver is not going to leave without you.'

Jill's friends were so embarrassed. Trying to truant was the most adventurous thing they had ever done. They were all petrified the story would get back to their parents. At least I didn't have that worry. Reluctantly, we all walked back down to the bus, accompanied by the boos, jeers and laughter of the forty teenagers already seated.

'You all ought to be ashamed of yourselves', the driver growled as we hopped on. 'I'll be checking behind there every morning from now on.'

As we drove to school, I sighed and looked out the window at the passing bush. That was the trouble when amateurs were involved, you always got caught. I decided that, from then on, I'd only take Jill with me.

It was also reasonably easy to leave school during recess and lunch-time. Our school was enclosed by bush on three sides. Keeping my eye on the teacher on playground duty, I would slowly edge my way towards the bush. Once I was really close, I would turn and run, then squat down behind a tree and wait to see if anyone was coming after me. If the coast was clear, I'd walk the three miles home, sticking to the cover of the bush and away from busy Manning Road. Pretty soon, a few other students caught on to the same idea. Sometimes, we'd come across one another in the bush, grin guiltily, and then press on, pretending we hadn't seen each other. Now and then, Jill came with me, but, in her opinion, the joy of missing school wasn't worth the long walk home.

One time, Jill talked me into allowing her best friend, Robin, to accompany us. I thought this was a bit risky, because Robin's father was the mathematics teacher. Sure enough, the head happened to be driving along Manning Road that morning, spotted us in the bush, picked us up and took us back to school. Poor Robin copped the worst. 'You, of all girls', he scolded her. 'We expect it of the Milroys, but not of girls of your calibre.'

The school began enforcing stricter rules in an attempt to reduce the high rate of truancy by some of its students. Mum had been threatened with the Truant Officer many times. To her, this was as bad as having a policeman call. So she began to try and make us stay at school all day.

She was in a difficult situation, because, while she wanted us to have a good education and to get on in the world, she was also sympathetic to our claims of being bored, tired or unhappy. Also, I knew it wasn't the fact that we truanted so much that upset her, but that now and then we got caught. Getting caught inevitably brought us to the personal attention of the school staff, which also meant that, in some way, she lost face in their eyes. Like most people, I suppose, Mum liked other people, especially those who were educated, to think well of her.

She was particularly upset after one visit to our Head. He had shown her three different sets of handwriting, all purporting to be hers, and all excusing either Jill or me from a morning or afternoon at school. 'You've got to get yourselves organised', she told us crossly, 'if you're going to forge notes from me, at least do it in the same style'.

The longer I stayed at school, the more difficult I became and the more reluctant Mum became to support my truanting. She was tired of the Head and the Guidance Officer ringing her up. I sympathised with her. I was sick of visiting the Guidance Officer myself. I felt very much on the defensive in these meetings, because I knew they were based on the premise that there was something wrong with me. In my view, this was totally unfounded. Consequently, my interviews with the Guidance Officer tended to be fairly short, mainly due to my lack of response. Mum was finally advised to allow me to leave school early and let me become a shop assistant.

However, one day, Mum actually encouraged Jill and me to miss school. There was a wonderful sale on and she said that, if we could manage to sneak off in the afternoon, she would buy us some new clothes.

The day of the sale also happened to be Sports Day, which gave me a brilliant idea. Jill and I were playing softball that afternoon and we had a friend who was a really good hitter. We arranged for Dawn to belt a beauty out over the embankment. Jill and I made sure we were both fielding in that area and when the ball flew over, we dived eagerly after it. Racing down the embankment, we grabbed the ball, flung it back, then headed for Mum's car, which was parked in the street nearby.

The following Monday, Mum was called to the Head's office once again and Jill and I with her. After speaking to Mum privately, we were called in.

'This is a most serious matter, girls', the Head said sternly, 'I have even considered calling the police in'.

We were stunned. He ordered us to sit down. I sneaked a look at Mum, but she was staring at the opposite wall.

'Now', he continued, 'I've had a talk with your mother and I appreciate that she has a difficult task raising you without the help of a husband, so I'm prepared to be lenient this time. You're the eldest, Sally, I know I can count on you to be responsible. If you will tell me the name of the young man who picked you and your sister up, nothing more will be said.'

I could feel my eyes grow suddenly large in my face. My mouth began to quiver at the corners and my stomach rippled. But I managed to murmur that I had nothing to say.

The Headmistress was then called in and gave Jill and I a talk on how easy it was to besmirch our reputations.

Ten minutes later, Mum was on her way home and we were back in class. I felt quite proud of myself. The Head had applied considerable pressure, and I hadn't cracked. Just like my Dad in the war. He'd been questioned by the Gestapo about his friends and he hadn't let them down. Well, I hadn't let Mum down, either. And boy, was she relieved.

Chapter Fourteen

RATHER PECULIAR PETS

Mum had slowly built up a collection of stuffed animals, reptiles and birds. Her favourites were two long snake skins, one of which still had the head and fangs intact, though a trifle flattened. Then there were an Irish pheasant, an echidna, a turtle, an eagle, eight frogs playing different musical instruments and numerous crocodiles of varying shapes and sizes.

Mum was passionately interested in the world of nature, and avidly watched any television programme dealing with cruelty to animals. She would sit in her favourite chair by the fireside and, between sobs, decry the brutality of man. The fact that, while she did this, she was surrounded by a small, but growing, collection of glassy-eyed, taxidermied creatures never bothered her. Her passion was for the dead as well as the living.

One evening as she sat engrossed in a programme about the extinction of the Tasmanian tiger, I crept slowly around the darkened room. Mum failed to notice my movements, because she always insisted on watching television with the light turned off. She reckoned it made it more like the movies. By the time I returned to my own chair, I had managed to turn the faces of her entire collection towards her. When the Tasmanian tiger disappeared for good, Mum was feeling quite emotional. Consequently, when I suddenly turned on the light, pointed to the other occupants of the room and said, 'Mum, LOOK!', she completely broke down. The sight of all those glazed, accusing eyes was just too much, she fled to the kitchen.

After a good sob, she returned ready to berate me. By this time, I'd taken up residence in her fireside chair and was engrossed in a quiz show. She confronted me with, 'Sally, you sod of a kid, don't ever do that to . . .', then, noticing that her entire collection was now standing in a small group, warming themselves by the fire, she paused in her tirade and asked, 'What are they doing there?'.

'Poor things are cold', I replied with a straight face. She was too big a woman not to see the humour of the situation. Between bursts of 'You're terrible', she giggled uncontrollably.

Mum seemed to like owning peculiar things, so none of us was surprised when, one day, she turned up with a stray dog that she had rescued from being run over on a busy city street. To everyone else, he looked like a shaggy, black mongrel, but in Mum's eyes, Curly, as she had named him, bore a close resemblance to a rare Bedlington terrier she'd read about in *Pix* magazine.

Mum received support for her views from an unexpected quarter, our neighbour. He commented to Mum that Curly was a rare sight. Mum had mistaken this comment for a compliment. The next time she was conversing with our neighbour, she brought up the subject of Curly again.

'Unusual, isn't he?' she said smugly.

'You got a prize one there, Glad', nodded our neighbour in agreement, 'it's not every day you can pick up a dog that looks like a cross between a toilet brush and a pipe cleaner!'.

Mum was terribly upset, but when she told us what happened, we all burst out laughing. I agreed with our neighbour. I had genuine doubts about what Mum maintained was Curly's fine pedigree. I tried to point out to her how close-set his little black eyes were, and how his only pursuits were of the basest nature.

Nothing would dampen Mum's enthusiasm. It didn't matter what horrible and degrading act Curly performed; in Mum's eyes, he was still a gem of a dog. She maintained that his many eccentricities were related to his long pedigree, just as in the human population, those who are especially talented may sometimes have an unusual side to their natures.

One of his most embarrassing habits was to greet newcomers to our home with a unique ritual of his own. He simply focused his zealous, close-set, black eyes on his intended victim and, in a flash, rammed his wet, black nose into their crotch, sniffing deeply. Mum's initial reaction to this extraordinary behaviour was one of wanton laughter, but then, she'd never been attacked.

She rationalised his actions by pointing out that since Curly had been with us, the number of Mormons, Jehovah's Witnesses and Avon ladies knocking on our door had decreased.

One evening, Mr Willie came round to visit and to inform us that he would soon be moving to Victoria. He was sorry he was leaving, but would make sure we got a nice Legatee in his place.

We were all rude to Mr Willie that night, and, after he left, Mum told us she was ashamed of our behaviour. She didn't understand that we felt abandoned. He'd called us his second family.

It wasn't long before our new Legatee rang to say he'd be popping around in an hour or so to visit us. Anxious to make a good impression, Mum rapidly tidied up the house. This was done in her usual manner by shoving all the clothes and junk scattered over the floor into the wardrobes and under the beds. Anything she couldn't find a spot for was simply screened from view by closing the door. With five children who never tidied up after themselves, and who were always playing some imaginary game that involved the use of sheets, blankets, blocks of wood and kitchen utensils, it was a handy trick. By the time she finished, it looked quite neat, and one would never suspect the mountain of gear stowed away.

Our new Legatee arrived promptly at six p.m., and knocked loudly on the door. Curly, who had just finished his usual dinner of curried chops and was about to embark on his favourite dessert, warm Weetbix, generously topped with sugar, pricked up his furry, flea-bitten ears and darted to the door.

'Sally, grab him', Mum yelled as she hurled an old dishcloth in a futile attempt to halt his frenzied exit. By the time I caught up with Curly, he was leaping up and down at the front door, whining and yelping in eager anticipation. I grabbed him by the scruff of the neck and dragged him down the hall and into Mum's bedroom.

'For God's sake, make sure you shut him in, Sally!' Mum whispered urgently as she hurried past. I gave Curly's backside a quick shove with my foot and, despite his growls and snapping teeth, managed to pull the door shut just as Mum said to our guest, 'Hello, please come in. Sorry to keep you waiting, I didn't hear you knock.'

'That's quite all right, Mrs Milroy', responded our visitor politely, 'think nothing of it'. And then, seeing me, he added, 'Aah, now this must be your daughter. No mistaking the resemblance, eh?'

'Er, yes . . .' Mum replied as she cast an anxious glance to her bedroom door, 'this is my eldest daughter, Sally.'

'Hello', I smiled. I could just make myself audible above Curly's fervent whining, scratching and yelping.

'You have a dog, Mrs Milroy? Got one myself, nice little fellow, good company. No need to lock yours up just because I'm here.' Mum smiled politely, then, looking helplessly at me, she said, 'Oh no, no, he's all right, he likes being in there, doesn't he, Sally?'.

'Er yes . . .', I muttered, totally amazed at Mum's comment. I eyed our puzzled guest compassionately. I could picture his dog: clean, trimmed and well-trained. Not an unkempt, uncouth mongrel like Curly with a brain the size of a dehydrated pea.

'Come and meet the rest of the family', Mum said as she grasped his arm and quickly changed the subject.

'Yes, yes, of course. That's what I'm here for.'

I led the way into our lounge-room, where my brothers and sisters were waiting quietly. I halted abruptly when Mum shrieked, 'Oh my God!'.

Somehow, Curly had freed himself, and, with unparalleled speed, he zapped out of the bedroom, down the hall and up between our guest's half open legs. Our visitor, who was only a short man, leapt to his tiptoes and clutched the wall behind him. Mum, her fingers desperately digging into Curly's matted fur, yelled, 'Down Curly, down!'. All to no avail. He was abnormally strong for a small dog.

'Hey, hey, hey', our victim spluttered as he leapt repeatedly in the air in response to Curly's probing nose.

'You disgusting dog, you're just disgusting!' Mum scolded as, with one final heave, she tore him away and tucked him firmly under her arm.

'I don't know what's got into him', she said unconvincingly. 'He's normally such a good dog, he's never done anything like this before. I'm so terribly sorry.' Still apologising, Mum lugged Curly out through the kitchen and onto the back verandah.

To his credit, our Legatee, having straightened his clothes and regained some of his composure, struggled on.

Following me into our lounge-room, he solemnly introduced himself to my brothers and sisters, who had hurriedly reseated themselves. Then, with a shaky sigh of relief, he carefully lowered himself into our battered green lounge.

'And how are you doing at school, Jill?' he enquired politely, turning slightly in his chair. A flatulent noise followed. Jill managed to stammer, 'Oh f. .fine. . .good'.

It would have been less embarrassing if our Legatee had been able to control his nervousness and sit still. Each of his movements, however slight, were accompanied by flatulent noises of varying pitch. It was one of the hazards of sitting on our vinyl lounge. We had all complained to Mum about the lounge before, but now, following Curly's attack, the noises seemed peculiarly appropriate. Our guest's plucky attempts at conversation met with little response. We were all desperately trying to control the laughter that threatened to bubble forth whenever we opened our mouths.

When Mum finally returned, she could see things weren't going too well and it took only a few minutes for her to realise why. Four brief sentences and she excused herself on the pretext of making a cup of tea. If she'd stayed any longer, she'd have broken her own code of etiquette and burst into a fit of giggles.

Fifteen minutes later, she calmly returned with a tray laden with hot cups of tea and a plate of mixed biscuits. Placing the tray on the wrought iron table she'd bought at the school fete, she said warmly, 'Would you like a biscuit with your cup of tea?'.

Thankful for the diversion, our guest responded eagerly with, 'Aah yes, Mrs Milroy, thank you', and, rising very, very slowly from his chair, he bent down to retrieve a Gingernut.

Suddenly there was chaos. Curly had slipped unseen through the doorway and struck again. Gingernuts, Milk Desserts and Chocolate Slice biscuits scattered themselves all over the floor. The hot tea from the upturned cups and saucers splashed downwards, slowly melting the Chocolate Slice biscuits and staining Mum's floor rug. Mum leapt over the table shouting, 'Aaarrgh Curly, you bloody stupid dog! STOP IT!'

Our Legatee was virtually helpless, he was pinned between the table and his seat by Curly sniffing as though his life depended on it. The very act of straightening up caused buttocks to come together, giving Curly's persistent black nose added advantage. The thought of sitting quickly down was too horrible for him to contemplate.

By the time Curly was finally removed, his little furry chest was heaving spasmodically, as it did during one of his asthma attacks. Mum tucked him under one arm and admonished, 'You're an animal, Curly, just an animal'. She had a habit of stating the obvious.

Much to Curly's disappointment, the gentleman never returned. A few weeks later, we were informed that we had been appointed another Legatee. Whether he heard about Curly from his predecessor I don't know, but he rarely visited, preferring instead to communicate by telephone or letter.

Chapter Fifteen

A BLACK GRANDMOTHER

On the fourteenth of February, 1966, Australia's currency changed from pounds, shillings and pence, to dollars and cents. According to Mum and Nan, it was a step backwards in our history. 'There's no money like the old money', Nan maintained, and Mum agreed. They had both been shocked when they heard that our new money would not have as much silver in it as the old two-shilling, one-shilling, sixpence and threepence. They influenced my views to such an extent that, when we were given a free choice for our creative writing essay at school, I wrote a long paper on how the country was going to rack and ruin because we were changing our money.

'It'll go bad, Glad', said Nan one night, 'you wait and see. You can't make money like that, it'll turn green.'

Then I noticed that Nan had a jar on the shelf in the kitchen with a handful of two-shilling pieces in it. Towards the end of the week, the jar was overflowing with sixpences, threepences, one-shilling and two-shilling pieces. I could contain my curiosity no longer.

'What are you saving up for, Nan?'

'Nothin'! Don't you touch any of that money!'

I cornered Mum in the bath. 'Okay Mum, why is Nan hoarding all that money? You're supposed to hand it over to the bank and get new money.'

'Don't you say anything to anyone about that money, Sally.'

'Why not?'

'Look, that money's going to be valuable one day, we're saving it for you kids. When it's worth a lot, we'll sell it and you kids can have what we make. You might need it by then.'

I went back in the kitchen and said to Nan, 'Mum told me what you're up to. I think it's crazy.'

'Hmph! We don't care what you think, you'll be glad of it in a few years' time. Now you listen, if anyone from the government comes round asking for money, you tell them we gave all ours to the bank. If they pester you about the old money, you just say you don't know nothin'.

You tell 'em we haven't got money like that in this house.'

'Nan', I half laughed, 'no one from the government is gunna come round and do that!'.

'Ooh, don't you believe it. You don't know what the government's like, you're too young. You'll find out one day what they can do to people. You never trust anybody who works for the government, you dunno what they say about you behind your back. You mark my words, Sally.'

I was often puzzled by the way Mum and Nan approached anyone in authority, it was if they were frightened. I knew that couldn't be the reason, why on earth would anyone be frightened of the government?

Apart from Art and English, I failed nearly everything else in the second term of my third year in high school. And Mum was disgusted with my seven per cent for Geometry and Trigonometry.

'You've got your Junior, soon. How on earth do you expect to pass that?'

'I don't care whether I pass or not. Why don't you let me leave school?'

'You'll leave school over my dead body!'

'What's the point in all this education if I'm going to spend the rest of my life drawing and painting?'

'You are not going to spend the rest of your life doing that, there's no future in it. Artists only make money after they're dead and gone.'

'Suits me.'

I gave up arguing and retreated to my room. Mum never took my ambition to be an artist seriously. Not that she didn't encourage me to draw. Once when I was bored, she had let me paint pictures all over the asbestos sheets that covered in our back verandah. Nan had thought it was real good: 'Better than getting the housing to do it.'

I sighed. Nan believed in my drawings.

The following weekend, my Aunty Judy came to lunch. She was a friend of Mum's. Her family, the Drake-Brockmans, and ours had known each other for years. 'Sally, I want to have a talk with you about your future', she said quietly, after we'd finished dessert.

I glared at Mum.

'You know you can't be an artist. They don't get anywhere in this world. You shouldn't worry your mother like that. She wants you to stay at school and finish your Leaving. You can give up all idea of Art School because it's just not on!'

I was absolutely furious. Not because of anything Aunty Judy had said, but because Mum had the nerve to get someone from outside the family to speak to me. Mum walked around looking guilty for the rest of the afternoon.

It wasn't only Mum and Aunty Judy, it was my Art teacher at school, as well. He held up one of my drawings in front of the class one day and pointed out everything wrong with it. There was no perspective, I was the only one with no horizon line. My people were flat and floating. You had to turn it on the side to see what half the picture was about. On and on he went. By the end of ten minutes, the whole class was laughing and I felt very small. I always believed that drawing was my only talent, now I knew I was no good at that, either.

The thought of that horrible day made me want to cry. I was glad I was in my room and on my own, because I suddenly felt tears rushing to my eyes and spilling down my cheeks. I decided then to give up drawing. I was sick of banging my head against a brick wall. I got together my collection of drawings and paintings, sneaked down to the back of the yard, and burnt them.

When Mum and Nan found out what I'd done, they were horrified. 'All those beautiful pictures', Nan moaned, 'gone for ever'. Mum just glared at me. I knew she felt she couldn't say too much, after all, she was partly responsible for driving me to it.

It took about a month for Mum and I to make up. She insisted that if I did my Junior, she wouldn't necessarily make me go on to my Leaving. I, like a fool, believed her.

Towards the end of the school year, I arrived home early one day to find Nan sitting at the kitchen table, crying. I froze in the doorway, I'd never seen her cry before.

'Nan . . . what's wrong?'

'Nothin'!'

'Then what are you crying for?'

She lifted up her arm and thumped her clenched fist hard on the kitchen table. 'You bloody kids don't want me, you want a bloody white grandmother, I'm black. Do you hear, black, black, black!' With that, Nan pushed back her chair and hurried out to her room. I continued to stand in the doorway, I could feel the strap of my heavy school-bag cutting into my shoulder, but I was too stunned to remove it.

For the first time in my fifteen years, I was conscious of Nan's colouring. She was right, she wasn't white. Well, I thought logically, if she wasn't white, then neither were we. What did that make us, what did that make me? I had never thought of myself as being black before.

That night, as Jill and I were lying quietly on our beds, looking at a poster of John, Paul, George and Ringo, I said, 'Jill . . . did you know Nan was black?'.

'Course I did.'

'I didn't, I just found out.'

'I know you didn't. You're really dumb, sometimes. God, you reckon I'm gullible, some things you just don't see.'

'Oh . . .'

'You know we're not Indian, don't you?' Jill mumbled.

97

'Mum said we're Indian.'

'Look at Nan, does she look Indian?'

'I've never really thought about how she looks. Maybe she comes from some Indian tribe we don't know about.'

'Ha! That'll be the day! You know what we are, don't you?'

'No, what?'

'Boongs, we're Boongs!' I could see Jill was unhappy with the idea.

It took a few minutes before I summoned up enough courage to say, 'What's a Boong?'.

'A Boong. You know, Aboriginal. God, of all things, we're Aboriginal!'

'Oh.' I suddenly understood. There was a great deal of social stigma attached to being Aboriginal at our school.

'I can't believe you've never heard the word Boong', she muttered in disgust. 'Haven't you ever listened to the kids at school? If they want to run you down, they say, "Aah, ya just a Boong". Honestly, Sally, you live the whole of your life in a daze!'

Jill was right, I did live in a world of my own. She was much more attune to our social environment. It was important for her to be accepted at school, because she enjoyed being there. All I wanted to do was stay home.

'You know, Jill', I said after a while, 'if we are Boongs, and I don't know if we are or not, but if we are, there's nothing we can do about it, so we might as well just accept it'.

'Accept it? Can you tell me one good thing about being an Abo?'

'Well, I don't know much about them', I answered. 'They like animals, don't they? We like animals.'

'A lot of people like animals, Sally. Haven't you heard of the RSPCA?'

'Of course I have! But don't Abos feel close to the earth and all that stuff?'

'God, I don't know. All I know is none of my friends like them. You know, I've been trying to convince Lee for two years that we're Indian.' Lee was Jill's best friend and her opinions were very important. Lee loved Nan, so I didn't see that it mattered.

'You know Susan?' Jill said, interrupting my thoughts. 'Her mother said she doesn't want her mixing with you because you're a bad influence. She reckons all Abos are a bad influence.'

'Aaah, I don't care about Susan, never liked her much anyway.'

'You still don't understand, do you', Jill groaned in disbelief. 'It's a terrible thing to be Aboriginal. Nobody wants to know you, not just Susan. You can be Indian, Dutch, Italian, anything, but not Aboriginal! I suppose it's all right for someone like you, you don't care what people think. You don't need anyone, but I do!' Jill pulled her rugs over her head and pretended she'd gone to sleep. I think she was crying, but I had too much new information to think about to try and comfort her. Besides, what could I say?

Nan's outburst over her colouring and Jill's assertion that we were

Aboriginal heralded a new phase in my relationship with my mother. I began to pester her incessantly about our background. Mum was a hard nut to crack and consistently denied Jill's assertion. She even told me that Nan had come out on a boat from India in the early days. In fact, she was so convincing I began to wonder if Jill was right after all.

When I wasn't pestering Mum, I was busy pestering Nan. To my surprise, I discovered that Nan had a real short fuse when it came to talking about the past. Whenever I attempted to question her, she either lost her temper and began to accuse me of all sorts of things, or she locked herself in her room and wouldn't emerge until it was time for Mum to come home from work. It was a conspiracy.

One night, Mum came into my room and sat on the end of my bed. She had her This Is Serious look on her face. With an unusual amount of firmness in her voice, she said quietly, 'Sally, I want to talk to you'.

I lowered my *Archie* comic. 'What is it?'

'I think you know, don't act dumb with me. You're not to bother Nan any more. She's not as young as she used to be and your questions are making her sick. She never knows when you're going to try and trick her. There's no point in digging up the past, some things are better left buried. Do you understand what I'm saying? You're to leave her alone.'

'Okay Mum', I replied glibly, 'but on one condition'.

'What's that?'

'You answer one question for me?'

'What is it?' Poor Mum, she was a trusting soul.

'Are we Aboriginal?'

Mum snorted in anger and stormed out. Jill chuckled from her bed. 'I don't know why you keep it up. Why keep pestering them? I think it's better not to know for sure, that way you don't have to face up to it.'

'I keep pestering them because I want to know the truth, and I want to hear it from Mum's own lips.'

'It's a lost cause, they'll never tell you.'

'I'll crack 'em one day.'

Jill shrugged good-naturedly and went back to reading her *True Romance* magazine.

I settled back into my mattress and began to think about the past. Were we Aboriginal? I sighed and closed my eyes. A mental picture flashed vividly before me. I was a little girl again, and Nan and I were squatting in the sand near the back steps.

'This is a track, Sally. See how they go.' I watched, entranced, as she made the pattern of a kangaroo. 'Now, this is a goanna and here are emu tracks. You see, they all different. You got to know all of them if you want to catch tucker.'

'That's real good, Nan.'

'You want me to draw you a picture, Sal?' she said as she picked up a stick.

'Okay.'

'These are men, you see, three men. They are very quiet, they're hunting. Here are kangaroos, they're listening, waiting. They'll take off if they know you're coming.' Nan wiped the sand picture out with her hand. 'It's your turn now', she said, 'you draw something'. I grasped the stick eagerly.

'This is Jill and this is me. We're going down the swamp.' I drew some trees and bushes.

I opened my eyes, and, just as suddenly, the picture vanished. Had I remembered something important? I didn't know. That was the trouble, I knew nothing about Aboriginal people. I was clutching at straws.

It wasn't long before I was too caught up in my preparations for my Junior examinations to bother too much about where we'd come from. At that time, the Junior exam was the first major one in high school, and, to a large extent, it determined your future. If you failed, you automatically left school and looked for a job. If you passed, it was generally accepted that you would do another two years' study and aim at entrance to university.

Mum was keen on me doing well, so I decided that, for her, I'd make the effort and try and pass subjects I'd previously failed. For the first time in my school life, I actually sat up late, studying my textbooks. It was hard work, but Mum encouraged me by bringing in cups of tea and cake or toast and jam.

After each examination, she'd ask me anxiously how I'd gone. My reply was always, 'Okay'. I never really knew. Sometimes, I thought I'd done all right, but then I reasoned that all I needed was a hard marker and I might fail. I didn't want to get Mum's hopes up.

Much to the surprise of the whole family, I passed every subject, even scoring close to the distinction mark in English and Art. Mum was elated.

'Now, aren't you pleased? I knew you could do it. Mr Buddee was right about you.'

Good old Mr Buddee. I didn't know whether to curse or thank him. Now that I had passed my Junior, I sensed that there was no hope of Mum allowing me to leave school. I should have deliberately failed, I thought. Then, she wouldn't have had any choice. Actually, I had considered doing just that, but, for some reason, I couldn't bring myself to do it. I guess it was my pride again.

Chapter Sixteen

WHAT PEOPLE ARE WE?

Fourth year high school was different to third year. It was supposed to be a transitory year where we were treated more like adults and less like difficult teenagers. Even our classes were supposed to be structured to mimic the kind of organisation we might find later in tertiary institutions. I was a year older, but I was still the same person with the same problems. I felt this was also true of school. The changes were only superficial. However, some deep and important things did happen to me that year.

One day, I happened to bump into a girl who I'd been friendly with in my Sunday School days. She invited me to a youth meeting to be held at a nearby church hall.

'Aw, no thanks, Sharon. I won't come.'

'Look, it's not going to be anything like you might imagine', she said confidently. 'Nothing to do with religion, just some Chinese food and a bit of a get-together, that's all.'

'You sure?'

'Positive.'

'Okay, I'll come. I know some other kids who like Chinese food. I might bring them, too.'

'Great. See you there.'

I arrived at the meeting with seven girls from around our neighbourhood and two from school. The food was quite good, and, even though everyone else there ignored us, we enjoyed ourselves. When everyone had finished stuffing themselves, a chap stood up and said, 'We have a Mr McClean here to give us a little talk. I'd like you all to be quiet while we listen to what he has to say.'

Uh-oh, I thought. Here it comes. I looked towards the back of the hall, the door was closed and there were two elderly gentlemen standing in front of it. I was trapped. I could feel my insides twisting themselves into a knot. I knew if Mr McClean turned out to be half as boring as some of the teachers I'd had in Sunday School, my friends would never forgive me.

Mr McClean stood up and smiled nicely at us all. 'I'm here to talk to all you young people about your future', he said. Your eternal future, I mouthed quietly in unison with Mr McClean. I'd heard it all before. It was going to be a long night.

As he continued, I began to think of other things, like the new clothes Mum had promised to buy me, the latest quiz show on TV and the way Jill seemed to be able to whip up an outfit on our old treadle machine in no time at all.

Suddenly, there was someone talking to me. I knew it wasn't Mr McClean. I looked around in a furtive kind of way, trying to see who it was. All eyes were fixed on the speaker, there was no one new in the room.

'Who are you?' I asked mentally.

With a sudden dreadful insight, I knew it was God.

'What are you doing here?' I asked. I don't know why I was surprised. It was a church hall, after all.

It had to be Him because the voice seemed to come from without not within, it transcended the reality of the room. I couldn't even see my surroundings any more. I was having an audience with Him, whom I dreaded. The mental images that I had built up of Him so far in my life began to dissolve, and in their place came a new image. A person, overwhelming love, acceptance and humour. What Nan'd call real class. In an instant, I became what others refer to as a believer.

i joined the local youth group after that. I was full of ideas for making the meetings and outings we went on more interesting, but it was difficult to change the pattern that had been set in motion so many years before. I became friendly with a girl a few years older than me. She was reasonably conservative, but less so than the other girls I'd met, and she had an excellent sense of humour. I could never understand why a lot of the girls at church considered cracking jokes unladylike. Thank heavens Pat wasn't like that.

One day, she said to me, 'You know, no one here can figure out why you like Youth Group so much, but hate church. What's the difference?'

In Pat's eyes, one was a natural extension of the other, but to me, church was practically the antipathy of Youth Group. I always felt uncomfortable in church, it was so formal and lacking in spontaneity. The sermons were full of cliches and things I didn't understand. To me, church was like school, more concerned with red tape than the guts of the matter.

I think Mum was relieved that I was finally channelling my energies into what she saw as something creative. Up until then, she hadn't been sure how I'd turn out. Now she hoped that, with the encouragement of people at church, I would begin to lead a more productive and less rebellious life. She was wrong.

One night, one of the deacons of the church asked if he could talk to me. I was friendly with his daughter and he seemed like a nice man, so I agreed.

'You and Mary are having quite a lot to do with one another, aren't you?' he asked.

'I suppose so, but we're not best friends.'

'No. I know that, but you see a lot of each other at Youth Group and church.'

'Yeah.'

'Well, Sally', he smiled, 'I want to ask a favour of you'.

'Sure, anything.'

'I'd like you to stop mixing with Mary.' He smiled his charming smile again.

'Why?' I was genuinely puzzled.

'I think you know why.'

'No, I don't.'

'You're a bad influence, you must realise that.' Believe it or not, that was one part of my character I was unaware of.

'What do you mean?' I wanted him to spell it out.

'This is Mary's Leaving year, the same as yours. I don't want her mixing with you in case she picks up any of your bad habits.'

Aaah, I thought. He's heard about my truancy.

'What about after Leaving?' I asked meekly. I sensed there was more to this than just that.

'No. I don't think so. Really, it'd be better if you broke off your friendship entirely. You do understand, don't you', he said in an incredibly charming way.

'Oh, I understand', I replied. I was amazed that he could have such a charming manner and yet be such a dag.

'Good girl, I knew you would.' He was relieved. 'Oh, by the way. I can count on you not to say anything to Mary, can't I? You'll find a way of breaking things off between you, won't you?'

I nodded my head, and he walked off.

I was hurt and disappointed. He was a deacon, I'd looked up to him. I was lucky I had my pride, it came to my rescue yet again. I didn't need people like him, I decided.

It was about that time that I began to analyse my own attitudes and feelings more closely. I looked at Mum and Nan and I realised that part of my inability to deal constructively with people in authority had come from them. They were completely baffled by the workings of government or its bureaucracies. Whenever there were difficulties, rather than tackle the system directly, they'd taught us it was much more effective to circumvent or forestall it. And if that didn't work, you could always ignore it.

That summer, the State Housing decided to paint the exterior of all the houses in our street. A decision that really panicked Nan. She made sure the front and back doors were kept locked so they couldn't come inside, and she spent most of the day peeping out at them from behind the curtains.

I tried to reason with her, but to no avail. The fact that State Housing employees had only ever called to collect the rent or carry out routine maintenance meant nothing to Nan. For her, they were here to check on us, and the possibility of eviction was always there, hanging over our heads like some invisible guillotine.

I thought back to all the years she had spent buttering up the rentmen. Each rent day, Nan would go through the same routine. She rose early and spent all morning cleaning the house, not that she ever intended letting the rentman in. It was just a way of relieving all her nervous tension. Then she washed and dried our best cup and saucer and arranged a plate of biscuits in tempting display. After that, she hunted for a milk jug that didn't have a crack in it. Her final touch was to plump up the cushion we had sitting on the chair on the front porch. She wanted him to be comfortable.

And the whole time Nan was preparing morning tea, she'd grumble under her breath, 'That bloody rentman! Who does he think he is, taking up my time like this. Doesn't he know I've got work to do?' Of course, once he arrived, it was a different story.

'You're here at last', she'd smile, 'sit down, you must be tired. They shouldn't make you walk so far.'

Why did she do it? I asked myself. Why was she afraid? It was a free country, wasn't it? I decided I'd try and talk to her again. Try to explain how things worked.

After Nan had given the painters a slap-up morning tea, I cornered her out the back, where she was raking up leaves. 'Nan', I said suspiciously, 'I think I've just realised why you've been treating the rentman like royalty all these years. You've been bribing them, haven't you?'

'I don't know what you're talking about, Sally.'

'Yes, you do. All these years, you've been frightened that we'd get evicted. That's why you've been buttering up the rentmen. You thought if it came to the crunch, he might put in a good word for us.'

'Good men have collected rent from this house over the years, Sally. Don't you go running down the rentmen.'

'You know I'm not running down the rentmen, Nan, I'm just trying to talk about all this.'

'Talk, talk, talk, that's all you do. You don't do any work.'

'Nan', I said, in a reasonable tone of voice, 'I don't think you understand about the house we rent'.

'What do you mean', she muttered as she kept her head down and continued to rake.

'Well, you only get evicted if you don't look after the place. For example, if we were to smash a wall or break all the windows, they might think about throwing us all out, but 'otherwise, as long as we pay the rent, they let you stay.'

'Hmmph, you think you know everything, don't you?' she replied bitterly. 'You don't know nothin', girl. You don't know what it's like for people like us. We're like those Jews, we got to look out for ourselves.'

'What do you mean people like us? We're just like anybody else, aren't we? I didn't even know you knew Jews existed, how on earth could we be the same as them?'

'In this world, there's no justice, people like us'd all be dead and gone now if it was up to this country.' She stopped and wiped her mouth with a men's handkerchief. Her eyes looked tired and wet.

'Nan', I said carefully. 'What people are we?'

She was immediately on the defensive. She looked sharply at me with the look of a rabbit sensing danger. 'You're tryin' to trick me again. Aaah, you can't be trusted. I'm not stupid, you know. I'm not saying nothing. Nothing, do you hear.'

I suddenly felt terribly sad. The barriers were up again. Just when I thought I was finally getting somewhere. 'Nan', I coaxed, 'I'm not trying to trick you. I just want to know what people we are, that's all.'

'I'm not talking, I'm not talking', she muttered as she dropped her rake and put her hands over her ears.

I sighed and walked back to the house. Inside, I felt all churned up, but I didn't know why. I had accepted by now that Nan was dark, and that our heritage was not that shared by most Australians, but I hadn't accepted that we were Aboriginal. I was too ignorant to make such a decision, and too confused. I found myself coming back to the same old question: if Nan was Aboriginal, why didn't she just say so? The fact that both Mum and Nan made consistent denials made me think I was barking up the wrong tree. I could see no reason why they would pretend to be something they weren't. And Nan's remark about the Jews had confused me even more. I knew a lot about the Jews because of the war and Dad. In my mind, there was no possible comparison between us and them.

Chapter Seventeen

MAKE SOMETHING OF YOURSELF

Mum was always a hard worker and had plenty of drive, but, in a small way, she was also proving to be quite a successful business woman. She had been doing so well for many years working as a florist that, in 1967, with the help of a loan from her old friend Lois, she was able to buy her own florist's business. Things were now really looking up, financially.

But I am certain Mum would have been more contented if she could have seen greater evidence that some of her own drive and ambition was rubbing off on her children.

'You want to make something of yourself', Mum said to me one night when she was going on about wanting me to do well in my Leaving. She had sensed that there was more chance of me failing than passing.

I was fed up with hearing that phrase. Mum and Nan were always harping on about how us kids must make something of ourselves.

'I've got no ambitions', I replied hopelessly. 'I can't see myself doing anything.'

'You've got plenty of talents, you just haven't discovered them yet.'

'Talents? God, Mum, there are more important things than what talents you've got. I feel pressured by everything else.'

'There's no need for dramatics. You've got a good life, what's there for you to worry about?'

How could I tell her it was me, and her and Nan. The sum total of all the things I didn't understand about them or myself. The feeling that a very vital part of me was missing and that I'd never belong anywhere. Never resolve anything.

I suppose it wasn't surprising that I returned to my final year in high school with a rather depressed attitude. This naturally led to a great deal of initial truanting, which both helped and hindered the inner search I seemed to have unwittingly begun on.

One lunch-time at school, I was talking about families with one of the girls in my class. When I mentioned mine and said how ordinary they were, she burst out laughing.

'You really think your family's normal?'

'Course they're normal. What's so unusual about them?'

'Everything! You've got the most abnormal family I've ever come across. Don't get me wrong, I like your mother, I really do, but the way you all look at life is weird.'

My class-mate continued to chuckle on and off for the rest of the lunch hour. I never asked her to explain further, I was too embarrassed.

Not long after that, I was off school with a genuine illness, a bout of the summer flu. As I lay sprawled, stomach-down, on my bed, reading one of Jill's *True Romance* magazines, I gradually became aware of a conversation Nan was having with the rentman on the front porch.

'Just look at that beautiful sky and those fluffy, white clouds over there', she said. 'Isn't it wonderful, what God has made?'

I smiled at the tone of her voice, it was the one she always used when she wanted to impress religious people. Nan was a shrewd judge of character. It took only a few minutes for her to sum up a person and then to direct her conversation and behaviour accordingly.

'Yes, Nanna, it's wonderful. You know, I've lived most of my life in the country, and, now I'm in the city, I miss the birds and animals.'

'Yes', interrupted Nan eagerly when she realised she was on to an influential topic. 'And look at that black crow over there and all those maggies, God made them, too.'

Following her lead, the rentman added, 'Yes, and the grass and trees'.

'That's right', Nan continued, 'and here are you and I, both white, and we couldn't do that!'.

My initial reaction to Nan's comment was one of silent, uncontrolled laughter, but within minutes, my feelings of amusement had see-sawed down to one of deep sadness.

Why did she want to be white? Did she really equate being white with the power of God, or was it just a slip of the tongue? I realised, with sudden insight, that there must have been times in her life when she'd looked around and the evidence was right before her eyes. If you're white, you can do anything.

One day, I answered a knock at the door and found two well-dressed, middle-aged ladies smiling at me benignly.

'Is Nan in?' they asked politely.

'Er, no. She's out the back. Actually, she's busy.'

'Oh. Well dear, we're from the Jehovah's Witness Church and, each week, we call here and have a little talk and a cup of tea with your Nanna. We think she's a wonderful old lady, so generous and kind. Every week, she gives us a small donation for our church.'

'She does?'

'Yes. Well, it's like a donation. We give her the *Watchtower* and, for a very small price, we sell her copies of our other leaflets, too.

She said she just loves reading them.'

'She did?'

'Anyway, dear, we won't keep you.' I think they sensed I wasn't going to open the door any wider. 'Will you tell Nan we called? Here are some leaflets for her to read. You can have them free this time because she's such a wonderful old lady. Please give them to her with our love.'

'Yes', I said, taking the leaflets and closing the door.

I took them out the back to where Nan was busy in the garden.

'Nan', I said, as if speaking to a naughty child. 'You haven't been encouraging those ladies from the Jehovah's Witness Church, have you?'

Nan chuckled wickedly. 'They think I want to become a Jehovah's Witness, Sally.'

'I know they do. Why did you tell them you've been reading their magazines?' Nan couldn't read or write, even though she tried to disguise the fact.

'Oh pooh, I just said that so they'd bring me some more. You got some more of their papers there?'

'Yeah. I didn't give them a donation, though. They said you could have them for nothing because you're such a wonderful old lady.' My sarcasm wasn't lost on her.

She grinned, then said, 'Feel them, Sally'.

'Feel what?'

'The papers.'

I looked, dumbfounded, at the leaflets in my hand. 'They feel soft', I said.

'That's right!' Nan grinned triumphantly. And then, lowering her voice, she whispered, 'They'll make the most marvellous toilet paper, Sally. I've got boxes of those magazines in my room. It'll save your mother a lot of money!'

I had realised by now that, when it came to economy, Mum's and Nan's ideas were rather peculiar. I was now used to wearing men's jumpers, and shoes with the toes stuffed with newspaper. When I was little, Nan had had to make do with the same clothes year in and year out and there were times when they had both gone without their own tea just to feed us, so I suppose I shouldn't have been surprised by the intensity with which they hoarded everything under the sun.

Initially, hoarding had been a practical necessity. I understood that, but what amazed me was that as our financial situation improved, so their tendency to hoard gained momentum. Before very long, they were both avid collectoholics.

Mum and Nan had always argued, but when it came to disputes over their different stockpiles, the comments became quite pointed. Nan referred to Mum's as broken-down junk, while Mum considered Nan's as good for nothing. Fortunately, there was something they did both agree on, the value of tools.

When Dad was alive, he'd hoarded tools; after he died, Mum and Nan continued to hoard tools, even though there was little use for them. Nan loved tools. They gave her status, and Mum regularly contributed weird and wonderful implements to Nan's growing collection.

One afternoon, she returned home from an auction with a large scythe. Nan was really excited, she commented that it was better than a lawnmower.

'That's a bloody stupid thing to buy her', I berated Mum. 'You know her eyesight's not too good. She might chop a leg off.'

Mum dismissed my fears with a wave of her hand, maintaining that, as Nan had used one when she was younger, it was perfectly safe. My curiosity was piqued. I tried to picture Nan as a young girl, swinging a scythe. Where would she have used a scythe, and why? I trooped out to the backyard, where Nan was busily hoeing into some long grass.

'Hear you used one of those things when you were younger', I said casually.

'Oh yes', she replied as she swung away. 'Good for weeds and grass. Kept the garden neat.'

'Whose garden?'

'What?'

'Whose garden?'

'You never stop, do you. You come sneakin' up, tryin' to trick me. You never been interested in gardens before, Sally!' She turned and continued to hack away. Our conversation was at an end.

At the end of first term, our Physics teacher gave the class a little talk.

'It's interesting', he said, 'only two more terms to go and I can already tell which of you will pass or fail. And I'm not just talking about Physics. In this class, most of you will pass. Then there are a few who are borderline, and one who will definitely fail.' He looked with pity at me. 'I don't know why you bother to turn up at all. You might as well throw in the towel now.'

Everyone laughed. I was really mad. Up until then, I hadn't cared whether I passed or failed. I'll prove you wrong, you crumb, I thought.

During second term, I made sporadic attempts at study. Once the August holidays were over, I began in earnest. I knew it wasn't going to be an easy task. I lacked the photographic memories of my two sisters, and I was way behind in my work. As usual, Mum tried to encourage me by bringing every snack imaginable.

Instead of having a good night's sleep before each exam, I kept myself awake by drinking strong coffee and tried to cram as much extra information into my brain as possible. By the end of my exams, I knew I'd passed English, History and Economics, I was doubtful about Chemistry and I was almost certain that I had failed Physics, Maths

1 and Maths 2.

I confided none of my fears to Mum. I figured she'd be disappointed soon enough. I needed five subjects to score my Leaving Certificate and I was confident of only three. It seemed all my hard work had been for nothing.

Mum gave me what she considered good advice for every teenager.

'Now that you've finished your exams, you want to go out and let your hair down a bit.' I knew she thought it wasn't normal for a girl my age to be spending so many nights at home.

'Look, Mum, will you give it a rest?' I yelled. I'd had a short fuse since my exams. 'I just want to sit here and be left in peace!'

Poor Mum, she now had within her family two extremes. On the one hand, there was me attending prayer meetings, and on the other, there were Jill and Bill who, like normal teenagers, spent their weekends raging about Perth. Bill had just completed his Junior Certificate exams.

Every Saturday night, they returned home as drunk as skunks. And they always managed to convince Mum that their vomiting was due to food poisoning, not booze. I just used to look at Mum sadly. I knew deep down she couldn't really believe it was food poisoning. It was just that she didn't want to face the possibility that one of us might turn out like Dad.

I was becoming very worried about my soon-to-be-published Leaving results. The results were printed every year in the *West Australian* and I thought this was terrible because it meant your shame was made public. Sometimes, other people knew even before you whether you'd failed or not. I could cope with the public exposure myself, but what about Mum? She'd always boasted to the neighbours about how bright all her children were. It would be a real slap in the face if they should see her eldest daughter's name in print with a string of fails after it.

There was only one thing to do, disappear. I volunteered to help out at some church camps for young children, it meant I would be away when the results came out.

Camp proved an interesting experience for me. I'd always enjoyed the company of small children. I had a group of ten to look after, and two of the girls were Aboriginal. They talked to me about their lives at home and what part of the country their Mums and Dads had come from. I seemed to have a natural affinity with them. That wasn't to say that I didn't get on well with the others, but I felt that I had a special insight into the Aboriginal girls.

A few days before the results were due to come out, Mum rang to see how I was and to ask what bus I was coming home on.

'I'm not coming', I told her firmly. 'They're short of helpers here so I'm staying on.'

'Don't you want to read your results in the paper?'

'I'm in Rockingham, Mum, not Africa, they get the paper down here, too.'

'Sally', she said suspiciously, 'you're not staying away because you think you've failed?'

'We-ell . . .'

'Oh, what's to become of you?' Mum wailed.

'Don't go weepy on me, Mum', I implored, 'I might have passed'.

We both hung up at the same time. Make a liar out of me, God, I prayed. Mum deserves some success in life.

My prayer was answered, because the day the results came out, I received a long, mushy telegram from Mum, extolling my superior intelligence and patting me on the back for passing five subjects. By the time I returned from camp, she had convinced herself that I'd go to university and become a doctor.

She was very disappointed in my decision to never study again. I told her I was sick of people telling me what to do with my life. I wanted to work and earn some money. I wanted to be independent.

'But Sally', she protested, 'you're the first one in our family to have gone this far. Why can't you go to university? What about becoming a doctor or a vet? When you were little, you loved looking after sick animals.' I opened my mouth to protest, but Mum cut me off with, 'Now I know you were always worried about having to treat a sick snake, but I'm sure that'd be rare and you could always sedate them'.

'Mum', I groaned, 'I don't give a damn about sick snakes. I just don't want to do any more study.'

'So you've come all this way for nothing? You're too stubborn for your own good. You'll regret it one day, you mark my words.'

'Oh stop complaining, you're lucky I lasted this long. Aren't you pleased you'll be having a bit of extra money coming in?'

'I never worried about the money. All that work', Mum bemoaned.

Shortly after that, I began attending Saturday afternoon basketball matches. Not to play, just to watch. By then, as a result of camp, I'd made some good friends with girls from other churches. When their games were finished, we'd stroll down and watch the boys' basketball.

For a while, I'd been hearing about a girl who attended a church a few suburbs from mine who was supposed to have a great personality and sense of humour. I was keen to meet her. Firstly, because I hadn't met many girls with a great sense of humour, and secondly, because I'd come in on quite a few conversations about this girl that had ended in, 'Yeah, but she's got a great personality', or, 'Yeah, but she's nice, isn't she?'. I wondered what was wrong with her.

When we finally met, I understood. I can't remember her name, but she was a very dark Aboriginal girl. We became friends and I enjoyed her company on Saturday afternoons.

One day, she told me she was leaving.

'What do you mean, leaving?' I asked. 'Where are you going?'

'I'm going back to live with my people.'

111

'Your people?' I was so dumb.

'Yes. I'm going back to live with them. I want to help them if I can.'

I was really sorry I wouldn't be seeing her any more. And I wondered who her people were and why they needed help. What was wrong with them? I was too embarrassed to ask.

Chapter Eighteen

THE WORKING LIFE

Towards the end of summer, in 1969, I managed to secure a job as a clerk in a government department. It was an incredibly boring job. I had nothing to do. I begged my superiors to give me more work, but they said there was none. I just had to master the art of looking busy, like they did. A couple of weeks, I was even forced to work overtime, not that there was anything to do, but they were all working overtime and they said it would look bad if I didn't, too. In desperation, I took to hiding novels in government files; that way, I could sit at my desk and read without everyone telling me, 'Look busy, girl. Look busy!'

I became so bored that, one day, I took a dress pattern to work. I laid it out on a large table in our office and began cutting. My immediate boss walked up behind me.

'You're cutting out a dress?' he said incredulously.

'Well, I've nothing else to do', I replied.

'Oh dear', he said softly, 'oh dear, dear me', and disappeared. He returned a few minutes later with the section head.

'What's this? What's this? What are you up to now, girl?' he said crossly. 'Last week, you were drawing dragons on all our estimate folders and now you're here with this. Do you know what you're doing?'

'I'm cutting out a dress.'

'Don't get smart with me, girlie. Put it all away, what if the Super walked in, how would it look? I don't mind you reading, but you can't come to work and expect to sew.' I sighed and packed up my things.

I lasted there about six months and then I resigned. And I thought school was boring. That was my first experience of being employed and I hadn't liked it one bit. It was an important experience for me, because it taught me something about myself that I had been unaware of. I wasn't going to be satisfied with just anything. And I wasn't lazy.

I had been unemployed about four months when I decided that it was time I began looking for another job. I was sick of sitting around at home with little to do.

I found a job as a laboratory assistant. For some reason, my new

113

employer assumed that as I had studied physics and chemistry at school, I must have known something about them.

My job was to analyse mineral samples from different parts of Western Australia for tin, iron oxide, and so on.

I accidentally disposed of my first lot of samples, so, in desperation, I invented the results. My boss was quite excited. 'Hmmm', he said as he looked over my recording sheet, 'these aren't bad. Good girl, good girl!'

I felt so guilty, I imagined that, on the basis of my analysis, they might begin drilling straight away in the hope of a big strike. I took more care after that.

The women I worked with all had strong personalities. Our boss was hardly ever in so we all took extended lunch hours and had long conversations about whatever came into our heads. I was very impressed with the whole group. They were the first females I'd met who actually had something to say.

To my delight, there was one English woman, Joan, who loved taking the mickey out of her superiors. One day, our boss returned to find us all tearing around the office in a mad game we'd invented. He berated everyone, especially the older women, for not setting a good example to me.

Joan was not to be outdone. She took a black Texta pen from his desk, painted a small, Hitler-type moustache under her nose and said, in a thick German accent, 'I gif ze orders round here!'. Then she saluted. She was a natural mimic, it was difficult not to laugh. The boss felt he couldn't fire her, because she was an excellent geologist.

The other women were just as interesting as Joan. One of them confided to me that she was schizophrenic. It was a confidence that failed to enlighten me, I just wondered what country she came from.

One day, I returned to the office from my lunch hour to find everyone abnormally subdued. Our office was going to be moved away from the city.

No one was keen on this, because it meant the whole company, instead of maintaining small branches here and there, would be under one roof. We would all have to knuckle under and behave. I decided to resign.

My boss offered me a rise in pay if I stayed. He said I was the best laboratory assistant they'd ever had.

The decision was taken out of my hands when I suddenly developed industrial acne as a result of being allergic to the chemicals I was using.

By the time I left the laboratory job, I had developed an interest in psychology. I had looked the word schizophrenic up in my dictionary and found out it was not a nationality after all.

I was more realistic about myself, now. I realised that the chances of me finding a job I was really happy in were remote. I needed to do further study. I decided to enrol in university for the following year, along with Jill who, having now completed her Leaving, was keen to study Law.

Chapter Nineteen

HOME IMPROVEMENTS

Home improvements were a long time coming to our house. Now that I was getting older and had more experience of the world, I wanted our home to be more like everyone else's. Not that I wanted our lifestyle to change, rather, I was hoping that Mum might be persuaded to spend a bit of money and install some modern conveniences.

It wasn't difficult to persuade her to spend money, but it was just about impossible to talk her into spending it on something really practical. There were some things I found increasingly difficult to live with. Like the pink chip heater in the bathroom and the way Nan boiled up all our clothes in the copper.

The copper was good in that your clothes always came out clean, if a trifle shrunken. What was not good was the fact that numerous cigarette burns and holes gradually appeared in every item due to Nan's incessant smoking. Even Mum was becoming fed up. She went so far as to maintain that Nan deliberately burnt holes in the dresses she didn't like. And, knowing how cantankerous Nan could be, I wouldn't have put it past her.

The final straw came for me one morning when I put on a lovely new dress Mum had bought me from the second-hand shop, only to discover two sizeable holes burned in the material that was supposed to cover my left breast. When I stuck out my chest and angrily pointed out to Nan where the damage was, she just laughed and said, 'That colour doesn't suit you anyway!'.

And then, one evening, Mum returned from work cross and embarrassed.

'Just look at my skirt.' I glanced down at Mum's skirt. There, just about in the centre of where her bottom would be, was a sizeable hole.

It was a blessing in disguise, really, because, the following afternoon, Mum went out and bought a twin tub washing machine and installed it in the laundry.

'You're only to use the copper for boiling the dogs' blanket in', she told Nan crossly, 'from now on, the clothes are washed in this machine.

116

I won't have any more holes in my dresses.'

Nan was reluctant to use the machine. It ran off electricity and she feared that, combined with the water, she'd get electrocuted. Even when I explained to her that all the wires were covered up and that it was perfectly safe, she still refused to touch it. In desperation, Mum finally gave her an ultimatum: use the machine or give up smoking while she washed. Now giving up smoking for any length of time to Nan was like cutting off an arm or a leg. She agreed to have a go at the machine.

To our amazement, not only did new holes begin to appear in our clothes, but the old ones got larger as well. Mum was furious. She berated Nan for still using the copper, but, to our surprise, Nan maintained that she had been using the twin tub.

'Well, show me what you do', asked Mum suspiciously as she accompanied Nan to the laundry.

Ten minutes later, Mum returned and collapsed in giggles next to me on the lounge. Apparently, Nan had been using the machine, but the whole time it was chugging away, she stood over it to make sure nothing went wrong. Now and then, she would plunge in the stick she used to stir the copper with, retrieve different items of clothing, and closely inspect them to make sure they were clean. That was when the fatal ash fell.

The pink chip heater in our bathroom had been a thorn in my side for years. Jill, Bill and I had all pleaded with Mum to have a new hot water system installed, but Mum was adamant that she couldn't afford one. We knew this was just an excuse, because with Mum's florist business doing well, and the loan paid off, we were now better off than we'd ever been.

Great skill and ingenuity were required to maintain a consistent trickle of hot water from the shower, which was positioned over the bath. In fact, it was only possible by one of two methods. The first required team-work. A leisurely soak could be enjoyed if someone else could be persuaded to man the heater and continually feed it with small wood chips and pieces of scrunched-up newspaper while you showered. The second method was more modest, but less convenient. Three buckets of wood chips were placed near the heater. As the water coming from the shower cooled, you leapt naked from the bath, taking care not to slip on the bare cement floor, threw a few handfuls of chips into the heater, and leapt back under again.

The issue finally came to a head one Saturday afternoon when a friend of mine asked if he could shower at our place before going out that evening. Coming from a wealthy Victorian family, for some reason, he assumed that everyone's bathroom was the same. Funnily enough, we assumed the same thing, and so began to matter-of-factly explain the workings of our chip heater.

I watched as my friend's ready smile slowly changed to dismay, and then, just as readily, back to a lopsided grin.

'Stop', he cried. 'Stop having me on!'

The culture shock Jeff experienced when he saw our heater was enough to send Mum running to the nearest gas appliance centre in shame.

I often found myself sandwiched between Nan's cantankerous nature and Mum's strange approach to home improvements, like the night I helped Mum remodel our lounge-room.

From a bin of specials in a wallpaper shop, Mum had purchased eight rolls of chocolate-brown Paisley print wallpaper. It wasn't nearly enough to cover all the walls, but Mum reasoned that it was better to have one feature wall of Paisley print than none at all. It would give our place a bit of class.

Having paid out for wallpaper, she wasn't about to pay out for glue, buckets, rollers or a ladder. Instead, she dragged out a large tin of glue from the laundry, which she mixed up in the bath. Our ladder was three pine crates piled on top of one another near the wall, and as for rollers, well, as Mum so succinctly pointed out, what were hands for?

I was given the dubious honour of running down the length of the hall that joined the bathroom to the lounge-room with each length of soggy, gluey wallpaper. As I entered the lounge-room, I had to make a frenzied leap onto the top of the pine crates and slap the wallpaper against the wall, aiming it as close as possible to the ceiling line. Mum's part in this was to hurriedly press the paper down as I held it. Once she'd patted the bottom part on, I pressed down the top part. Then I climbed down from the crates and the whole process started all over again.

By the time three panels were plastered to the wall, the whole hall was also plastered with glue and bits of Paisley print that had torn off and I was beginning to feel distinctly sticky and generally doubtful about the whole thing. Unfortunately, Mum wasn't one to admit to failure. She urged me on with comments like 'It's beautiful, Sally, you're so clever with your hands' and 'We'll have the best house in the street after tonight!'.

At one stage, Nan came in and, seeing us balancing on top of the crates completely obscured by the wallpaper, which had somehow flopped backwards over our heads, commented, 'I'm livin' in a nut house! You two are the silliest buggers I know.' Mum blew her top and Nan left, chuckling. She was always pleased when she upset someone.

By midnight, we'd finished the full length of the wall. There were still uneven pieces left over at either end, but we decided that they could wait until morning to be snipped off.

The following morning, Mum and I went in to admire our handiwork. Nan was already in the lounge-room, pacing up and down, eyeing the wallpaper, with Curly close on her heels. He was giving it the occasional lick. I think he liked the glue.

'Come on, Nan', Mum coaxed, 'it looks lovely, doesn't it?'.

Nan smiled smugly, 'Oooh yes . . . you've got one bit going one way and the next bit going the other. You are clever, Glad.' Then, she turned to Curly and said, 'Come on boy, I'll give you your milk. You don't want to stay in here with these silly buggers.'

Nan was right, the pattern was all mixed up. Mum salvaged some pride by muttering, 'We can say we did it that way deliberately'.

Mum continued her attempts at updating our house the following month, when Cyril came to stay.

Cyril was an elderly friend of mine whom I had met at church. Now we children were getting older, we often brought friends home to stay. Nan wasn't happy about the situation, but Mum felt that by welcoming our friends, she was helping us keep on the straight and narrow.

Cyril was an Englishman, and he prided himself on his ability to cope with the Australian climate. During the summer, when we relished cold showers, cool drinks, shady verandahs, and even the dog had an ice cube in his milk, Cyril would be out in the midday sun, clad only in baggy shorts and lace-up shoes. Nan's comments of 'Come inside you silly man', and 'Hmmph, thinks he's a blackfella' went unheard as Cyril busied himself with some particularly hot, sweaty task.

'You know what they say', I said to her. 'Only mad dogs and Englishmen go out in the noonday sun.' I must've impressed her, because with a jerk, she pulled open the louvres and ordered Curly inside.

When Cyril had first arrived at our place, he'd only planned to stay overnight. He had no fixed abode, but resided anywhere he could find a friendly face and somewhere to park his van. However, the following morning, he regaled Mum and Nan with comments like 'I don't know where I'll go from here' and 'I'm worried about that knock in my back axle, I really shouldn't be driving around'. Battlers themselves, it would have been against their natures to do anything but offer him a temporary home.

Being a practical sort of man, Cyril assured Mum that it would take him no more than a few days to discover what was causing the knock in his back axle. Mum, a shrewd sort of woman, was mentally noting all the odd jobs around the house that needed a man's attention.

Mum's suggestion of putting a sliding flywire door in the gap in our enclosed back verandah was eagerly taken up.

Cyril hated spending money and Mum loved a bargain, so, in no time at all, a fourth-hand sliding door, profusely patchworked with bits of florist wire, and painted psychedelic blue with paint discarded at the local tip, was installed.

But a fly-free verandah had to be weighed against the difficulty we all experienced in actually getting in and out. The railings were slanted so the door would be self-closing, but the heavy jarrah frame made

119

it a race against time to whip down the three back steps without guillotining an arm or a leg. Nan's bruises and Curly's whines bore testimony to Cyril's ingenuity gone wrong.

Cyril attempted to rectify his mistake by placing a stopper inside the railing, and a weight to one side of the door to slow it down. There was no thought of repositioning the railings, the basic principle was, after all, a good one. Finally, Nan came up with the best solution. She propped the door permanently open with two red bricks, and the flies returned.

Cyril's next project was the side gate. Mum had been warned continually by the local council to keep the dogs in the yard. She presented this problem to Cyril and he immediately set about producing the cheapest, most functional gate in the southern hemisphere.

For weeks, he haunted auctions, rubbish tips, junk yards and second-hand shops in search of materials. One night after tea, he unfolded a neat drawing of how he envisaged the gate would look. I peered over his shoulder at the sketch. It was large and fancy, in a word, ostentatious, and Mum loved it. Nan failed to see how he could get something like that out of the heap of metal beds and wire bases he'd stockpiled in the yard.

For the next four days, Cyril cut, welded, heated, moulded and re-welded different pieces of metal. The final production was five foot wide and five and a half foot high, and it bore no resemblance to the original drawing. Cyril proudly told Mum that he had let his innate creativity flow, altering the design as he went along.

I stood eyeing the monster in awe. I suddenly and desperately wished he'd discover what was causing the knock in his back axle and leave before Mum could ask him to do anything else.

By the time Cyril finished the gate, his stay of two to three days had stretched into six weeks. And his search for the elusive knock had led to a complete dismantling of his van, which was strewn in various stages of disassembly down our drive. It was a mystery to us how he still managed to find some part of it to sleep in.

No sooner would one mechanical problem be solved than another would begin. Cyril's concern for his back axle passed to the exhaust system, the wheel bearings and, eventually, to the engine itself. We began to sense that it was going to be a lifetime job.

I'm happy to say that Mum bore the brunt of it. The words 'Now you take my van. . .' were now a cue for the rest of the family to melt slowly away. Mum was the only one too polite to do so. Her punishment for such courtesy was long sessions with Cyril, during which he explained the intricacies of modern motor mechanics to Mum's mechanically feeble brain.

Nan, in particular, was getting fed up with him. Habits that had at first seemed humorous now became more and more irritating.

'He's digging in for the winter', she commented ominously to me one day.

Nan discovered that she had an intense dislike of classical music. Actually, she hadn't known what classical music was until she met Cyril. Now, every morning, as though fired with a missionary zeal to educate, he roused us all with loud bursts of ROM, POM, POM, POM! ROM, POM, POM, POM!

Nan decided that his passion must be curbed, especially before six in the morning.

Initially, she countered his attacks by turning up her transistor radio full blast. It failed to register against his stereophonic cassette with four speakers.

I suggested to Nan that she tackle Cyril directly and simply ask him to turn his music down. 'He can only say no and I don't think that's likely, because he's on our territory, so it's only fair that he considers our wishes.'

'You can't do that, Sally', she said in a shocked voice. 'You can't go asking people to do things.'

It seemed we were at an impasse. Situations such as these had been resolved in the past by Mum and Nan simply wearing their opposition down and thus avoiding confrontation, but, in Cyril, they'd met their match. So, for the next few weeks, the music continued louder than ever, and Nan's progressively more militant comments passed unnoticed.

I could see that, as far as Cyril was concerned, subtlety was a word he'd never discovered in his well worn English dictionary, which was surprising, because he often looked up long, complicated words to include in his everyday language. This habit, rather than adding to the quality of his conversation, served merely to lengthen it.

Then, one afternoon, I watched with curiosity as Nan shuffled towards Cyril's semi-complete van. I knew she was a woman with a mission.

I listened as she gave Cyril a brief introduction into the mysteries of animal health. Then she mentioned Curly, her four-footed favourite. I glimpsed Cyril's sympathetic nod as she described Curly's hearing problem.

'Well, these things happen as we get older, Nan, I'm going a bit deaf myself.'

Nan persevered, intimating that Curly was all right a few months ago. 'Funny how it's come on all of a sudden. I'm worried about him, Cyril, if his ears don't get better soon, I'm afraid he won't hear the cars when they toot at him and he'll get run over.'

Now Cyril was a stickler for convention and he couldn't understand why anyone would let their dog have his afternoon sleep in the middle of the road. So, consequently, he replied: 'You know, Nan, it's not right that he should be out at all. He's not licensed.'

Nan was getting pretty fed up by this stage, so she said gruffly, 'Never mind about his licence, what about his ears?'.

'Well, why don't I take him up the vet for you?' Poor Cyril, he was

121

trying, but he'd missed the point again.

'A vet', Nan exploded almost immediately. 'Curly doesn't need a vet! I know what's wrong with him, it's your music. Rom, pom, pom, pom every morning, Curly can't take it, he's only little. He's not even drinking his milk.'

As Nan's tirade continued, Cyril's ruddy face grew ruddier and ruddier. To top it all off, Curly, sensing that he was being discussed, came and stood next to Nan's bare legs, peering up at Cyril through the mound of black hair that hung over his eyes. That was enough for Cyril. He retreated slowly backwards, up two steps and inside his van. I heard him splutter a promise that he would turn his music down. Nan smiled, thanked him and shuffled back down the drive with Curly at her heels. 'Aah, you're a good dog, you can have your milk, now.'

That evening, as soon as Nan retired to bed, Cyril began recounting the story of their conversation to Mum. He'd nearly finished, when it suddenly dawned on him that Mum was not responding in her usual gregarious manner. Normally, she laughed at anything, even at things other people didn't consider funny. Mum possessed the kind of laugh that began as an infectious giggle but, in moments, was a full-blown roar. Minutes of silent chewing passed.

Finally, Mum placed her knife and fork in the centre of her plate and said seriously, 'How kind of you, Cyril, to play that beautiful music of yours softly from now on. I've been worried about Curly's ears for a while now myself, perhaps they'll improve with time.'

It took six months before Cyril's van was almost completely restored. One very warm morning, he was busy working on the engine in the front of our yard. Nan had been in and out, taking him glasses of cold water to keep him going. 'I don't want to have a mad Englishman on my hands', she confided. Cyril had a bald patch on the top of his head and Nan was worried about the sun affecting his brain.

At lunch-time, Nan stormed into my room and interrupted my day-dreaming by saying crossly, 'Will you look what he's done? You go out and tell him off, Sally. You tell him we don't want any of that business around this house!'

'What are you talking about, Nan?'

'It's still there', she muttered, peering through my bedroom curtains.

'What's still there?' I said as I moved up behind her. All I could see was the van and Cyril's hot, sweaty, half-naked body.

'Will you just look where he's put his shirt, look!' Cyril's shirt was spread out neatly across the rose-bush in the front of our yard. 'It's disgusting', Nan said as she continued to eye him through the curtains. 'Does he think that's a clothes-line? Puttin' his dirty old shirt where everyone can see. You mark my words, Sally, the neighbours'll think there's blackfellas living here!'

Nan turned and stormed out the front. I heard a ripping noise as she tore Cyril's shirt from the rose-bush. Then, she stormed back inside,

leaving Cyril gazing after her, his mouth wide open.
  He left the following week.

Chapter Twenty

A NEW CAREER

Mum was both surprised and pleased when I began university in February. But while I phrased my new academic ambition in terms of I never want to work again, Mum took it to mean I was, at last, getting somewhere in the world.

I found university to my liking. I was amazed that none of the lecturers checked to see whether you turned up or not. Even missing tutorials wasn't a deadly sin. I spent many long afternoons in the library, reading books totally unrelated to my course. Then there were hours in the coffee shop, discussing the meaning of life, and days stretched out in the sun under the giant palms that dotted the campus, thinking about what a wonderful climate we had.

Jill was more conscientious than me. It was probably just as well we weren't both doing Arts, because I would have led her astray. She was enjoying studying Law and she'd made some new friends.

I was studying on a Repatriation scholarship and while there was never any money left over, my needs were small. I'd never been one to indulge in following all the fashion trends, and apart from my bus fares and lunches, I had few expenses.

I found travelling to university in winter terrible. I hated the cold. I had to catch two buses and they rarely connected in time for me to transfer immediately from one to the other. On really wet, stormy days, I stayed at home. I would sit in front of the fire all day, watch television, and read my latest book from the library. Nan always brought me in a huge lunch.

It amazed me that, after all those years, she was still trying to fatten me up. I and my brother David were her only failures.

The only day she didn't make my lunch was rent day. She was always too busy bustling around preparing the rentman's morning tea to bother with me then. One morning, she was being particularly fussy. It was a new rentman's first visit and I knew Nan wanted to impress him.

Soon, she was sitting on the front porch having a cup of tea with him. They took extra long that morning. I assumed it was because

Nan was spending time buttering him up. When she returned inside, the large plate of biscuits she'd laid out was completely empty.

'Goodness me, he must have liked that lot.'

Nan smiled. It was a triumph. 'He loved them. That poor man was so hungry, he ate the lot! He asked me what brand they were, said he wanted to buy some for his own place, but I didn't know.' Nan shoved a paper and pencil into my hands. 'Write down the name for me. The empty packet's over there on the bench.'

I walked over to the cluttered bench top and began rummaging through the various items jumbled on top. 'There's nothing here, Nan.'

'Hmph! Your eyesight's worse than mine. Look, just near the teapot.'

'What? This one?' I leant weakly against the side of the bench.

'What are you laughing for?'

With an unsteady hand, I held the empty packet as close as I could to her face. Her mouth dropped open in shock as her gaze took in the half-torn picture of a fox terrier.

'No supper for Curly tonight, Nan', I choked.

Over the next few months, the fact that Nan's eyesight was failing became obvious. Sometimes, she mistook the salt for the sugar or the deodorant for the flyspray. While we complained, Mum was prepared to tolerate all these little mistakes, until, one evening, Nan made a fatal error.

It was Friday night and, as usual, Mum had collapsed on the lounge in front of the TV. She preferred sleeping on the lounge to her own bed, maintaining that television was both relaxing and good company. She was completely covered in several layers of a tartan rug, only her frizzy mop of black, curly hair protruded.

It was way past tea-time when Nan entered, carrying a quivering mass of dog food. It was a brown jellied concoction made up of bits of liver and other less recognisable chunks of dubious origin. I watched curiously as Nan paused in the doorway and peered intently into the semi-darkness. Her squinting eyes paused for a moment on me. I don't know whether she actually registered my presence, or saw me merely as part of the large green chair I was sitting in. I was about to speak when she turned and, halting abruptly, stared hard at the lounge. She leaned forward slightly, her eyes narrowing in concentration, and then, following two quick strides towards the lounge, she croaked in exasperation, 'There you are, Curly, you stupid dog, didn't you hear me calling you?'.

I suppose I should have said something, however, my sense of humour got the better of me.

'Now come on, Curly', Nan growled, 'it's no use pretending you're not there.' She moved closer and held out the bowl. 'Come on, eat up. I'm not standing here all night!' Nan shoved the food deeper into what she was convinced was Curly's black, furry face.

I watched, entranced, as, prodded into consciousness, the tartan mass

125

that was Mum slowly began to move. Nan, sensing that Curly was at last responding, said, 'Good boy. Good dog. Come and eat it up!'

With one wild fling, Mum emerged. Her frizzy, black hair was covered with small chunks of jellied meat.

'Glad?' croaked Nan in disbelief.

'You stupid bloody woman', Mum spluttered, 'what the bloody hell do you think you're doing?!'.

I burst into laughter and Nan, realising she'd made a terrible mistake, made a hurried exit.

It was only after Mum had shampooed her hair and settled back on the lounge with a hot cup of tea that she was able to laugh.

Three sharp barks at the front door then let us all know that the recalcitrant Curly was outside and eager to come in. I opened the door and he pattered in, whining, a sure sign that he was hungry. Nan poked her head around the kitchen doorway and whispered, 'Is that Curly, Sally?'.

'I think so', I laughed, 'unless Mum barks, too'.

Nan chuckled, then said, 'Come on, Curly, you naughty boy. Where have you been? Glad nearly got your tea!'

'She did it deliberately, you know, Sally', Mum said as soon as I re-entered the lounge-room. 'She's an old devil. Her eyesight's not that bad. You leave a five-cent coin on the floor and I bet you she's the first one to pick it up!'

However, the following week, Mum bought Nan a pair of old binoculars. Nan was really excited. All of a sudden, she could see things that, apparently, had been blurred for years.

By the time I'd been at university a term, I was finding it very difficult to study at home. Apart from the high noise level and general chaos, I had no desk to work at, and, being disorganised myself, I was always losing important notes and papers, which I had to replace by photocopying someone else's.

Then when the August holidays came around, it suddenly dawned on me that if I was to pass anything, I would have to actually do some work. The trouble was I'd missed out on so much I didn't know where to begin.

My first attempts at a concentrated effort were rather futile, because I had to keep interrupting my study to call out, 'Turn down that radio!' or, 'The TV's too loud!' or, 'Will you all shut up, I'm trying to study!'.

After a week or so of constant yelling and arguing, I came to the realisation that it was impossible to change my environment. I decided to try and change myself instead. I found that if I tried really hard, I could work amidst the greatest mess and loudest noise level, with no bother whatsoever. I just switched off and pretended I was the only one in the house.

This was no mean feat, because our house was always full of people.

Many of my brother David's friends would just doss down on the lounge-room floor, they loved staying overnight. David had just begun high school that year. It never occurred to any of us to tell Mum there'd be someone extra for tea. We just assumed that she'd make what she had go a little bit further. I have to admit I was one of the worst offenders, but Mum never complained. She always told us, 'Your friends are welcome in this house'.

My technique for passing my exams that first year was simple, I crammed. The knowledge I gained was of little use to me afterwards, because as soon as my exams were over, I deleted it from my memory. Why clog up my brain with unnecessary facts and figures? I passed that year with a B and three C's. Mum was pleased, but urged me to spend more time studying so I could score A's, like Jill.

My brother Bill also had important exams that year, his Leaving. Unfortunately, he was not successful. However, he was able to find employment fairly quickly as a clerk with the Public Service.

I decided that I would like to spend my second year at university living away from home. Mum was mortified by the idea. I would be the first to leave the family nest. She urged me to reconsider.

After weeks of tearful arguments, she relented and said that if the Repatriation Department agreed to pay my fees, I could go. Fortunately, they did agree, and I was soon ensconced in my own little room in Currie Hall, a co-educational boarding-house just opposite the university.

Now for most of my teenage years, Mum had been concerned over my lack of interest in boys. I had had plenty of good friendships with the opposite sex, but never a real romance. She was worried I would end up an old maid, and she, an old lady with no grandchildren. But now that I was living in a co-ed college, she suddenly started worrying that I would develop an interest I couldn't control and join the permissive society.

It was difficult for Mum to let me grow up. She often visited me at Currie Hall, but she always left in tears. One night, we had a huge argument because I wouldn't kiss her goodbye. I thought she was expecting a bit much, wanting me to kiss her in front of ten male students gathered around the exit to my building. I had an image to maintain. Eventually, I asked Mum not to come and see me at all if she was going to break down. It was too exhausting.

I had great difficulty seeing through my second year. I had developed an intense dislike of the subject I was majoring in. I was dismayed when, at our first tutorial, I discovered that a good deal of our laboratory work involved training white rats. Rats were one of the few animals I disliked.

I managed to avoid handling Fred, as we dubbed him, by agreeing to do all the recording for the group, instead. However, after a few sessions, my tutor noticed my aversion and insisted that I, also, handle

Fred. He maintained there was nothing to it. There was a mutual antagonism between Fred and me of which my tutor was totally unaware.

Patiently, he demonstrated once again how to handle him. Then, placing Fred back in his maze, he insisted that I copy his actions. I looked down at Fred and he looked up at me. We both knew what was coming.

I attempted to pick him up, just as I'd been shown, but, in seconds, Fred had turned and sunk his teeth into my wrist.

Some good did come from this experience. Apparently, Fred was always so upset after a session with me that the tutor banned me from handling him, otherwise it was impossible for the group that followed to do anything with him.

Apart from Fred, I was sick of trying to master statistics. I had a mental block when it came to any form of mathematics. 'Rats and Stats', I complained to a fellow student one day, 'I came here to learn about people'. I wasn't the only student who was disgruntled. Many complained, but to no avail. I got to the stage where I was ready to pull out of university completely. However, I was going out with Paul, a schoolteacher, by then, and he persuaded me to stick it out.

I met Paul through his brother, with whom I had been friends for many years. In fact, Bruce had lived with our family for a while. He was like a brother to me and also a favourite of Nan's. Bruce was a lot like my brother Bill.

Nan never disappeared when Paul or Bruce were around. She actually seemed to enjoy their company. Paul commented once that Nan reminded him of many of the old people who had looked after him up North. I just nodded. It never occurred to me at the time to think about who those people were.

In a short period, Paul and I got to know each other well, spending a lot of time together. We discovered that we had a lot in common. I liked the artistic side of his nature and he seemed to find my wit amusing. Also, he fitted into our family well.

Paul had spent his childhood in the north-west, living mostly at Derby. His parents were missionaries, as were his grandparents and many of his relatives. When Paul was thirteen, his family moved to Perth, where his parents started a hostel for mission children who came to the city to attend high school. Paul found high school very difficult at first, because, apart from the normal adjustments all children have to make and the fact that he had come from such a vastly different environment, he had a language problem. He only spoke pidgin English.

By the end of the second term of my third year at university, we'd fallen in love and decided to get married. This came as a real shock to Mum, because I had always told her Paul was just another good friend. It kept her off my back. It took a few weeks before the fact that we meant what we said actually sank in. Then Mum reacted more normally: she panicked.

I added to her trauma by telling her I'd decided to be married in our backyard. This immediately prompted her to worry about how she could manage to lock up all the chooks so they didn't molest my wedding guests. And, of course, there was the problem of Curly.

Mum pushed one panic button after another over the following weeks. The drive was too sandy, the grass too prickly and nearly dead, she didn't have enough chairs or glasses or plates. How much food would we need, where did she get it from, how many guests would be coming. I told her that there'd only be about one hundred people. I thought this would allay her fears, but it only served to heighten them. She began asking me questions like are they big eaters or small eaters, drinkers or non-drinkers and so on. In the end, I said to her quite sternly, 'Pull yourself together. You're the mother of the bride, you've got to stop worrying and get organised. Think of it as a challenge!'

It was the best advice I could have given her. There was nothing Mum loved more than a challenge.

Our wedding date was set for two months hence, and, as the days passed, Mum swung into action like a real trooper. Every morning and night, she watered the grass in an attempt to coax back the green colour normally associated with lawn. However, as the day of judgement drew closer, she became obsessed with the yard, specifically, the drive. For some reason, it became the focal point of all her worries.

One afternoon, a huge load of gravel was deposited on our verge. And three days later, a three-foot high cement roller, weighing in the vicinity of a ton, arrived. In the meantime, Bill had agreed to help rake out the gravel over the drive, but when he arrived to see the cement roller, he looked at Mum in disgust and said, 'What the bloody hell is that?'.

'It's to help flatten the gravel. You know, make it more like bitumen.'

Bill scratched his head and breathed out. 'Yeah . . . and how are we going to pull it up and down?'

Mum was not to be put off. 'Look, it's got these two sticks poking out, I thought you boys could strap yourselves between them and pull it along.'

'Mother dear', he said between clenched teeth, 'if you think I'm gunna strap myself to that bloody thing, you've got another think coming. Sorry Sal', he said as he turned to me, 'not even for you'.

'That's okay, Bill, it was Mum's idea.'

'Yeah, well. That's pretty obvious, isn't it?'

'God, Bill, it wouldn't hurt you.' Mum was offended. 'You know the wedding's soon and I'm worried about the drive.' Bill was not to be persuaded. He had this knack of recognising the futility of Mum's schemes right from the start.

When Mum approached David the following day, he was more sympathetic. After she pleaded with him, he promised to give it a go.

129

It was nearly a hundred degrees in the shade the day he strapped himself to the roller. Mum cheered him on with cold glasses of lemonade and comments like 'You're the only one who does anything for me, David'. This kept him going for a couple of hours, however, as the temperature continued to rise, his strength sapped.

'I'm not doin' any more, Mum. Bill was right, it's a bloody stupid idea!'

'But you can't leave the drive like that', Mum protested, 'it's all uneven'.

'You pull it, then', he shouted. 'Have you any idea how heavy it is? Well, have you?' As weak as he was, he still managed to raise his voice loud enough to cower Mum into silence.

Mum spent the following week working on me. Whenever she saw me, she told me in detail how bad the drive was and hinted that Paul might like to take a turn.

The following Saturday, after lunch, we led him like a lamb to the slaughter.

Mum, anxious to get him started, positioned herself between the straps and, with grunts and groans, indicated what was expected of him. Paul looked desperately at me. I looked at the roller. Mum departed down the drive, stomping on the uneven bits in an attempt to press them down.

'Please?' I pleaded as she continued to make scuffling noises.

'All right', he relented. And, removing his shirt, he strapped himself to the roller and began to slowly move after Mum.

'Oh Paul, that's good', Mum encouraged. 'You're much better than David.'

He laboured admirably for two hours. But finally, he staggered inside, dripping with sweat, and collapsed on the lounge.

'Listen, Sal', he gasped, 'I don't care if people get their feet dirty or if their shoes stick in the gravel. They can break their bloody ankles for all I care. I'm not pulling that roller another inch.'

Just then, Mum entered with more lemonade. 'Drink this, you're a silly boy working in that heat. You're lucky you didn't dehydrate.' Paul choked on the lemonade and then looked at Mum in amazement.

'It wasn't my idea to flatten out the gravel.'

'You've done a wonderful job, Paul. Hasn't he, Jill?'

Jill burst out laughing and fled to the kitchen.

'That'll do for now, Paul', Mum said kindly. 'It's too hot to work any more. Perhaps you could finish it off tomorrow?' Paul's stunned silence was enough to send Mum scurrying after Jill.

'Is she always like this?' he asked me pitifully.

'No.'

'Thank God for that.'

'Normally, she's worse.'

Chapter Twenty-One

OWNING UP

My wedding day, the ninth of December, 1972, dawned bright and sunny. I nicked into town early that morning to buy a wedding dress. I found an Indian caftan that I liked, it was cream with gold embroidery down the front. I was pleased because it was lovely and cool. It was becoming obvious that the day was going to be a stinker. By the time I got home, the temperature was over the hundred-degree mark.

My Aunty Vi arrived early to help. Aunty Vi had been a close friend of Mum's in her teenage years and they were both florists. Although they hadn't seen much of one another over the years, they still maintained a friendship on the basis of an occasional lunch date or phone call.

Mum welcomed her with open arms. 'I need help with all the flowers', she said excitedly. Our laundry was jammed with buckets and buckets of cut flowers.

'Mum', I complained as I tried to fight my way through the buckets to the toilet, 'you won't need all these flowers, and what on earth are these for?' I called as I spied a huge carton of plastic roses.

Mum poked her head around the laundry door and said crossly, 'Never mind what they're for. You just stay out of the way and mind your own business!'

I was suspicious by then. 'You're not up to anything silly, are you, Mum?'

'Of course she isn't', Nan grumbled as she came to her rescue. 'Now you hurry up and go to the toilet and get out of here. We've got work to do.'

'Well, listen Nan', I said, 'whatever else you get up to, make sure you lock up the chooks, won't you? And I don't want Curly interfering with anyone.'

'Oh, the chooks are all right', she replied. 'They're having their scratch around now. I'll pen them up before anyone comes. Curly's going to be in my room.'

'Why don't you go and have a shower, dear', Mum interrupted, 'you look hot'. Just then, Paul's parents arrived. I made the introductions and then decided that a shower mightn't be a bad idea.

I wandered into my room to get my towelling dressing-gown and gather up my things.

Just as I was about to head for the shower, Bill came in. 'Sal', he said, 'I think we'd better have a talk. There's something I'd like to say to you.'

'Sure Bill, what is it?'

'I just wanted you to know this. If Paul doesn't ever do the right thing by you, you just let me know. I'll fix things up.'

'I'll remember that, Bill', I said, 'but Paul's a nice bloke, I don't think we'll have any problems'.

'Yeah, well, just thought I'd say that to you, okay?'

'Thanks, Bill.' Bill left, and I couldn't help thinking that Mum's prophecy after Dad died had finally come true. Bill really was the man of our house. I felt very lucky. I had a wonderful family.

When I emerged from the shower, cooler and cleaner, I found Mr Morgan busily stacking up glasses in the kitchen. Mrs Morgan had disappeared and so had everyone else. I wandered out the back and, to my surprise, saw Mum, Aunty Vi and Mrs Morgan squatting on their knees in the dirt. They were surrounded by buckets and buckets of cut flowers. 'That's right, Margaret', Mum said coaxingly to my future mother-in-law, 'just stick them straight in like that. No one will know the difference.'

'I'll go round and do the front', said Aunty Vi as she picked up two buckets and shuffled around the side of the house. Just then, Nan joined them. 'I've put all those plastic roses in the front garden, Glad', she said. 'They do look beautiful. You'd think they were real.'

Oh no, I thought. They can't be doing this! I raced back in through the house and out to the front. Garishly coloured flowers of all descriptions were stuck in what had previously been bare earth. They stood straight up, their faces towards the sun.

Mum appeared behind me. 'Oh Sally, what are you doing here?' she asked nervously.

'MUM! How could you??!'

'Well, I told you I was worried about the garden', she replied lamely.

'It's so embarrassing! How could you ask Margaret to help? What an introduction to our family! Honestly, Mum, this is one of the stupidest things you've ever done!'

'But the garden looks lovely, now. No one will know they're standing there with no roots.'

'It's a stinking hot day. They'll keel over in half an hour.'

'No, they won't. Nan's keeping the sprinkler on them right up till the guests start arriving.'

'Oh, Mum', I wailed, 'you'll never change!'.

By this time, she was looking hot and bothered and extremely harrassed. 'Look', I said, weakening, 'I'll pretend I didn't see the flowers, but at least make sure Curly and the chooks are kept out of the way. I don't want anything else happening, okay?'

'Yes, dear.'

Everything seemed to go smoothly after that. The wedding ceremony was brief and to the point.

After the ceremony was over, I went in search of Nan. I'd been concerned that, with the yard full of people she considered strangers, she might pull one of her disappearing acts. Mum had already explained to her that it was important she be seen as she was the grandmother of the bride. It took me a while to locate her.

I finally found her behind our old garden shed, crying.

'Nan, what's wrong?'

'You kids don't need me any more', she sobbed, 'you're all grown up now'.

'But we still need you', I replied, trying to reassure her. She shook her head and continued to cry.

'Would you like me to get Mum?' I asked anxiously.

She nodded.

So I patted her arm and went and explained to Mum about Nan and she went to comfort her. She persuaded Nan to go inside the house, where she settled her down with a cup of tea. I felt at a loss. It seemed it never mattered what I did, it was always the wrong thing.

The rest of the afternoon wasn't too traumatic. Little things like the chooks and dogs running wild and a few guests ending up drunk didn't seem to matter. Everyone enjoyed themselves immensely and quite a few people commented that it was the most unusual wedding they'd ever been to. Mum took this as a compliment.

It was close to midnight when the last guest finally left. No one had wanted to go home.

'I did all right, didn't I, Sally?' Mum asked smugly.

'Yeah', I replied, 'maybe you should go into the catering business'.

'I was thinking that myself!' I glanced at her in fear. We both laughed.

Shortly after my wedding, I found out that I had passed all my units at university except psychology. I wasn't surprised. I disliked the work I was doing so much that I hadn't bothered to study for my exams. I decided to change my major for the following year, but Paul talked me out of it. 'You'll have to repeat', he said.

'Repeat?' I was disgusted at the thought. Another year with the rats was almost too much to bear. However, when I looked at the alternatives, I realised that I could be jumping from the frying-pan into the fire. Also, I'd heard that there was some human content in third-year psychology. So I decided to persevere.

Towards the end of the summer vacation, Paul and I moved into a run-down old weatherboard house in South Perth. The toilet was miles down the back of the yard, only one gas burner worked on the stove, the hot water system wasn't even as decent as the old chip heater we'd had at home, and the place was infested with tiny sand fleas. After living in there a few weeks, we also discovered that there were rats residing underneath the floor-boards. For some reason, none of this seemed to bother us. We thought the place had character and it was adventurous being on our own.

And I was learning new skills, like how to cook and make beds. Considering what a good cook Nan was, it might have been expected that I'd have more flair. I was hopeless. Nan had never allowed us to cook as children, the kitchen was her own private domain. And as for helping around the house, well, that was quite unheard of. There had been occasions when Jill and I had attempted to wash up the dishes, but Nan had always shooed us away with the comment 'You stay out of my kitchen'.

To Nan's credit, she had taught me how to light a fire, chop wood, gut chickens and look after sick animals. However, I found these were skills I rarely had to use now.

After a while, Jill moved in with us and then two other friends as well. We were a happy little group. Most of our evenings were filled with Bob Dylan music, poetry and long discussions about current world issues. It was a lovely time in my life.

The day the university year began, I had to force myself to attend. I was convinced I was going to fail again. Many times, I came near to giving up my course entirely, but Paul always talked me into continuing. He gave me the impression that some of my attitudes were very immature. That was quite a shock. I had never thought of myself as being immature before.

Now that Jill and I were once again living in the same house, we often had long talks about our childhood. And the subject of Nan's origins always came up.

'We'll never know for sure', Jill said one night. 'Mum will never tell us.'

'Hmmn, I might start pestering her again. We're older now, we've got a right to know.'

'What does Paul think?'

'When I asked him whether he thought Nan was Aboriginal, he just laughed and said, "Isn't it obvious? Of course she is." ' Paul, of course, had been brought up with Aboriginal people.

'I don't think we can really decide until we hear Mum admit it from her own lips.'

'That'll be the day.'

A few weeks later, Mum popped in for her usual visit, laden with fattening cakes and eager to tell me about the latest bargain she'd bought at auction. I'd been to too many auctions with Mum in the past, I knew that many items that looked like bargains at first glance turned out to be a total waste of money on closer inspection. The auctioneers had become so used to Mum buying things no one else would buy that they often knocked things down to her without taking any bids from the floor.

'One-o-four will have it', they'd shout, as a hammer without a handle or a duplicating machine that didn't duplicate came up for grabs. 'You'll have it, won't you, one-o-four, you buy anything for a dollar.' One-o-four was Mum's permanent bidding number.

'Come out to the car and see what I've bought,' Mum said excitedly. 'You won't believe it.' That was the trouble, I never did.

As she opened up the back of the car, she said generously, 'You can have whatever you like, there's plenty here'. Mum always bought in bulk.

Apart from the usual assortment of rusty tools and various other odds and ends, Mum had, in fact, actually bought something useful. There was a box of Indian-made cheesecloth shirts. Although, as it turned out, there were also seven other boxes that had to be picked up later. Approximately one hundred and forty shirts in all.

'I'll sell what we can't use at Trash and Treasure', Mum said. It wasn't a good suggestion, Mum always came home from those markets with more than she had taken.

'Aargh! I don't even want to think about it. Let's go and eat that cake you brought.'

We went in and settled down in the kitchen and I made a cup of tea. Mum was soon in a relaxed and talkative mood.

Then, after a while, there was a lull in the conversation, so I said very casually, 'We're Aboriginal, aren't we, Mum?'.

'Yes, dear', she replied, without thinking.

'Do you realise what you just said?!' I grinned triumphantly.

Mum put her cake back onto her plate and looked as though she was going to be sick.

'Don't you back down!' I said quickly. 'There's been too many skeletons in our family closet. It's time things came out in the open.' After a few minutes' strained silence, Mum said, 'Why shouldn't you kids know now? You're old enough, it's not as though you're little any more. Besides, it's different now'.

'All those years, Mum', I said, 'how could you have lied to us all those years?'.

'It was only a little white lie', she replied sadly.

I couldn't help laughing at her unintentional humour. In no time at all, we were both giggling uncontrollably. It was as if a wall that had been between us suddenly crumbled away. I felt closer to Mum then than I had for years.

Chapter Twenty-Two

A BEGINNING

I was very excited by my new heritage. When I told Jill that evening what Mum had said, she replied, 'I don't know what you're making a fuss about. I told you years ago Nan was Aboriginal. The fact that Mum's owned up doesn't change anything.' Sometimes, Jill was so logical I wanted to hit her.

'Jill, it does mean something, to have admitted it. Now she might tell us more about the past. Don't you want to know?'

'Yeah, I guess so, but there's probably not much to tell.'

'But that's just it, we don't know. There could be tons we don't know. What other skeletons are lurking in the cupboard?'

'You always did have too much imagination!'

'I'm going to keep pestering her now till she tells us the whole story.'

'She won't tell you any more.'

'Maybe not', I replied, 'but the way I look at it, it's a beginning. Before, we had nothing. At least now, we've got a beginning.'

'Mum's right about you, you should have gone on the stage.'

When Mum popped in a week later with a large sponge cake filled with chocolate custard, I was ecstatic. Not because of the cake, but because I had a bombshell to drop, and I was anxious to get on with it. I made coffee for a change and I waited until Mum was half-way through a crumbling piece of sponge before I said, 'I've applied for an Aboriginal scholarship'.

'What?!' she choked as she slammed down her mug and spat out the sponge.

'There's an Aboriginal scholarship you can get, Mum. Anyone of Aboriginal descent is eligible to apply.'

'Oh Sally, you can't', Mum giggled, as if speaking to a naughty child.

'Why can't I', I demanded, 'or are you going to tell me that Nan's really Indian after all?'.

'Oh Sally, you're awful', Mum chuckled, and then she added thoughtfully, 'Well, why shouldn't you apply? Nan's had a hard life.

Why shouldn't her grandchildren get something out of it?'

'Exactly', I replied.

I don't think Mum realised how deep my feelings went. It wasn't the money I was after, I was still receiving the Repatriation scholarship. I desperately wanted to do something to identify with my new-found heritage and that was the only thing I could think of.

When I was granted an interview for my scholarship application, Mum was amazed. I think she expected them to ignore me. She was very worried about what I was going to tell them. Mum always worried about what to tell people. It was as if the truth was never adequate, or there was something to hide.

She had been inventing stories and making exaggerated claims since the day she was born. It was part of her personality. She found it difficult to imagine how anyone could get through life any other way, so consequently, when in response to her question about my interview, I answered, 'I'm going to tell them the truth', she was flabbergasted.

I was successful in my scholarship application, but for the next few months, I was the butt of many family jokes. We all felt shy and awkward about our new-found past. No one was sure what to do with it or about it, and none of the family could agree on whether I'd done the right thing or not. In keeping with my character, I had leapt in feet first. I wanted to do something positive. I wanted to say, 'My grandmother's Aboriginal and it's a part of me, too'. I wasn't sure where my actions would lead, and the fact that Nan remained singularly unimpressed with my efforts added only confusion to my already tenuous sense of identity.

'Did Mum tell you I got the scholarship, Nan?' I asked one day.

'Yes. What did you tell them?'

'I told them that our family was Aboriginal but that we'd been brought up to believe differently.'

'What did you tell them about me?'

'Nothing. So relax.'

'You won't ever tell them about me, will you, Sally? I don't like strangers knowing our business, especially government people. You never know what they might do.'

'Why are you so suspicious, Nan?' I asked gently. She ignored my question and shuffled outside to do the garden. A sense of sadness suddenly overwhelmed me. I wanted to cry. 'Get a grip on yourself, woman', I muttered. 'You don't even know what you want to cry about!'

Slowly, over that year, Mum and I began to notice a change in Nan. Not a miraculous change, but a change just the same. Her interests began to extend beyond who was in the telephone box opposite our house, to world affairs. Nan had always watched the news every night on each channel if she could, but now, instead of just noting world disasters, she began to take an interest in news about black people.

If the story was sad, she'd put her hand to her mouth and say,

'See, see what they do to black people'. On the other hand, if black people were doing well for themselves, she'd complain, 'Just look at them, showing off. Who do they think they are. They just black like me.'

About this time, Nan's favourite word became Nyoongah*. She'd heard it used on a television report and had taken an instant liking to it. To Nan, anyone dark was now Nyoongah. Africans, Burmese, American Negroes were all Nyoongahs. She identified with them. In a sense, they were her people, because they shared the common bond of blackness and the oppression that, for so long, that colour had brought. It was only a small change, but it was a beginning.

In a strange sort of way, my life had new purpose because of that. I wondered whether, because Jill and I had accepted that part of ourselves, perhaps Nan was coming to terms with it, too. I was anxious to learn as much as I could about the past. I made a habit of taking advantage of Mum's general good nature.

'Where was Nan born, Mum?' I asked her one day.

'Oh, I don't know. Up North somewhere.'

'Has she ever talked to you about her life?'

'You know she won't talk about the past. She says she can't remember.'

'Do you think she does remember?'

'I think so, but she thinks we're prying, trying to hurt her.'

'Mum, is there anyone who could tell me anything about Nan?'

'Only Judy.'

'Who? Aunty Judy?'

'Yes.'

'Why would she know anything about Nan?'

'Nan worked for their family.'

'In what capacity?'

'Oh, you know, housework, that sort of thing.'

'You mean she was a servant?'

'Yes, I suppose so.'

'How long did she work for them?'

'Oh, I don't know, Sally. Why do you always bring this up? Can't we talk about something else?' Nearly all of our conversations ended like that.

Amazingly, I passed my psychology unit at the end of that year, I even scored a B. I was looking forward to my final year because there was quite a large slice about people in the course and that, after all, was what I'd come to learn about.

By now, both Jill and I had many friends at university. All our lives, people had asked us what nationality we were, most had assumed we were Greek or Italian, but we'd always replied, 'Indian'. Now, when

---

* *Nyoongah* — the Aboriginal people of south-west Australia. (Derived from man or person). Also the language of these people.

we were asked, we said, 'Aboriginal'.

We often swapped tales of what the latest comment was. A few of our acquaintances had said, 'Aaah, you're only on the scholarship because of the money'. At that time, the Aboriginal allowance exceeded the allowance most students got. We felt embarrassed when anyone said that, because we knew that that must be how it seemed. We had suddenly switched our allegiance from India to Aboriginal Australia and I guess, in their eyes, they could see no reason why we would do that except for the money.

Sometimes, people would say, 'But you're lucky, you'd never know you were that, you could pass for anything'. Many students reacted with an embarrassed silence. Perhaps that was the worst reaction of all. It was like we'd said a forbidden word. Others muttered, 'Oh, I'm sorry . . .' and when they realised what they were saying, they just sort of faded away.

Up until now, if we thought about it at all, we'd both thought Australia was the least racist country in the world, now we knew better. I began to wonder what it was like for Aboriginal people with really dark skin and broad features, how did Australians react to them? How had white Australians reacted to my grandmother in the past, was that the cause of her bitterness?

About half-way through that year, 1973, I received a brief note from the Commonwealth Department of Education, asking me to come in for an interview with a senior officer of the department. I was scared stiff.

Two days later, I sat nervously in the waiting area. I had pains in my stomach. I always got pains in my stomach when I was nervous. I'd been for interviews before, but always with more junior staff of the department. The senior people never usually concerned themselves with trifling matters like students, they were more concerned with important things, like administration. Several people walked past and eyed me curiously. I suddenly had the distinct impression that something was very wrong

'You may go in now', the woman at the reception desk suddenly said.

'Thanks', I smiled and walked slowly into the office.

'Mrs Morgan', the senior officer said as I sat down. 'We'll get straight to the point. We have received information, from what appears to be a very reliable source, that you have obtained the Aboriginal scholarship under false pretences. This person, who is a close friend of you and your sister, has told us that you have been bragging all over the university campus about how easy it is to obtain the scholarship without even being Aboriginal. Apparently, you've been saying that anyone can get it.'

I was so amazed at the ridiculousness of the accusation that I burst out laughing. That was a great tactical error on my part.

'This is no laughing matter! This is a very serious offence. Have you lied to this department? I want to hear what you have to say for yourself.'

I felt very angry. It was obvious I had been judged guilty already, and I knew why. It was because Jill and I were doing well. The department never expected any of their Aboriginal students to do well at tertiary studies. They would have considered it more in keeping if we both failed consistently.

'Who made the complaint?'

'I can't tell you. We promised confidentiality.'

'It was no friend of ours.'

'This person is a student and knows you both extremely well.'

'But that doesn't add up. If they know us really well, they would have been to our home and met my grandmother and mother, in which case they'd never have made this complaint.'

'Is that all you have to say?'

'You've obviously already judged me guilty, what else can I say?'

'I expected more than that from you. You don't seem very keen to prove your innocence. You do realise that this is a most serious offence?'

I'd had it by then. 'Look', I said angrily, 'when I applied for this scholarship, I told your people everything I knew about my family, it was their decision to grant me a scholarship, so if there's any blame to be laid, it's your fault, not mine. How do you expect me to prove anything? What would you like me to do, bring my grandmother and mother in and parade them up and down so you can all have a look? There's no way I'll do that, even if you tell me to. I'd rather lose the allowance. It's my word against whoever complained, so it's up to you to decide, isn't it?'

My heart was pounding fiercely. It was very difficult for me to stand up for myself, I wasn't used to dealing with authority figures so directly. No wonder Mum and Nan didn't like dealing with government people, I thought. They don't give you a chance.

The senior officer looked at me silently for a few minutes and then said, 'Well, Mrs Morgan. You are either telling the truth, or you're a very good actress!'

I was amazed, still my innocence wasn't to be conceded.

'I'm telling the truth', I said crossly.

'Very well, you may go.' I was dismissed with a nod of the head. I was unable to move.

'I'm not sure I want this scholarship any more', I said. 'What if someone else makes a complaint? Will I be hauled in here for the same thing?'

The senior officer thought for a moment, then said, 'No. If someone else complains, we'll ignore it.'

Satisfied, I left and walked quickly to the elevator. I felt sick and I wasn't sure how much longer my legs would support me. It was just as well I'd lost my temper, I thought. Otherwise, I wouldn't have defended myself at all. It was the thought that somehow Mum and Nan might have to be involved that had angered me. It had seemed so demeaning.

Once I was outside, I let the breeze blowing up the street ease away the tenseness in the muscles in my face. I breathed deeply to steady myself and walked slowly to the bus stop.

What if I had been too shy to defend myself, I thought. What would have happened then? I had no doubt they would have taken the scholarship away from me. Then I thought, maybe I'm doing the wrong thing. It hadn't been easy trying to identify with being Aboriginal. No one was sympathetic, so many people equated it with dollars and cents, no one understood why it was so important. I should chuck it all in, I thought. Paul was supporting me now, I could finish my studies without the scholarship. It wasn't worth it.

I wanted to cry. I hated myself when I got like that. I never cried, and yet, since all this had been going on, I'd wanted to cry often. It wasn't something I could control. Sometimes when I looked at Nan, I just wanted to cry. It was absurd. There was so much about myself I didn't understand.

The bus pulled in and I hopped on and paid my fare. Then I headed for the back of the bus. I just made it. My eyes were becoming clouded with unshed tears and if the bus had have been any longer, I would have probably fallen over in the aisle. I turned my face to the window and stared out at the passing bitumen. Had I been dishonest with myself? What did it really mean to be Aboriginal? I'd never lived off the land and been a hunter and a gatherer. I'd never participated in corroborees or heard stories of the Dreamtime. I'd lived all my life in suburbia and told everyone I was Indian. I hardly knew any Aboriginal people. What did it mean for someone like me?

Half-way home on the bus, I felt so weighed down with all my questions that I decided to give it all up. I would telephone the department and tell them I wanted to go off the scholarship. I didn't think my family would care what I did, they'd probably be relieved I wasn't trying to rock the boat any more. They could all go on being what they'd been for years, they wouldn't have to cope with a crazy member of the family who didn't know who she was. That's what I'd do. And I'd do it as soon as possible. I wasn't a brave person.

Just then, for some reason, I could see Nan. She was standing in front of me, looking at me. Her eyes were sad. 'Oh Nan', I sighed, 'why did you have to turn up now, of all times'. She vanished as quickly as she'd come. I knew then that, for some reason, it was very important I stay on the scholarship. If I denied my tentative identification with the past now, I'd be denying her as well. I had to hold on to the fact that, some day, it might all mean something. And if that turned out to be the belief of a fool, then I would just have to live with it.

When I told Jill about my interview, she was amazed. 'I'm glad it was you and not me', she said. 'I couldn't have said what you did. I'd have let them think I was guilty. I can't stick up for myself like that.'

'I don't know how I did it, either', I replied. 'But you know what, I'm really glad I did. From now on, I'm going to say more, be more assertive.'

'Heaven help us!'

'Who do you think dobbed me in?'

'Dunno. It makes you suspicious, though.'

For the next few weeks, we watched all our friends closely, searching for any small signs of guilt and betrayal. There were none.

'I give up', I told Jill one lunch-time, 'if we keep watching everyone, we'll never trust anyone again, better to forget it'.

On the weekend, I told Mum what had happened. She was very upset, much more upset than I had anticipated. She took it as a personal slight on herself.

Nan took an interest in the proceedings as well. She wasn't angry, just very pessimistic. 'You shouldn't have done it, Sally', she growled. 'You don't know what they'll do now. They might send someone to the house. Government people are like that. Best to say nothing, just go along with them till you see which way the wind blows. You don't know what will happen now, you mark my words.'

'Oh don't be stupid, Nan', Mum yelled. 'She did right to defend herself. No one's going to come snooping around. Times have changed'.

'You're stupid, Glad', Nan grunted, and before Mum could reply, she shuffled out to her bedroom.

'You're going to be in for it tonight, Mum', I sighed. 'She's going to be in a real lousy mood.'

'I don't know why she gets like that', Mum said. 'She's frightened, you see. She's been frightened all her life. You can tell her things have changed, but she won't listen. She thinks it's still like the old days when people could do what they liked with you.'

'Could they, Mum?'

'What?'

'Do what they liked with you?'

'Oh, I don't know. I don't want to talk now, Sally. Not now.'

However, my run-in with the Education Department did produce some unexpected results. Mum suddenly became more sympathetic to my desire to learn about the past. One day, she said to me, 'Of course, you know Nan was born on Corunna Downs Station, don't you?'

'I've heard her mention that station', I replied, 'but whenever I've asked her about it, she clams up. Remember when David got that map of the north and showed her on the map where Corunna Downs was? She was quite excited that it was on a map, wasn't she? Yet, she still won't talk.'

'I know. It really upsets me, sometimes.'

'Mum, who owned Corunna Downs?'

'Judy's father.'

'I didn't know that. What was his name?'

'Alfred Howden Drake-Brockman.'

'Fancy that. I suppose that's why Judy and Nan are so close. That and the fact that Nan used to work for the family.'

'Yes. Nan was Judy's nursemaid when she was little.'

'Tell me the other things she used to do then, Mum.'

'I remember she used to work very hard. Very, very hard . . . Oh, I don't want to talk any more. Maybe some other time.'

For once, I accepted her decision without complaint. I knew now there would be other times.

Even though I was married, I saw my family nearly every day. There were such strong bonds between us it was impossible for me not to want to see them. Just as well Paul was the uncomplaining sort.

One Saturday afternoon, I was over visiting Mum when she asked me to help her with Curly. 'He's in one of his cantankerous moods', she said. 'He won't come inside, see what you can do with him.'

I eyed Curly in disgust from my standpoint on the front porch. He was lying in the middle of the road as usual. All morning, cars had been tooting at him, all to no avail. Curly moved for no one.

'You'll get run over, Curl', I called in my Let's Be Reasonable voice. 'You'd better come in.' Still no response.

'I don't think he'll come in, Mum', I replied. 'I wish Paul were here, he always obeys Paul.'

'You don't think he's going deaf in his old age', Mum asked with a concerned look on her face.

'Naah, just stupid.'

'He's a good dog, Sally', she protested. 'You shouldn't talk about him like that.'

'I think you'd better go inside, Mum', I advised. 'He'll never listen to me with you standing there.' Mum disappeared and I called once again to the flat layer of black fur lying on the road.

'Curl, Mum's gone now. If you don't come in, I'm gunna drag you in.' Curl raised his head slightly and growled. I knew what that meant. As soon as I touched him, he'd bite me. I'd been through this before.

'Listen, you bloody mongrel', I yelled.

But before I could continue my tirade, Nan came up behind me and said, 'Don't say that, Sally, it hurts me here', she patted her chest. 'Fancy, my own granddaughter sayin' that. I never thought you'd be the one.'

'You're as bad as Mum', I complained. 'I'm not allowed to say anything.'

'I been called that', Nan replied. 'It makes you feel real rotten inside.'

'It's no use you going on, Nan', I said without listening, 'he is a

143

bloody mongrel!'.

'Don't! Don't!' she said, as though I was inflicting some kind of pain on her.

'Nan', I reasoned, 'someone has got to be firm with him or he'll get run over one day'.

'What are you talkin' about, Sally?'

'I'm talking about Curly', I replied in exasperation, and then paused. 'Why, what are you talking about?'

Nan gazed towards the oval directly opposite our house. Just where the bitumen ended and the grass began sat a small Aboriginal boy, I recognised him as belonging to a house around the corner from us. He was intent on some sort of game.

'Nan!' I said in shock. 'You don't think I was calling that little fella a bloody mongrel, do you? Oh Nan, I'd never call a kid that. That's a terrible thing to call anyone. How could you think I'd do such a thing?'

'I've heard them called that. It's not right, they got feelings.'

'Nan, did you say you'd been called that?'

She put her hand over her mouth.

'Who was it, Nan? What rotten bugger called you that?'

'Don't want to talk about it, Sally', she shook her head.

'You've been called that more than once, haven't you, Nan?' She ignored my question and turned to go inside. Half-way through the doorway, she stopped and said, 'Sal?'.

'Yeah?'

'Promise me you won't ever call them that? When you see a little bloke like that, think of your Nanna.'

I nodded my head. I was too close to tears to reply. I wished I could wipe memories like that from her mind. She looked so vulnerable, not like her usual complaining self. It was times like that I realised just how much I loved her.

Chapter Twenty-Three

A VISITOR

After I graduated from university, I continued post-graduate studies in psychology at the Western Australian Institute of Technology.

My brother David was also successful in completing his Leaving exams that year, and now Helen was the only one of us still at school. She was in third year high school.

Mum and I had many small conversations about the past, but they weren't really informative, because we tended to cover the same ground. Sometimes, Mum would try and get Nan to talk. One day, I heard Nan shout, 'You're always goin' on about the past these days, Glad. I'm sick of it. It makes me sick in here', she pointed to her chest. 'My brain's no good, Glad, I can't 'member!'

Mum gave up easily. 'She's been like that all her life', she complained to me one day, 'she'll never change. When I was little, I used to ask about my father, but she wouldn't tell me anything. In the end, I gave up.'

'Who was your father?'

'Oh, I don't know', she replied sadly, 'Nan just said he was a white man who died when I was very small'.

I felt sad then. I promised myself that, one day, I would find out who her father was. She had a right to know.

In 1975, I gave birth to a daughter, Ambelin Star. The family was very excited, it was our first grandchild. Mum cried when she saw her, so did Nan. Now, instead of collecting antiques, Mum started buying up toys and children's books.

I passed my course at WAIT and decided to give up study for a while and concentrate on being a wife and mother.

I continued to prompt Nan about the past, but she dug her heels in further and further. She said that I didn't love her, that none of us had ever loved or wanted her. She maintained that Mum had never looked after her properly. In fact, she became so consistently cantankerous that she gradually drove us all away. Everyone in the family got to the stage where, if we could avoid seeing Nan, we would.

145

Paul and I also became fed-up with city life at this time, so we thought we'd try the country for a while. Paul's parents were now living in Albany on a small farmlet, so we moved down to Albany for twelve months.

Jill had now left university and was helping Mum run her florist shop. She had had enough of study for a while, although she did return later and completed an Arts degree.

My brothers were now both working, Bill was up North with a mining company and David in the city with a firm of auctioneers. David was also working at night and in the evenings as a musician with a rock and roll band.

In 1976, Helen successfully completed her Tertiary Admittance Examination. The TAE had replaced the Leaving examination.

In 1977, lack of money and poor employment prospects drove us back to Perth, where Paul began his own cleaning business. He had resigned from teaching when we moved to Albany. And I became pregnant with my second child that year and was very sick, spending a number of weeks in hospital.

Because of these various factors, my search for the past seemed to have reached a standstill from 1975 to 1978.

By the time I'd had my second child, Blaze Jake, in 1978, a change was beginning to take place in our family. Nan's brother, Arthur, began making regular visits. He was keen to see more of Nan now they were both getting older. And he was very fond of Mum.

'Who is he?' I asked, when I found him parked in front of the TV one day with a huge meal on his lap.

'You remember him. Arthur, Nan's brother. When you were little, he visited us a couple of times, remember?'

I cast my mind back and suddenly I saw him as he had been so many years before. Tall and dark, with a big smile.

'Is he her only brother?' I asked. 'No other relatives hidden away in the closet?'

'No', Mum laughed, 'he's the only one that I know of. He's a darling old bloke, a real character. I think Nan's jealous of him.'

'That'd be right! Great, to think they're seeing each other after all these years.'

'It's wonderful', Mum said with tears in her eyes. 'I've told him to come and stay whenever he likes.'

'Mum', I said slowly, 'you don't think he could tell us about the past? About Nan, I mean.'

'I think he could, if we can get him to talk. He tells some wonderful stories. Go and talk to him.'

It took a while for me to get close to Arthur. He loved Mum, but he was wary of the rest of us. He wasn't quite sure what to make of us, and he wasn't quite sure what we made of him. If he had have known how insatiably curious we were about him and his past, he would probably have been scared off.

But on one of these early visits, he unexpectedly did provide us with a very vivid picture from the past. Some old photographs of Nan, taken in the nineteen twenties. Nan had always refused to allow any of us to take her photograph, so it was exciting to be able to see her as a young woman. Nan, however, was not impressed.

It became very obvious in a very short time that Nan and Arthur were brother and sister, because they fought like cat and dog. When Arthur was around, Nan behaved like a child. She was jealous because Mum loved him and enjoyed his company. She was also frightened of what he might tell us.

'Don't listen to him', she told us one day when he was half-way through a story about the old times, 'he's only a stupid old man, what would he know? He'll tell you wrong!'

'Is she goin' on again', Arthur said to Mum. He loved pretending Nan wasn't there. 'You know what's wrong with her, don't you?' he whispered. 'She's jealous.'

'You silly old man', she grumbled, 'who do you think you are. Nobody's interested in your stories. You're just a silly old blackfella.'

'Aah, you'll have to think of a better name than that to call me', he smiled, 'I'm proud of bein' a blackfella. Anyway, you're a blackfella yourself, what do ya think of that?!'

Nan was incensed. No one had called her a blackfella for years. She bent down to him and said, 'I may be a blackfella, but I'm not like you. I dress decent and I know the right way to do things. Look at you, a grown man and you got your pants tied up with a bit of string! You don't see me goin' round like that.'

'Git out of here', he said as he shook his fist at her, 'leave us alone, we want to talk'.

Nan wandered off, but she was back fifteen minutes later to check on what he was saying.

'You're like a bag of wind', she complained as she stood in the doorway of the lounge-room. 'Blow, blow, blow! Don't you ever shut up?'

'I feel sorry for you', Arthur replied sympathetically, 'you got my pity. You don't have a good word to say about anyone, not even your own daughter. I tell you this, this is a warning, one day I'm gunna get a young wife. I'll bring her round here and then you won't dare to talk to me like that.'

Nan always laughed whenever Arthur talked about getting himself a young wife to look after him in his old age. 'No one would have you', she hooted. 'Young girls are smart these days, they see you comin' and they run like a willy-willy. Who'd want a silly old blackfella like you, you got no money.'

'You don't know what I got', Arthur replied. 'I got all my land up in Mukinbudin, that's more than what most blackfellas got.'

'Your land, your land', Nan mimicked him. 'I don't want to hear about your land no more. I bet all the kangaroos eat your crops.'

That was the last straw as far as Arthur was concerned. Nan's comment had hit close to home and she knew it. He'd told her about a part of his land that he kept uncleared so the wildlife could prosper in peace, now she was using this confidence against him.

'I'm tellin' you nothin', no more', he said. 'We'll ignore her. Tell her to go, Glad', he added to Mum. 'We don't want her in here. She's been with whitefellas too long!'

'Now, Nanna', Mum said in her Let's Be Reasonable voice, 'Arthur is your only brother, whenever he comes, you pick a fight with him. You're both getting old, it's time you made up. He doesn't want to listen to your complaints all the time.'

Nan was determined to remain perverse. 'And we don't want to hear his stories either', she said forcefully. 'He goes over and over the same old thing. He wasn't the only one hard done by.'

'No, he wasn't', Mum replied, 'but at least he'll talk about it. You won't tell us anything. Whenever we ask you about the past, you get nasty. We're your family, we've got a right to know.'

'Glad, you're always goin' on about the past. You and Arthur are a good pair, you don't know what a secret is.'

'It's not a matter of secrets, Nan', Mum reasoned. 'You seem to be ashamed of your past, I don't know why. All my life, you've never told me anything, never let me belong to anyone. All my life, I've wanted a family, you won't even tell me about my own grandmother. You go away and let Arthur talk, at least he tells me something.'

Nan opened her mouth to reply, but Arthur cut her off with, 'If you don't go, Daisy, I'll tell them your Aboriginal name'.

Nan was furious. 'You wouldn't!' she fumed.

'Too right I will', said Arthur. Nan knew when she was beaten, she stormed off.

'What is it?' both Mum and I asked excitedly after she'd gone.

'No, I can't tell you', he said, 'it's not as if I wouldn't like to, but Daisy should tell you herself. There's a lot she could tell you, she knows more about some of our people than I do.'

'But she won't talk, Arthur', Mum replied. 'Sometimes, I think she thinks she's white. She's ashamed of her family.'

'Aah, she's bin with whitefellas too long. They make her feel 'shamed, that's what white people do to you. Why should we be 'shamed, we bin here longer than them. You don't see the black man diggin' up the land, scarin' it. The white man got no sense.'

I sat and listened to many conversations between Mum and Arthur after that. Whenever he turned up for a visit, Mum would ring me at home and say, 'He's here!', and I would go rushing over.

On one such afternoon, I wandered out to the backyard to find Nan and Arthur under a gum tree, jabbering away in what sounded to me like a foreign language. I sat down very quietly on the steps and listened. I prayed they wouldn't see me.

After a few minutes, Nan said, 'My eyes aren't that bad, Sally, I can see you there, spyin' on us'.

'I'm not spying', I defended myself. 'Keep talking, don't let me stop you.'

'We're not talkin' no more', Nan said. 'You hear that, Arthur, no more!'

Just then, Mum came out with a tray full of afternoon tea. After she'd given them their tea and cake, I followed her inside.

'Mum', I said excitedly, 'did you hear them? They were talking in their own language!'

'What, Nanna too?'

'Yep! And not just a few words, she was jabbering away like she always talked like that. I wouldn't have thought she'd remember after all these years.'

'Sally, are you sure you're not making this up?'

'No! Honestly Mum, I heard them!'

'But it must be years since she used her own language. Fancy, her remembering it all this time.'

'It's a ray of hope, Mum', I said. 'She could have easily forgotten it, a language needs to be used to be remembered. It must mean it was important to her. She might turn into a proud blackfella yet.'

'Don't you ever give up?'

'Where there's life, there's hope, Mum.'

Over the following weeks, whenever I saw Nan, I'd bring up the topic of her language. She was very defensive at first and would lose her temper with me, but, after a while, she gradually came round. One day, she said, 'Hey, Sally, you know what goombo is?'.

'No, what', I grinned.

'Wee, wee.'

Nan chuckled and walked off.

She told me many words after that, but I could never get her to say a sentence for me. It would be a long time before I would learn to be content with the little she was willing to give.

Chapter Twenty-Four

WHERE THERE'S A WILL

'I'm going to write a book.' It was the beginning of 1979, a good time for resolutions.

Mum looked shocked. 'Another new scheme, eh?' she asked sarcastically. She was used to my wild ideas.

'Not just a scheme this time, Mum', I said determinedly. 'This time, I'm really going to do it.'

'Is it going to be a children's book?'

'Nope. A book about our family history.'

'You can't write a book about our family', she spluttered, 'you don't know anything!'.

'Aah, but I'm going to find out, aren't I?'

'How?'

'I don't know, some way.'

'Well, don't expect any help from Nan, you know what an old bugger she is. It's only since Arthur's been visiting that she's let a few things drop.'

'Where there's a will, there's a way, Mum', I replied light-heartedly. 'I've got plenty of will.'

'Oh Sally', she groaned, 'I wish you wouldn't start on these new ideas. You get everyone all fired up and then you don't carry through. Well, I'm not going to worry about you writing a book. You'll soon lose interest.'

'Wanna bet?'

Mum took me more seriously the following week when I bought a typewriter and started to type. As she watched my jerky two-finger effort she said, 'It'll take you a lifetime to do a page at that rate'.

'No, it won't. I'm going to teach myself how to type, it's just practice. I'll get quicker.'

'What are you typing, anyway?'

'I'm putting down what I know. It's not much, but it's a start. Then I'm going to try and fill in what I don't know, and I expect you to help me.'

'I can't help you. I don't know anything.'

'You only THINK you don't know anything. I'm sure if you searched those hidden recesses of your mind you'd come up with something.'

'It's no use counting on me, Sally.'

'You're as bad as Nan, sometimes! You've got to help me, you're my mother, it's your duty.'

'No need to be so dramatic. You know I'd help you if I could.'

'But you can help me, Mum. You've spent all your life with Nan. You must be able to tell me something about her. What seems unimportant to you could be a really good lead for me. For example, how come Nan and Judy are so close?'

'I've already told you, Nan was Judy's nursemaid. Judy was quite sick as a child, I suppose that drew them closer together.'

'How come Nan was their nursemaid and not someone else?'

'Oh, I don't know. I told you Nan came from the station that Judy's father owned.'

'Yeah, that's right', I said slowly. 'You know, I think I'll go and talk to Judy. I don't know why I didn't think of it before. There, you see, you've given me a lead already!'

'Goodness, I don't think that's much of a lead. Judy won't tell you anything, her and Nan love secrets.'

'No harm in trying.'

'What are you going to ask her?'

'Oh, I'll ask her about the station and why they chose Nan to come down to Perth. I'll ask her about Ivanhoe, too.' Ivanhoe was a grand old house in Claremont situated on the banks of the Swan River, where Nan had spent much of her working life.

'I went to Battye Library the other day, Mum.'

'What for?'

'It's a history library. Western Australian history. I wanted to read up about Aborigines.'

'Oh', Mum said keenly, 'did you find out anything interesting?'.

'I sure did. I found out there was a lot to be ashamed of.'

'You mean we should feel ashamed?'

'No, I mean Australia should.'

Mum sat down. 'Tell me what you read.'

'Well, when Nan was younger, Aborigines were considered sub-normal and not capable of being educated the way whites were. You know, the pastoral industry was built on the back of slave labour. Aboriginal people were forced to work, if they didn't, the station owners called the police in. I always thought Australia was different to America, Mum, but we had slavery here, too. The people might not have been sold on the blocks like the American Negroes were, but they were owned, just the same.'

'I know', Mum said. There were tears in her eyes. 'They were treated just awful. I know Nan . . . ' She stopped. 'I better get going, Sal,

I've got to go to work early tomorrow.'

'What were you going to say?'

'Nothing.'

'Yes, you were.'

'It's nothing, Sally, nothing. You make a mountain out of a molehill.'

'No Mum, you make molehills out of mountains.'

'I don't want to talk about it now. Maybe later. You'll have to give me time. If you want my help, you'll have to give me time.'

I could see Mum was quite upset.

'Okay, I'll give you all the time you want, as long as you help me.'

'I'll try', she sighed, then added: 'You seem determined to do this'.

'I am.'

'I'm not sure it's a wise thing. You don't know who you might offend, you go barging in, you've got no tact. You might find yourself in deep water.'

'I can swim.'

'If you want to talk to Judy, it'll only upset Nan. She's getting older, when she finds out you want to write a book, she'll be really upset, and she'll make my life hell. Can't you just leave the past buried, it won't hurt anyone then?'

'Mum', I reasoned, 'it's already hurt people. It's hurt you and me and Nan, all of us. I mean, for years, I've been telling people I'm Indian! I have a right to know my own history. Come to think of it, you've never gotten around to telling me why you lied to us about that. About being Indian.'

'Oh, let's not go into that, I've had enough for one night.' Mum rose quickly to her feet. 'See Judy if you like, but don't upset Nan.'

'You want to come with me when I see her?'

'No.'

'Just thought I'd ask. Hey, I meant to tell you, I got a copy of your birth certificate the other day.'

Mum sat down just as quickly. 'How did you do that? I didn't know you could do that.'

'It's easy. You just apply to the Registrar General's Office. I said I wanted it for the purposes of family history. I tried to get Nan's and Arthur's, but they didn't have one. Hardly any Aboriginal people had birth certificates in those days.'

'Sally . . .' Mum said tentatively, 'who did they say my father was? Was that on the certificate?'

'There was just a blank there, Mum, I'm sorry.'

'Just a blank?' Mum muttered slowly. 'Just a blank. That's awful, like nobody owns me.'

I hadn't anticipated Mum being so cut up about it. I felt awful. She'd known all her life that Nan had never married.

'I'm really sorry, Mum', I said gently. 'I got your certificate because I thought it might give me some leads, but it didn't. Except that you were born in King Edward Memorial Hospital. That's unusual, because I wouldn't have thought they'd have let Aboriginal women in there in those days.'

'Is that where I was born?'

'Yep. You sure were.'

'Well, at least you've found out something, Sally.'

'You've asked Nan who your father was, haven't you?'

'Yes.'

'Maybe Judy would know.'

'She probably does', Mum sighed, 'but she won't tell. I asked her once and she just kept saying, "It's in the blood", whatever that means.'

'I bet you never asked her straight out. You beat round the bush too much. Why don't you corner her and say, "Judy, I want to know who my father is and I'm not leaving here till I find out" .'

Mum grinned. 'I couldn't do that, I'm not brave enough. Anyway, he couldn't have cared less about me or he would have contacted me by now. And when Nan needed help, there was no one. He can't be much of a man.'

'You know, Mum, just on a logical basis, it must be someone who mixed with the mob at Ivanhoe in Claremont.'

'You reckon?'

'Yeah. It makes sense. Did any single blokes ever stay there?'

'No. Jack Grime lived there for years, but it wouldn't have been him.'

'Why not?'

'He was high up in the social circle, an English gentleman. His brother's son is one of the Queen's vets, now.'

'Oooh, perhaps you'd better buy a corgi!'

Mum laughed.

A few days later, I rang Aunty Judy. I explained that I was writing a book about Nan and Arthur and I thought she might be able to help me. We agreed that I would come down for lunch and she said she could tell me who Nan's father was. I was surprised. I had expected to encounter opposition. Perhaps I wanted to encounter opposition, it fired my sense of injustice. I felt really excited after our talk on the telephone. Would I really discover who my great grandfather was? If I was lucky, I might even find out about my grandfather as well. I was so filled with optimism I leapt up and down three times and gave God the thumbs up sign.

My day for lunch at Aunty Judy's dawned, and was too beautiful a day for me to fail. Mum had agreed to drop me in Cottesloe where Judy was now living, and mind the children while we had our talk.

'Can't I come, Mum?' Amber wailed as we pulled up out the front of Judy's house.

'Sorry, Amber', I replied, 'this is private'. I leapt from the car, all vim and vigour. 'Wish me luck, Mum.'

During lunch, we chatted about diet, health foods and the impurities in most brands of ice-cream, then Aunty Judy said, 'You know, I think I have some old photos of your mother you might be interested in. I'll have to dig them out.'

'Oh great! I'd really appreciate that.'

'I'll tell you what I know about the station, but it's not a lot. You know, a relative of ours published a book a while ago and they got all their facts wrong, so you better make sure you get yours right.'

'That's why I'm here. I don't want to print anything that's not true.'

After lunch, we retired to the more comfortable chairs in the lounge-room.

'Now, dear', Aunty Judy said, 'what would you like to know?'.

'Well, first of all, I'd like to know who Nan's father was and also a bit about what her life was like when she was at Ivanhoe.'

'Well, that's no problem. My mother told me that Nan's father was a mystery man. He was a chap they called Maltese Sam and he used to be cook on Corunna Downs. He was supposed to have come from a wealthy Maltese family, I think he could have been the younger son, a ne'er-do-well. My mother said that he always used to tell them that, one day, he was going back to Malta to claim his inheritance. The trouble was he was a drinker. He'd save money for the trip and then he'd go on a binge and have to start all over again. He used to talk to my father, Howden, a lot. He was proud Nanna was his little girl.'

'Did he ever come and visit Nan when she was at Ivanhoe?'

'Yes, I think he did, once. But he was drunk, apparently, and wanted to take Nanna away with him. Nan was frightened, she didn't want to go, so my mother said to him, you go back to Malta and put things right. When you've claimed your inheritance, you can have Daisy. We never saw him again. I don't know what happened to him. Nan didn't want to go with him, we were her family by then.'

'Did you meet Maltese Sam?'

'Oh, goodness, no. I was only a child. My mother told me the story.'

'How old was Nan when she came down to Perth?'

'About fifteen or sixteen.'

'And what were her duties at Ivanhoe.'

'She looked after us children.'

'Aunty Judy, do you know who Mum's father is?'

'Your mother knows who her father is.'

'No, she doesn't. She wants to know and Nan won't tell her.'

'I'm sure I told your mother at one time who her father was.'

'She doesn't know and she'd really like to. It's very important to her.'

'Well, I'm not sure I should tell you. You never know about these things.'

'Mum wanted me to ask you.'

Aunty Judy paused and looked at me silently for a few seconds. Then she said slowly, 'All right, everybody knows who her father was, it was Jack Grime. Everyone always said that Gladdie's the image of him.'

'Jack Grime? And Mum takes after him, does she?'

'Like two peas in a pod.'

'Who was Jack Grime?'

'He was an Englishman, an engineer, very, very clever. He lived with us at Ivanhoe, he was a friend of my father's. He was very fond of your mother. When she was working as a florist, he'd call in and see her. We could always tell when he'd been to see Gladdie, he'd have a certain look on his face. He'd say, "I've been to see Gladdie", and we'd just nod.'

'Did he ever marry and have other children?'

'No. He was a very handsome man, but he never married and, as far as I know, there were no other children. He spent the rest of his life living in Sydney, he was about eighty-six when he died.'

'Eighty-six? Well, that couldn't have been that long ago, then? If he was so fond of Mum, you'd think he'd have left her something in his will. Not necessarily money, just a token to say he owned her. After all, she was his only child.'

'No, there was nothing. He wasn't a wealthy man, there was no money to leave. You know Roberta?'

'Yes, Mum's been out to dinner with her a few times.'

'Well, she's the daughter of Jack's brother, Robert. She's Gladdie's first cousin.'

'Mum doesn't know that, does Roberta?'

'Yes, she knows. She asked me a year ago whether she should say something to your mother, but I said it'd be better to leave it.'

'Perhaps Mum could talk to her.'

'Yes, she could.'

'Can you tell me anything about Nan's mother?'

'Not a lot. Her name was Annie, she was a magnificent-looking woman. She was a good dressmaker, my father taught her how to sew. She could design anything.'

Our conversation continued for another half an hour or so. I kept thinking, had Mum lied? Did she really know who her father was? Was she really against me digging up the past, just like Nan? I had one last question.

'Aunty Judy, I was talking to Arthur, Nan's brother, the other day and he said that his father was the same as yours, Alfred Howden Drake-Brockman. Isn't it possible he could have been Nan's as well.'

'No. That's not what everyone said. I've told you what I know; who Nan's father is. I'm certain Arthur's father wasn't Howden, I don't know who his father was.'

'Arthur also told me about his half-brother Albert. He said Howden was his father, too.'

'Well, he went by the name of Brockman so I suppose it might be possible, but certainly not the other two.'

'Well, thanks a lot, Aunty Judy, I suppose I'd better be going, Mum will be here any minute. She's picking me up.'

'You know who you should talk to, don't you? Mum-mum. She's still alive and better than she's been for a long time.' Mum-mum was a pet name for Aunty Judy's mother, Alice.

'She must be in her nineties by now', I said. 'Do you think she'd mind talking to me?'

'No, I don't think so, but you'd have to go interstate, she's in a nursing home in Wollongong. You could probably stay with June.' June was Judy's younger sister, Nan had been her nursemaid, too.

'I'll think about it, Aunty Judy. Thanks a lot.'

'That's all right, dear.'

I walked out to the front gate and, just as I opened it, Mum pulled up in the car.

'How did you go?' she said eagerly.

'All right', I replied. 'Mum, are you sure you don't know who your father is? You've lied about things before.' It was a stupid thing to say, Mum was immediately on the defensive.

'Of course I don't know who my father is, Sally. Didn't you find out, after all?' She was disappointed. I felt ashamed of myself for doubting her.

'No Mum, I found out. It was Jack Grime, and Roberta is your first cousin.'

'Oh God, I can't believe it!' She was stunned.

'Can you remember anything about him, Mum? You're supposed to look a lot like him.'

'No, I can't remember much, except he used to wear a big gold watch that chimed. I thought it was magical.'

'Judy said he used to visit you when you were working as a florist, can you recall any times when he did?'

'Well yes, he popped in now and then, but then a lot of people did. I was a friendly sort of girl. Sometimes, I would go and have lunch with him at Ivanhoe, that was after Nan had left there. To think I was lunching with my own father!'

An overwhelming sadness struck me. My mother was fifty-five years of age and she'd only just discovered who her father was. It didn't seem fair.

'Mum, are you going to say anything to Nan?'

'Not now, maybe later, after I've had time to think things over. Don't you say anything, will you?'

'No, I won't. Does she know I've been to see Judy?'

'Yes, she knew you were going. She's been in a bad mood all week. Did you find out anything else?'

'Judy says Nan's father was a bloke called Maltese Sam. That he came from a wealthy family and wanted to take Nan away with him.'

'Maltese Sam? What an unusual name. I've never heard anyone talk about him. Arthur's coming tomorrow night, I'll ask him what he thinks. Of course, you know who he says is Nan's father, don't you?'

'Yeah, I know. Judy doesn't agree with him.'

The following evening, Mum and I sat chatting to Arthur. After we'd finished tea, I said, 'I visited Judith Drake-Brockman the other day, Arthur'.

'What did you do that for?'

'Oh, I thought she might be able to tell me something about Corunna Downs and something about Nan.'

'You wanna know about Corunna, you come to me. I knew all the people there.'

'I know you did.' I paused. 'Can I ask you a question?'

'You ask what you like.'

'Judy told me Nan's father was a chap by the name of Maltese Sam, have you ever heard of him?'

'She said WHAT?'

Arthur was a bit hard of hearing sometimes, so I repeated my question.

'Don't you listen to her', he said when I'd asked again. 'She never lived on the station, how would she know?'

'Well, she got the story from her mother, Alice, who got the story from her husband, Howden, who said that Annie had confided in him.'

Arthur threw back his head and laughed. Then he thumped his fist on the arm of his chair and said, 'Now you listen to me, Daisy's father is the same as mine. Daisy is my only full sister. Albert, he's our half-brother, his father was Howden, too, but by a different woman.'

'So you reckoned he fathered the both of you.'

'By jove he did! Are you gunna take the word of white people against your own flesh and blood? I got no papers to prove what I'm sayin'. Nobody cared how many blackfellas were born in those days, nor how many died. I know because my mother, Annie, told me. She said Daisy and I belonged to one another. Don't you go takin' the word of white people against mine.'

Arthur had us both nearly completely convinced, except for one thing, he avoided our eyes. Mum and I knew it wasn't a good sign, there was something he wasn't telling us. So I said again, 'You're sure about this, Arthur?'.

'Too right! Now, about this Maltese Sam, don't forget Alice was Howden's second wife and they had the Victorian way of thinking in those days. Before there were white women, our father owned us, we went by his name, but later, after he married his first wife, Nell, he changed our names. I'll tell you about that one day. He didn't want to own us no more. They were real fuddy-duddies in those days. No white man wants to have black kids runnin' round the place with his name. And Howden's mother and father, they were real religious types, I bet they didn't know about no black kids that belonged to them.'

We all laughed then. Arthur was like Mum, it wasn't often he failed to see the funny side of things.

When we'd all finally calmed down, he said, 'You know, if only you could get Daisy to talk. She could tell you so much. I know she's got her secrets, but there are things she could tell you without tellin' those.'

'She won't talk, Arthur', I sighed. 'You know a lot about Nan, can't you tell us?'

He was silent for a moment, thoughtful. Then he said, 'I'd like to. I really would, but it'd be breakin' a trust. Some things 'bout her I can't tell. It wouldn't be right. She could tell you everything you want to know. You see, Howden was a lonely man. I know, one night at Ivanhoe, we both got drunk together and he told me all his troubles. He used to go down to Daisy's room at night and talk to her. I can't say no more. You'll have to ask her.'

'But Arthur, what if she won't tell us?'

'Then I can't, either. There's some things Daisy's got to tell herself, or not at all. I can't say no more.'

After he left, Mum and I sat analysing everything for ages. We were very confused, we knew that the small pieces of information we now possessed weren't the complete truth.

'Sally', Mum said, breaking into my thoughts, 'do you remember when Arthur first started visiting us and he said Albert was his full brother?'.

'Yeah, but that was before he knew us well.'

'Yes, but remember how he almost whispered when he told us the truth about Albert? He didn't want to hurt the feelings of any of Albert's family and he loved him so much I suppose he thought it didn't matter.'

'Yeah, I know. You think there might be more to Nan's parentage.'

'It's possible.'

'There's another possibility. Howden may have been her father, but there could be something else, some secret he wants to keep, that is somehow tied in with all of this. Perhaps that's why he didn't look us in the eye.'

'Yes, that's possible, too. And I can't see why he wouldn't tell us the truth, because he knows how much it means to us. I don't think we'll ever know the full story. I think we're going to have to be satisfied with guesses.'

'It makes me feel so sad to think no one wants to own our family.'

'I know, Mum, but look at it this way, just on a logical basis, it's possible he was her father. We know he was sleeping with Annie, and Arthur said that even after he married his first wife, he was still sleeping with Annie, so he could have sired her.'

'Yes, it's possible.'

'Well, that's all we can go on then, possibilities. Now Judy said Jack Grime was your father, but maybe he wasn't. He was living at Ivanhoe at the time you were born, but that doesn't necessarily mean he fathered you, does it?'

'Oh God, Sally', Mum laughed, 'let's not get in any deeper. I've had enough for one night.'

Chapter Twenty-Five

PART OF OUR HISTORY

A few days later, I popped in to see Mum. Nan told me she'd just gone up the shops and would be back in a few minutes. I decided to wait. I wasn't intending to say anything to Nan about my trip to Judy's, I wasn't in the mood for an argument. Uncharacteristically, she began following me around the house, making conversation about whatever came into her head. I suddenly realised that she was anxious to hear what Judy had told me, but I decided to let her sweat it out and bring up the topic herself.

Finally, after half an hour of chatting about the weather, the cool-drink man and Curly's arthritis, she blurted out, 'Well, what did she tell you?'.

'Who?' I asked innocently.

'You know, Judy. Mum told me you'd been to see her.'

'Do you want me to tell you what she said?'

'I don't care, if you want.' Nan shrugged her shoulders. We both went and sat down in the lounge-room. After we'd made ourselves comfortable, I said, 'Well, she told me that you were the nursemaid at Ivanhoe.'

Nan grunted. 'Hmmph, that and everything else.'

'You've always worked hard, haven't you, Nan?'

'Always, too hard.'

'Judy also said your father was a bloke called Maltese Sam.'

'What did she say?' Nan looked astonished.

'She said your father was called Maltese Sam, and that he visited you at Ivanhoe and wanted to take you away with him. Do you remember anyone visiting you there?'

'Only Arthur, and that wasn't till I was older.'

'There was no one else, you sure?'

'I'd know if I had visitors, wouldn't I? I'm not stupid, Sally, despite what you kids might think.'

'We don't think you're stupid.'

Nan pressed her lips together and stared hard at the red-brick fireplace

160

directly opposite where we were sitting.

'Nan', I said gently, 'was your father Maltese Sam?'.

She sighed, then murmured, 'Well, if Judy says he is, then I s'pose it's true'. I looked at her closely, there were tears in her eyes. I suddenly realised she was hurt, and I felt terrible, because I'd caused it. I decided to change the subject. I began to talk about my children and the latest naughty things they'd been up to. We had a chuckle, and then I said, 'Wouldn't you have liked to have had more children, Nan?'. She shrugged her shoulders and looked away.

'Think I'll do some gardening now, Sal', she said. 'Those leaves need raking up.'

She left me sitting alone and confused in the lounge-room. What was she hiding? Why couldn't she just be honest with us? Surely she realised we didn't blame her for anything. Surely she realised we loved her? I swallowed the lump that was rising in my throat. One thing I was sure of: before this was over, Mum and I would have shed more than our fair share of tears.

When Mum returned from the shop, she said, 'Have you spoken to Nan?'.

'Yes, but only about Maltese Sam. I don't think she thinks he was her father, but she won't say anything. See if you can get her to talk, later.'

'God, she's an old bugger!'

'I know, but the bit about Maltese Sam upset her. Better leave it for a few days before you tackle her.'

'I tell you what, I'll get a few days off work and make a big fuss of her and then, when she's in a good mood, I'll ask her about it.'

So three evenings later, after they'd finished eating a big roast dinner, Mum said quietly, 'Don't go and watch television yet, Nan, I want to talk to you. Sit with me for a while.'

'I'm not talking about the past, Gladdie. It makes me sick to talk about the past.'

Mum persisted, in spite of this protest, and said, 'I'm only going to ask you one question. Then you can do whatever you like, all right?' Nan sat still. 'Now, you know Sally's trying to write a book about the family?'

'Yes. I don't know why she wants to tell everyone our business.'

'Why shouldn't she write a book?' Mum said firmly. 'There's been nothing written about people like us, all the history's about the white man. There's nothing about Aboriginal people and what they've been through.'

'All right', she muttered, 'what do you want to ask?'.

'Well, you know when you write a book, it has to be the truth. You can't put lies in a book. You know that, don't you Nan?'

'I know that, Glad', Nan nodded.

'Good. Now, what I want to know is who you think your father

161

was. I know Judy says it was Maltese Sam and Arthur says it was Howden. Well, I'm not interested in what they say. I want to know what you say. Can you tell me, Nan, who do you think he really was?'

Nan was quiet for a few seconds and then, pressing her lips together, she said very slowly, 'I . . . think . . my father was . . Howden Drake-Brockman'.

It was a small victory, but an important one. Not so much for the knowledge, but for the fact that Nan had finally found it possible to trust her family with a piece of information that was important to her.

Mum gave Nan a week to recover before tackling her about Jack Grime. She'd been trying to spend more time at home and, in a gentle way, talk about the past.

Finally one evening, she said, 'Nan, I know who my father was'. Nan was silent. 'It was Jack Grime, wasn't it, Nan?' Silence. 'Wasn't it, Nan?'

'Judy tell you that, did she?'

'Yes.'

'Well, if that's what she says.'

'But was he, Nan?'

'I did love Jack.'

'What happened then, Nan, tell me what happened. Why didn't it work out?'

'How could it? He was well-off, high society. He mixed with all the wealthy white people, I was just a black servant.'

Nan ignored Mum's pleas to tell her more and disappeared into her room, leaving Mum to cry on her own.

When Mum and I talked about this later, Mum said, 'You know, he probably was my father, Nan obviously had a relationship with him. If he was, I feel very bitter towards him. There's never been any acknowledgement or feeling of love from him. I was just one of the kids. Later, when he moved east with Judy's family, he never wrote, there were no goodbyes, I never saw or heard from him again. All I can remember is that he used to tell wonderful stories, he was like a childhood uncle, but definitely not a father.'

We hoped that Nan would tell us more about the past, especially about the people she had known on Corunna Downs. Mum was anxious to hear about her grandmother, Annie, and her great grandmother, and I was keen to learn what life had been like for the people in those days. To our great disappointment, Nan would tell us nothing. She maintained that if we wanted to find out about the past, we had to do it without her help. 'I'm taking my secrets to the grave', she told Mum and I dramatically, one day.

Over the next few years, Arthur continued to visit regularly and to talk in snatches about Corunna. Sometimes, he'd say to Nan, 'Daisy, come and sit down. Tell your daughter and granddaughter about the past, tell them what they want to know.'

162

But Nan maintained a position of non-co-operation, insisting that the things she knew were secrets and not to be shared with others. Arthur always countered this statement with, 'It's history, that's what it is. We're talkin' history. You could be talkin' it, too, but then, I s'pose you don't know what it is.'

Nan hated Arthur hinting that she might be ignorant, so she replied vindictively, 'You always makin' out you're better than anyone else. Well, you're not! You're just a stupid old blackfella, that's you!'

Arthur was incensed. Raising his voice, he said, 'You're a great one to talk. Here I am in my nineties and I can read the paper and write my own name, too. I been educated! I'm not like you, you're just an ignorant blackfella!'

Nan was mortally offended. For a few seconds, she was lost for words, then she shouted, 'I don't know why I bother with you! You're always picking fights. You know they were s'posed to send me to school. It's not my fault I can't read or write. It hasn't done nothin' for you, anyway. I been listenin' to you, you can't even make up a good story!'

When Mum had finished waving goodbye to Arthur, she went in search of Nan. 'I'm fed up', she said crossly. 'You're the one that picks the fights, you're jealous. He's your own brother.'

'He shouldn't have said that to me', Nan replied in a grumbly sort of way. 'I can't help it if I can't read or write.' Nan looked sad and Mum was lost for words. It wasn't until then that anyone realised how deeply she felt about the whole thing.

'Lots of people can't read or write', Mum said gently, 'white people, too. It's not important. It doesn't make you any better than anyone else'.

'Yes, it does', Nan muttered, 'I always wanted to learn. Oh, go away, Gladdie, leave me in peace.' We all avoided mentioning anything to do with reading or writing after that, we didn't want Nan to think we were looking down on her.

The next time I saw Arthur, he asked me to tell him about the book I was writing.

'I want to write the history of my own family', I told him.

'What do you want to do that for?'

'Well, there's almost nothing written from a personal point of view about Aboriginal people. All our history is about the white man. No one knows what it was like for us. A lot of our history has been lost, people have been too frightened to say anything. There's a lot of our history we can't even get at, Arthur. There are all sorts of files about Aboriginals that go way back, and the government won't release them. You take the old police files, they're not even controlled by Battye Library, they're controlled by the police. And they don't like letting them out, because there are so many instances of police abusing their power when they were supposed to be Protectors of Aborigines that

163

it's not funny! I mean, our own government had terrible policies for Aboriginal people. Thousands of families in Australia were destroyed by the government policy of taking children away. None of that happened to white people. I know Nan doesn't agree with what I'm doing. She thinks I'm trying to make trouble, but I'm not. I just want to try to tell a little bit of the other side of the story.'

Arthur was silent for a few seconds, then he said thoughtfully, 'Daisy doesn't agree, I know that. I think she's been brainwashed. I tell you how I look at it, it's part of our history, like. And everyone's interested in history. Do you think you could put my story in that book of yours?'

'Oh Arthur, I'd love to!'

'Then we got a deal. You got that tape recorder of yours? We'll use that. You just listen to what I got to say, if you want to ask questions, you stop me. Now, some things I might tell you, I don't want in the book, is that all right?'

'Yes, that's fine. I won't put anything in you don't want me to.'

'Before we start, there's something else. I don't want my story mixed up with the Drake-Brockmans'. If you're goin' to write their story as well, I'll have none of it. Let them write their own story.'

'Agreed.'

It took three months or more to record Arthur's story. We went over and over the same incidents and, each time, he added a little more detail. He had a fantastic memory. Sometimes when he spoke, it was like he was actually reliving what had happened. We became very close. There were times when I worried that I was working him too hard, but, if I slacked off, he'd say, 'We haven't finished yet, you know'. He was always worried about my cassette recorder. I had to check it each time to make sure it was working. 'You don't want to miss nothin' ', he'd remind me. 'Those batteries get low.' Even if the batteries were new, I still had to check.

One night, after I'd spent a long session with Arthur, I fell into bed, exhausted. That night, I had a dream. I knew he was going to die.

'What's wrong?' Paul asked me the following morning when I burst into tears over my cornflakes.

'It's Arthur', I sobbed, 'he's going to die.'

'Aw, Sal', Paul said, 'what makes you think something like that'.

'I dreamt about it last night.'

'Just because he's old doesn't mean he's about to die'.

'He is. I know he is.'

'You and your intuition, you've been wrong before.'

'Not about this. I think he knows he's going, that's why he wants to get his story done.'

'Well, if he is, there's nothing you can do about it. The best thing is to finish his story, seeing it means so much to him.'

'Yeah, I know.'

Later that day, I rang Mum.

'Mum, it's about Arthur.'

'Oh yes. What's up?'

'I don't know how to say this, Mum.'

'What's wrong??'

'I had a dream last night. He's going to die soon. We've got to get his story finished.'

'Oh Sally, Arthur's not going to die, the doctors have only just given him a clean bill of health.'

'No Mum, I'm very sure about this.'

'Are you sure your dream wasn't about Nan? She's the one that hasn't been feeling well.'

'No, Mum. It's the old boy. And you know how keen he is about his story. We've got to drop everything and spend as much time as we can with him. Paul said he'll mind the kids. You'll have to take me over to see him.'

'I wish you'd gotten your licence when you were younger.'

'I'll get it one day. Anyway, it gives you something to do.'

'I'm always running you around places.'

'Your life would be dull without me, Mum.'

'I suppose you're right. Sally . . . do you think he knows?'

'Yes. You watch his face the next time he talks, it's got a sort of glow about it, like maybe he can see something we can't. A glimpse of heaven, maybe. It's like he's not really here, any more.'

'It's funny you saying that. I noticed the other night he was different. He's still the same old Arthur, but changed somehow.'

'Yeah . . .' I could tell by the tone of Mum's voice that if we pursued this conversation any further, we'd both start crying.

So it was that I spent the next few weeks non-stop recording everything I could. When we finished, we were both pleased.

'We've done it', Arthur laughed. 'We've done it! I got no more story to tell, now.'

'I can't believe it', I said. 'We've actually finished.'

'I got a good story, eh?'

'You sure have.'

'You think people will read that?'

'Of course they will, and they'll love it. If they don't, they've got no heart.'

'Now, if only you could get Daisy to talk.'

'I don't think she ever will, Arthur.'

'Aah, she's too set in her ways. She's funny about secrets. She doesn't understand history.'

'Yeah, well, I'll keep hoping.'

'What you gunna do now, you gunna type that all up?'

'Yep. I'll finish typing all the cassettes. Then I'll put it all together, because we've got bits and pieces all over the place.'

165

'Aah, I been wantin' to get this done all my life. Different people, they say, "Arthur, we'll write your story", but none of them come back to see me. Aah, I'm better off without them. It's better your own flesh and blood writes something like that.'

'Yeah, I think you're right. You know I'm going to Sydney, don't you?'

'I heard about that. What you goin' over there for?'

'I want to meet Alice Drake-Brockman, she's still alive, you know. I thought I'd ask her about her old days and who Mum's father is.'

'You think she'll remember me?'

'I think so.'

'Say hello to her for me.'

'I will. I'm only going for a week, when I get back, we can talk some more.'

'Too right. 'Cause you know I'm going back to Mucka, don't you?'

'No. I thought you were going to stay in Perth a bit longer.'

'I got a yearning for that place. My own home, my land. I been away too long. Can you understand that?'

'Yes.'

'Anyway, I told you my story now. You'll look after it, won't you?'

'Yes, of course I will.' I couldn't say any more. I had a lump in my throat. I knew he wanted to die on his own land.

Chapter Twenty-Six

LINKS WITH THE PAST

'Are you sure it's wise, going to Sydney now, Sal? Why don't you wait till after the baby's born?' It was now 1982 and I was six months pregnant with my third child.

'It's too important to wait, Mum. Alice is in her nineties, how do I know she'll be alive in three months' time?'

'Yes, but you know all that trouble you had when you were carrying Blaze, you nearly lost him.'

'I'll be fine, Mum. Don't worry.'

The following week, I flew to Sydney and then caught the bus to Wollongong. Aunty June, Judy's sister, and her husband, Angus, met me at the bus station. I felt very nervous. The last time I'd seen them, I was a child, now I was a woman with a mission.

I could not have had two kinder hosts. They did everything to make me feel at home. We swapped many funny yarns and stories about home.

Alice Drake-Brockman was in a nearby nursing home. She was ninety-three and in the best of health. Aunty June took me to the home and explained who I was and why I was there.

'You look a lot like your mother', Alice said, 'now, tell me, how is Daisy?'.

'She's fine, getting old, though. Her eyesight isn't too good.'

'It's been years since I've seen her.'

'Yes, I know.'

'So you want to know a bit about Corunna, eh?'

'Yes, would you mind if I asked you a few questions?'

'Ooh no, go ahead.'

'Can you tell me who Nan's father might have been, Alice?'

'Oh yes. Your great grandfather was a Maltese, I think he came from a wealthy family, but was the younger son. He was always saying he must go back and right his affairs in the old country. He had good blood in him, but he never got past the nearest pub. One time, I think he managed to get as far as Carnarvon, but then he spent all his money

167

and had to come back again.'

'Did you ever meet Nan's mother?'

'Oh yes! She was a born designer. On the hard ground, she'd cut out dresses, leg-o'-mutton sleeves and all. She could design anything. I didn't get to know her well, because I left the station, and, when I left, I took Daisy with me. Annie had said to me shortly before, "Take her with you, mistress. I don't want my daughter to grow up and marry a native, take her with you." It was at her request that I took Daisy. Of course, what I was doing was illegal, you weren't supposed to bring natives into Perth. The magistrate said, "I can't give you permission to take her, because that's against the law, but the captain can't refuse her passage". She was fourteen years of age when she came with me and terrified of the sea, she'd never even seen a boat, living inland all those years. I became a well known authority on native affairs after that. I was quoted in the *Herald*. I said, "Make a test case out of me". When I was prosecuted, they said, "How do you plead, guilty or not guilty?". My husband stood up and said, "Guilty M'Lord". They asked us our reasons and I told them her own mother had said, "Don't leave my daughter here, take her with you". I brought other native girls in after that. I'd train them, then find friends who wanted one. I provided quite a few.'

'What was Corunna Downs Station like then?'

'Well, I can't tell you a lot about that, because I was only there once. After my husband sold Corunna, he bought Towera, that was about nine hundred miles away. When my husband was on Corunna, all the squatters were asked to send boys down to school, I suppose that was when Albert and Arthur went down. Albert came back to work at Corunna, but Arthur ran away. He had ambitions of his own. Corunna Downs was named by my husband. There is a poem, "Corunna". He was reading a book at the time with the natives, and in it was a poem about Corunna, I think it was in Spain, so he named the station after that. When I went to Corunna, there were about forty natives working for us. Every Sunday night, we'd roll the piano out onto the verandah, it'd be cold, so we'd have a big log fire out in the open. The natives would sit around and we'd have a church service and a sing-song. The natives just loved it. They lived for it. At nine o'clock, we'd stop. Then, they'd all be given cocoa and hot buns. That was their life. The natives never liked to work. You had to work with them if you wanted them to work. They always wanted to go walkabout. They couldn't stand the tedium of the same job. We used to change their jobs. Daisy always had that tendency. She'd get tired of one job, so I'd say, "Come on, let's chuck the housework", and we'd go shopping.'

'Did Nan ever see her mother again?'

'Yes. I sent her back for a holiday with Howden. I said, "Take her back for a holiday, let her see her mother". She went back by boat. She saw them and she was happy, but, by then, we'd become her family.'

'What were her duties at Ivanhoe?'

'Oh, housework, that sort of thing. She was always good with Granny, she'd just come quietly and take her shoes off after lunch when it was time for her to have her afternoon sleep. She was simply devoted. No white trained nurse had better experience. She grew up loving us and we were her family, there were no servants. It was just family life. She couldn't read a clock, but she knew the time better than any of us. She knew everybody's handwriting that came to the place.'

'Why did she leave Ivanhoe?'

'Why? The police came and took Daisy from me. She was manpowered during the war. No one could have any home-help, I wasn't allowed to have her. She was a wonderful cook. Later, she rented a little house near the Ocean Beach Hotel. I gave her quite a lot of furniture, brooms and things, that I could do without. That's how she supplied herself.'

'Can you tell me who my mother's father might have been?'

'No. I couldn't tell you. He must have been white, maybe a station hand. When Daisy was pregnant, I was absolutely ignorant. My husband said to me one night, "I think you'd better get up, Daisy seems to be in pain". She slept in a room just off ours, it was his dressing-room, we turned it into a room for Daisy. She was groaning and I said, "What's up, Daisy?". She said, "I don't know, mistress, but I think I'm going to have a baby". I hadn't any idea. She was wearing loose dresses. I called Betty, she was about sixteen at the time. I said, "Betty, had you any idea?". "Yes, of course I had, Mum", she said. Well, I was absolutely ignorant, so I rushed over in the car to the hospital, knowing that Nurse Hedges would be there. I told her and she said, "Look, don't wait to get permission. Go home and pack for her and get her to the midwifery hospital. They won't be able to refuse her." So I went and packed a suitcase and took her to the hospital. The baby was born a few hours later, but who the father was, we never found out. Gladys was always a beautiful girl. She went to Parkerville, we took her there. That was a home run by the Church of England sisters, it was a charity home for the ones that had no parents, we sent Gladys there. She grew up with just as nice manners as anybody could wish. Later, when she was grown up, I said to the florist in Claremont, "Will you take this girl?". They said, "No, we wouldn't. We couldn't take a native, because you know they're forbidden." I said, "Will you take her on trial for me, I just can't bear to think of her becoming a servant somewhere". So they took her on trial to please me, and they kept her as one of the family. She looked like a lovely Grecian girl. She never looked back. You see, she was so well brought up by those Church of England sisters. It was only through my being an old scholar that I was able to get her in. It was very hard to get her in.'

When Alice finished talking, I felt a little stunned. All my life, I'd been under the impression that Mum had lived with Nan at Ivanhoe.

It was a shock to me to discover that she'd been placed in a children's home. Why hadn't she told us? I decided I would ask her as soon as I got back.

'Well, it's been very interesting talking to you', I smiled. 'I've heard a lot about you over the years. Can I come and see you again some other time?'

'Any time you like, dear.'

I spoke with Alice again after that, and she told me a little more about Corunna and the early days. I was pleased I'd made the trip, even though I hadn't come up with a great deal of new information.

In talking to Alice, it dawned on me how different Australian society must have been in those days. There would have been a strong English tradition amongst the upper classes. I could understand the effects these attitudes could have had on someone like Nan. She must have felt terribly out of place. At the same time, I was aware that it would be unfair of me to judge Alice's attitudes from my standpoint in the nineteen eighties.

On my return from Sydney, Mum met me at the airport. 'What did you find out?' was her first eager question.

'Quite a lot', I replied. 'I'm really glad I went. I never found out anything startling, but I think sometimes you learn more from what people don't tell you than from what they do.'

On the way home in the car, I described my trip in detail to Mum. I never mentioned her being in Parkerville Children's Home. I wasn't sure how to tackle her about that.

The following day, I left with Paul and the children to spend two weeks at Lancelin, a small fishing town north of Perth. It was the first real holiday we'd had for a long time. When I returned to Perth, I felt refreshed and ready to tackle Mum.

On my first day back, I popped round to visit Jill. Jill was living in Subiaco, sharing a house with Helen, and was still working in Mum's florist shop. I was quietly sipping a cup of coffee when she suddenly said, 'Oh goodness, I forgot! You don't know, do you?'

'Know what?'

She shrugged her shoulders in a helpless kind of way. 'It's Arthur', she said. 'He's dead. He died a few days ago. He went home to Mukinbudin and, apparently, he just had a heart attack and died virtually straight away.'

I wanted to cry, but I couldn't. I felt too shocked. I knew he wanted to go, but the reality of never being able to talk to him again was very painful. He was one of the few links I had with the past.

I saw Mum that afternoon. 'You've heard about Arthur, haven't you?' she said.

'Yeah, I heard. Did you see him before he went to Mucka?'

'Yes.'

'When?'

Mum looked a bit awkward. 'The night before you came home from Sydney.'

'Was he still in Perth then?'

'Yes.'

'I wish I'd seen him.'

'He wanted to see you, too.'

'Why, what did he say?'

'I think he came round to say goodbye. He knew he was going to die once he got to Mucka, he wanted to see us all one last time. He really wanted to see you, Sally. I was supposed to take you around the night you got home.'

'Aw Mum, why didn't you?'

'You looked so tired when you got off the plane, and I was worried about the baby. I knew he'd keep you up late, talking. That's why I never told you, I knew if I did, you'd insist on going over there.'

'Oh Mum, he might have wanted to tell me something.'

'I don't think so, dear. I'm sorry. He knew you cared about him and you'd make sure people read his story, he knew that, so don't go upsetting yourself.'

'Yeah, I guess so. When's the funeral?'

'In a couple of days' time, you coming?'

'Yeah, I'll come. I hate funerals.'

I went with my brother Bill and Mum. I couldn't feel sad for him any more. I knew he was tired of this life, and I knew he was happy. When we got home, we described the funeral to Nan. She hadn't wanted to go, she hated people looking at her. Nan had a good cry, then she said, 'Well, I can't be too sad for him, he wanted to go. I got no brother now.' After that, she rarely mentioned him.

It was about a week after Arthur's funeral that I decided to tackle Mum about Parkerville Children's Home. She had never told any of us she'd been brought up in a home. She'd always led us to believe that she'd spent all her childhood at Ivanhoe. It wasn't that she'd actually lied about it, it was a sin of omission more than anything else.

I popped the question over afternoon tea. Mum was shocked. But before she had time to gather her wits, I said, 'You deliberately misled us. All these years, I thought you were brought up at Ivanhoe with Judy and June. Why on earth didn't you tell us the truth?' It was yet another tactical error; if Mum hadn't been on the defensive before, she certainly was now.

'You're making a big deal out of nothing', she replied. 'I spent holidays at Ivanhoe. Anyway, there's nothing to tell.'

'Oh, come on, Mum, this is me you're talking to, not some stranger off the street! You think I can't tell when you're hiding things? I know you too well. I want you to tell me what it was like.'

'I told you before, Sally', she said in a very annoyed way, 'there's nothing to tell. You're a terror for taking the bull by the horns. Who told you I was brought up in Parkerville, anyway?'

'Alice told me. How did you think I felt, finding out like that. I was shocked.'

'You didn't say anything to June, did you?'

'Of course not, but it was all I could think about. You're lucky I didn't ring you up and abuse you over the phone. You're supposed to be helping me with this book and here you are, hoarding your own little secrets. And you complain about Nan.'

'All right, all right! I'll tell you about it, one day.'

'Now?'

'No, not now. And you promise me you won't tell any of the others.'

'I'll only promise that if you'll promise to spill the beans one day. I mean soon, not in ten years' time, I could be dead by then.'

It was difficult for me to decide how next to trace my family history. Nan and Mum had united. Now that Mum was feeling threatened, she suddenly found she had more in common with Nan than she'd ever imagined.

Consequently, I spent the next few months transcribing Arthur's cassettes and putting his story together. It was very important to me to finish his story. I owed him a great debt. He'd told me so much about himself and his life, and, in doing so, he'd told me something about my own heritage.

When I had completed it all, I rang Mum.

'It's finished', I said when she answered the phone.

'What's finished?'

'Arthur's story.'

'Can I come and read it?'

'That's what I'm ringing you for.'

172

ARTHUR CORUNNA'S STORY

(c. 1893 — c. 1950)

My name is Arthur Corunna. I can't tell you how old I am exactly, because I don't know. A few years ago, I wrote to Alice Drake-Brockman, my father's second wife, and asked her if she knew my age. She said that I could have been born around 1893-1894. Later, her daughter Judy wrote to me and said I could have been born before that. So I guess I have to settle for around there somewhere. Anyway, I'm old, and proud of it.

The early years of my life were spent on Corunna Downs Station in the Pilbara, that's in the north of Western Australia. We called the top half of the station, where I lived, Mool-nya-moonya. The lower half, the outstation, we called Boog-gi-gee-moonya. The land of my people was all round there, from the Condin River to Nullagine, right through the Kimberleys.

After my people had worked for so long on the station, they were allowed to go walkabout. We would go for weeks at a time, from one station to another, visiting people that belonged to us. We always went to Hillside, that was Dr Gillespie's station. The eastern part of Western Australia, that's different. We call that Pukara. Our land was Yabara, the north.

My mother's name was Annie Padewani and my father was Alfred Howden Drake-Brockman, the white station-owner. We called him Good-da-goonya. He lived on Corunna Downs nine years before marrying his first wife, Eleanor Boddington. She had been a governess in the area. While on the station, he shared my Aboriginal father's two wives, Annie and Ginnie.

Ginnie, or Binddiding as we called her, was a big built woman. She was older, argumentative. She bossed my mother around. I used to cry for my mother when she was in a fight. I'd run round and grab her skirts and try and protect her from Ginnie. Ginnie only had one child by Howden, and that was my half-brother, Albert.

My mother was small and pretty. She was very young when she had me. I was her first child. Then she had Lily by my Aboriginal father. Later, there was Daisy. She is my only sister who shares with me the same parents. I was a good deal older than her when they took me away to the mission, she was only a babe in arms, then. My mother was pregnant with other children, but she lost them.

My Aboriginal father was one of the headmen of our tribe. He was a leader. He got our people to work on the station and, in return, he was given a rifle, tea, tobacco and sugar. He was a well-known man, tall and powerful. Many people were scared of him. Sometimes, he would go walkabout, right down to Fremantle, then up through Leonora, Ethel Creek and back to Corunna Downs. Men were frightened of him because he was a boolyah man*.

My uncle and grandfather were also boolyah men. For centuries, the men in my family have been boolyah men. I remember when my grandfather was dying, he called me to him. I was only a kid. He said, 'You know I can't use my power to heal myself. I will pass my powers into you and then I want you to heal me.' He did this, and I ran away and played, even though he was calling me. I was only a kid, I didn't understand. My grandfather died. It wasn't until years later that I began to learn just what powers he had given me.

One day, my uncle said to my mother, 'Never worry about Jilly-yung. (That was my Aboriginal name.) Never worry about him, I will look after him when I'm dead. I will always be close to him. He may not know I am there, I may be a bird in the tree or a lizard on the ground, but I will be close to him.' That was my Uncle Gibbya. He was married to Annie's sister.

My Uncle Gibbya was a powerful rainmaker. He didn't always live on Corunna Downs. One day when he was visiting our people, Howden said to him, 'You can work with me on the station as long as you can make it rain.' My Uncle Gibbya said, 'I will make it rain. Three o'clock this afternoon, it will rain.' Howden looked at the sky, it was blue and cloudless. He shook his head. Later that day, white clouds began to gather, like a mob of sheep slowly coming in. At three o'clock, it rained. My Uncle got his job. He was the best rainmaker in the area.

On the station, I wasn't called Arthur. I had my Aboriginal name, Jilly-yung, which meant silly young kid. When I was a child, I copied everything everyone said. Repeated it like a ninety-nine parrot. The people would say, 'Silly young kid! Jilly-yung!'

I loved my mother, she was my favourite. My mother was always good to me. When others were against me, she stood by me. She used to tell me a story about a big snake. A snake especially for me, with pretty eggs. 'One day', she said, 'you will be able to go and get these eggs'. I belonged to the snake, and I was anxious to see the pretty snake's eggs, but they took me away to the mission, and that finished that. It was a great mystery. If I had've stayed there, I would have gone through the Law, then I would've known. I didn't want to go through the Law. I was scared.

When we went on holidays, we called it going pink-eye, my Aboriginal father carried me on his shoulders when I was tired. I remember one

---

* *Boolyah man* — person who has attained a high degree of knowledge and who has special perceptive and combative skills. Also more commonly known as a *Maban*.

time, it was at night and very dark, we were going through a gorge, when the feather foots*, ginnawandas, began to whistle. I was scared. The whistling means they want you to talk. They began lighting fires all along the gorge. After we called out our names, my family was allowed through.

One day, I took a tomato from the vegetable garden. I'd been watching it for days. Watching it grow big and round and red. Then, I picked it and Dudley saw me. He was Howden Drake-Brockman's brother and we called him Irrabindi. He gave orders for my Aboriginal father to beat me. Maybe he had his eye on that tomato, too.

I was beaten with a stirrup strap. I spun round and round, crying and crying. I was only a kid in a shirt in those days. My Aboriginal father never hit me unless an order was given. Then, he had to do it, boss's orders. He was good to me otherwise, so I never kept any bad feelings against him.

Dudley Drake-Brockman wasn't like Howden. They were brothers, but they were different. Dudley was a short little man. He couldn't ride. He was cruel and didn't like blackfellas. My people used to say about Dudley ngulloo-moolo, which means make him sick. We didn't want him there. In the end, he got sick and died.

I used to play with Pixie, Dudley's son. We used to fight, too, but I never beat him. I was afraid of his father. My mother used to say to me, 'Jilly-yung, never beat Pixie in a fight. When he wants to fight, you walk away.' She was a wise woman.

Howden was a good-looking man, well liked. He could ride all the horses there, even the buck jumpers. Old Nibro told me that. He used to help him break them. There was one big, black horse he named Corunna. He would always ride him when he went out baiting dingoes.

I remember Howden used to dance on his own in the dining-room. He'd be doin' this foxtrot, kicking his leg around with no partner. I used to watch. There was a big dining-room then, and a great, huge fan that we had to pull to cool people off who were eating there. They gave us a handful of raisins for doing that.

We had other jobs on the station besides pulling the fan. For every tin full of locusts we killed with a switch, we got one hard boiled lolly. I remember once, I was a tar boy for the shearers. In those days, it was blade shearing, not like the machines they have now. The shed was stinking hot and the click, click, click of the shears made a rhythmic sound. I couldn't help goin' to sleep. Next thing I knew, I got a smack in the face. They were all singin' out TAR! TAR!, and I was asleep. When the girls brought down the dishes of cakes and buckets of tea, I made sure I was there. I wasn't going to sleep through that.

---

* *feather foot (Ginnawandas)* — similar to the *Boolyah* or *Maban*. Person with special (magic) powers, often used for purposes of retribution. Similar also to *kadaicha man*.

177

Archie McGregor was one of the few white men on the station, he married Mr Richards' sister. Mr Richards was a big-wig in Marble Bar. Archie worked on the windmills and the pumps. When the pumps went bung, Archie had to go down in the deep well and fix them. He was the one that taught Albert and me how to build windmills. Those windmills were a terrible height. They had to be to catch the wind. I thought he was teachin' us things so we could help run the station one day. I was wrong.

When Howden married Eleanor Boddington, he built another house. He didn't stay living with Dudley. He built it by himself, too. He was a carpenter.

You know, he was a cowboy as well, because he had these two big pistols. He pulled them out, BANG! BANG!, firing at the tree, tryin' to shoot it. They were old muzzle loaders, like the ones the Yanks use in cowboy films. You put the powder in and a bit of lead and the cap in afterwards. Then it revolved and you went BANG! BANG!, just like that! He used to hit this tree way down near the toilet. The bullets would bounce off. He was a smart man, I tell you.

I spent a lot of my time on the station with my brother, Albert, and my sister, Lily. When we were kids, we'd run round finding lizards, sticking our fingers in the holes in the ground and wood. One time I did that, it was a snake. A snake won't chase you to bite and kill you. They just want to get away. You only get bitten if you tread on them, they're just protectin' themselves. People always try to kill snakes whenever they see them. They should leave them alone. You point a gun at a snake and he'll get goin', he knows what you goin' to do.

Albert was older than me and they started educatin' him early. Mrs McGregor, Archie's wife, was the teacher. She trained Albert to write on a slate with chalk. He had to speak English and learn the white man's ways and table manners. The other children weren't taught, only Albert and, later, me. She also gave us what you call religious instruction. We learnt all about the saints. She had a big roll of colour pictures that we used to look at.

I went with my mother everywhere until they rounded me up to be educated. When I heard they were after me, I ran away. I didn't want to be educated. Also, I thought they wouldn't give me any meat at night-time. They caught me in the end, put me with Albert and Mrs McGregor. I wasn't allowed to talk blackfella after that. If I did, Dudley beat me. I liked my language, but I got a good hiding if I spoke it. I had to talk English. When I was sleeping on the homestead verandah, I used to call to my mother in my own language, 'Save me meat'.

Of course, when they caught me, Albert could already talk English. He used to study at the cook's table. One night, the cook was a bit late with our supper. Albert said, 'Go tell him.'

'Tell him what?' I said.

'Tell him to hurry up with the tucker.'

'Give me hurry up tea!' I shouted. I should have said, 'Hurry up and give me tea!', but I didn't know. Anyhow, the old cook came down and chased me round and round the kitchen. I was gone through the door with the cook chasin' after me! He never caught me, I was too quick.

That was Albert. He was always puttin' things into my head, but he never did anythin' wrong himself.

Albert lost two fingers because of me. I chopped them off in the tank machine. He stuck his fingers in to try and stop the cogs going round. I turned the handle and chopped them off. They used that machine to make tanks. You put in a straight bit of iron and bend it to make a boomerang circle. You only need three or four sheets to make a tank. Fancy, me choppin' his fingers off. We were just messing around, I didn't know he had his fingers in there.

When we were being educated, Albert and me slept on the homestead verandah. We had a bed side by side. Some nights, I'd wet my bed and jump into his. I'd dream someone was hitting me so I'd fight them in bed, I'd punch them and call out, then when I looked at my bed, I found it was wet.

Even though Albert was the older one, I took no notice of him. I was the mischievous one. He was too frightened to do anything, sometimes he needed protecting.

I knew all the people on the station, they was a good mob. There was Chook Eye, Wongyung and Mingibung. They were housegirls. They used to take in cups of tea and look after the house. Then there was Tiger Minnie, she used to help Howden bait the dingoes. No one could bait like her. Then there was Sarah, she was a big woman, she helped look after the garden. She grew pumpkins and cabbages for the cook and shooed the birds away. She was half-caste, like me. When her own baby was born, it was nearly white. A white blackfella. We all reckoned those extra babies belonged to either old Fred Stream, or Sam Moody, the cook.

We used to call Sam Moody backwards, Moody Sam. He was a white man and a good cook. He'd cook bread, cut it in big slices and give it to the natives through the small kitchen window. He cooked meat, too. We'd all get bread and slices of meat. We'd poke our billies through that little window and get tea, too. If Moody Sam didn't cook, we'd get slices of mutton, make a fire outside and cook it ourselves. For extra meat, my people used to catch kangaroos and wild turkeys and fish from the creek. We'd go down to the creek and we'd stand with our legs bent and apart, then we'd catch them between our knees. We'd grab them with our hands and throw them on the bank.

Old Fred Stream, I think he was German. He used to take me on trips to Condin. Corunna Downs wool used to be stored there, ready to be loaded on the sailing ships bound for Fremantle. The stores were great big sheds and they housed goods as well as wool. One time, Fred Stream told me there were two saddles to be picked up, one for me and one for Albert. When they pulled them out, the rats had chewed away the straps. Those rats ate anything.

I don't know if Condin is used now they have a railway to Port Hedland. In those days, it was just surveyed. I never went back to see the new railway, or anything else.

On the way back to Corunna Downs, we camped at DeGrey Station. You should have seen all the pretty dresses come runnin' to meet our wagon. There was red, pink and green, all the colours of the rainbow. They was all runnin' to come and see me, too. I was only a little fella, I wasn't much in those days.

Some of the people there had pet pigs. They sold two to Fred Stream. Before we reached Corunna Downs, he knocked one on the head and cooked it in the ashes. I reckoned he was cruel, to eat a little pig like that! I couldn't look at him and I couldn't eat it. I kept thinking, fancy killing such a little pig. He was only a baby.

The next day, we came to a freshwater well and stopped to water the team. There were goats runnin' all over the place. Big ones, little ones, young ones, old ones. Fred Stream watched all these goats, then he said, 'You want a goat?'. I said, 'NO!'. I didn't want him to catch and kill no baby goat. Anyhow, he rounded up a kid and a billy and when we got to Corunna Downs, we let them go. I don't know what happened to them. I couldn't take a little baby goat away from his mother. I'm funny like that. I take after my old grandfather, I'm tender-hearted. I don't believe in stealing anything from its mother.

I remember one time when I was very small, it must have been Christmas, because there was so much food on the table on the verandah. All kinds of food laid out on this big table. I kept thinking to myself, I should eat more, I should eat more. I should finish it off. I knew I wasn't goin', to see food like that again for a long time. I just kept lookin' at all that food, thinkin' what a shame it was to go away and leave it. Even though my belly was already aching, I made myself eat more. A while later, I brought it all up. My belly was swollen and I just couldn't keep it in! You know, it must have been Christmas, because I was all dressed up in a shirt and pants that day.

There were always corroborees at Corunna. You needed special permission to watch them. We used to go with Howden. I hadn't been put through the Law by then, because I was still too young. That happens when you are fourteen or fifteen. I didn't want to go through the Law. I used to say, 'Don't let them do that to me, Mum'. I didn't want to be cut this way and that. For the real black ones, it was compulsory. I was half-caste, so I could be exempted. The women were just marked on the chest. Just one mark, here in the middle. That was their ceremony.

In those days, the women were given to you when you were only a baby. They had Old Dinah picked out for me. She used to help in the garden. She's dead and gone now, probably still waitin' for me in heaven. She was old enough to be my mother. I suppose, later, I could have had Helen Bunda for my wife. She was half-caste, too, and very clever with her hands. Her mother was Nellie, or Moodgjera. Her father was a bullock driver.

There was some wonderful wildlife on Corunna Downs. There was one little bird, he was a jay or a squeaker, he'd sing out three times and then the rains would come. He was never wrong. While he was there, there was always a good feed, but when he was gone, drought! When the little frogs sang out, we knew it was going to rain. They were lovely colours, white and brown with black spots. They were all different, there wasn't one the same. They used to get into the cooler and we'd have to clean it out. They was all natural animals. Wonderful creatures. There were no insecticides then to kill the birds. That's why the blackfellas want their own land, with no white man messin' about destroyin' it.

All the people round there, we all belonged to each other. We were the tribe that made the station. The Drake-Brockmans didn't make it on their own. There were only a few white men there, ones that fixed the pumps and sank wells by contract. The blackfellas did the rest.

I remember seein' native people all chained up around the neck and hands, walkin' behind a policeman. They often passed the station that way. I used to think, what have they done to be treated like that. Made me want to cry, just watchin'. Sometimes, we'd hear about white men goin' shooting blackfellas for sport, just like we was some kind of animal. We'd all get scared, then. We didn't want that to happen to us. Aah, things was hard for the blackfellas in those days.

One day, I'd like to go back to Corunna Downs, see what improvements there are. I believe it was used for a military base during the war. When I was there, Brockmans built a hump and stuck a flagpole in it. Whenever any visitors came, they raised the Union Jack.

Aah, I always wish I'd never left there. It was my home. Sometimes, I wish I'd been born black as the ace of spades, then they'd never have took me. They only took half-castes. They took Albert and they took me and Katie, our friend. She was put in Parkerville. She had a big doll with her when she went, Albert had me. Others went, too. I was about eleven or twelve.

When I left, Lily cried and cried. She was only little, but she ran away and hid, no one could find her. I was her favourite. She was full blood, real black, so they didn't want to take her. Daisy was only a baby, she didn't know what was goin' on.

They told my mother and the others we'd be back soon. We wouldn't be gone for long, they said. People were callin', 'Bring us back a shirt, bring us this, bring us that'. They didn't realise they wouldn't be seein' us no more. I thought they wanted us educated so we could help run the station some day, I was wrong.

When they came to get me, I clung to my mother and tried to sing* them. I wanted them to die. I was too young, I didn't know how to sing them properly. I cried and cried, calling to my mother, 'I don't want to go, I don't want to go!'. She was my favourite. I loved her. I called, 'I want to stop with you, I want to stop with you!'. I never saw her again.

---

* *sing* — to sing an incantation which is believed to have the power to kill the person against whom it is directed.

When we left Corunna Downs to come to the Swan Native and Half-Caste Mission, we had to travel through Marble Bar and then to Port Hedland. We caught the ship, the *Ballara*, me, my brother Albert, Pixie and Dudley Drake-Brockman. Albert and I travelled steerage. Sometimes, I'd sneak out and head towards the front end of the boat to see what was going on. Dudley Drake-Brockman would always catch me and shout, 'Get back to where you belong!'.

It was a fine day when we arrived in Fremantle. We were taken straight to the mission, it was situated near the banks of the Swan River in Guildford.

The first thing they did was christen us. Canon Burton and Sophie McKintosh, I think she was the matron, were our godparents. We were christened Corunna, they didn't give us our father's name. That's when I got the name of Arthur. Albert had always been called Albert and he stayed that way.

For a long time, I was very worried about my mother. She had always been good to me. She loved me. Albert didn't seem to mind so much, I think he was too frightened to mind anything. You see, we couldn't understand why they'd taken us away. We weren't their family. The mission wasn't anyone's family. They called us inmates, then, all us kids, we were all inmates, just like a prison.

We soon found out that there were bullies at the mission. I suppose you get them everywhere. There was one that wanted to try us out. I was worried about Albert, I knew he couldn't fight his way out of a paper bag. He was bigger than me, older than me, yet I knew they could belt him up and tie him in knots. I had to take his part. I'd tackle whoever was beating up Albert and finish them off. They never tackled me again and they learnt not to touch Albert, because he was my brother.

There was one bully there, he had everyone bluffed except me. He'd throw stones at me, call me names, but he'd never tackle me. When it came to knuckles, I got my fist in first.

I was different to Albert. I was made different. I could fall off a horse, do anything and there was never nothing damaged or broken, even if I landed on a rock. I'm like rubber, you can bounce me anywhere. Albert wasn't like that. He used to get sick a lot. I cried for him when he was sick. He was my brother.

One man that worked on the mission, Mr Ferguson, he said about

Albert and me, 'These boys have been well brought up. They say thank you for everything.' We even said thank you when they gave us a hiding.

They soon learnt I could work at the mission. I was reliable. They could give me a job and I'd do it, no matter what. I had ten hurricane lamps to clean. I cleaned the glasses, then filled them with kero. I was the mailman and the milkman, too. I delivered milk and eggs to Mr and Mrs Anderson in Guildford. Then, I'd continue on to Thompson's place, that was just over the railway line, they bought our milk, too. There were lots of people who bought things from the mission. I was the only one who was allowed to collect mail from the Midland post office. They sent me because I was the fastest walker.

If Matron needed any medicine, she sent me. She'd give me a letter to take to the chemist, Webb was his name. One time while I was waiting in the chemist shop, a lady started talking to me, she was waiting, too. She told me what she was there for and what was wrong with her. There was this wrong with her and that wrong with her. She had so many things wrong with her I was amazed she was still alive. All this time she was talking, she was drinking lemonade. It was a real hot day. She told me all her troubles and I just sat there and listened and looked at her lemonade. She didn't even offer me one drop.

After Albert and me had been there a while, the mission was visited by a man called Governor Bedford. He was an Englishman, a grey-headed thing. After his visit, the darker kids were separated from the lighter kids. He didn't like us being together.

Before the Governor's visit, they built a building close to the bridge and near the brickyard. It looked like an ark to us, so we all called it Noah's Ark. We all thought that was fitting, because we was all in there together, white ones, black ones. We liked sharing that ark. Governor Bedford didn't like it one bit. He separated us all out. The light-coloured ones had to go where the girls were and the girls were moved to the west side of the mission.

Funny thing was, they put Freddy Lockyer in with the white kids. He had fair hair and fair skin, but really, he was a white blackfella. He didn't want to go, he wanted to stay with us blackies, he belonged to us, but they made him go. I said to him, 'You're not black enough to stay with us, you have to go'. I felt sorry for him. He was really one of us.

There was always a boundary between the girls and the boys. They had to sit one way and we had to sit the other. Apart from when we played, you had to follow the boundary and stick to your side. When the girls were older, they were put into service as housegirls and maids for anyone who wanted one. Once the boys reached adolescence, they were completely separated from the girls and put in a nearby orphanage. I suppose they were worried we might chase them.

184

After a while, the bigger boys started running away to Moora. They were brought back, but if they ran away a second time, the mission people would try and find work for them with the farmers up there. They were all well taught by then. I was still there when nearly all the older boys from the orphanage had run away. The only one left was Pinjarra Frank.

Bob Coulson was another man who worked on the mission. He was a good man with a hammer. I used to watch him. If he saw any cats sneakin' around the chicken house, he'd corner them and hit them on the head with a hammer. A cat only had to look at him and he was a goner.

Coulson wasn't a big man, but he had a nose like a devil. He used to be a soldier and he often showed us his bayonet. He was full of bluff. I think he was afraid the blackfellas might tackle him one day, that's why he kept on showing us his bayonet. He always wore his shirt sleeves rolled up, ready for action.

Corunji was Coulson's dog. He was a nice, old dog. We used to give him a slice of bread, now and then. One day, we were going into Guildford on deliveries and Corunji followed us. We had to cross the railway line, and when a train came, old Corunji started running and barking and chasing the engine. He must have slipped, because his foot went under the wheel and his leg was cut off. We were all crying, 'Corunji, Corunji. Poor old Corunji!' We ran all the way back to the mission to tell Coulson what had happened. He got on his bike and cycled back to the railway line, we all followed. Poor old Corunji was still lyin' there, just lookin' at us as if to say, 'Can't you help me?'. Coulson got off his bike, walked over to Corunji, put his hand over his snout, pulled out his hammer and hit him over the head. Then, he got on his bike and cycled back to the mission. He just left him lyin' there. He did that to his own dog. Like I said, he was a good man with a hammer. I couldn't help thinking if he'd do that to his own dog, he might do that to me, one day. When he wasn't looking, I kept an eye on him. I didn't trust him after that.

Coulson had three children of his own. He told us once he used to beat his own son with a stick wrapped round the end with barbed wire. His daughters were called Mabel and Audrey. His wife was an olden-day lady. At least, that's how I remember her. There was nothing pretty about her. She was just a plain sort of Englishwoman. We didn't have much to do with her. All she did was look after her house and keep an eye on the girls. Apart from that, she didn't stick her big nose anywhere. I don't think she was very loving to her kids. They were always coming around and talking to us.

When I was in my fourth year at the mission, Coulson caught me and some other boys outside the mission boundaries. We were playing in a public picnic area near the river. It was a popular spot and we were hoping to find some money that people might have dropped. When he found us, he was real mad. He ordered us back to our dormitory, he said he was going to give us a beating. You can imagine how scared we all were. He was so angry, we'd never seen him that angry, we were frightened of what he might do to us.

We didn't go back to the dormitory, we ran all the way to Midland, to the police station. You see, the police were called Protectors of Aborigines in those days, so we thought we might get some protection from them. We all ran inside the station and told the policeman what Coulson was going to do to us. We thought he might help us, we were only kids. He listened to what we had to say, then he said, 'Get back to the mission! It's none of my business what happens to you!' We didn't know what to do.

As we came out of the station, Coulson came riding down the road on his bike. He spotted us, rounded us up and walked us back to the mission.

By this time, he was just about boiling over. He shoved us all in a dormitory, locked the door and told us to strip off. Then, when we were naked, he raced around the dormitory like a madman, beating us with a long cane over the head and body. He didn't care where he hit us, he just beat us and beat us till we bled. There was bits of blood everywhere. We were all crying, some of the boys were screaming, 'No more, no more. No more, master!' He liked you to call him master.

I was the only one that didn't cry out. He came over and grabbed me and said, 'Arthur, I've never had to beat you before, but BY GOD I'm going to give it to you now!' He beat me and he beat me, but I wouldn't cry for him. He beat me harder and harder, my thighs were running with blood and I still wouldn't cry for him. He was very, very angry, but I wasn't going to give him the satisfaction of making me cry.

After that, I decided that, when my wounds were better and I could walk again, I would run away. Albert could stay there if he wanted to, but I didn't want to be skinned and belted around. I'm real old now and I can still show you the scars from that beating. My wounds took a long time to heal. I was in a bad way.

I think Coulson felt guilty for beating me so hard, because, later, he took me for a train ride to visit his sister and her husband. They had a butcher's shop. It made no difference to me, I still didn't trust him. I was glad that I hadn't cried for him. I was pleased that, when I ran away, I'd be rid of him.

Pinjarra Frank and Tommy decided to come with me. I wanted Albert to come, too, but he was too frightened. He thought that, if we ran away and we got caught, Coulson might beat him the way he'd beaten me.

We told all the mission kids we intended to head towards Geraldton. Other boys had run away in that direction, so it would make our story

186

seem likely. We didn't tell anyone we really planned to head towards the goldfields. It was a good plan, because, that way, if any of our friends were asked questions, they didn't have to lie. We'd told them all just to say what we said.

We did run away. I must have been about fifteen or sixteen, then.

Coulson didn't stay at the mission long after that. He was sacked. I guess the Anglican mob that ran the mission began to realise that all the boys had been running away because of the way Coulson had been treating them. Maybe the other kids told them what Coulson had done to me.

I was sorry to leave Albert behind. After I left, he had no one to protect him and he got sick again. They sent him to hospital. Then, Howden came down and took him back to Corunna Downs. Dudley was dead by then. As far as I know, Albert worked there until it was sold to Foulkes-Taylor. Then, Albert went to Dr Gillespie's station, Hillside. A lot of people went to Hillside. They knew that Foulkes-Taylor was a hard man.

I heard people was looking for me, I heard Howden was looking for me, but I was gone. I didn't want to be found. And I wasn't having anything more to do with school.

A lot of things happened to me after I left the mission. First off, we had to cross over the railway line, we knew that. We walked and walked until we came to this big tunnel going over the line, we were amazed, we'd never seen it before. We all peered down, the inside got darker and darker and there was a tiny little opening at the end. Pretty soon, a train came past, it went straight into that tunnel, we all called out, 'STOP, STOP!', but it went straight in anyway and came out the other end with no trouble at all. We all thought a long time about that.

We walked for a long time after we crossed the railway line, we were very careful not to be seen. Finally, we got to Parkerville and camped in the bush there for a rest. Suddenly, a man appeared out of nowhere. 'What are you boys doing here?' he growled. We jumped up, scared out of our wits. We told him our story and showed him the scars on our legs. We only had shorts on so you could easily see them. He felt sorry for us. 'Stay where you are, boys', he said. 'I'll get you something to help you on your way.' He came back with some bread and dripping and a box of matches so we could light a fire at night and keep warm.

After that, we kept walking until it was dark. Luckily, we came across an old abandoned house. It was falling down, but it was better than nothing. We got some old, dry gum leaves and sticks from the bush and lit a fire. Then, we settled down for the night. There was an occupied house further down the hill, but we'd been careful to avoid it.

We was just all driftin' off to sleep, it was a cool, clear night, when suddenly, we heard a woman's voice drift by on the wind. 'I tell you, Bill, there's someone in that old house, I can see the smoke coming through the roof!' We all looked up, there was no roof. We quickly put the fire out and sat close together, ready to run if we had to. Then, the man's voice drifted by, 'Shut up woman! You mind everyone's business but your own!' Their light went out and we never heard anyone. We didn't light the fire again, even though we were cold. It was a long time before any of us slept.

Early next morning, we made our way to the railway line. There was a goods train waiting there. I took my two boomerangs and walked up to the engineer. 'Please mister', I said, 'will you swap two boomerangs for a ride on your train?'. 'No!' he said.

When the train pulled out, we jumped on a wagon that was only half full. The train passed through Northam and we finally ended up

188

at Kellerberrin. We didn't know where the train was headed, but riding on that wagon was a lot better than walking.

At Kellerberrin station, the station master spotted us. He came running over and hauled us down. 'You're the boys that are wanted by the police, aren't you?' he said. He had his hand on my shoulder, I wondered what he was going to do with us. He looked us over real good and then said, 'Right boys, you see that building over there, that's the police station. I want you boys to go and present yourselves to the constable, he'll know what to do with you.'

He pointed again to the small building further down the track and sent us on our way. We walked slowly down the track, we wasn't sure if he was watching us or not. When we got near some bush, we veered off and ran for our lives.

No one chased after us, so, after a while, we stopped. We were starving hungry by then. We found some mouldy bread and an old milk can. We ate the bread and scraped out what was left from inside of the can, then we set off again.

We kept following the railway line. Just as the sun was setting, we reached Hines Hill. We were dog tired by then. We sat down at the bottom of a hill to rest. Suddenly, we spotted a tall man coming slowly down the hill towards us. The sun was in our eyes, so we were frightened he was a policeman, but we were too tired to get up and run.

He walked right up and said, 'What are you boys doing here? Where have you come from?' We told him our story, he looked at the scars on our legs and shook his head. He told us he was a farmer. We asked him if he could give us some flour to make damper and some tea and sugar. He went away and came back with some tucker. He warned us to be careful, he said the police had been asking about us.

After he left, we built a fire in the bush, we still had a few matches left and we wanted to fill our bellies real quick.

Just as we were making damper, a man appeared from nowhere and shouted, 'What are you boys up to?'. He said he was the station master from Hines Hill and he'd spotted our smoke and tracked us down. We were scared, tired and starving, we didn't have the heart or the strength to run away. We waited for him to tell us he was going to turn us in to the police. He walked up close to us and looked us up and down. 'Where'd you boys get those scars?' We told him our story and he took pity on us. 'Put out that fire, boys', he said. 'I'll take you to a friend of mine. You'll eat better there.'

We followed him through the bush, we were too tired to care where he took us. We ended up at a small house. It was owned by a contractor with three daughters. He was a widower. They sat us down at a table inside the house. They took us inside, just like that. Wasn't that something? The girls giggled when they looked at us. They cooked us a big meal and we were allowed to eat as much as we liked. Can you believe that? It was sure better than damper, they even let us sleep the night there.

The next morning, Tommy decided to strike off by himself. He was from the goldfields and he wanted to get back home. He missed his people. Pinjarra Frank and me didn't know what to do. We thought we'd just keep on walking.

Then, the contractor came to us and said, 'Boys, how'd you like to stay with me for two weeks and help with some fencing? I can't pay you, but you'll have your tucker.' That was good enough for us. We didn't have anywhere else to go.

We helped with the fencing and whatever else he wanted doing. The two weeks turned into over a month and we were still there. The girls cooked us good meals. They were allowed to play with me, but not with Pinjarra Frank. He was real dark and he didn't work as hard as me.

One day, a man came by. He was a good-looking man with a big moustache. He came in a sulky, all dressed up. At first, when I saw him coming, I thought he was a policeman, and I nearly ran away. He pulled up at the house and said to the contractor, 'I'm after a boy who can ride. I hear you've got two boys, can they ride? There's jobs going if they can.'

'I can ride', I said. I prayed the horse wouldn't throw me as soon as I jumped on. The contractor said, 'Stay with us, we're fond of you. Let Pinjarra go.' He was a good man, that contractor, but his house was close to the railway line and, all the time I'd been there, I'd been lookin' over my shoulder, wonderin' when the police would catch up with me. I decided to go with the stranger. McQuarie was his name.

McQuarie climbed down from the sulky and unhitched two horses from the back. 'On you get', he said. Pinjarra leapt on, but they had to give me a leg up, I was too small. I clung on to the reins and mane and prayed with all my heart I wouldn't fall off. For twenty-five miles, McQuarie drove the sulky, and for twenty-five miles, I bumped up and down, barely hanging in the saddle. Jig-jog, jig-jog, I went. My bottom and the insides of my legs were painful sore. I kept telling myself the next hill would be the last one, but they kept going on and on. We went through forest country, they were clearing for a new settlement, then one more hill, then Nungarin. The sun had set by then. It was tea-time. That was my first start in life.

The next day, McQuarie's son Ernie came to me and said, 'Come on, I'll show you the ropes. I hear you need some riding lessons.' That day, I learnt to canter so my body didn't jolt around so much. My legs and bottom were still sore, but I wasn't giving up that easy.

Ernie took me out to one of the runs and we stopped at a lake. He reined his horse in, climbed down and lay on the grass. I did the same. I thought he was going to tell me about the run. He said nothing.

He pulled his hat down over his eyes, took out a plug of tobacco from his pouch and rolled a big, fat cigarette. Then he smoked it real slow. All the time, he was looking at the lake. When he finished, I sat up. I thought, now he's going to tell me about the run. He didn't even look at me, he just lay back, pulled a book out from his pocket, and started to read. He turned each page real slow and deliberate like. I sat looking at the lake. We stayed like that all day, not talking, just laying there. When it was dark, he said, 'Right, let's go'. They were the only words he said to me. We rode back to the station and had tucker.

I had tucker in the kitchen. The white workers sat at one table, the blacks at another. McQuarie and his family ate in the formal dining-room. That night, I slept in the stripper. I lifted up the top and crawled inside. Later, I got an old sheepskin for a mattress and, sometimes, I had a blanket, too, if there was one to spare. Later on, they floored the barn ready for barn dances and I slept in there with the horses. I reckon I must have slept in that barn for well over two years.

The following day, Ernie took me to a different run. It was a long way out. By and by, he reined in his horse, climbed down and sat on the ground. He pulled out a plug of tobacco and rolled another big, fat cigarette. We did the same thing we had the day before.

The third day was the same, except in a different place. I soon learnt that Ernie was not only lazy, but greedy, too. He never shared anything. Not his tobacco, not his food, nothing. You could be starving and he wouldn't offer you anything. Later on, McQuarie built a store and Ernie would sneak in there and eat big tins of peaches when we were supposed to be boundary riding. He never offered me a drop. He'd open up a big tin of peaches and scoop them out with a spoon. He'd lean against the counter, look me straight in the eye and eat some more.

Eventually, Ernie ran the store and all the farmers who lived nearby bought on credit, payable after harvest. No one paid their debts, Ernie kept on eating and eating and the store went bankrupt.

As for me, I decided never to worry about tucker. When I was out all day, minding the cattle, they only gave me one piece of bread and a thin slice of pork. The meat was so thin that, if you held it up to the sun, you could see through it.

After I'd been there a while, McQuarie told me I was now a stockman. From then on, I took my orders from him. He said my conditions were five bob a year, my horse and saddle, board and tucker. I never did get that five bob a year, but then, I wasn't worried about wages. I had a home.

In three years, I was head stockman and mustering cattle all over the district. It was pioneer days, then. They were just clearing Nungarin and the railway line wasn't even there, only the earthworks.

When there was no stock work to be done, I spent my time grubbing boab tea-tree and clearing more land ready for cropping. Other times,

I did errands for McQuarie, driving him and his friends here and there in the sulky.

All this time, I went under the name of Marble. I thought it might give me some protection from the police, they were still looking for me. McQuarie told me, 'Marble, if you ever see the police round here, you hide, and I'll tell them to take Pinjarra Frank, instead. I'll send you word when they've gone.'

McQuarie reckoned Pinjarra didn't work as hard as me. Thing was, they didn't want him, he was real black. They wanted me.

Even though Pinjarra was older than me, I was his boss. Pinjarra was lazy, and, in the end, McQuarie gave him the sack.

McQuarie was a good man, he never growled at me. I remember once, I was in the barn putting blinkers on a horse, I had to climb up onto the manger to do it. I was only small. It took me a long time to grow. McQuarie came in and saw me and laughed, 'Hey Marble', he said, 'when are you going to grow?'. I didn't say nothin'. I'm like a tree that never been watered. I just thought to myself, yeah, I don't get enough to eat.

Dick McQuarie, the other son, used to give me clothes. They were always too big, but I just rolled them up till I grew into them. They fitted me for years.

Sometimes, McQuarie would ask me to drive a visitor around or help someone with work they were doing. Everyone wanted me in those days.

I remember this fella Baird. They call the shop he owned in Perth Myers, these days. It used to be called Bairds. He came to Nungarin once to help build a house for his brother. I took him out with his tools and he got interested in me. One day, he said, 'Would you like to come to Perth, Marble? I'll look after you, give you a good schooling.' I started to think about that hiding I got at the mission. That was supposed to be schooling. I thought, nobody's going to school me again. Now, if he had've said, 'Marble, what if I take you back to Corunna Downs?', I might have gone, but school, that was where they gave you a good hiding for doing nothing. Seems funny, thinking about it all now. If I'd have taken his offer, I might have ended up as a shopwalker for Bairds.

I decided to stay with McQuarie. He never said, 'How long are you gunna be?'. I was my own boss. He never gave me any money and I never worried about it. I was just growing up and there was nothing to spend money on.

One chap McQuarie had me drive around was a big squatter from Victoria, by name of Syd Stock. I had to take him by buggy to his brothers in Nungarin. One night, we was sitting by the fire, the air was real cool and quiet like, when he turned to me and said, 'Would you like to come back to Victoria with me, Marble? I've got stations there and horses and buggies, too. You can work on one of my stations.'

I looked at him, he was a good man. The kind of man I liked. Then I said, 'No. I don't want to go far away from the north. I might never come back. This land is my home.'

Now, that could have been an opportunity missed. He was an old man and he trusted me. I was young, then, with no ties, just a young, working man. He might have given me a station. I knew he was a good man, because, whenever we went to the hotel, he never put me outside or cast me away like most white men. Where he went, I went. He kept me with him always. Treated me like his equal. That was a rare thing in those days. A thing to be treasured.

Everybody seemed to like me, then. I couldn't make out why. I'd look in a mirror and what'd I see. Me. An ugly bloke like me. What did they see in me? But each time someone asked me to go with them, I said no.

One day, Dick said to me, 'Come on, Marble, we'll take you to the Northam Show'. They gave me new clothes and everything. They stayed in their Aunty's pub, the Shamrock Hotel, and I camped in the horses' manger nearby. I wasn't very big. I used to sit on the beer cases outside the hotel and eat my tucker.

I loved that Show. They had merry-go-rounds and all sorts of things I hadn't seen before.

I met a bloke there, Jack Gollan was his name. He was an announcer at the races and owned delivery stables in Northam. He used to come and talk a lot to me after we met. He wanted me to work for him, too.

When I went to the Show week races, it was the only time I hit the boss for some money. Dick said to the boss, 'Give me some money', so I said, 'Me too, boss'. He gave me half a sovereign. When we got to the races, I gave it to a bloke to put on a winner for me. I never saw that half-sovereign again.

I had to watch from outside, they said I didn't have enough money to bet and pay my entry fee to the races as well. Inside, they had two big pots of hot dogs boiling up. I could smell them and I was real hungry. My money was gone, so what could I do. Later, two blokes in a sulky came through from New Norcia. They gave me a ride back to the pub.

As far as crops go, 1911 was a good harvest for nearly everyone. It was never as good after that. Dry conditions seemed to set in. Good rain fell in some places, like Bruce Rock. The farmers there were getting two bags to the acre, but it was lighter soil. If you were cropping in heavy soil, it was like trying to plough without hitching up the horses. Things got bad and we took three hundred head of cattle further north, trying to find better grazing and water.

It was July 1912, miners were finding gold at Paynes Find, then. There was traffic on the roads. When the bit of water we found finally

193

dried up, we took the cattle back to Nungarin. In the end, we had to sell most of them.

We kept working McQuarie's station, but things got worse and worse. The first time McQuarie went broke was because everyone owed him money. All the farmers were in debt to him and none of them could pay their bills. The bailiff came to sell off the stock and the machinery. All the other farmers got together and agreed not to bid against McQuarie. He used his sister's money and got everything back for ten shillings or a pound. The bailiff didn't know what to do. McQuarie was the only one bidding, the others were just standing around, watching.

After that first time, McQuarie got the other farmers to help him clear a lot of land for extra cropping. He wasn't going to get nothin' out of that crop, just enough to pay his bills. Jackatee and me cleared even more land and put in more crops. We pulled out big boab trees, raked the roots together and burnt them. Then, we put the crop in. Jackatee was a good worker. He was real black. At night, we'd boil our billy in the bush and cook pancakes for tea on the forge. That was all the tucker we had. He was a good friend, old Jackatee.

Anyway, turned out the crop was better than before, but still not good enough to save McQuarie. A bad drought came and finished him off. There was no water, no feed for the animals. Dick and me had to shoot poor old Bess. She was a good horse, but there was nothin' for her to eat. What stock there was was in bad condition. We had to lift them all up between sticks and a chain to treat their sores. Then we let them go. Poor buggers. There was no food. Some of them were too far gone to be helped.

McQuarie said to Dick, 'Dick, you can stop on the station. There's plenty of seed and super. You could put in another crop.' Dick said, 'No fear, I'm not doin' that. There's a war comin', I'm off to fight.' Ernie left, too. They were very lucky, because they could have been shot. They came back at the end of the war and stayed with their Aunty.

I stopped with McQuarie till he was real broke. The farmers still owed him money and the bailiff was coming again. Dalgetys sold him up. They didn't worry about the man battling on the land, they just wanted their money. And if the land didn't come into fruition like it should, they sold you up. I finally left with Jackatee in 1913. There was no food for me then, either.

We went into Nungarin, trying to find work. We'd do anything. One chap saw us in the street and asked us to help him load a truck. He gave us threepence. Threepence, for all that work! We bought some bread and ate it. We were starvin' hungry. A big load of sandalwood came in and the storekeeper came over and said, 'You boys want work loading that sandalwood?'.

'Yes', we said. We were desperate, we didn't ask the pay.

When we finished loading twelve ton of sandalwood, he gave us half a crown. Then, we gave it back to him in his store for some sardines and biscuits and that was the end of that. It seems like the whitefella doesn't want the blackfella to get a foot in this world.

I had no money, no job. I was about twenty, twenty-one then. I could see I couldn't live in Nungarin. I decided to strike out for Goomalling. There were two friends of mine who wanted to go there, too, Billy One Moon and Hunting Maggie. Hunting Maggie was blind. Billy was her husband and he used to lead her along the road with a stick. I called them Aunty and Uncle. I wasn't in my home country and I thought if any other natives asked who I was, it would give me some protection.

By the time we were three or four miles out of Nungarin, McQuarie pulled up behind us in a buggy. 'Hey, Marble', he said, 'I want you to drive me to Hines Hill and the bailiff wants a boy to help round up stock'.

'Righto', I said. I told my friends I would meet them later.

After I got back from Hines Hill, I rounded up the stock. They were no trouble. I had a bad time with my old pony. She wanted to stop with me. She didn't want to go in the corral with the others. I thought McQuarie might say, 'Take her, Marble, she's your horse', but he didn't. I nearly cried when I saw her go.

After that, the bailiff said, 'You want another job?'.

'Too right', I said. 'I got no job.'

'Good', he said. 'I want you to shepherd the sheep near the pub till we're ready to truck 'em.'

While I was minding the sheep, a man came up and spoke to me.

'When you finished working for that bailiff, how about coming and working for me? I'll give you ten bob a week plus board.'

'That's all right by me!' I said. It was the most I ever been offered.

After they trucked the sheep, the bailiff gave me thirty shillings. That was more than I expected. I picked up my swag and went over and saw Dick McQuarie.

'Dick', I said, 'how much you want for that old bike of yours?'.

'My old bike? Well, let me see, about thirty bob would do.'

I gave him my thirty bob and wheeled the bike across the railway line to Hancock's place. A local had imported the bike years ago from England and sold it to Dick. It had no tyres or tubes. I didn't mind. I had a bike and I was looking forward to my new job.

From 1913 till 1916, I worked for Hancock. In all that time, I got no pay, only my tucker, and I worked damn hard. I never saw that ten bob a week he promised me. Most of the time I was there, I was freezing cold. We just lived in an old bough shed. There was no proper place to sleep and, in winter, the wind cut right through you. There was no getting away from it, no matter where you sat. I used to get old gallon tins and fill them with hot water, tie bags around them, then strap them to my feet. My feet felt the cold the most. Like ice, they were. I never had shoes. The tins gave some relief. I tell you, it's hard to keep warm in an open bough shed.

Most of my working time was spent clearing the land, seeding and cropping. It was hard work, but I was used to it. In between times, I made mud bricks for a hut with a chimney and fireplace. I used to tread the mud with my bare feet, and when a stick tickled my foot, I'd pull it out. If I didn't, the brick would crack. The bricks started to mount up. We dug out a hole in the ground and I built a cellar with a nice big chimney inside to throw out the heat. Winter came and we'd used all the bricks, so we slept in the cellar. It sure was warmer than that shed. I felt like a king that winter.

While I was at Hancock's, I managed to get tyres and tubes for my bike. I fixed that bike up real good, oiled it and kept it nice. In my spare time, I'd ride all over the countryside, wherever my legs would take me, round and round they'd go, pushing those pedals to goodness knows where. I never planned on going anywhere in particular. I just liked riding round, looking at the land and the bush. It was what you'd call my entertainment. I met lots of different people when I was out. Most of them was friendly. 'Gidday', they'd say, or, 'Mornin' '. Course, you got some that weren't interested in talkin' to you, but I never let them worry me. I loved that bike, it made me feel real grand.

It was during my time at Hancock's that I met up with a Welshman named Davy Jones. He was working on the Trans Line, out on the Nullarbor Plain, and now and then, he came to Nungarin to check on his land. It was at the time when Lord Kitchener had ordered all the States to be linked by railway line, in case of war. That way, they could help each other.

While Davy was working the Trans Line, the Land Department was trying to forfeit his land in Nungarin. That's why he visited Hancock so much. Davy couldn't write then, so he'd get Hancock to write letters for him. Excuses and reasons about why he was away and how he'd be working the land once the Trans Line was finished.

He didn't just talk to Hancock, he talked to me, as well. He seemed real friendly. More like a white blackfella, really. Sometimes when the three of us were together, I'd show off. I wasn't big, but I was strong and good with an axe. I'd say to Hancock and Davy, 'I'll drop this big tree with my axe before you even get back to camp'. Camp was about twenty feet away. They'd laugh and walk off, but I always did it. I wasn't afraid of work.

Towards the end of three years with Hancock, I could see I wasn't getting anywhere. The hut was built by then, but I was still just getting me tucker, no money. I wasn't going nowhere. 'Hancock', I said to him one day, 'how about paying me that money you owe me?'. He went real quiet and looked at me. The year was 1916, it was the middle of winter and there was a flood on. After a while, he said, 'Marble, you clear that forty acres of land I been wantin' cleared and I'll give you twelve pounds, no more, no less!'.

Now he'd tried to get all sorts of people to clear that land. Nobody could do it. It was covered with big logs and stumps, and with the flood on, it was worth more like one hundred pounds, not twelve pounds! Trouble was, I knew he had me and he knew, too. Where could I go, I had no money, no home. 'Right', I said, 'I'll clear the land for you, as long as you pay me. For three years, I been working for you, breaking my back and you never paid me yet. I got no choice, I got to stick with you or I got nothing.'

I don't think he believed I'd clear the land. He thought he'd have me there three more years, doing his work for him, building his house. He didn't know me. I worked from three hours before sunrise till sunset, clearing and burning. During that time, the flood got worse and the railway line was nearly washed away. Every day, I was soaking wet. My feet were like blocks of ice. Sometimes, the rain drove down so hard I couldn't see in front of me, but I kept going. I wasn't going to give up, it was my only way out. The job took me three weeks. I cleared that land by myself when no other man would, or could.

I showed Hancock the land, then asked him for my money. He couldn't believe I'd done it. He thought he'd beaten me. He didn't give me the money right away, but he kept me waiting, waiting, hoping I'd forget about it. He knew I'd leave soon as he gave me the money. I kept asking him for my pay. In the end, he went to Perth and got the money from the bank. Then, he took out fifteen shillings a week board for the three weeks it had taken me to clear the land.

Despite the flood, 1916 was a good year for most farmers. There'd been drought earlier on, and maize, lucerne and crushed fodder had been imported from Argentina. There was none to be had around Northam.

We couldn't get any from New South Wales, either.

When Micky Farrell heard I'd left Hancock, he offered me work carting two hundred tons of chaff for twenty-five shillings a week. There were two wagons and a steam cutter and fifteen men on the job, but only me doing the carting. I wasn't afraid to work. The work with Micky only lasted two weeks. After that, I was looking for work again. Mr Williams gave me a job harvesting. I got two pounds a week for that. When that job wound up, I didn't know what I was going to do. I just hoped something would turn up. That was when I met up with Davy Jones again. I hadn't seen him for quite a while. He told me he'd finished working on the Trans Line.

'Marble', he said, 'why don't you come and share farming with me. You buy the horses and harness and come and work my land with me.'

'All right, Dave', I said, 'that suits me fine'. I had nothing else to do. I bought the horses and the harness and teamed up with Davy Jones.

He would've been stuck if he hadn't got me. He was a failure. He'd tried cropping his land before, but left it too late. He spent all his time putting in crops for Micky Farrell and Mr Lochlan to earn some money, but by the time he was free to put in his own crop, the season was just about at an end. Of course, the hot weather came. The crop only rose six inches before it was burnt off and that was the end of that.

When I started with Davy, I put in two hundred acres with my team. They were a good team, hard-working animals. As hard as me. I bought their feed and watered them and looked after them real well. That year, we had the best crops in the district. One paddock gave ten bags to the acre, the other seven bags. The lowest yield we got was eighteen bushels to the acre. From then on, we never looked back. All our crops were bumpers, right through till 1923.

Davy Jones became Mr Davy Jones of the Nungarin district. He was independent, now. He didn't have to work for no one. When he was working on the Trans Line, he had a tiny little purse he kept with him in camp. It had all his money in it. Now, he was banking with Lloyds of London. He had money in his pockets and I had money in mine, but not as much. It was his land, but I did all the work. The only thing I owned was the team. My share after harvest was one quarter, Davy got the rest.

I saved all my money, never spent a penny. Pretty soon, I had enough to buy a farm. I bought a nice little farm in Mukinbudin.

I'll never forget Mucka when I first saw it, there was nothing there. A few houses now and then, but nothing more. Later, I had the first truck there and I used to cart water for the townspeople from ten miles out. They didn't even have a pub till years later.

My name was good right through the district. Everyone knew I was a good worker. Later, I had six men working for me, clearing my land. I paid them out of a cheque book. I was the only farmer in the area to have a cheque book. All the other farmers were mortgaged to the bank, they had no say in their crop. They were all jealous of me, a black man, doing better than what they were. When I first bought the farm, they all made fun of me. 'Where are you going to get stock from?' they'd call. 'What would you know about farming?' they'd yell. They thought I knew nothin'. I proved them wrong.

Anyway, before long, I was working my own farm as well as share farming with Davy. Things were going real well for me. One day, Davy came up to me and said, 'Listen Marble, you've got your farm in Mucka now, what about if you just stick to that and I give Bill Bradley a go. You know, the bloke that's working for Hull's. I'd like to share farm with him.'

I didn't know what to say. Davy was my friend. It wasn't that I was thinking about the extra money, it just seemed that Davy didn't want me with him any more, after so long together. Davy was standing there and I kept looking at the ground. In the end, I said, 'All right Dave, if that's what you want to do. I can handle the lot myself, but if that's the way you want it, I can pull out and go home.'

That year, I put in my last crop with Davy. Bill and Mrs Bradley moved in with Davy while the crop was still growing.

Every Sunday, Mrs Bradley would come out and look over the crop. 'Ooh, what a lovely crop, Marble', she would say. She wasn't a bad woman.

One day, she said to Davy, 'Mr Jones, look at them clouds up there, it looks like they could bring a hailstorm'.

'You don't know what you're talking about, woman, we don't get no hailstorms round here', said Davy.

That was Sunday morning. Ten o'clock Sunday night, the rain came, and the thunder and lightning and the hail, as well. The hail took the crop right off. There wasn't one head left, even the trees were stripped bare. They looked dead, standing there with no leaves on.

Davy heard the noise of the hail. It was pitch black outside apart from the lightning. He'd been sitting by the fire when it started, and when the hail came, he didn't even stop to put on a coat. Just lit up the lantern and rushed down to the crop. There he was in the pouring rain, running up and down, in and out, trying to see how many heads were left. All you could see was his lantern bobbing up and down. The lightning flashed once and I saw him. He was soaking wet and he couldn't believe it was really hailing.

I think God must have been looking after me. Something told me to get insured that year. I had never been insured before. I came out with my quarter and Dave got nothing.

Davy's bad luck continued. The next year, he put his own crop in, but forgot to seed with super, and it died off. The following year, Bill

Bradley put the crop in for him, but Davy was in the same position he was in before he joined up with me. He still had no team and had not bothered to buy one, so this meant he had to take off Hull's crop and Micky Farrell's before he could have the use of their team to take off his own crop. He only just made it.

If Davy had've stuck with me, I'd have had his crop off early on and my own as well. No one could work a team the way I could. It was me that gave him his start. I did all the work, he just stood back and collected the money.

By the time the thirties came round and the Depression hit, he wanted me back. I was married by then. I had responsibilities. Davy said, 'You can bring your wife, too, Arthur'.

I was going by my real name, now. I left Marble behind when I left Davy. Now I was Arthur Corunna, farmer of Mukinbudin.

After I left Davy in the twenties, some important things happened to me. In 1925, I went down to Perth. I'd heard that my little sister Daisy was living at Ivanhoe. Ivanhoe was a big house in Claremont on the banks of the Swan River. Daisy was a servant there, living with our father, Howden Drake-Brockman, and his second wife, Alice.

I was keen to see Daisy again. She was my sister, my family. I wanted my little sister Daisy to know she had a brother who was getting on in the world.

I hardly recognised her when I saw her. When they took me from Corunna Downs, she was only a baby, with real white blonde hair, and now, here she was, a grown woman, with black frizzy hair. She was small and pretty, like our mother, Annie. I was sure glad to see her.

When I first called in at Ivanhoe, Mrs Drake-Brockman was out. Later that day, she came home to find me sitting in the kitchen doorway, talking to Daisy, my legs stretched out onto the verandah. You see, I'd finally started to grow. I was a big man. I wasn't small no more.

After seeing Daisy again, I took to visiting her as often as I could. One year, I hired a buggy and pair for two shillings and took her to the Show. We thought we were real grand, travelling along in that thing. I took her to the races and on picnics, everywhere. Daisy loved the horses. Nothing she liked better than seeing those wonderful animals go for their lives round the track. We both loved horses.

Helen Bunda, our cousin, used to come, as well. She was in service with another white family. She did the most beautiful needlework. She was a clever woman with her hands.

I made friends with a chap in Perth, Mr McKenzie. He was a real nice man. He'd lend me his car so I could pick up the girls and take them on outings. I always returned his car safe and sound. He knew he could trust me.

Judith, June and Dick Drake-Brockman were only little, then. I used to give them horsey rides when I was at Ivanhoe and scare them by chasing them round the lawn. Daisy was their nursemaid.

On one of my visits to Ivanhoe, Alice Drake-Brockman gave me a little dog. She told me Foulkes-Taylor had given it to her when he bought Corunna Downs, but she didn't want it. I called him Pixie, after Dudley's son, that was his nickname. I took that little dog with me wherever I went. He was a good little dog. I've always had a tender

201

spot for little creatures like that.

When I saw Daisy again in 1925, it was also the first time I'd seen Howden since I'd run away. I wondered what he'd say to me. I wondered if I'd be welcome. Mrs Drake-Brockman said I could sleep with Daisy in her room. When Howden came home, he came straight to Daisy's room. He knocked on the door and came in and shook me by the hand real hard. He hadn't changed. He looked older, more tired, but apart from that, he was just the same. I was a grown man, too, now. We were both men. 'I'm pleased to see you, Arthur', he said. I didn't know what to say.

After that, whenever I stayed in Perth, I always slept in Daisy's room. At night, we had long talks, catching up on the news. I went and saw a lawyer and made a will, leaving all my earthly goods to Daisy. I wasn't married, then. She was my only family.

Sometimes when I was in Perth, I'd ride on the electric trams. DING! DING! DING! they'd call out and then change back the other way. I wasn't going nowhere in particular, I just loved to listen to that noise.

I went on the trains, too. In those days, you could go from Merredin to Perth for seventeen shillings. From Kununoppin to Perth was the same. I loved riding on the trains. I felt like I was someone important, being able to get on, pay my fare and sit there like a king until I got off at the next stop.

In 1927, I got a letter from Howden. I hadn't seen Daisy for a while. I'd been busy on the farm. The letter asked if I'd like to have Daisy with me. It said they didn't want her no more and they wondered if I could come and get her. Too right, I thought. Nothing I'd like better.

I went over and talked to one of my neighbours. He was a white man, but a good man, young and single. He was well off, too, and I knew he'd treat Daisy right. I asked him if he wanted a wife. He asked who I had in mind. I told him about Daisy and how pretty she was and how hard she worked and what a good wife she'd make. He said, 'Arthur, any sister of yours is all right by me'. I knew I had him, then. I didn't want Daisy just marrying anyone. I wanted someone I could trust, someone who would treat her real nice. She was my family. My little sister.

I finished what I had to do on the farm and was all set to go get Daisy when another letter arrived. It said they'd changed their minds and I couldn't have her after all. I was disappointed, so was the farmer next door.

In December 1927, I heard Daisy had had a baby girl. It was news to me. I wondered, then, if that was why they'd changed their minds. They must have found out she was pregnant. I'd have had her still. I wish she'd come to me, baby and all. I love kids.

Early in 1928, Howden died. He'd been a sick man for some time. Personally, I think he left his heart in Corunna. Howden saw Daisy's baby before he died. They called her Gladys. He held her in his arms and said, 'She's very beautiful'. She was one of the most beautiful babies I'd ever seen.

Shortly before his death, Howden mailed me a whole pile of photos that had been taken on Corunna Downs. I guess Howden figured no one else would want old pictures. That was why he sent them to me. It was the only thing he ever gave me.

Apart from Daisy, the other thing I discovered in the twenties was boxing. Actually, boxing and wrestling. I was good at both, but I didn't know it till then. When I was a kid, old Fred Stream learned me a bit. He knew they were going to send me to the mission and he reckoned if I didn't learn something, I'd get a hiding.

I was a farmer, I wasn't trained for fighting, but one punch from me and I could flatten them. I used to know Riley. His son was a referee and he had a boxing and wrestling tent. He used to travel all round Perth and up the Nor'west.

Riley said, 'If I trained you, I reckon you'd be middleweight champion of the world'. They always let me in the Show free because they knew I was a good fighter. I didn't want to be a boxer.

Whenever the Shows came round Nungarin, I'd put in for the boxing and wrestling. Sometimes, they were too scared to take me on. I remember one bloke took a long look at me and then said, 'I'm not taking you on, mate. I seen a bloke look like you once before. He gave me a terrible time.' I missed out, that year.

One year in the late twenties, the hotel manager from Mucka said, 'Arthur, you want to take my beer on your truck into the Show and sell it for me?'. I was one of the few men who had a truck in the district. I thought, why not? I loaded up the truck, threw a tarp over the grog and drove to Nungarin. I spent the night in the hotel there. Everything was booked up to the pub in Mucka, my board and tucker. I was a white man, then, not black. It was a king's life.

Once inside the Show, I sold the beer from the truck, and all the time, I could hear these men, singing out, singing out. They were boxers and wrestlers and they were singing out for men to come and challenge them. When all the beer was sold, I thought, I'll have a go. I walked over, put my hand up and yelled, 'Hey! Over here, I'll have a go!'

While I was standing there, a bloke came up to me and pushed me on the shoulder. He was one of the trainers. I'd seen him before. 'You can't wrestle, mate', he said. I just grabbed him, clothes and all. Lifted him up and dropped him. Pinned him to the dirt. 'What do you think of yourself now, mate?' I said. 'WHO can't wrestle??' He went for his life, dirt all over him. The men in the ring had seen what happened and they wouldn't take me on after that. I looked too tough.

There was a boxer I remember well, Jack Yakem. He was white and he fought in the Royal Show, everywhere. He lived for fighting. He used to stick out his chest and strut round the ring like a rooster round the hens and yell out, 'My name's Jack Yakem! I CRACK'em, you STACK'em.' Everyone was scared of him. Anyway, he was the same weight as me and I thought, Arthur . . . have a go.

When they let me into the ring, the crowd was full round us, urging us on, calling out. They all wanted to see me get beat. Jack didn't waste no time. He started pummelling me in the ribs with his fists.

After a few minutes, I thought, I've had enough of this. I hit him fair over the earhole and dropped him right there. He went flying, flat to the ground. The crowd roared.

Anyhow, he got up and I dropped him again. Eleven times I dropped him, quick with my fists. He never knew when I was going to hit him! I'd drop him, then wait for him to get up, then drop him again!

I won that fight, but they never gave me any money. It was always the same. Later when I got home, I took my singlet off, I was black and blue all round my ribs where he'd pummelled me. I don't know what colour he was.

I was a hard nut to crack, when I was young. My life was full of sport.

When I was young, I had girls runnin' after me all the time. I was a good catch and they all wanted me. Trouble is, I was like my old grandfather, tender-hearted. I wouldn't go with any girl, because if I got her into trouble, I'd have to marry her. Other blokes were different. They'd take a girl out, get her into trouble and then let her go. Have another one and let them go. I ain't got no stock like that. I saw to it that I didn't. Only my own, what I'm going to have, that's how I am.

In the old days, you were nobody unless you were somebody important. And when they announced your engagement, they took your photo and everything and put it in the paper. I was worried about that. I thought to myself, when I get engaged, what can I say? Who could I say I was and who was my father? I decided I'd trick them all, if they ask me, I'd say, 'Well, my father is Mr Corunna from Corunna Downs Station'. That's what I would put in the paper and no one would know any better. No one would know about Howden and Annie and how they wasn't married white man's way. You see, they were very particular about such things in those days.

There were times when I could have protected myself through the name of Brockman, but I never did. Howden never gave me nothin'. I've only got one good father and he's in heaven. No matter which way the wind's blowin', he's there with you.

Before I married my wife, Adeline, she came to me and said, 'Arthur, I've seen a fortune teller and she told me I'm going to marry you. She also told me what your life will be like and that, one day, somebody will rob you of your farm.'

I said, 'Nobody's goin' to rob me. They'll get this fist if they try!' I was gettin' on in years, about thirty-five, and I'd been thinkin' I should marry, but when Adeline said that, I thought, better not get married or I'll be losin' my farm.

Still, I couldn't stay single for ever, so I thought the only fair way was to put all the girls' names in a hat. I figured the name that I picked out would be my wife. Me and my mates put all the girls' names we knew into an old felt hat. I thought, well, Helen Bunda's name could come out. She was my cousin and her name was in there. I wanted a small girl, not a big woman. Someone like my mother.

One of my mates held the hat up and I picked out a slip. On it was written Adeline Wilks!

'That can't be the one', I said, 'she's plump. Let me have another go.'

We mixed the papers round real good, they held up the hat and I chose another one, Adeline Wilks again.

'Those papers ain't mixed up right', I said, 'give me one more go'. This time, we gave those papers a mixin' they'll never forget. They held up the hat once more.

'Last time', I said. I closed my eyes, put my hand in and pulled out a slip, Adeline Wilks! I gave up.

'Well, if she's the one I got to have, so be it', I said. I think the spirit of her people must have chosen her for me.

We were married in the early thirties in Perth in St Marys Cathedral by Bishop Prindiville. She was a Catholic and I was an Anglican. I agreed to bring up the little ones as Catholics. It didn't seem important, all one God, after all.

Shortly after we were married, I was out in the paddock, diggin' roots. It was a hot day, the sweat was pourin' off me. Anyhow, I was diggin' away, diggin' away, when, suddenly, I was struck blind. I closed my eyes and opened them, but I couldn't see nothin'. I closed my eyes real tight and opened them again, but I still couldn't see. I could feel my hand on my face, but I couldn't see it. I sat down and closed my eyes and stayed there for a while, real still like.

That's when I knew Annie was dead. My poor old mother who I hadn't seen since they took me away was dead. I stood up and opened my eyes, I could see again, but Annie was dead. She was so small and pretty, I wish I'd seen her again, just one more time.

The first farm I had in Muckinbudin was hard work. My house was only a bit of tin. I had to cut great big sleepers on drums with a handsaw for the roof. No electricity or water. We had to go over the line if we wanted water.

Men teased me when I bought the farm, they didn't want a blackfella movin' in.

'Where you gunna get stock', they said. I just ignored them. When I should have had sheep, they wouldn't give me any, because my colour wasn't right. Everybody else got them, not me.

I was on my own, a black man with no one to help him. I done all the fencing myself, bought everything, the dam, too. Paid money to men to clear land. I chopped all the fence posts, dug out the holes and, when there was nothing else to do, helped clear the land. I made sure I owed no one, I didn't want no mortgage. You mortgage a place and you're beat. They've got you then, just over a lousy little bit of money.

After I'd improved the farm, a bloke wanted to buy it. Jack Edwards was his name. He already had other farms and he wanted mine as well. You see, the white man gets greedy, he wants to take everything.

We sold the farm bare for four thousand pounds. He told me he wanted to rent it for so many years till he got his money together. So he gave me four hundred pounds the first year and said he couldn't give me any more till he'd made some more money out of my farm so he could pay for it. There was no stipulation in our agreement that my horses and machinery went with the land, but soon I found he was takin' my horses and machinery and workin' his other farms with them as well as mine.

He had big ideas and big ways. He put in one season and had a good crop, but the following year, the Depression hit and he said he couldn't go through with the sale.

I said, 'Well, Jack, if you can't go through with it, you replace everything on the farm the same as you got it, the horses in the same quantity, the machinery in good gear, collars and harness and everything'. He done all that, but two horses he never replaced, I let him off on that.

With the Depression, the price of wheat fell to ten shillings a bushel and then to five shillings. I had two boys, Arthur and Manfred, by then, and in 1934, my third son, Albert, was born. My crop yielded eight bags to the acre that year, but, at five bob a bushel, it didn't amount to much. All we got out of it was a pram for Albert.

In 1936, my daughter, Norma, was born and life was real hard. I'd do anything to make a few bob then, anything to keep my wife and family. I picked roots at a shilling an acre, I cleared five hundred acres of mallees* for seven pounds. I burnt mallees for charcoal to sell to gas producers. By gee, some men were mean, then, they'd pinch my roots and my charcoal. I was doin' the work and they was gettin' the profits.

Ever since the Depression, I've voted Labor. When the Labor Government got into power, we got another two shillings a bushel.

It was during this time that I owed money on my header**. I was the first farmer in the distrct to have a truck and the first to buy a header. My header came down by train. Tug Wilson, who ran the post office at Mucka and was also an agent for Wesfarmers, took a photo of it. I was makin' history, you see.

I think I must have been somethin' out of the ordinary, to be a

---

* *mallee* — various Australian species of *Eucalyptus*, having a number of almost unbranched stems arising from a large underground root stock. Found mainly in semi-arid regions. Also, an area of scrub land where the predominant species of plant is mallee.

** *header* — a form of reaping machine which cuts off and gathers only the head of a grain crop.

black man ahead of everybody else.

Anyway, Wesfarmers summonsed me over the header. When Wesfarmers first started, I bought me bags, me super, everything, off Wesfarmers and I paid them every time. It was little men like me that made Wesfarmers, I even had one of their men come and service my machinery, and now they were summonsing me over the header.

First, a policeman came and said, 'We've got to sell you up!'.

'Oh yeah', I said, 'what are you goin' to sell'.

'All your goods and chattels', he said.

I laughed. 'You needn't worry about that', I said, 'I got no goods and chattels!'.

Anyway, when the summons came, I went down to Perth to see a lawyer who came from Bunbury, Howard Barth. He rang Wesfarmers and said, 'Believe you're takin' Corunna on about the debt he has. You want to fight him, you have to push it through me!'

I could have stuck to the header, if I'd wanted. I had a good crop and was goin' to use it to take it off. In the end, I said, 'Take the rubbish of a thing away!'. I'd never had any debt with them before, I'd always paid my way. The one time I'm short and they won't help me.

Later on during the Depression, the Agricultural Bank served a summons on me for owin' them one thousand three hundred pounds, I'd had to mortgage my farm with them to get by. They sold up everything, all my machinery, except my horses. I had nowhere to keep them, they were strayin' everywhere and the bloke who'd taken on my farm said he was goin' to shoot them if I didn't take care of them. I had to round them up and sold them for three pounds a head to be shot for pig feed. Can you tell me that was fair, for all my pioneering days, to be treated like that?

The Depression didn't do no favours for my neighbour who'd had four farms, either. He had to sell up, he left the district for good. I had to take my family and start again on new, uncleared land. It's hard for the black man to get ahead. Struggling under all disabilities, I went on in hardship on my new land.

My neighbours in Mucka were a mixed bag, some good, some very bad. There was a man that give me a lot of trouble, he was mean, he didn't like blacks. He's dead and gone now, God finished him. That man used to shoot my horses and pigs.

One day, he was in town and he said to one of my neighbours, 'Have you managed to get Arthur off his farm, yet?'. He went on and on, talkin' to my neighbour about how two white men can easily get rid of one black man. My neighbour never said a word, he just let him ramble on, then he said, 'You're talkin' to the wrong bloke. I don't want Arthur off his farm.'

You see, he thought he was going to turn this man against me, but this man was my friend. I'd helped him when things went wrong. When he was in hospital, I'd helped cut his hay and shear his sheep. He was my mate. Whenever I wanted a wagon or anything, he'd say, 'Take what you like, Arthur'. If I wanted hay, he'd give it to me. Later, he married and moved to Arthur River. He took all his cows and his wife and family and moved on. His name was William Arthur Bird and he was a good man.

Now, you take the bloke opposite. He was the one that give me all the trouble. He was only livin' on what he could steal off me. He was the one bad egg in the nest. He was mean. He was the only man I knew who spent a penny and saved a shilling.

He put a fence right round the lake so he could steal my sheep. Got his son to lift up the bottom fence at the bottom dam and mix my sheep with his. I lost a lot of sheep that way. He used to have meetings at his place, tryin' to be a big shot, sayin' he was the first man with Corriedale sheep. In the end, he had no Merino at all, only Corriedale, my Corriedale!

When the sheep came back to my land, he summonsed me. I had no earmark on my sheep, only a woolbrand. He put his own earmark on my sheep and then accused me of stealin' them. The police came out and saw my Corriedale sheep runnin' back to me.

I went down to Perth and saw a lawyer. When I told him what was going on, he said, 'You let me handle this'. While I was sittin' there, he rang the police.

'What's this I hear about Corunna being accused of stealing sheep?' he said.

I don't know what the policeman said, I couldn't hear, but my lawyer replied, 'You speak to me like that again, man, and I'll have you in gaol! Any further action on this has to go through me, I'm Corunna's lawyer. We're going to fight you on this!'

After that, they dropped the case against me. They knew they couldn't win. I wasn't stealin' those sheep, they was just comin' home.

I never did nothin' mean to the men who robbed me. You got to leave God to do His own work.

No one could ever rightly accuse me of stealin', because everything I got I paid for. I didn't want no one sayin' to me, 'You in debt, we got to sell you up!'. You see, they'll get you if they can. They'll follow you to the last ditch, even the government. You got to be a blackfella to know what the pressure is from the government.

They never even treated the blackfellas right during the war. I heard of this native bloke, he went and fought for the country overseas, when he came back he still wasn't a citizen, he had to get an exemption certificate. And he wasn't even allowed to vote. That's the white man's justice for you. You see, the black man remembers these things. The black man's got a long memory.

They took a lot of natives away to Palm Flats, Moore River, during the war, old ones and all. Neville* was still the Protector of Aborigines. Any blackfella that had dealings with Neville got no good word to say about him. He wasn't protectin' the Aborigines, he was destroyin' them!

These poor blackfellas they took away had to live in a compound with soldiers around them. They took natives from Nungarin and the goldfields, too. The young girls would say to the soldiers, 'Why you worried about us for, we not your enemies, Australia's our country'. The soldiers couldn't do anything, it was their business to keep them there. So in the end, the girls made love to the soldiers and got away.

Anyone who escaped, they sent trackers after them. They'd catch them, beat them up and put them back in gaol. Our own country and we not free. They didn't let no one out till the end of the war.

I don't know why they didn't lock me up, too. Maybe they didn't think of me as a real blackfella. They seemed to go for the real dark ones, the ones out of work and battlin' for a livin'. The real bushies, too. I heard a rumour that they were worried the Japanese would get hold of the bushies and the bushies would lead them through the interior. I'd be no good to them. I'd be lost myself, probably.

Aah, it seems funny, lookin' back now. Mucka was a good place to live in the old days. People were more friendly, they needed each other. The black man was workin' for the farmers, gettin' paid in tea, flour and sugar. Blackfellas cleared the land, put crops in, pulled sandalwood. I remember the lake country used to be full of dingoes, the blackfellas used to track them, hunt them down. Aah yes, no one can say the blackfella didn't do his share of work in Mucka. They helped make it what it is today, I hope they won't be forgotten.

---

* *Neville* — Mr A.O. Neville, Chief Protector of Natives, Western Australia, 1915-1940. Widely credited as a principal advocate and force behind an active policy of miscegenation in Western Australia through the 1930s. The legal removal of 'half-caste' Aboriginal children from their mothers was part of this policy.

Well, I'd like to finish my story there. That's the important part. I been livin' in Mucka for years now. I got my children all growed up and my farm is comin' along real nice. I still put a crop in and I got my pigs and there's plenty of the wildlife on my place. The wildlife always got a home with me.

I wish I could give advice for the young blackfellas of today, but I can't. Each man has to find his own way.

You see, the trouble is that colonialism isn't over yet. We still have a White Australia policy against the Aborigines. Aah, it's always been the same. They say there's been no difference between black and white, we all Australian, that's a lie. I tell you, the black man has nothin', the government's been robbin' him blind for years.

There's so much the whitefellas don't understand. They want us to be assimilated into the white, but we don't want to be. They complain about our land rights, but they don't understand the way we want to live. They say we shouldn't get the land, but the white man's had land rights since this country was invaded, our land rights. Most of the land the Aborigine wants, no white man would touch. The government is like a big dog with a bone with no meat on it. They don't want to live on that land themselves, but they don't want the black man to get it, either. Yet, you find somethin' valuable on the land the Aborigine has got and whites are all there with their hands out.

Those Aborigines in the desert, they don't want to live like the white man, owin' this and owin' that. They just want to live their life free, they don't need the white man's law, they got their own. If they want water in the Gibson Desert, they do a rainsong and fill up the places they want. If it's cold, they can bring the warm weather like the wind. They don't need the white man to put them in gaol, they can do their own punishment. They don't have to hunt too hard, the spirits can bring birds to them. Say they want a wild turkey, that turkey will come along, go past them and they can spear it. Kangaroo, too. They don't kill unless they hungry, the white man's the one who kills for sport. Aah, there's so much they don't understand.

Now, if I had been born a white man, my life would have been different. I'd have had an education the proper way, without the whipping. As it is, I got to take my papers to someone who's educated

212

to get me through. Some things aren't understandable to me. Now I got some of my grandchildren educated, they help me. If I'd have been a wealthy farmer, I'd have given all my kids a real good education.

I'm a great grandfather now and proud of it. Only thing is, Daisy beats me there, she's got more great grandchildren than me. I got to catch up with her. I'm proud of my kids, I'm proud of my whole family. Daisy's family and my family, we special, I got healing powers, but Daisy's got them stronger than me. You see, it runs in our family. The spirit is strong in our family. When I die, someone will get my powers. I don't know who. They have to have a good heart, and live a simple life. Otherwise, you're a motor without petrol. Your power comes from above. You can't cure yourself. You got to use that power to help others.

I'm at the end of my story now. To live to ninety, that's an achievement. I haven't really felt the effect of old age, though, of course, the visibility's gone away a bit, but me mind is not so bad. I've had everything a man could want, really. A little bit of sport and a little bit of music. I'm an entertainer. You take me anywhere and I'll join in, could be playing the mouth organ or anything. I'll give it a go. Everybody liked me, that's what beat me, even some of the men I worked for.

Now my life is nearly over, I'm lookin' forward to heaven. I'll have a better time up there. I'll be a little angel, flyin' around, lookin' after stars and planets, doin' the spring cleaning. God is the only friend we got. God the father, God the son and God the Holy Spirit. You stick to Him, He's the only one. Don't listen to what others tell you about God, He's the best mate a man could have. You don't have Him, you don't have no friend at all. You look away from God, you go to ruin.

Take the white people in Australia, they brought the religion here with them and the Commandment, Thou Shalt Not Steal, and yet they stole this country. They took it from the innocent. You see, they twisted the religion. That's not the way it's supposed to be.

I look back on my life and think how lucky I am. I'm an old fella now and I got one of my granddaughters lookin' after me. That's something, these days. And I got Daisy's granddaughter writin' my story. I been tryin' to get someone to write it for years, now I'm glad I didn't. It should be someone in the family, like. It's fittin'.

I got no desires for myself any more. I want to get my land fixed up so my children can get it and I want my story finished. I want everyone to read it. Arthur Corunna's story! I might be famous. You see, it's important, because then maybe they'll understand how hard it's been for the blackfella to live the way he wants. I'm part of history, that's how I look on it. Some people read history, don't they?

213

Chapter Twenty-Seven

WHERE TO NEXT?

'It's a wonderful story.' Mum had tears in her eyes when she finished reading Arthur's story.

Like me, Mum now felt that at last we had something from the past to hang on to. And, for Mum in particular, there was something to be proud of.

However, in an odd way, we also experienced a sense of loss. We were suddenly much more aware of how little we knew about Nan and about the history and experiences of our own family. We were now desperate to learn more, but there appeared to be few obvious leads left.

After much thought, I decided that our best course was to return to Nan and Arthur's birthplace, Corunna Downs.

Paul thought this was a wonderful idea, he loved the North and he also could see no other way forward for us. He hoped we could persuade Nan to go with us.

When I told Mum about the idea, she wasn't very positive.

'You can't go up there. It's a silly idea, you don't know anyone. Nan won't want you to go.'

'Nan doesn't want me to do anything! All my leads have dried up, Mum, that's all there is left, now.'

When I approached Nan about the idea of going up North, she was disgusted.

'You're like your mother, you like to throw money away. All you'll be lookin' at is dirt. Dirt and scrub.'

I ignored her and said, 'Why don't you come with me? You might meet some of your old mates up there.'

'Haa!' she laughed and shook her head in disbelief, 'I'm too old. Too old to go bush now. You think I got young legs? Look at them!'

'They look all right to me, Nan. They've been holding you up for over seventy years, no reason to think they'll give out on you now. Besides, you'll be in the car most of the time.'

'I don't like cars and I'm too old to go bush. It's a waste of money, you're chasin' the wind. You go up there and the cyclone'll get you.'

Just then, Mum entered the fray. All this time, she'd been quietly observing Nan's reaction.

'Nan's right, Sally', she said, much to Nan's surprise. 'You shouldn't spend that money just to look at dirt. What will it achieve? There's no one up there we know. What are you going to do, anyway, walk up to strangers in the street and ask them if they knew Daisy or Arthur Corunna?'

'Yep', I replied. 'I'll take my tape recorder, who knows what we will find out.' Mum's face changed from disbelief to laughter in a matter of seconds.

'You're really determined to do this, aren't you?' she said in a rather hoarse voice.

'You know me, Mum.'

'You know', Mum said wistfully, 'I've always had a hankering to go North'.

'Who said anything about taking you? I mean, all you'd be doing is looking at dirt. You don't want to go two thousand kilometres for that.'

'You're not leaving me here?!'

'I don't want to be dragging a reluctant mother around', I said. 'No, it wouldn't work. You stay here with Nan. I'll go with Paul and the kids.'

'I'm coming and that's that!' she said.

Nan suddenly interrupted. 'You two, you're both nuts! You, Glad, you're like the wind, you blow here and you blow there. You got no mind of your own!'

'Well, Nan, maybe Mum'll chase the cyclones away!'

Over the following few weeks, I made arrangements for our trip. We decided to go in the May school holidays, that way the children could come and Paul, who was a teacher, could do most of the driving. As the weeks passed, Mum became more and more excited.

'Maybe we will learn something', she said one afternoon as we pored over a map of Western Australia.

'Of course we will, and even if we don't, it's a good holiday.'

'What are you hoping to find at Corunna?'

'Oh, I don't know.' I felt awkward talking about why I wanted to see Corunna, even with Mum. 'I guess I want to see if there are any of the old buildings left. Buildings that might have been there in Nan's day. And I want to look at the land. I want to walk on it. I know that sounds silly, but I want to be there, and imagine what it was like for the people then.'

Mum nodded, there were tears in her eyes. I tended to cover up my feelings with a rather brusque manner, Mum used humour to hide hers. We'd both been very emotional lately.

After a few minutes, Mum said, 'What if they won't let us on the station? We don't know who owns it now, they mightn't like strangers going out there.'

'Well, I'll ring and arrange it before we leave Perth.'

'You mean you'll ring the people on Corunna?' Mum said in surprise. 'You can't ring up someone you don't know!'

'Can you think of something better? I'll just introduce myself and explain why we'd like to come out.'

'Ooh, I couldn't do that. I don't think you should, either, maybe we should forget it.'

'No way, I'm not asking you to do it, I'll do it. It's important to you to see the old place, isn't it, Mum?'

'Yes, very important.'

'Then we'll do it.'

As the time for us to leave drew near, Nan became more and more outspoken in her opposition. Apart from threatening us with cyclones, flooded rivers and crocodiles, she tried to convince us that, while we were away, something terrible would happen to her.

'There'll be no one to look after me. It's no use saying the others will check on me, because they won't. Anything could happen to me, I could pass out in the toilet and no one would know.'

'Now, Nan, don't be silly', Mum coaxed. 'You'll have Beryl here.' Beryl was a friend of Mum's and had looked after Nan before. 'And Jill and Bill will both be calling in several times during the week. And David and Helen will be able to see you on the weekends. I'm leaving you plenty of money, if you need anything, Beryl will get it up at the shop.'

'You know my heart's not too good, Gladdie, you'll be sorry if you go away and I die.'

'You've been dying ever since I've known you', Mum said firmly. Nan, sensing that, for once, Mum was not going to be moved, shuffled off with her hand over her supposedly weak heart.

True to form, Nan began developing aches and pains the following week, along with other vague symptoms. One morning, she stayed in bed.

'I think this is the beginning of something serious', she muttered when Mum took her in her breakfast. Poor Mum couldn't help feeling sympathetic, Nan looked so old and, in Mum's mind, really sick.

'I think it's genuine, this time', she told me despairingly the following evening. 'I think she really has got something wrong with her.'

'Have you called the doctor?'

'Of course I haven't!'

'You can't make a proper diagnosis without calling the doctor. If she's faking, she'll recover quick smart, and if she's really sick, she should have a doctor look at her.'

'But she always gets so upset when I talk about getting the doctor

216

in.'

'And she knows you won't call her bluff. Look Mum, how many years has Nan been having these convenient illnesses? Every time you want to go away, she gets sick. Now listen, if she's really sick this time, then, of course, you can't leave her. But do you want to miss out on going North just because of a fake illness?'

'Of course I don't. You're right, I've never been firm with her.'

When Mum returned home that night, she told Nan that, if she wasn't better in the morning, she was going to call the doctor. Nan was silent.

'You can't go on like this, dear', Mum said. 'I'm very worried about you, you're the only mother I've got and I've got to take good care of you. It's no use me going with Sally when you're sick. I'd never forgive myself if something happened to you. If the doctor says it's serious, then I'll stay here and look after you. I just hope they won't put you in hospital, that's all.'

'Are you really going to call the doctor, Glad?' Nan croaked shakily. 'I'm sure I only need rest.'

'You might need medicine, antibiotics or something like that. It's the only way. Now, you snuggle down and I'll bring you in a cup of tea.'

'Don't bother', Nan pouted. 'I've already had one. I'd be lyin' here thirsty all night if it was up to you.'

'I was only away half an hour and, besides, you said you were too weak to get out of bed.'

'I am weak. I had to force myself. Oh, go away and leave me alone, I need my sleep. You always come and bother me when I'm tryin' to sleep.'

Nan's recovery had begun.

Over the next week, we organised the last details of our trip. We obtained a video camera to film the trip so that we could show Nan and my brothers and sisters when we returned.

Amber and Blaze were terribly excited. Zeke was only six weeks old, the only thing that excited him was milk. The children were convinced that going North was as adventurous as exploring deepest, darkest Africa. Nan had convinced them that they'd encounter giant snakes and huge crocodiles every step of the way. Blaze had a bit of rope packed in his bag, he wanted to catch a pet.

For a long time now, I'd been continually reminding Mum that she could only take a minimum of luggage. We were driving up in a small self-contained campervan and we needed every inch of space.

But the night before we were due to leave, Mum arrived with a station wagon full of gear. Amber and Blaze laughed and laughed when they saw her drive in. Paul failed to see the funny side. He just put his head in his hands, muttered, 'I can't believe it', and assigned me the task of sorting through it all.

Despite strenuous objections, as we hauled everything from the back of her car, I began to make two piles, one for necessities, the other for luxuries. I tossed the pick, shovel and bucket on the unwanted pile. I was sure Mum would have no luck hunting for gold with that lot. Also on this pile went the shotgun that didn't shoot, two eiderdowns, a sack of potatoes and two suitcases of clothes. Mum had bought an outfit for every occasion imaginable. We realised then that her definition of roughing it was very different to ours. We decided to take the case of apples and the cartons of Deb Instant Mashed Potato, as well as the boxes of dehydrated peas and corn. It seemed a waste not to use them, though we did wonder how on earth we could eat our way through so much.

By late that evening, we'd finished packing. Mum decided to sleep in the van, just in case anyone pinched it. Paul grinned hopefully when she mentioned this possibility.

Five o'clock the following morning, we were on our way.

Chapter Twenty-Eight

RETURN TO CORUNNA

By the time we arrived in Port Hedland, we were eager to begin our investigations. We'd been told to look up an older gentleman by the name of Jack, as he knew a lot of people in the area and might be able to help us.

As soon as we saw Jack, we liked him. He was very friendly. I explained who we were, why we'd come to see him and asked if he could tell us anything about the Brockman or Corunna families. We were amazed when he told us that Albert Brockman had been his good friend and that they'd worked together for many years.

'Jiggawarra, that's his Aboriginal name, that's what we all call him up here. Now, he had a brother and a sister that were taken away. They never came back. I think the brother was called Arthur.'

'That's right!' I added excitedly, 'and the sister was called Daisy, that's my grandmother'.

'Well, I'll be', he said, with tears in his eyes. 'So you've come back! There's not many come back. I don't think some of them are interested. Fancy, you comin' back after all these years.'

'Are we related to you, then?'

'Well, now, which way do you go by, the blackfella's way or the white man's way?'

'The blackfella's way.'

'Then I'm your grandfather', he said 'and your mother would be my nuba*, that means I can marry her'. Mum laughed. We felt excited at discovering even that.

Jack went on to explain that he was, in fact, Nanna's cousin and that his mother's sister had been on Corunna in the very early days and had married one of the people from Corunna.

'I could have been there myself as a young baby', he added, 'but that's too far back to remember. I was born in 1903 and worked on

---

* *nuba* — a person who is in the correct tribal relationship to another person for the purpose of marriage.

Corunna from 1924 onwards. Foulkes-Taylor owned it then. They was a real good mob, that Corunna lot, but, slowly, they started drifting away. They didn't like the boss.'

'What about Lily?' Mum asked, 'did you know her?'. Lily was Nan and Arthur's half-sister.

'Lily? I'd forgotten about her. Oh yes, I knew Lily, she was a good mate of mine. So was her bloke, Big Eadie. He was a Corunna man, too. Aah, we used to have a lot of corroborees in those days. We'd all get together and have a good old corroboree. I can't explain to you how it made us feel inside. I loved the singing, sometimes we'd get a song and it'd last for days. Lily was a good singer, you could hear her voice singin' out high above the others. All those people are gone now. I suppose Arthur and Daisy are dead, too?'

'Arthur is, but my mother is still alive', replied Mum.

Jack was very moved. 'Why didn't you bring her with you?'

'We tried', I replied 'but she reckoned she was too old to come North. Said her legs wouldn't hold her up.'

Jack laughed. 'That's one thing about mulbas*', he said, 'they can find an excuse for anything! She's one of the last old ones, you know. Gee, I'd like to meet her!'

'Maybe she'll come next time', I said hopefully. 'Did Lily have any children, Jack?'

'No. She wanted to. She was good with kids. Looked after plenty of kids in her time. She could turn her hand to anything, that woman. How many kids did Daisy have?'

'Only me', Mum said sadly. 'I'd love to have come from a big family.'

'Ooh, you ask around', Jack laughed, 'you'll soon have so many relatives you won't know what to do with them. You'd be related to a lot up here.'

'Really?'

'Too right. You might be sorry you come!'

'There was another sister', I interrupted, 'I think she was full blood, but died young, her name was Rosie'.

'That'd be right. A lot of full bloods died young in those days.'

'I can't believe we've met you', I sighed. 'All these people have just been names to us, talking to you makes them real. We didn't think anyone would remember.'

'Aah, mulbas have got long memories. Most around here remember the kids that were taken away. I should have been taken myself, only the policeman took me in after my mother died. Then he farmed me out to other people so I was able to stay in the area.'

'I suppose it wasn't often that happened.'

'No. I was one of the lucky ones.'

---

* *Mulbas* — the Aboriginal people of the Port Hedland/Marble Bar area of Western Australia. (Derived from man or person.)

'Did you know a bloke called Maltese Sam?' Mum asked.

'Oh yeah, he's dead now.'

'Could he have been my mother's father?'

'No, no, not him. I couldn't tell you who her father was. Maybe the station-owner. There's plenty of pastoralists got black kids runnin' around.'

I asked Jack if there was anyone else we should talk to.

'You fellas go and see Elsie Brockman, she's your relation, Albert's wife.'

'Are you sure?' Mum asked in astonishment, 'I thought they'd all be dead by now'.

'Oh, Albert's been gone a while, but Elsie's still here. Only be as young as you', he said to Mum. 'Then there's a big mob in Marble Bar you should see, and Tommy Stream in Nullagine. Any of you fellas speak the language?'

'No', I replied, 'but Arthur could and Daisy can. They wouldn't teach us.'

'Shame! There's mulbas here know their language and won't speak it. I'm not ashamed of my language. I speak it anywhere, even in front of white people.'

'Do you speak the same language as my mother?' Mum asked.

'I speak four languages. Light and heavy Naml, Balgoo and Nungamarda and Nybali. Your mother's language would be Balgoo, but she would speak Naml, too. All those old ones from Corunna spoke both. Those two languages are very similar.'

Mum and I exchanged glances. We were going to tackle Nan about that when we got home.

'You mob sure your granny never came back?'

'Not that we know of, why?'

'Well, I recall meeting a Daisy in '23. I was workin' between Hillside and Corunna at the time. Never seen her before. It was like she appeared outa nowhere. Took her from Hillside to stay at Corunna. She had family there she wanted to visit. Half-caste she was, pretty, too. She was pregnant, baby must have been near due.'

'I don't think it'd be her', I replied.

'Well, I just wondered.'

I was wondering, too.

It was all too much. Our heads were spinning, we seemed to be inundated with new information. The children were becoming restless, so Paul suggested that we go and have some lunch and talk over what to do. We said goodbye to Jack. It seemed awful, leaving him so soon. We'd only just met and we really liked him. We promised to call back in if we had the opportunity.

Over lunch, we talked about Elsie Brockman. Mum and I both felt it was probably a different person. We reasoned that, as Uncle Albert had been the oldest and quite a bit older than Nan, it would be unlikely for his wife to only be in her fifties. It would have made her, at the very least, thirty years younger than Albert. We decided to go to Marble Bar, instead.

Fortunately for us, we arrived in Marble Bar on pension day. This meant that most of the people were around town somewhere.

A group of old men were sitting patiently under a tall, shady tree in the main street, waiting for the mail to arrive. We parked nearby and walked over and introduced ourselves. Jack had told us to ask for Roy.

'We're looking for Roy', I said.

'I'm him', replied an elderly man with a snow-white beard, 'what do you want?'.

'Gidday', I smiled and held out my hand. 'I'm Sally and this is Paul and my mother, Gladys.' We shook hands all round. 'We're trying to trace our relatives', I explained, 'they came from Corunna, went by the names of Brockman or Corunna. We heard you worked on Corunna.'

'Not me! I worked on Roy Hill and Hillside, but you'd be related to Jiggawarra, wouldn't you? I worked with him on Hillside, he built the homestead there, a good carpenter. A good man.'

Another older man interrupted. 'Who are these people?' he obviously asked in his own language.

'Brockman people', Roy replied.

'Oh yes', the other smiled, 'your mob's from Corunna. You'd be related to most of the people round here, one way or another.'

'You lookin' for your mob now?' another asked kindly.

'Yes', I replied. 'My grandmother was taken from here many years ago.'

'That's right', he agreed, 'hundreds of kids gone from here. Most never come back. We think maybe some of them don't want to come home. Some of those light ones, they don't want to own us dark ones.'

'I saw picture about you lot on TV', chipped in another. 'It was real sad. People like you, wanderin' around, not knowin' where you come from. Light coloured ones wanderin' around, not knowin' they black underneath. Good on you for comin' back, I wish you the best.'

'Thank you', I smiled, 'we are like those people on TV. We're up here trying to sort ourselves out.' Then, turning back to Roy, I said, 'Did you know Lily, Roy?'.

'What do you want to know for?'

'She's my Aunty', Mum said proudly.

Roy was taken aback for a minute. 'That's right, I forgot about that.'

'Go on, Roy, tell them about Lily', the others teased.

Roy shook his head. 'I'm not sayin' nothin'. I'm not sayin' a word about Lily.' The other men chuckled. Lily was now a closed topic of conversation.

'What about Maltese Sam?' I asked.

'Maltese? He's finished with this world now.'

'I was told he was my grandmother's father, you know, the father of Jiggawarra's sister.'

'No, no, that's not right', said Roy.

'You got that wrong', others chorused, 'who told you that?'.

'Oh, just someone I know in Perth.'

'How would they know, they not livin' here', replied another. 'We all knew Maltese, it's not him, be the wrong age.'

'Do any of you know who her father might have been?' I asked quietly.

There was silence while they all thought, then Roy said, 'Well, she was half-caste, wasn't she?'.

'Yes.'

'Then it must have been a white man. Could have been the station-owner. Plenty of black kids belong to them, but they don't own them.'

Just then, we were interrupted by a lady in her fifties. 'Who are you people?' she asked as she walked up to our group.

'Brockman people', Roy said crossly, 'we're talkin' here!'.

'You Christian people?' she asked Mum.

'Yes.'

'I knew it', she replied excitedly, 'I knew it in my heart. I was walkin' down the street when I saw you people here and I said to myself, Doris, they Christian people, they your people. Now, what Brockman mob do you come from?'

'My mother is sister to Albert Brockman', explained Mum.

'Oh, no! I can't believe it. You're my relations. My Aunty is married to Albert Brockman.'

'She's not still alive, is she?' I asked quickly.

'Yes, she's livin' in Hedland. She was a lot younger than him.' Mum and I looked at each other. We were stupid. We should have believed what Jack told us.

'Come home and have a cup of tea with me', urged Doris. 'I'll ring Elsie and tell her about you, she won't believe it!'

We thanked the men for their help and said goodbye.

As we walked down the main street, Doris said, 'You're lucky you didn't come lookin' for your relations any earlier, we've only all just been converted. Those Warbos* people came through and held meetings. It's made such a difference to this town, there's not many drunks, now.'

Doris made us a cup of tea when we got to her place and we encouraged her to talk about the old days. She said she could remember Annie, Nan's mother, from when she was a small child and that she thought she'd died somewhere in the thirties at Shaw River.

'All the old people had a little camp out there', she explained to

---

* *Warbos* — Name used by Aboriginal people of the Port Hedland/Marble Bar area of Western Australia for the Aboriginal people of the Warburton Ranges area.

us. 'There was nowhere else for them to go. All the old Corunna mob died out there.'

'Did Lily die out there, too?' Mum asked.

'Yes, she did.'

'Roy wouldn't tell us anything about Lily.'

Doris chuckled. 'That's because she was one of his old girlfriends. He doesn't like to talk about his old girlfriends.' We all laughed.

Just then, another lady popped in. She was introduced to us as Aunty Katy. She was Elsie's sister. We all shook hands and began to talk again.

'Lily was very popular around here', Aunty Katy told us. 'She could do anything. Everyone liked her, even the white people. She never said no to work.'

'How did she die?' Mum asked.

'Now, that's a funny thing', replied Aunty Katy, 'she came back from work one day and was doing something for one of the old people, when she dropped down dead, just like that! It was a big funeral, even some white people came. Poor old darling, we thought so much of her.'

'She married Big Eadie from Corunna Downs, but there were no children', added Doris.

'You know, if your grandmother was Daisy, then her grandmother must have been Old Fanny', said Aunty Katy. 'I'm in my seventies somewhere, but I can remember her, just faintly. She was short, with a very round face, and had a habit of wearing a large handkerchief on her head with knots tied all the way around.'

I smiled. Mum just sat there. It was all too much.

Just then, the rest of the family arrived. Trixie, Amy and May. We shook hands, then sat around and had a good yarn. In the process, we learnt that Nan's Aboriginal stepfather had been called Old Chinaman and that he had indeed been a tribal elder on Corunna and had maintained this position of power until the day he died. Also, Annie had had a sister called Dodger, who had married, but never had any children. We also learnt that Albert had been a real trickster, even in his old age.

We all laughed and laughed as funny stories about Albert's pranks kept coming, one after the other. By the end of the afternoon, we felt we knew Albert nearly as well as them.

Just as the sun was setting, Doris said, 'You fellas should go and see Happy Jack. He knew Lily well. She worked for his family for many years. He lives down near Marble Bar pool.'

We were anxious to learn as much as we could, so we took Doris' advice and headed off in search of Happy Jack.

One look at Jack's place and it was obvious that he was an excellent mechanic. His block was strewn with many mechanical bits and pieces, as well as half a dozen landrovers that he was in the process of fixing.

We explained who we were and showed him some old photos Arthur had given us of the early days. At first, he didn't seem to take in what we were saying, but when it finally dawned on him who we were, he was very moved.

'I just can't believe it', he exclaimed, 'after all these years'.

'I know you don't know us, Jack', I said, 'but it would mean so much to us if you could tell us about Lily, we know very little and we would like to be able to tell Daisy about her when we go home'.

'I'm happy to tell you anything I know', he said as we settled ourselves around his kitchen table. 'She was a wonderful woman. A wonderful, wonderful woman. She worked for my family for many years. You know, she's only been dead the better part of fifteen years, what a pity she couldn't have met you all.'

'We wish we'd come sooner', I replied. 'Doris told us so many of the old ones have died in recent years.'

'That's right. And that Corunna mob, there was some very good people amongst that mob. They were all what you'd call strong characters, and that's by anyone's standard, white or black. Now, my family, we started off most of the tin-mining in this area. We would go through and strip the country, and all that old Corunna mob would come behind and yandy* off the leftovers. I think they did well out of it. We were happy for them to have whatever they found, because they were the people tribally belonging to that area. It was like an unwritten agreement between them and us. Now and then, others would try and muscle in, but we wouldn't have any of that, it belonged to that mob only. We let them come in and carry on straight behind the bulldozers. It gave them a living. We were very careful about sacred sites and burial grounds, too, not like some others I could mention. The old men knew this. Sometimes, they would walk up to us and say, 'One of our people is buried there'. So we would bulldoze around it and leave the area intact.

'Now Lilla, that's what a lot of us called her, not Lily, Lilla. She was a great friend of my mother's. She worked in the house and was a wonderful cook. Later when I married, she helped look after my kids, too. She had a fantastic sense of humour. You could have a joke with her and she'd laugh her head off. All the descendants of that mob are interlocked now, they're all related around here, I can't work it out. It's worse than my own family. What's Daisy like, is she fairly short?'

'Yes.'

'Yes, Lilla was like that. Though mind you, in her later years, she became a fairly heavy woman, must have been good pasture she was

---

* *yandy* — a process of separating a mineral from alluvium by rocking in a shallow dish.

225

on. She was wonderful to the old people, even though she was old herself, she worked really hard looking after them. We used to call her The Angel. She was what you'd call a Black Nightingale, really, and I mean that in a dedicated way. Some of those old ones at Old Shaw camp couldn't move off their mattresses, they were crippled. That didn't worry Lilla, she'd heave them off and heave them back on again. If she got into trouble, she'd come and see one of our family, because she knew we were on the radio and could get the Flying Doctor in. You see what I mean, she was a beautiful old woman, a very gentle woman, and when she died, I felt very sad, because I felt a thing was lost from amongst the people then.

'Is there anyone else we could talk to who might help us?' I asked after a few minutes' silence. I was amazed at how steady my voice seemed. All I wanted to do was cry, but my voice sounded so firm and steady, like it belonged to someone else.

'Yes', replied Jack thoughtfully. 'You should go to the Reserve and see Topsy and Old Nancy. Nancy is well into her nineties and Topsy well into her eighties, I think I remember them saying they were on Corunna very early in the piece, they might know your grandmother, they were great friends of Lilla's. The only thing is, they only speak the language, you'd have to get someone to interpret.'

'Thanks very much', I said. 'You don't know what this means to us.' We all had tears in our eyes then. While Jack had been speaking of Lilla, it was as though we'd all been transported back into the past. As though we'd seen her and talked to her. Lily was a real person to us now. Just like Albert was.

'Jack', I said as we left, 'would you mind if I put what you told me in a book?'.

'You put in what you like. I'm very proud to have known her. I'm extremely proud to have known that woman. The way she conducted herself, the way she looked after her own people, was wonderful. Your family has missed knowing a wonderful woman.'

'Thanks', I whispered.

We drove back to the caravan park in silence. Even the children were quiet. We unpacked the van and set up our things for tea. Once again, tea came out of a tin. I don't think we'd have cared what we ate. We wouldn't have tasted it. Mum and I couldn't help thinking of all the things we'd learnt about our family. Our family was something to feel proud of. It made us feel good inside, and sad. Later that night, Mum and I sat under the stars, talking.

'I wish I'd known them', Mum sighed.

'Me too.'

'You seem a bit depressed.'

'I am.'

'What about.'

'Dunno.' That wasn't true. I did know and Mum knew it. It was just that I needed a few minutes to collect my thoughts so I could explain without breaking down. Finally, I said, 'It's Lilla. I feel very close to her in the spirit. I feel deprived.'

'How do you mean?'

'Deprived of being able to help her. We could have helped her with those old people. I feel all churned up that she did all that on her own. She never had children, we could have been her children. I mean, when you put together what everyone's said, she was obviously working hard all day and then going out to camp and looking after the old ones, feeding them . . .' My voice trailed off. Mum never said anything.

I tossed and turned that night. The feelings I had about Lilla ran very deep, like someone had scored my soul with a knife. Too deep to cry. Finally, I turned to my old standby. 'Where is she now?' I asked. 'Where are Lilla and Annie and Rosie and Old Fanny? Where are the women in my family, are they all right? I wish I'd been able to help.' Suddenly, it was as if a window in heaven had been opened and I saw a group of Aboriginal women standing together. They were all looking at me. I knew instinctively it was them. Three adults and a child. Why, that's Rosie, I thought. And then the tears came. As I cried, a voice gently said, 'Stop worrying, they're with me now'. Within minutes, I was asleep.

The following morning, I awoke refreshed and eager to tackle the Reserve. The deep pain inside of me was slowly fading. It would be a long time before it was completely gone. I never told Mum what I'd seen. I couldn't.

I was, therefore, rather surprised when she took me aside and said quietly, 'What happened to you last night?'.

'I don't know what you're talking about.'

'Last night, something important happened to you. You were asleep, or at least I thought you were, then suddenly, I saw you standing with a group of Aboriginal women. I think there were three of them and a child. I knew you were trying to tell me something, something important, but I didn't know what.'

'Oh Mum', I sobbed, 'it was them!'. Her face crumpled. She knew who I meant.

'They're all right, Mum, they're happy.' She just kept nodding her head. Then she covered her face with her hands and walked silently away.

By lunch-time, we'd pulled ourselves together sufficiently to be able to tackle the Reserve. We'd asked an Aboriginal woman called Gladys Lee if she would come and interpret for us. Jack had recommended her, as she worked with the old people through the recently established Pipunya centre. She was very happy to do so.

Armed with our old photos, we went from house to house on the

Reserve, asking about Lilla. We drew a blank every time. I couldn't understand it.

Finally, we reached the last house. We stepped up onto the small verandah and Gladys showed the photos to two old ladies and then asked about Lilla. No, they didn't know her. Suddenly, I twigged from Gladys speaking that these two ladies were Topsy and Old Nancy. I asked Gladys to show them the photos again.

Topsy took a closer look. Suddenly, she smiled, pointed to a figure in the photo and said, 'Topsy Denmark'. Old Nancy took more of an interest then. After a few minutes, she pointed to the middle figure and said, 'Dr Gillespie'.

'That's right!' I said excitedly to Gladys. I pointed to the photo containing Nanna as a young girl and got them to look at it carefully. Suddenly, there was rapid talking in Balgoo. I couldn't understand a word, but I knew there was excitement in the air. Topsy and Nancy were now very anxious about the whole thing.

Finally, Gladys turned to me with tears in her eyes and said, 'If I had have known Daisy's sister was Wonguynon, there would have been no problem'.

'Who's Wonguynon?' I asked.

'That's Lilla's Aboriginal name. We only know her by Wonguynon. I loved her, she looked after me when I was very small. I used to run away to her and she'd give me lollies and look after me until my parents came. She was related to my father. I am your relation, too.'

Topsy and Nancy began to cry. Soon, we were all hugging. Gladys and I had tears in our eyes, but we managed not to break down. Topsy and Nancy pored over all the photos I had, chuckling and laughing and shaking their heads. They explained, through Gladys, that they had been on Corunna when Nan had been taken. They'd all cried then, because they were all very close.

'They lived as one family unit in those days', Gladys explained. 'They lived as a family group with Daisy and Lily and Annie. This makes them very close to you. They are your family. Daisy was sister to them. They call her sister, they love her as a sister.'

By this time, we were all just managing to hold ourselves together. I tried not to look at Gladys as she explained things, because I was trying to keep a tight lid on my emotions. It wasn't that I would have minded crying, it was just that I knew if I began, I wouldn't be able to stop. It was the only way to cope.

Later, we retraced our steps back down through the Reserve, stopping at each house in turn and asking about Wonguynon. It was totally different, now, open arms, and open hearts. By the time we reached the other end of the Reserve, we'd been hugged and patted and cried over, and told not to forget and to come back.

An old full-blood lady whispered to me 'You don't know what it means, no one comes back. You don't know what it means that you, with light skin, want to own us.'

We had lumps in our throats the size of tomatoes, then. I wanted desperately to tell her how much it meant to us that they would own us. My mouth wouldn't open. I just hugged her and tried not to sob.

We were all so grateful to Gladys for the kind way she helped us through. Without her, we wouldn't have been able to understand a word. Our lives had been so enriched in the past few days. We wondered if we could contain any more.

The following day, we decided to go to Corunna Downs Station. Doris offered to come with us, as she knew the manager out there. Also, she was worried we might take the wrong track and get lost.

The track to Corunna was very rough. Apparently, it was the worst it had been for years. After an hour of violently jerking up and down, we rounded a bend and Doris said quickly, 'There's the homestead'.

When we reached the main house, Trevor, the manager, welcomed us with a nice hot cup of tea and some biscuits. We explained why we were there and he happily showed us over the house. To our surprise and delight, it was the same one Nan and Arthur had known in their day. We saw where the old kitchen had been, the date palm Nan had talked about, and, further over in one of the back sheds, the tank machine in which Albert had lost his fingers. I suppose these would be items of no interest to most people, but to us, it was terribly important. It was concrete evidence that what Arthur had told us and what Nan had mentioned were all true.

There were no Aboriginal people on Corunna now. It seemed sad, somehow. Mum and I sat down on part of the old fence and looked across to the distant horizon. We were both trying to imagine what it would have been like for the people in the old days. Soft, blue hills completely surrounded the station. They seemed to us mystical and magical. We easily imagined Nan, Arthur, Rosie, Lily and Albert, sitting exactly as we were now, looking off into the horizon at the end of the day. Dreaming, thinking.

'This is a beautiful place', Mum sighed. I nodded in agreement. 'Why did she tell me it was an ugly place? She didn't want me to come. She just doesn't want to be Aboriginal.' We both sat in silence.

We stayed on Corunna until late in the afternoon, then reluctantly drove back to Marble Bar. We wanted to stay longer, but our time was so limited and we now had many other leads to follow.

We all felt very emotional when we left from Doris' house. She looked sad. She'd rung Aunty Elsie and told her we were coming to see her before we returned to Perth. Doris had also suggested that we see Tommy Stream in Nullagine and Dolly and Billy in Yandeearra.

Just as we were leaving, Doris said, 'You know, I've got a stone from the old days. It's a bit hollow in the middle, they used it for grinding seeds out in the bush. You think Daisy might like that? She'd know what it was for, it might mean something to her.'

'I'd love it myself', replied Mum.

'Me too', I chipped in.

Doris laughed. 'Take it, then. It's from a time we don't see around here any more. You show it to Daisy, it's fitting she should have it.'

With a mighty heave, Paul picked it up and deposited it in the back of the van. It was very heavy.

'Are you sure it'll be all right there, Paul?' Mum asked anxiously.

'It's a rock, Mum', Paul grinned. 'There's not much you can do to damage a rock.'

Just to be sure, Mum wrapped an old kitchen towel around it to cushion it from any bumps in the road. She wanted to preserve it just the way it was. It was a precious thing.

We kissed everyone goodbye and headed off towards Nullagine. Mum and I were both a bit teary. Nothing was said, but I knew she felt like I did. Like we'd suddenly come home and now we were leaving again. But we had a sense of place, now.

Tommy Stream was a lovely old man. After we introduced ourselves, we explained who we were and why we had come. He told us that he was Nanna's cousin and had been on Corunna Downs when she had been taken away.

'I remember', he said softly, 'I was younger than her, so when she left, I was only a little fella, but all the people cried when she left. They knew she wasn't coming back. My kids would be related to you', he told Mum, 'they'd be like your cousins'.

Mum asked again about Maltese Sam. It was a ghost from the past she wanted very definitely settled.

'That's not right', replied Tommy after she suggested Maltese might be Nan's father. 'I knew Maltese, he wasn't her father. I don't know who her father was, but it wasn't him.'

We talked a little more about the old days, and when it began to grow dark, we decided to head back to the Nullagine caravan park. The children were tired and hungry. We thanked Tommy for talking to us. Like Doris, he suggested that we visit Billy and Dolly Swan at Yandeearra, we decided we would head that way the following morning.

Yandeearra was a long drive away, so we set out as early as we could. We telephoned ahead to let the people know we were coming and also to ask permission to come. We didn't want to intrude. Peter Coppin, the manager, was pleased for us to visit and welcomed us all on our arrival.

Before we had met anyone else, an older lady came striding towards us.

'Who are you people?' she asked.

Mum explained who we were. The older lady suddenly broke into a big smile and hugged Mum.

'You're my relations', she cried, 'Lily was my Aunty, dear old thing. I knew you were my people. When I saw your car, I just knew. Something told me I was going to see some of my old people today. No one said anything to me, I just knew in my heart.' We were amazed. Dolly then pointed to Amber and Blaze and said, 'You see those kids, they got the Corunna stamp on them. Even if you hadn't told me, I could tell just by looking at those kids that you lot belong to that old mob on Corunna.'

Dolly introduced us to Billy and we sat and talked about the early days and who was related to who. He was very pleased that we'd been to see Tommy Stream as well as the Marble Bar people. He explained that others had come through, trying to find out who they belonged to.

'We try to work it out', he told us kindly, 'we tell them best we can, but some of them we just can't place. And that makes us feel bad, because we think they could belong to us, but we don't know how. Now, I know exactly who you fellas are so there's no trouble there, I can tell you straight. You belong to a lot of the people here. My children would be your relations. Tommy, he's close, and others, too, then there's some that you're related to but not close, if you get what I mean. You still related to them, though.'

We stayed the night at Yandeearra. The following morning, Billy and Dolly said, 'We couldn't sleep. We tossed and turned all night, trying to work out which group you belong to. Tell us about where you from again.'

We went through all that we knew again, very slowly. Then Peter Coppin came over and joined in the discussion. They worked out that Dolly was Aunty to Mum, so the groups could be worked out from there.

'There are four groups', explained Peter, 'Panaka, Burungu, Carriema and Malinga. Now, these groups extend right through. I can go down as far as Wiluna and know who I am related to just by saying what group I'm from. We hear that further up north, they got eight groups. We don't know how they work it out, four is bad enough.' We all laughed.

Then Billy said, 'I think we got it now. You', he said as he pointed to me, 'must be Burungu, your mother is Panaka, and Paul, we would make him Malinga. Now, this is very important, you don't want to go forgetting this, because we've been trying to work it out ever since you arrived.'

Dolly and Peter agreed that those groups were the ones we belonged to.

'You got it straight?' Billy asked.

'I think so', I laughed, as I repeated the names.

'Good!' he said, 'because some of the ones that come up here get it all muddled up. We want you to have it straight, because it's very important. We don't want you to go getting tangled up in the wrong group.'

'Well, I'm glad we got that sorted out', added Peter, 'now you can come here whenever you like. We know who you belong to now. If you ever come and I'm not here and they tell you to go away, you hold your ground. You just tell them your group and who you're related to. You got a right to be here same as the others.'

'That's right', agreed Billy strongly. 'You got your place now. We've worked it out. You come as often as you please. There's always a spot here for you all.'

We all felt very moved and honoured that we'd been given our groups. There was no worry about us forgetting, we kept repeating them over and over. It was one more precious thing that added to our sense of belonging.

We were all sad when we left Yandeearra the following day. We'd been very impressed with Yandeearra and the way Peter managed the community. It was a lovely place.

Our next stop was Aunty Elsie's place in Hedland. She had a lovely home overlooking the ocean.

I don't think she could take in who we were at first. She had had little contact with Arthur and Nan, though Albert had talked about them a lot, she told us. As we talked, things began to fall into place. We were surprised at the likeness of some of Aunty Elsie's grandchildren to our own family. We explained how we thought everyone we were related to must be dead and how we couldn't believe she was really Uncle Albert's wife. Aunty told us that she'd been many years younger than Albert when they'd married. There were four children, Brian, William, Claude and Margaret. Aunty was, in fact, roughly the same age as Mum, so they had a lot in common. We showed her photos of the family and laughed once again about all the tricks Uncle Albert played on everyone. Aunty also told us how Uncle Albert had owned his own truck and what a hard worker he'd been. It was a trait that seemed to run in the family.

By the time we finally left, we'd gotten to know her really well. Aunty gave us a big fish for our tea. We promised we would come to Hedland again and asked her to visit Perth so she could meet the rest of the family. We felt very full inside when we left. It was like all the little pieces of a huge jigsaw were finally fitting together.

The following day, it was time to head back to Perth, but there was one last stop to make. Billy and Dolly had told us to call in and visit Billy Moses at Twelve-mile, just out of Hedland. We were all exhausted by this stage, but we didn't want to miss out on anything, so we gathered together the last remnants of our energy and drove out to Twelve-mile.

When we arrived, we were told that Billy and Alma had gone shopping and no one knew when they'd be back, but we could wait near his house if we wanted to. Only five minutes had passed, when a taxi pulled in, bearing Billy and Alma.

They eyed us curiously, obviously wondering who we were and why we were waiting near their house. I felt embarrassed, what if Billy didn't know us after all? I decided to take the bull by the horns. I walked forward and held out my hand.

After introducing myself, I explained slowly who we were and why we had come. He listened seriously, trying to take in everything I said. Suddenly, his face lit up with a heart-warming smile and he said, 'You my relations! Yes, you've come to the right place. You my people. I am your Nanna's cousin.' There were tears in his eyes. I held his hand warmly. Alma smiled and said, 'You must be his relations'.

We walked back to his house and sat down for a chat. Billy said, 'I can't believe it. Some of my people coming all the way from Perth just to visit me. You always come here. You can come and live here, I'm the boss. This is your place, too, remember that.' We began to talk about the old times and Billy explained how he, too, was taken away at a young age.

'I was very lucky', he told us, 'I came back. I made it my business to come back and find out who I belonged to. It was funny, you know, when I first came back, no one round here would talk to me. You see, they weren't sure who I was. They were trying to work it out. I'd walk down the street and they'd just stare at me. Then one day, an old fella came into town, he saw me and recognised me. He spoke up for me and said, that fella belong to us, I know who he is. I know his mother. After that, I never had any trouble. They all talk to me, now. I belong here. It's good to be with my people. I'm glad you've come back.'

We were glad, too. And overwhelmed at the thought that we nearly hadn't come. How deprived we would have been if we had been willing to let things stay as they were. We would have survived, but not as whole people. We would never have known our place.

That afternoon, we reluctantly left for Perth. None of us wanted to go, Paul included. He'd been raised in the North and loved it. We were reluctant to return and pick up the threads of our old lives. We were different people, now. What had begun as a tentative search for knowledge had grown into a spiritual and emotional pilgrimage. We had an Aboriginal consciousness now, and were proud of it.

Mum, in particular, had been very deeply affected by the whole trip.

'To think I nearly missed all this. All my life, I've only been half a person. I don't think I really realised how much of me was missing until I came North. Thank God you're stubborn, Sally.'

We all laughed and then, settling back, retreated into our own thoughts. There was much to think about. Much to come to terms with. I knew Mum, like me, was thinking about Nan. We viewed her differently, now. We had more insight into her bitterness. And more than anything, we wanted her to change, to be proud of what she was. We'd seen so much of her and ourselves in the people we'd met. We belonged, now. We wanted her to belong, too.

Chapter Twenty-Nine

SOMEONE LIKE ME

When we arrived back in Perth, Nan was really pleased to see us, and so was Beryl. Nan had gone through all the money Mum had left her and had had Beryl on the go non-stop, running up to the shop for chocolate biscuits and putting bets on the TAB.

'I knew you'd all be safe', Nan said when she saw us. 'I been praying the cyclones wouldn't get you.'

We rounded up the rest of the family the following day and insisted on showing the video we had made of our trip. Much to our dismay, the film turned out to be pretty mediocre. It suffered from the faults common to most home movies. Lack of focus, zooming too quickly and panning too slowly.

Throughout the filming of Corunna, I watched Nan. She was taking a keen interest in the old buildings.

'There's the old date palm', she said. 'That used to be the garden down there. That's the old homestead, that part over there, that's where they had the kitchen.'

When it was all over, Nan said, 'Fancy, all those old buildings still being there, I didn't think there'd be anything left. What about the tank machine, Sally?'

'Yep! But the manager had tied it up so it couldn't be used. He was worried one of his kids might stick their fingers in it.'

'Ooh yes, it'd be dangerous.'

Mum told Nan what all the old boys had said about Lily. Nan laughed and laughed. 'Ooh yes', she chuckled, 'that was Lily, all right. She was the sort of person you couldn't help liking, she had a good heart, did Lily.' I was amazed, Nan had never talked about Lily like that before.

Over the next few days, Mum talked at length with Nan about the different people we had met. Nan feigned disinterest, but we knew it was just a bluff. She was desperately interested in everything we had to say, but she didn't want to let her feelings show. In many ways, she was a very private person.

One night when they were alone, Mum told her how Annie and

a lot of the other older ones from Corunna Downs had died at Shaw River. 'She had Lily', Mum said. 'She devoted herself to the old ones. Annie wasn't alone when she died, she had some of her people with her.' Nan nodded. There were tears in her eyes. Her lips were set.

'Do any of them remember me?' she asked wistfully.

'They all do', Mum said, 'they all remember you. Do you remember Topsy and another woman called Nancy? They said they lived with you and Annie on Corunna.'

Nan looked shocked. 'They still alive?' she asked in disbelief.

'Yes.'

Nan just shook her head. 'I'm going to bed', she muttered. Mum laid down and cried herself to sleep.

A few weeks later, I tackled Nan about being able to speak two languages, she was unwilling to discuss the subject. When I told her about the different skin groups, she said crossly, 'I know all that, I'm not stupid'. She wouldn't be drawn further. There'd been a slight change, a softening, but she was still unwilling to share the personal details of her life with us.

When Mum and I got together, we couldn't help reminiscing about our trip.

'Well, we found out one thing', said Mum, 'Maltese Sam definitely wasn't Nan's father'.

'That's right. Though it doesn't necessarily mean Howden was, either.'

'No, I know. Probably, we'll never really know who fathered her.'

'Do you reckon Jack Grime really is your father?'

'Oh, I don't know, Sally', Mum sighed. 'When I was little, I always thought Howden was my father, isn't that silly?'

'Howden? Why did you think that?'

'I suppose because he was Judy and June and Dick's father. I guess because I was little and didn't understand, I assumed he was my father, too. You know how it is when you're a kid.'

'Yeah, I could see how you might think that. You were all living there at Ivanhoe.'

'Yes.'

'Aunty Judy said you're the image of Jack Grime, though, that'd be some sort of proof, wouldn't it?'

'Oh, I don't know, people can look like one another, but it doesn't mean they're related.'

'Yeah. Hey, I know. I've got a photo of Jack, a big one, why don't we look at it, see if you do look alike?'

'I don't want to do that.'

'Go on! We'll hold it up to the big mirror in my room, you can put your head next to it and we'll see if you do look like him.'

'Oh, all right', Mum giggled, 'why not?'.

Within minutes, Mum and I and the photo were all facing the large mirrors in the doors of my wardrobe.

'Well, that was a dead loss. You don't look anything like him, even taking into account the fact that you've put on weight. There's no resemblance there at all.'

'He doesn't look like any of you kids, either, does he?'

'Naah', I agreed. 'Hang on a tick and I'll get another picture.'

I returned quickly. 'Okay', I said, 'face the mirror'.

Mum fronted up to the mirror and tried not to laugh. She felt silly.

Suddenly, I held up a photograph of Howden as a young man next to her face. We both fell into silence.

'My God', I whispered. 'Give him black, curly hair and a big bust and he's the spitting image of you!'

Mum was shocked. 'I can't believe it', she said. 'Why haven't I ever noticed this before, I've seen that picture hundreds of times.'

'I suppose it never occurred to you', I replied.

'You don't think it's possible he was my father?'

'Anything's possible. But he couldn't be yours as well as Nan's. You know, features can skip a generation. Say he was Nan's father, well you could have inherited those looks from that.'

'Oh, I don't know, Sally', Mum sighed. 'It's such a puzzle. You know, for nearly all my life, I've desperately wanted to know who my father was, now, I couldn't care less. Why should I bother with whoever it was, they never bothered with me.'

'But that's been the recent history of Aboriginal people all along, Mum. Kids running around, not knowing who fathered them. Those early pioneers, they've got a lot to answer for.'

'Yes, I know, I know, but I think now I'm better off without all that business. All those wonderful people up North, they all claimed me. Well, that's all I want. That's enough, you see. I don't want to belong to anyone else.'

'Me either.'

We walked back to the lounge-room. After a few seconds' silence, Mum said, 'Sal . .?'.

'What?'

'Aw . . . nothing. It doesn't matter.'

'I hate it when you do that. Come on, out with it.'

'We-ell . . . You know the Daisy that Jack said he'd met? You don't think that could have been Nanna?'

'Dunno. I asked her the other day if she'd ever been back North, but she just got mad with me.'

'It might have been her', Mum said tentatively, 'Alice did tell you she'd gone back once'.

'But if it was her, it was in 1923 and she would have been pregnant. Mum . . . do you think you might have a brother or sister somewhere?'

She nodded.

'But surely Nan would have told you?'

'Not if she wasn't allowed to keep it.'

'This is terrible.' I eyed her keenly. 'There's something you're not telling me, isn't there?'

Mum composed herself, then said, 'The other night when I was in bed, I had this sort of flashback to when I was little. I'd been pestering Nanna, asking her why I didn't have a brother or a sister, when she put her arms around me and whispered quietly, "You have a sister". Then she held me really tight. When she let me go, I saw she was crying.'

I couldn't say anything. We both sat in silence. Finally, Mum said, 'I'm going to ask her'.

A few days later, Mum broached the subject with Nan, only to be met with anger and abuse. Nan locked herself in her room, saying 'Let the past be'.

'I'll never know, now', Mum told me later. 'If she won't tell me, I'll never know.'

'You mustn't give up! What does your gut feeling tell you?'

'Oh Sally, you and your gut feelings, you're like a bloody detective. How do I know my gut feeling isn't pure imagination?'

'What does it tell you?' I persisted.

She sighed. 'It tells me I've got a sister. I've had that feeling all my life, from when I was very small, that I had a sister somewhere. If only I could find her.'

'Then I believe what you feel is true.'

Mum laughed, 'You're a romantic'.

'Crap! Be logical, she could still be alive, if she was born in 1923, she'd be in her sixties, now. Also, if Nan had her up North, she could have been brought up by the people round there or a white family could have adopted her.'

'Sally, we don't even have a name. It's impossible! You talk like we'll find her one day, but it's impossible.'

'Nothing's impossible.'

'Could you talk to Nan?'

'Yeah, but she won't tell me anything. I'll let her cool down a bit first.'

'There's been so much sadness in my life', Mum said, 'I don't think I can take any more'.

'You want to talk about it?'

'You mean for that book?'

'Yes.'

'Well . . . ', she hesitated for a moment. Then, with sudden determination, she said, 'Why shouldn't I? If I stay silent like Nanna, it's like saying everything's all right. People should know what it's been like for someone like me.'

I smiled at her.

'Perhaps my sister will read it.'

238

GLADYS CORUNNA'S STORY

(1931 — 1983)

I have no memory of being taken from my mother and placed in Parkerville Children's Home, but all my life, I've carried a mental picture of a little fat kid about three or four years old. She's sitting on the verandah of Babyland Nursery, her nose is running and she's crying. I think that was me when they first took me to Parkerville.

Parkerville was a beautiful place run by Church of England nuns. Set in the hills of the Darling Ranges, it was surrounded by bush and small streams. In the spring, there were wildflowers of every colour and hundreds of varieties of birds. Each morning, I awoke to hear the kookaburras laughing and the maggies warbling. That was the side of Parkerville I loved.

That was my home from 1931 when I was three years old. I was only able to go back to my mother at Ivanhoe three times a year, for the holidays.

There were two sections at the Home. The older children's section, where all the houses were named after people who had donated money, and Babyland Nursery. I don't think that was named after anyone.

Babyland was really just a cottage surrounded by verandahs. Inside was a kitchen with a large wood stove, some small tables and chairs and high chairs for the really little ones. There was only one dormitory and it was filled with lots of little iron beds that sat close to the floor. They were very neat and tidy in Babyland. You were only allowed to play inside on real wintry days. Normally, they made us all sit out on the verandahs, that was so you didn't mess up the rooms once they'd been cleaned.

Every morning, the older girls came over to bathe us. We were always cold from the night before because we still all wet our beds. I dreaded bath time because of the carbolic soap and the hard scrubbing brushes. The House Mother used to stand in the doorway and say, 'Scrub 'em clean, girls'. We'd cry, those brushes really hurt. Our crying always seemed to satisfy her, she'd leave, then. As soon as she left, the girls would throw the brushes away and let us play. It got that way that we'd start crying as soon as the House Mother appeared in the doorway.

Our clothes were kept in a big cupboard and the girls dressed us in whatever fitted.

I guess that was one of the few times when I was lucky to be black, because the older Aboriginal girls always gave us black babies an extra kiss and cuddle. That gave me a wonderful feeling of security, I'll always

241

be grateful for that time. You see, even though we weren't related, there were strong ties between us black kids. The older white girls never seemed to care about anyone, and our House Mothers weren't like real mothers, they just bossed us around, they never gave you a kiss or a cuddle.

Every morning, I'd sit on the verandah with my friend Iris, she was fat like me. She had very white skin and her freckles stood out like they'd been daubed on with a paintbrush. The older girls called her Chalky, because she was so pale. She always seemed to be unhappy, she had an awful cough and her feet were blue. We didn't have shoes. She loved to sit close to me. We'd play games with the odds and ends of toys that were scattered over the verandah. If we walked around the verandah, she liked to hold my hand. We always stuck together, if there were two of you, the others didn't pick on you so much.

After school, the older girls would come back and carry me around. I used to sit on the verandah and press my face against the wooden railing that faced the school oval. It always seemed to be such a long time before they came. When the bell rang, they'd all come running over, fighting about whose turn it was to carry me. I felt sorry for Iris then, no one ever wanted to carry her. I wished the big girls would play with her, too, but she was always coughing, and I was so busy enjoying the attention that I soon forgot her.

After tea, the girls would dress us in our night clothes. They were a one-piece suit with a square piece that buttoned at the back so we could go on the potty. They had feet in so they kept our toes warm.

Every little bed in the dormitory had a grey or dark green blanket on it and we had to kneel down beside our beds and say our prayers. After that, the lights were turned out and some of the smaller kids had their cots pushed closer to the House Mother's bedroom so she could hear them if they got sick in the night.

I remember one night hearing Iris cough and cough. I dozed off again and was awakened by the light being turned on and people walking in and out. When I got up in the morning, Iris was gone. I felt very lonely, sitting on the verandah that day. I asked the others if they'd seen her, they said she was sick and had been taken to hospital. I felt very sad.

A few weeks after that, when I was playing on the verandah by myself, she just appeared out of nowhere. She was all dressed up in a white lace dress and she was happy, she wasn't coughing any more. She smiled at me and I smiled at her and then she left. I felt better then, I knew that, wherever she'd gone, she was all right.

When I was five years old, I was sent to George Turner. It was a house opposite Babyland, across a wide expanse of gravel. I had been told to go and see my new House Mother, there were no goodbyes to my friends, they just sat playing on the verandah as usual.

I stumbled down the front steps and began slowly walking across the gravel with my little bundle of clothes. I tried to walk on the clumps of dandelions to keep my feet clean, but they ran out when I reached the rainwater tank, after that, it was just black sand.

When I finally reached the gate of George Turner, I was too scared to open it. I just stood there shyly. I was worried about my feet. In Babyland, it had been very important that you kept your feet clean, that was why we were never allowed off the verandahs, and now here I was with black, sandy feet. I was sure my new House Mother would be very cross with me.

Suddenly, one of the older girls came up to the gate. I felt relieved when I recognised her, she was one of my friends. She took me by the hand and led me up to Miss Moore, who was waiting on the verandah.

Miss Moore showed me over the house, she said I was one of twenty-five children who would be staying here. She explained to me that the boys slept on one side of the verandah and the girls on the other, with a blind lowered in the middle to make a division. We each had a small cupboard for our own personal things and a small mirror so we could see to comb our hair in the morning. I was amazed in that all the time she'd been talking to me, she hadn't once mentioned my dirty feet.

I was also surprised to see that all the walls in the dormitories were covered with huge framed pictures of film stars. Of course, I was too young to know then that they were film stars, I just thought they were pictures of Mummies and Daddies.

After Miss Moore had finished explaining things to me, she told me to put my things away in the cupboard. I never had much, just a few pieces of coloured easter egg paper and a one-legged teddy that I had hidden in my clothes and stolen from Babyland. All the way over, I had been worried that the teddy might fall out and they'd see it and take it back. I was glad he was still with me. I also had a hairbrush that my mother had given me. She liked me to look neat.

My little cupboard wasn't bare for long, I became a hoarder. I loved collecting silver paper from easter eggs. Sometimes, the big kids would give me some and I would sit for hours, trying to get the creases out. Then I'd stack them gently in an old chocolate box. I collected anything the older children were willing to part with, I wasn't fussy. I loved hair ribbons, sometimes one of the older girls would help me get dressed and they'd tie a ribbon in my hair to make me look pretty. I was so pleased. I'd show off to the kids who didn't have one.

I had nightmares at George Turner, I'd never had them in Babyland. Maybe it was the big bed, it was very high off the ground and when I was in it, it felt very empty. Also, I wasn't used to sleeping on the verandah. There were all sorts of noises that frightened me. The old canvas blinds would creak against their rope moorings, the nightbirds called to one another, and you often heard the wings of some large bird flapping past.

My bed was the last one on the verandah, next to the blind that divided the girls' section from the boys'. There was a large window just near my bed, I'd look through the window and see only darkness and eerie shadows.

Sometimes, I'd awake in the night with a heavy weight on my chest and my mouth would be all dry inside. I was sure there was someone sitting on the end of my bed. I'd lie under the blankets, too scared to move or breathe. I thought, if I lay still enough, they might go away. I hoped that, because I was only little and didn't take up much room, they might think the bed was empty. When I awoke in the morning, I'd look straight to the end of my bed to see if anyone was there. There was never anyone.

As I grew older, that fear disappeared. Maybe because I started to learn about Jesus. When I felt really scared, I'd look over the verandah to the tall gum tree nearby, and I'd see him there, watching me. I felt very protected. Sometimes, when I was sad, a light would shine suddenly inside of me and make me happy. I knew it was God.

Apart from these experiences, the thing that helped me most was the music I used to hear at night. As I grew older, I realised it was Aboriginal music, like some blackfellas were having a corroboree just for me. It was very beautiful music. I only heard it at night when I was feeling depressed. After I'd heard it, I knew I could go to sleep. It was that same feeling of protection.

I suppose it was healthy, sleeping on the verandah like that, but on wintry nights when there were lightning and thunder and the rain poured in, it was really scary. Of course, they pulled down the blinds all the way round to give us some shelter, but it was still frightening. I was sure one night I'd be struck by lightning. If it got too wet, we were allowed to drag our mattresses inside and sleep on the floor.

There were many times when I felt very lost. I knew I wasn't a baby any more. I knew I had to look after myself, now.

One day, after I'd been at George Turner for about a year, some of the older girls asked me if I'd like to go for a walk. It was really lovely in the bush. When I got tired, they took turns in giving me piggyback rides.

We walked deep into the bush on the far side of the Home. Sometimes, we'd disturb wallabies resting in the shade of the red gums. They'd hop a short distance away, they weren't upset by our presence, but their soft grey ears would twitch, making sure we didn't get too close.

'Let's head for the cemetery', one of the kids suggested.

'What's that?' I asked Enid, who was giving me a piggyback.

'It's where they put you when you die', she replied, 'there's lots of babies buried there'. She'd been there often. Apparently, all the kids liked going there. They told me they liked to read the names printed on the crosses. Sometimes, there'd only be a first name, like Rosie, with the age printed underneath.

Just as we were nearing the cemetery, I said to Enid, 'I thought you went to heaven with Jesus when you died'.

'You do', she replied. 'We're here now, down you go.' She eased me off her back and onto the ground.

I gazed at the little graves scattered here and there amongst the low clumps of red and pink bush. Then I followed Enid as she went from grave to grave, reading the names. Suddenly, she grabbed my hand.

'Look', she said, 'see this one, it's that little friend of yours, the one you had in Babyland. Iris, three years ten months.'

I gazed in shock at the little mound of earth beneath the small, white cross. Enid moved on, reading out the names of more babies as she went. I stood staring at Iris's grave. I suddenly realised that that was why she hadn't come back to Babyland, she'd died.

I picked up some buttercups and placed them on the top of the grave, like I always did when I found a dead bird in the bush and buried it. I tried to hide my tears from the others, but they noticed and started chanting, 'Look at the sookie bubba!'. Enid heard them and shouted, 'Leave her alone!'. Then she ran back to me and picked me up. 'It's all right', she said, 'your friend is happy in heaven'.

We had the same routine every morning at Parkerville. They woke us early by ringing a bell. The air was always cold and you never felt like getting up.

You made your bed, got dressed and swept down the verandahs. After that, it was time for breakfast. There was a large table inside the dining-room in the house, with long stools that slotted underneath, so they could be kept out of sight when not in use.

During winter, we always had a big open fire going, it got very cold in the hills. I remember, at night, we would hate leaving the fire to go out to our beds on the verandahs, they were so cold and draughty. I always tried to hide behind a chair, hoping Miss Moore wouldn't notice me. That way, I could huddle next to the fire all night. It was a trick that never worked, she always dragged me out and sent me off with the others.

Every morning, the boys got the wood for the stove in the kitchen and the older girls cooked the porridge. I never liked breakfast much, it was the weevils, they'd be there every morning, staring at me from my bowl of porridge. I covered them as much as I could with milk and sugar. Sometimes, I closed my eyes as they went into my mouth. I hated the thought of them being inside me. I'd love to have been able to forgo the porridge, but I was always too hungry to allow myself that luxury. Apart from a slice of bread and dripping, the porridge was all we got.

After breakfast, we cleaned up and then went to morning church before school.

At lunch-time, we all lined up and marched to the big dining-hall. Lunch was usually hot, like a stew. The meat sometimes smelt bad, especially in summer.

After school, we were allowed one slice of bread and dripping before going to afternoon church. Tea was usually cold meat and salad and, if we were lucky, jelly and custard.

Every Friday night, we had pictures. They were old silent movies and we really loved them. Often, the films were quite heart-rending tales about gypsies stealing a child from a family. Of course, by the end of the film, they'd all be reunited. I really identified with those films. We all did. I always thought of myself as the stolen child. In fact, I lived the part so whole-heartedly that it took me ages to come back to reality after the film had finished. We all loved any films about families. Pictures like that touched something deep inside us. It was every kid's secret wish to have a family of their own. But it was never something we talked about openly. During the week, we usually played the movies in our games.

One of the most terrible punishments they could inflict on us at the Home was depriving us of our Friday night picture.

The first thing we did on Saturday mornings was line up for a dose of Epsom salts. It was revolting. After that, it was clean-up time. We washed the kitchen floor, wiped down the stove and cleaned out the bath with a mixture of charcoal and cooking salt. The job I hated most was cleaning the table we ate breakfast on. It was covered in white pigskin and it showed every mark, we had to really scrub it to get it clean.

Our dining-room in the house was really large. Actually, it was really a dining and sitting-room. We had our big table at one end and there was a small table and chair at the other, where the House Mother sat and had her breakfast. We all envied Miss Moore, because she had real butter on her toast and plenty of scalded cream.

When it came to work, the boys had it real easy. The nuns considered looking after the house women's work. They still had that old-fashioned way of thinking. The boys never even helped with the floors. Though I didn't mind that, I loved polishing the floor.

They gave us large tins of yellow polish which was made at the Home, it was very thick. We'd tie old woollen jumpers to our feet, slop huge lumps of wax on the floor, and then zoom all over the place. It was better than roller skating. We often banged into one another as well as the wall. Miss Moore only came in and checked on us if someone started crying. No matter how bad you hurt yourself, you never cried, otherwise everyone got punished.

It didn't pay to upset Miss Moore, because she had a terrible temper and when she got angry, she could inflict terrible beatings.

The House Mothers never did any work, their job was to supervise. After we'd finished the house, we'd all march over to the laundry to wash our clothes. They had ladies in to do the linen, but we had to look after our own things.

My favourite time at the Home was Saturday afternoons. Once we'd finished our work, we were allowed to do as we pleased. If it was too cold for swimming, we'd go hunting for food.

I was always hungry. I was like Pooh Bear, I couldn't get enough to eat. My stomach used to rumble all the time. We loved to eat the wild cranberries that grew in the bush, they were sweet and juicy. Year after year, we went to the same bushes, they were always laden. Trouble was, the goannas liked them, too. You could be eating from one side, and a goanna from the other, you never knew until you met in the middle. I don't know who got the biggest fright.

At the back of the dining-room was a shed used for storing apples and root vegetables. The door was always locked, but there was a small window that we could easily climb through. We'd pinch some apples and potatoes and then nick off into the bush to our special tree, where we liked to play Mothers and Fathers.

It was a big, old red gum. It was dead and the trunk was split, so it was like a big room inside. We hid tins and bits of broken china that looked pretty. It was a very happy place. We'd light a fire with a thick piece of glass we kept hidden. We'd shine it onto a dry gum leaf and, before long, the wisp of smoke would start to rise. We'd throw some more dry leaves on and get it going really good before we put the potatoes on. When we thought they were ready, we'd haul them from the ashes by poking a long stick through them. Sometimes, we'd burn our tongues, because our mouths would be watering too much to wait. Often, the centre of the potatoes was raw, but we didn't care.

The best feed we had was gilgies. They were plentiful in the small pools and creeks around the Home. We caught them with a piece of old meat begged from the kitchen and tied to a piece of string. It took only a few seconds after you'd dropped the string into the water to catch a gilgie. When we'd caught nine or ten, we'd boil them up in an old tin. They were the best feed of all.

Most of my happiest times were spent alone in the bush, watching the birds and animals. If you sat very quiet, they didn't notice you were there. There were rabbits, wallabies, goannas, lizards, even the tiny insects were interesting. I had such respect for their little lives that I'd feel terrible if I even trod on an ant. We'd come across all sorts of snakes, green ones, brown, black. We used to pick the green ones up and flick them. I wouldn't pick them up now. We never touched the black or brown ones, if we came across those, we just walked away. Sometimes, the older boys used to kill the really big black snakes.

One day when I was on my own, I found some field mice under a rock near a honeysuckle vine. I often went to that vine, because the flowers were sweet to suck. It was almost as good as having a lolly. I thought the baby field mice were wonderful, they were pink and bald and very small. I decided it was a secret I'd keep to myself in case anyone harmed them.

As I sat looking at them, some boys suddenly appeared out of the bush nearby. When they saw what I was looking at, they ran over and pulled the mice out and held them high in the air, laughing and taunting me. They threw them to some kookaburras, who gobbled them up. I was really upset. I broke up the nest in the hope that the mother would never have babies again. I often checked under the vine after that, but there were never any mice.

I had a crying tree in the bush. It was down near the creek, an old twisted peppermint tree. The limbs curved over to make a seat and its weeping leaves almost covered me completely. You didn't cry in front of anyone at the Home, it wasn't done. You had to find yourself a crying place. A lot of the kids cried in their beds every night, but it wasn't the same as having some place quiet to go where you could make as much noise as you liked.

I'd sit for hours under that peppermint tree, watching the water gurgle over the rocks and listening to the birds. After a while, the peace of that place would reach inside of me and I wouldn't feel sad any more. Instead, I'd start counting the numerous rainbow-coloured dragon-flies that skimmed across the surface of the water. After that, I'd fall asleep. When I finally did walk back to the Home, I felt very content.

Saturday night was spent getting our clothes ready for church on Sunday. We ironed everything with those heavy flat irons you heated up on the stove. It was hard work, especially if you were little. Our clothes were always starched and ironed. We had to iron and iron until not one crease showed, it took ages.

I remember, one night, I went racing into the kitchen just as Miss Moore was coming through the door with a red-hot iron. It hit straight into my arm. I must have passed out, because when I woke up, I was in the Home Hospital with my arm all bandaged up and the Matron sitting beside me.

They'd got the old doctor who serviced the Mundaring district to come and look at me. He only came to the Home in emergencies. When he took the bandage off my arm, all I could see was raw meat, the skin had gone.

They kept me in hospital for four days. I was very lonely, no one else was sick. I think they felt sorry for me, because they let me sit out on the verandah with my arm in a sling. The other kids would sneak over and talk to me. The hospital was out of bounds, so they had to crawl through the big field of green peas opposite. I used to get cross with them because they used to take so long to crawl through that field. I knew they were all lying on their backs, eating the peas, and had forgotten about me.

I was lucky that I didn't get seriously ill too often. You didn't get on very well at Parkerville if you had something wrong with you and you couldn't take care of yourself. All the weaker kids got stood over, older kids picked on them. There were a lot of kids at the Home that were crippled with polio. I felt sorry for them. And you had to be dying not to go to school. If you stopped home, they gave you a dose of salts or castor oil. It cured everything, in those days.

One of the lowest points of my childhood was the time they took me to Princess Margaret Hospital to remove my tonsils. I was so frightened. I was all alone and I thought I was going to die.

I had to wear a nightie with the back all open. Everything smelt of carbolic soap, even the sheets. I hated that smell. They put me in a high iron bed and hardly anyone spoke to me. It was like being in a morgue.

I was very sick after the operation. I had no one to talk to, I cried and cried. I couldn't understand why my mother hadn't been to visit me, I thought perhaps they hadn't told her I was sick. She told me later that she couldn't get time off work and she couldn't come at night because of the curfew, which prevented Aboriginal people travelling after dark.

It was hard for her, then, and hard for me, too. Even when I was sick, I belonged to the Native Welfare Department. I wasn't even allowed to have the comfort of my own mother.

But just after this, something happened that really cheered me up. My Uncle Arthur visited. He'd come to see me once before at Parkerville when I was only very small. The memory I had of him was only dim, but it was important. I did love him and I knew he loved me. I also knew that if he could have taken me from there, he would. He was very important to me. He reminded me of my mother and home. Sometimes, I used to think that if he and Mum could live together, then I'd have a family. It wasn't to be.

He came and saw me once more after that, then never again. He was too busy trying to make a living for himself and his own family.

On Sunday afternoons, visitors were allowed to come. We used to wait and wait, we knew it was a long, uphill walk from the station, and we never knew whether someone was coming for us or not. That was the worst part. You hoped right up to the very last minute. I used to think, well, Mum will be here soon, I'll just wait a little bit longer. She'll be cross if she doesn't see me standing here, waiting for her. I remember some years when I only saw her twice at the Home.

If no one came, you put on a brave face and didn't cry. You pretended you didn't care, you just shrugged your shoulders and walked away. If one of your friends got visitors, you'd be so jealous. Of course, if you saw someone coming over the hill for you, you'd get so excited you'd just run.

A lot of kids at Parkerville had parents. Some had mothers, some had fathers. You'd do anything for kids like that, because you always hoped that they might ask you to come along and share their visitors.

It was hardest for the Aboriginal kids. We didn't have anyone. Some of the kids there had been taken from families that lived hundreds of miles away. It was too far for anyone to come and see them. And anyway, Aboriginal people had to get permits to travel. Sometimes, they wouldn't give them a permit. They didn't care that they wanted to see their kids.

Each time Mum came and saw me, she always had a bit of paper with her that said she was allowed to travel. A policeman could stop her any time and ask to look at that paper, if she didn't have it on her, she was in big trouble.

When Mum didn't visit me for a long time, I used to wonder if she'd forgotten me. But the only day she had any time off was on

Sunday, and then she had to cook the roast first. She never had any annual holidays, like some of the other servants did. I remember quite a few times when she told me she hadn't come because she couldn't afford the train fare. The only time she had the whole Sunday off was if the Drake-Brockmans went visiting for the day.

When I was still quite young, Sister Kate* left Parkerville and took a lot of Aboriginal children with her. I was very sad, because I lost a lot of my friends. There were a few lightly coloured Aboriginal boys left and they kept an eye on me. I don't know why I wasn't sent with Sister Kate, maybe it was because of the Drake-Brockmans, I don't know.

I think Alice Drake-Brockman thought she was doing a good thing sending me to Parkerville. Sometimes, she'd come up and bring Judy, June and Dick with her for a picnic. That was always in the spring, when the wildflowers were out. Dick and I got on well, we were very close. He treated me like his sister.

I loved it when they all came up, because the other kids were so envious. There was a lot of status in knowing someone who had a car. I thought I'd burst for joy when I saw the black Chev creep up the hill and drive slowly down the road, to halt at George Turner. All the other kids would crowd up close, hoping I'd take one of them with me. I'd jump down from the wooden fence we sat on while we waited and hoped for visitors and I'd walk slowly towards the car. I felt very shy, but I was also conscious of the envy of the others still sitting on the fence behind me. It was a feeling of importance that would last me the whole of the following week. I always promised the other kids that next time, I might take one of them. It made me king until the following Sunday, when someone might get a visitor who brought a box of cakes. Even so, cakes weren't as important as a car ride, because it was very hard to make a cake last a full week.

I often prayed for God to give me a family. I used to pretend I had a mother and a father and brothers and sisters. I pretended I lived in a big flash house like Ivanhoe and I went to St Hilda's Girls' School, like Judy and June.

It was very important to me to have a father then. Whenever I asked Mum about my father, she'd just say, 'You don't want to know about him, he died when you were very small, but he loved you very much'. She sensed I needed to belong, but she didn't know about all the teasing I used to get because I didn't have a father, nor the comments that

* *Sister Kate* — an Anglican nun who set up a Home for part-Aboriginal children in the 1930s. Initially, such children were sent to her by the Western Australian government authority responsible for Aborigines. Sister Kate's, as the institution became known, remains well known today as a hostel and support organisation for Aboriginal children and families.

251

I used to hear about bad girls having babies. I knew it was connected to me, but I was too young to understand.

I had a large scar on my chest where my mother said my father had dropped his cigar ash. I tried to picture him nursing me, with a large cigar in his mouth. I always imagined him looking like a film star, like one of the pictures the big girls had.

The scar made me feel I must have had a real father, after all. I'd look at it and feel quite pleased. It wasn't until I was older that I realised it was an initiation scar. My mother had given it to me for protection.

We used to have quite a few outings at the Home. We went to the pictures and put on concerts at different places to raise money.

One morning, we were all very excited, because we'd been told we were going to the zoo. I really needed something to get excited about then, because I hadn't seen my mother for ages and I felt very sad. Actually, it wasn't only me. Hardly any of the kids had had visitors, they all felt down. There hadn't even been people looking for kids to adopt.

People often came to the Home to look kids over for adoption. I don't think they realised how upsetting it could be for everyone. We all got excited, we wondered who'd be the lucky one to get a Mother and a Father. The visits usually came to nothing, the kids would end up being turned down and they'd cry themselves to sleep at night.

A friend of mine did get adopted. Everyone was surprised, because usually, once you'd reached the age of eight or nine, no one wanted you. This girl was eight, she was very pretty with blonde hair. A wealthy family took her, we thought she was very lucky. She'd only been gone a couple of years when she died. There was a big court case about it. She died of arsenic poisoning. None of us wanted to be adopted after that.

Going to the zoo gave everyone a lift. After breakfast, we marched to the station. When the old steam engine came chugging in, we were all so frightened we'd be left behind that we ignored the screams of our House Mothers and jumped on while the train was still going. If you were first on, you always saved a seat for your mates and everyone hoped that their little group would end up in a carriage without a House Mother. That way, you could scream as loud as you liked when you went through the tunnel at Swanview.

The zoo was really exciting, especially the elephants. I'd seen pictures of elephants dressed up in gold, with Indian princes sitting on their backs. I could imagine myself doing that. I always remembered to smile at the elephants, because I'd read in a book that they never forgot, and there was a story about a man who was cruel to them so they'd trampled him to death. I believed in playing it safe.

I felt a lot happier after my day with the animals. When we marched back to the ferry, we passed a house near the river where I knew old Aunty Mary and Uncle Ted lived. I'd been to visit them on the Christmas holidays with my mother, and, for some reason, it suddenly made me feel close to her.

We all settled down on the ferry and were soon chugging back across the Swan River. I had a seat right up near the water and I watched as the ripples came out from under the boat and slowly faded away.

Then I noticed another ferry coming across from the other side, so I leaned over to look to see how close it was going to come to our boat. To my surprise, I saw my mother sitting on the ferry, as pretty as ever in her blue suit. I couldn't believe it. I called out to her, I shouted and waved my arms. She must have known I was going to the zoo, I thought, but she's got the wrong time, she's going to miss me. She might go to see me at the zoo and I won't be there. I jumped up and down and called and called. My mother sat upright on the ferry, she never even turned her head in my direction.

Within minutes, our boats had passed, and I realised she hadn't heard me calling.

I sat back on the wooden seat and slumped into a corner. The other kids just looked at me, they never said anything. I forgot all about the elephants and bears and lions. All I could think about was my mother. The sadness inside me was so great I couldn't even cry.

By the time I'd been in George Turner a couple of years, I began to get as adventurous as the other kids. I became a bit of a leader and had my own little gang.

Also, I wasn't scared at night any more. I actually came to love that part of the night when all the wild horses raced through. There were a lot of them in the hills, in those days. When we heard them coming, we'd lean over the verandah and call out. They were so beautiful, some silver, some white, some black and brown. They were going down to the grassy paddocks on the other side of the hill. I suppose they were a bit like us kids in a way, they didn't belong to anyone.

They'd been featuring a run of Tom Mix films on Friday nights and we'd all gotten interested in the Wild West. Sometimes, we'd pretend the Home's dunny cart was an old chuck wagon. We all had great imaginations.

Our enthusiasm for the Wild West led to a new interest in the wild brumbies. We decided that if we were really going to be like the cowboys, we needed a horse, so we thought we'd lasso one when they went through at night. There was one catch, we had no rope.

The only rope that we knew of was on the flag the school hoisted every Anzac Day. We knew what cupboard the flag was kept in, so we drew sticks to see who would steal it. This was a practice we used to solve most of our problems. If you drew the long stick, you just accepted your fate, even though you were scared stiff.

Harry lost. Poor Harry, he was always getting into strife. It was just his luck.

After Harry had sneaked over to the school and pinched the rope off the flag, we all leant over the verandah railings and waited in the dark for the horses to come through. We were very excited. Unfortunately, they always came through late, near midnight, so a lot of the smaller kids fell asleep over the verandah railings.

Round about eleven thirty, we heard the rumble of their hooves and we knew they were on their way. Harry leapt up onto the railings and got his lasso ready. When the brumbies came flying past, he flung the rope out as high and as far as he could, but when the rope disappeared, so did Harry. We watched in awe as he sailed over the railings, screaming. Once the horses had passed, we all ran down and found him lying in the dirt with his arm broken. We grabbed the rope and hid it, then we went and woke Miss Moore.

'He was walking in his sleep', we told her innocently, 'he fell off the verandah and broke his arm'.

That turned out to be a good excuse. So we often used it after that when we were caught out of bed, playing dares.

I grew to love adventures, and I always knew I had to be brave, it didn't do to lose face in front of your friends.

There was an empty cottage where old Sister Fanny lived. Actually, she lived on a part of the verandah which was enclosed in hessian. It was very dirty and must have been very cold in winter. The inside of the cottage was used for visitors, who sometimes came and stayed overnight or for a few days.

All the kids were too scared to go near Sister Fanny, we all thought she was a witch.

One day, some kids from a rival gang dared me to go right up to her. I wanted to back down, but, being a leader, I couldn't. Also, I'd been shooting my mouth off about how brave I was, so I had to live up to it.

I sneaked up very slowly to the cottage until I found myself standing just outside the hessian door that hung from the old tin roof. The flap swayed back and forth in the breeze and I could see inside to the dirt floor. There was a large, black cat lying on the ground asleep. I was sure then Sister Fanny must be a witch, because everyone knew witches had black cats.

I was so busy watching the cat, I didn't notice Sister Fanny. She pulled the hessian aside, stuck out her old, wrinkled face and said, 'Haaa!'. I jumped back in shock. She had lank, uncombed shoulder-length hair and she looked very grubby. As I gazed at her face, I realised that she really did have one blue and one brown eye. The other kids had told me that, but I hadn't believed them.

'I just wanted to pat the cat', I said quickly.

'Come in, child, come in', she said in a thin, wobbly voice. I went inside and sat down and patted the cat. I thought if I patted it, it wouldn't hurt me.

Sister Fanny kept mumbling and walking around the room. I began to feel sorry for her, it was so shabby. There were just an old iron bed and boxes for furniture, nothing nice. I realised then she wasn't a witch, just a frail old lady.

After a few minutes, I got up, said goodbye and rejoined the other kids. They couldn't believe I'd actually gone inside, they all thought I was really tough.

'You saw the witch', they said, 'you saw the witch. What do you think, is she a real witch?'

'No', I replied, ' and don't go throwing any more stones at her place. She's just an old lady.'

'Yeah, but she's got one brown eye and one blue', said Tommy, 'only witches have eyes like that!'.

I couldn't deny that, but I knew in my heart she was just an old lady.

There were a number of adults who I became quite attached to, and used to visit regularly. I found I got on well with older people, perhaps because they often had food, usually biscuits or cakes.

I regularly visited the office lady, Miss Button, who had a little room behind the office, to ask her if she had any jobs she needed doing. She was a particular friend of mine. She would get me to dust down her mantelpiece and then she'd make me a cup of tea and give me a biscuit.

I was very excited when she went for a trip to England. She was always talking about England. Once, she'd shown me a map of the world and pointed out where England was. Just before she left on her trip, she promised me she'd send me a postcard from England. I couldn't believe it when it finally arrived. All the kids thought I must be really important to get a postcard from the country where the King and Queen lived, because, apart from God, they were the next ones we stood in awe of.

About this same time, I was adopted by the Northam Country Women's Association as a needy child, they decided that they would send me a gift at Christmas and on my birthday. A parcel arrived on my birthday, not long after Miss Button's card. I told all the kids that Northam was really in England and that my parcel had come from the King and Queen. I was lucky, because my present was a beautiful doll, and it looked English. It was the best birthday I ever had, even though the older kids said I was lying and that Northam wasn't in England.

While Miss Button was in England, I spent a lot of time visiting Miss Lindsay, another old girl who lived at the Home. She had a tiny weatherboard cottage half-way between the last house and the hospital. She'd always been a part of Parkerville, no one could remember when she first came there. She was English, and, whenever I visited her, I always took her a flower I'd pinched from the garden, because Miss Moore had told me that the British like flowers.

After Miss Lindsay had made a big fuss over my flower, she would go to her glass cabinet and take out a plate of small iced cakes. The first time I'd had a cake from Miss Lindsay, I'd taken a bite straight away and found, to my horror, that my fancy pink cake had cobwebs inside. I'd been really scared, I'd wanted to vomit. Had I swallowed a spider? Would I die? I'd thanked her quickly, then rushed outside.

For the next few days, I'd prayed that if I had swallowed a spider, it wasn't a poisonous one. By the end of the week, I was still alive, so I decided to start visiting Miss Lindsay again.

Now, being a little wiser, I was always hopeful, but ever cautious, of her cakes. I never ate the cake in front of her, now. I'd just thank her and then run out into the bush, where I'd carefully pull the cake

257

apart before placing any in my mouth. I don't know why I kept going back, because every cake she gave me had cobwebs inside. I guess I thought I'd have to get a good one off her, eventually. I kept going back, she kept giving me cakes and they always had cobwebs in them. I hate to think how old they must have been. It was a long time before I gave up. I loved food that much.

I was really pleased when Miss Button returned from her trip. She only ever had very plain biscuits, but at least they were fresh.

At the opposite end of the Home to where Sister Fanny lived was the farm. Mr Pratt lived there, another of my favourite old people, not because of food, though, but because he had a horse and buggy. The horse was called Timmy, he was big and black and beautiful. When he was attached to the buggy, he'd strut like a rooster, waiting to be admired and stroked. He was Mr Pratt's pride and joy, nobody else was allowed to ride him.

The old farmhouse was very tumbled down. Climbing roses had gone wild and covered most of the front yard, junk covered most of the back. Rusty machinery, tins, harnesses, old sheets of iron. If you needed anything at all, you could find it at the farmhouse.

The older boys went over there regularly to milk the cows. We used to follow them. We'd lay back on the bales of straw in the milking shed and beg the boys to squirt us with milk. I had my mouth open all the time, it was lovely, feeling that warm, creamy milk shoot in and down your throat. It really warmed you up on a cold day.

Whenever Mr Pratt did the garden at George Turner, I'd follow him around, continually chatting about this and that. I liked talking to grown-ups, and he was a darling old fellow.

One day, I was playing chasey with the others on the road, when someone yelled that I was wanted. I walked up the wooden steps and onto the verandah, little Faye was there, looking scared. 'Moore's in an awful temper', she said, 'what have you done?'. I mothered little Faye, she relied on me and I knew she was worried about me.

'I'll be all right', I replied. I patted her head and walked inside.

'Where's that bloody kid?' I could hear Miss Moore screaming from the kitchen. What had I done? When I saw her, her face was contorted with rage.

She grabbed me by the arm and started belting me across the head. It was nothing new, she'd given me beltings before. Sometimes, she hit me so much I'd go deaf for a couple of days.

She dragged me towards the large clothes cupboard. I started to cry, I didn't know what I'd done wrong. 'Get your clothes, you stupid girl', she screamed. I was so upset, my eyes were too full of tears to see my clothes. I grabbed at a dress and she hit me again and shouted, 'Your good clothes'. Then she started shaking me and screaming that I had to be ready in fifteen minutes to go in the car. Where was I

258

going? I felt very frightened, were they sending me away? What about my mother, would I ever see her again? I started to tremble and shake all over.

Miss Moore called out to Pat, my friend, to come and help me get my clothes out. I knew all the other kids would be outside listening to the goings-on. They kept out of reach when Miss Moore's temper was aroused. I tried to stop myself from crying, but I couldn't, I started to sob. 'Stop crying', she shouted, 'I didn't hurt you!'.

She sent me to the bathroom to dress and wash my face. I managed to get my clothes on, then I splashed my face with cold water, but I still couldn't stop crying. Everything had happened so suddenly, I didn't know what I'd done wrong. I wanted to vomit. I heard the car toot loudly out the front. Miss Moore hauled me out, picked up my bag of clothes and took me to the car. 'Stop snivelling', she said, 'you didn't do anything wrong'.

I hopped in the front next to Willie, the driver, Sister Dora sat in the back. Willie started up the engine, then glanced down to me and said kindly, 'Don't cry any more, your mother will be all right'. I was really frightened, then.

When we arrived at Ivanhoe, Alice Drake-Brockman took me to where my mother was lying in bed on the balcony. She looked terrible, her eyes were closed, I thought she was dead. I went to race towards her, but Alice restrained me and said, 'Ssssh, she's asleep'. I tiptoed over and touched my mother's hand, which was resting on the white coverlet. She opened her eyes, tears trickled down her face, she squeezed my hand.

The following day, she told me what had happened. They'd taken my Aunty, Helen Bunda, to hospital, but her appendix had burst and there was nothing they could do. They'd asked my mother to give blood. They'd taken the first lot, but it had jelled through carelessness, so they'd taken some more. 'They nearly killed me', she whispered, 'I'll never go to hospital again'.

I asked her about Aunty Helen and she said, 'Aunty Helen died. The doctor didn't care. You see, Gladdie, we're nothing, just nothing.' I felt very sad, and sort of hopeless. I didn't want to be just nothing.

I stayed at Ivanhoe a week. When the others were asleep, I would sneak into bed with my mother. She'd cuddle me, with silent tears wet on her cheeks. She seemed so unhappy that I'd cry, too, loving the comfort of her arms, yet sad at her tears.

I was upset that Aunty was dead, but I was glad Mum was getting better. Alice was very cross with the hospital. She made my mother eat to get her strength back.

One day, when Mum was lying propped up on the pillows, the men from the *Daily News* arrived to take her photo. We were all very excited when we got the paper. Judy showed Mum her photo and then read the article out to her. It said how she'd nearly sacrificed her life to

259

save her cousin's and how brave she was. I felt very proud.

Everybody knew what had happened when I went back to Parkerville, some of the kids had seen my mother's picture in the paper. Miss Moore patted my shoulder and said she was pleased to see me back, but I couldn't look at her after the way she'd treated me. I felt betrayed.

It wasn't long after that that Mr Pratt's horse, Timmy, died. I was playing in the garden when Mr Pratt rode by with the buggy and Timmy. I ran up to the fence and waved madly at him, he waved back.

Suddenly, one of the wheels of the buggy caught in a rut in the road, the buggy overturned and poor Timmy fell and broke his leg. I screamed when I saw it happen, there was Timmy lying on his side in the dirt.

Mr Pratt gently undid the harness and talked to him in a loving way to keep him calm. Miss Moore came out and pulled me inside. She said I wasn't to go out until she said I could. Later, I heard the sound of a gunshot ring out and I knew Timmy was dead.

A few days afterwards, Mr Pratt was climbing a ladder at the farmhouse, when he suddenly fell to the ground, dead. I've always thought that the loss of Timmy was too much for him to bear.

Easter was always a special time for me, I considered Good Friday the saddest day of the year. I couldn't understand how anyone could do such a horrible thing as to kill Jesus.

We'd attend church in the morning and it'd be stripped bare, except for a large cross on which was pinned the brass body of Jesus. The cross was positioned in front of the altar, and above the altar was a huge glass window which opened to the sky.

After the service, we'd all file out solemnly. On the way back to George Turner, we'd pass some of the graves of the early pioneers and that made Good Friday seem even more depressing.

Once we were back at the house, we weren't allowed to play or make a noise, it was a day of solemnity.

Easter Sunday would change all that, we'd have a special midday dinner and an easter egg. Kids who had relatives usually got visitors who brought more easter eggs. My mother usually came to see me and brought me an egg. It was a really happy day and I'd feel good because Jesus was alive again.

In the May holidays, I usually went to Ivanhoe. Willie would drive me down to Perth and I'd be met by Alice.

I was always pleased to see my mother and really excited that I was going to be with her for two whole weeks. She'd give me a hug and then take me into the kitchen for a glass of milk and a piece of cake.

I loved Ivanhoe and I really loved Judy, she was so beautiful and she always made a fuss of me. She liked to dress me up, but I'd cry when she insisted on putting big satin bows in my hair. I didn't want to look like Shirley Temple.

I remember one holiday at Ivanhoe when I was very upset. I was in the kitchen with my mother. She had her usual white apron on and was bustling around, when Alice came in with June. I couldn't take my eyes off June. She had the most beautiful doll in her arms. It had golden hair and blue eyes and was dressed in satin and lace. I was so envious, I wished it was mine. It reminded me of a princess.

June said to me, 'You've got a doll, too. Mummy's got it.' Then, from behind her back, Alice pulled out a black topsy doll dressed like a servant. It had a red checked dress on and a white apron, just like Mum's. It had what they used to call a slave cap on its head. It was

261

really just a handkerchief knotted at each corner. My mother always wore one on washing days, because the laundry got very damp with all the steam and it stopped some of it trickling down her face.

I stared at this doll for a minute. I was completely stunned. That's me, I thought, I wanted to be a princess, not a servant. I was so upset that when Alice placed the black doll in my arms, I couldn't help flinging it onto the floor and screaming, 'I don't want a black doll, I don't want a black doll'. Alice just laughed and said to my mother, 'Fancy, her not wanting a black doll'.

I clung to my mother's legs and cried and cried. She growled at me for being silly and bad-mannered in front of Alice, but I knew she didn't really mean it. I could hear the sadness in her voice. She understood why I was upset.

They told the story of this often at Ivanhoe. They thought it was funny. I still can't laugh about it.

It was terrible in the nineteen thirties, the Depression was on and people were so poor, especially Aboriginal people.

They would come along the river, selling props. These were long, wooden poles people used to prop up their clothes-lines.

I think they liked calling in to Ivanhoe, because Alice had said that my mother was allowed to give them a cup of tea and a piece of cake or bread. Alice was always generous with food.

I used to feel so sorry for these Aboriginal people, I wondered how they could come to be so poor. They had nothing, especially the old ones. A lot of them had been separated from the young ones, all their kids had been taken off them, they had no one to look out for them.

My mother loved it when they came, she'd sit on the lawn with them and they'd talk about how it used to be in the old days. My mother always gave them clothes and shoes, whatever she could find. When they left, she'd have tears in her eyes. It hurt her to see her own people living like that.

At Christmas, I also went to Ivanhoe. We'd all sleep out on the balcony at the rear of the house, we had a lovely view over the Swan River from there.

At the top of the house was a large attic which June was allowed to use as a playhouse, it was a lovely room. There were seats under the windows and dolls and a dolls' house. There were teddies and other toys and a china tea-set. We'd play tea parties and practise holding out our little fingers like grown-ups did. June's dolls were lovely, they were china and dressed in satin and lace.

It was strange, really, at the Home, nobody owned a doll. There were a few broken ones kept in the cupboard, but when you asked to play with them, you had to play in the dining-room until you'd finished. You were never allowed to take one to bed.

I was lucky, because I had a rag doll my mother had given me called

Sally Jane. I loved her very much. She was kept at Ivanhoe for me and Mum let me take her to bed every night.

On Christmas morning, we'd wake up early and check the pillowslips we'd hung on the ends of our beds the night before. Alice always gave me a new dress, with hair ribbons to match. Mother always made me doll's clothes and I would dress Sally Jane in one of her new dresses. We were very happy together, Judy, June, Dick and I. It was like having a family.

Every year after each of the holidays, I found it harder and harder to leave my mother and return to Parkerville. I couldn't understand why I couldn't live at Ivanhoe and go to school with Judy and June. You see, I hadn't really worked out how things were when your mother was a servant. I knew the family liked me, so I couldn't understand why they didn't want me living there.

I can't say I was really rapt in school, I used to gaze out the window a lot. And I was always getting into trouble. It wasn't that I was a cheeky child, it was just that everybody got into trouble, in those days.

Usually, I managed to get out of trouble by making up a good story, there were only a few occasions when I wasn't quick enough to think up something convincing. I think one of the reasons I survived was because I learnt to lie so well.

You see, if there was an argument or if something had been damaged, and it was your word against a white kid, you were never believed. They expected us black kids to be in the wrong. We learnt it was better not to tell the truth, it only led to more trouble.

The Home also taught us never to talk openly about being Aboriginal. It was something we were made to feel ashamed of.

One year, we had a school play that was a great success. It was shown to people from the surrounding districts and was greeted with great enthusiasm. I was chosen to play the part of the fairy princess.

Actually, it was lucky I was chosen to do anything, because the year before, I'd disgraced myself in public. I was in the choir and had quite a good voice, so they decided I could do a solo. When we gave our first public concert, I just looked at all those strange faces and froze. I opened my mouth, but nothing came out. Sister Dora, who was head nun at Parkerville, had been really embarrassed.

Sister Rosemary had chosen me to play the part of the fairy princess, and when Sister Dora objected, she said there was nothing to worry about, because I didn't have to say anything.

I had to wear a long, flowing gown with a jewelled crown on my head. I had to walk to the centre of the stage and then back to my throne while all the elves paid homage to me. I loved it. I decided that, when I grew up, I wanted to be a film star.

The play was so popular that the Home decided to put it on in a hall next to Christ Church Grammar in Claremont. We were all loaded onto a big cattle truck and off we went. The play went well, with lots of loud applause at the end. I was very proud, because all the Drake-Brockmans were in the audience and, more importantly, so was my mother.

When it was all over, we only had a moment for a quick hug before being loaded back onto the cattle truck and taken home again.

When I was about eleven, we got a new headmaster at Parkerville, Mr Edwards. He was different to the old headmaster, he didn't yell so much. He was a slightly built man with a big, bushy moustache. He was very kind in a lot of ways, but when he got near the older girls, he just couldn't control himself. He was always squeezing their legs and wanting to sit at their desks and help them with their work. Everyone just ignored it. There was no use complaining because no one would believe you.

He encouraged my interest in poetry and introduced me to algebra, I loved both those things. When he realised that I'd read all the poetry books in the library and knew many poems off by heart, he lent me some of his own books, including a set of Shakespeare's plays. I read all of them and loved every one. I suddenly found that school didn't have to be dull after all, it could be quite exciting. I was no longer a middle-of-the-class student, but progressed to the top.

I think it was because of Mr Edwards that I was one of the girls chosen to visit St Hilda's Girls' College for the day. It was a great honour to be allowed to visit St Hilda's. I was really excited, because I knew it was the school that Judy had been to.

The St Hilda's girls were supposed to give you a nice afternoon tea and then entertain you. But when I got to the school, one of the teachers said that, seeing as I had such nice manners, I would be allowed to go and sit with a girl who was sick. I was so disappointed.

Her parents picked me up and took me to their place. She had some rabbits, we looked at those for a while and then we just sat around for the rest of the day. It was really boring. Late in the afternoon, they drove me back so I could catch the bus to Parkerville. I'd been trying to be so polite and that's where it got me.

Even though I was older now, I was still getting into scrapes. We'd go out in our little gangs and steal fruit from the surrounding orchards.

I'll never forget one Sunday night, Mr Tindale, the minister, was preaching his usual hellfire and brimstone sermon, when he suddenly stopped and pointed to the audience. Then he said in a loud thundery voice, 'Whoever has been stealing apricots from the Johnson farm will go to hell! I want the gang who did it to come and see me tomorrow afternoon after school. If you take your punishment, there might be some hope for you.'

After that, he continued to rant and rave about the devil and bang his fist on the pulpit. Mr Tindale always wore long, flowing, black robes, so I could imagine just what the devil looked like.

Sister Dora loved his sermons, she would almost stand in her seat when he shouted that we were all going to hell and her eyes lit up whenever he mentioned the devil.

Anyhow, this time, I was really scared, because I felt sure he knew it was my gang that had been raiding the Johnson farm. My mind

265

was working overtime, what could I do? I hated being caned by Tinny, he always lifted the girls' dresses before hitting them, it was quite degrading. I'd managed to talk my way out of trouble a lot in the past, I was wondering what kind of story I could invent to get out of this one.

As we were filing out of church, Margaret, a girl from another gang, whispered to me, 'How the devil did he find out?'.

'Dunno.'

'I was sure no one had seen us pinch that fruit', she said. 'Guess we'll just have to face the music now, he obviously knows.'

'You', I said, 'were your lot stealing apricots from there?'.

'Yeah. And I'm not looking forward to the stick', Margaret grimaced.

I felt very close to her at that moment, I also felt very guilty. To compensate, I gave her half the chewing-gum from my mouth. She was very pleased, gum was hard to get.

When we were out raiding orchards, we often came across old tramps in the bush. Some of them had little makeshift huts they used to sleep in.

One of these tramps made us kids a swing. He did his best, but it was too high, so we'd climb up the tree and then leap on it and pretend we were Buck Rogers or Tarzan.

One day, we were banned from going to that part of the bush. The rumour was that a boy had hung himself there. The House Mothers said it wasn't true, but I think it was. They said the boy had been sent somewhere else. It made me feel very sad. I never went to that tree again. I think it could have happened, because, unless you could look out for yourself, you had a bad time. You could feel that low that you'd want to die.

Towards the end of the school year, we'd be given our annual treat to the pictures. We went by train to Perth, then marched up Plaza Arcade to the Royal Theatre in Hay Street.

All the other Homes would be there, too, Sister Kate's and Swanleigh. Some of the kids would be very excited, because they had brothers and sisters in the other Homes and it was the only time of the year they saw them.

I used to feel glad then that I was an only child, it always upset me to think that all they saw of the rest of their family was just a glimpse and a wave before we were all ushered into the theatre.

As we moved through the theatre doors, we were handed a paper bag containing sandwiches, a cake and lollies. It was such a treat.

I always tried to sit upstairs or under the balcony, but never in any other part of the theatre, because you got pelted with bits of leftover food. The yelling and screaming had to be heard to be believed, there was absolutely no control. The House Mothers tried, but there wasn't any point in them shouting at us, because we couldn't hear them.

I didn't go to Ivanhoe that Christmas. I was called into the office and told I wouldn't be going, because they had other people staying there. I couldn't understand this, I didn't take up much room. Sister Rosemary had tears in her eyes because I was so upset. 'Never mind, dear', she said, 'you'll be going to the beach'. It was no consolation. I felt really hurt, like no one wanted me.

The Home had a house at Cottesloe, it was a large, rambling one and was used mainly for holidays for children who had nowhere else to go. Each child was allowed to stay for two weeks. We went by train to Perth and then changed trains for Cottesloe, it was the longest train ride I'd ever had.

When we stopped at Claremont Station, I stuck my head out the window, hoping that, by some strange chance, my mother might be there. Of course, she wasn't.

The house at Cottesloe was so close to the beach it took only a few minutes to walk down. Every room was filled with beds so as many children as possible could fit in. The dining-room was packed with wooden tables and benches. We had plenty of food, even supper, and the kitchen staff let us help ourselves whenever we felt hungry.

By this time, I had made friends with a girl called Margot, she was a few years older than me and very pretty. One day, we were racing into the waves and laughing, when two boys came and joined us. I was completely tongue-tied, I couldn't think of a thing to say. Margot was full of confidence and spun them a story about us being on holiday from the country. You never told anyone you were from a Home because they looked on you as some kind of criminal.

When the other girls found out that we were seeing two boys, they looked at me through new eyes. I wasn't just a kid any more.

That night, I spent ages admiring myself in the bathroom mirror. I could see only my head and shoulders in my mirror at George Turner, so it was really wonderful to be able to look into this full-length one and see the whole of me. I was really surprised, because my figure had changed. I was taller and my stomach had almost disappeared. I'd carried it around with me for so long I wondered how it could have gone without me noticing it. My hair was a bit longer and it was black and curly. I realised suddenly that I really was pretty, people weren't just being polite saying that.

I felt more confident, seeing myself in this new light, but I stopped going to the beach with Margot. I wasn't keen on seeing those boys again.

I felt different after coming back from Cottesloe in the new year. Even Miss Moore treated me as an older girl, now. I was allowed to stay up for an extra half an hour after the little ones had gone to bed. Miss Moore let me read some of her magazines and she'd bring in her wireless and we'd listen to the news.

When I went out to bed, I'd tuck little Faye in, it was a habit I'd gotten into over the years. I felt really sorry for the little ones at George Turner, I had never forgotten how sad I'd been when I left Babyland. They often needed comforting at night. They'd turn their faces into the pillow and cry, because they knew if Miss Moore heard them, she'd give them a smack. She hated being disturbed at night.

I couldn't stand it if they cried too long, I'd take them into bed with me. Sometimes when they cried, they wet their beds, they were terrified of getting into trouble about it. I'd get up and change their beds and hide their wet sheets and pyjamas in the bottom of the laundry basket. They always wanted me to be their mother. I felt guilty because, sometimes, I used to get sick of them. They wanted to be babies all the time, but they didn't realise that I was only a kid, too.

One of my favourite jobs now was going over to Babyland and looking after the little ones. My friend Pat had a little sister there. There were four kids from her family at Parkerville and the terrible thing was they were all put in different houses.

Pat's baby sister thought I was her mother. She called me Mummy all the time and she said I smelt the same as the Mummy she'd had that had died.

I used to cry for all those little kids, sometimes. They had no one.

Even though I was twelve now, no one had told me the facts of life. We were totally ignorant about the things that could happen to our bodies. The older girls never told you anything, they'd just laugh and keep everything a secret.

We were all so innocent it would have been easy for someone to take us for a ride. We had no protection. There must have been cases of kids being molested, but I was lucky, it never happened to me. No one would believe you if you complained about things anyway, adults were always right, kids had no say.

I was also aware that I was changing, growing up, because boys who I had previously fought with now seemed embarrassed in my company. The old easygoing atmosphere had gone. I guess they were changing, too.

One Sunday, my mother visited. I could tell she was upset as soon as I saw her.

We went for a walk and she told me that Alice had asked her to leave Ivanhoe. 'She said she can't afford to keep me any more', she

268

said bitterly. 'How many years have I been working for that family and they can't afford to keep me!'

She was very hurt. I was cross and confused, in some ways, I had felt like part of the family and now Mum was no longer going to have anything to do with them. I felt very unsure of myself.

It was well known around Claremont what a good worker my mother was. I think people felt sorry for her for the way she'd been treated. A Mrs Morgan offered Mum a job as a live-in housekeeper and she said that I would be allowed to go and stay there on holidays. Mum was only too pleased to accept this offer. It was the first time she'd been out on her own in the world. She had always told me that she'd be at Ivanhoe for ever, that it was her home.

The Morgans were good to Mum. They gave her an increase in pay, she had a nice room and, for the first time in her life, annual holidays.

Going to Morgans' was the best thing that could have happened to her, she developed a new independence. It was a different atmosphere, they'd never had a servant before. They didn't have Victorian attitudes towards her. Also, this new job was like a proper business arrangement, it wasn't like being one of the family and not getting any time off.

I loved it when she was there, it meant she could come to the Home and spend her annual holidays with me. The nuns let her sleep in a room just off one of the school buildings and they let me sleep there, too. A couple of times, she brought the two Morgan girls, June and Dianna, up with her. They were nice girls and enjoyed all the bush around the Home.

In the morning, we'd walk down to the grocer's at the bottom of the hill. There was a deep creek that ran past the store, it was spanned by a wooden bridge. We'd cross the bridge and go into the store.

I could never take my eyes off the jars of lollies. There were jars and jars, all containing lollies of all sizes and colours. Hard boiled striped candy-sticks stood on the front counter and, next to them, large tins of mixed loose biscuits. Mum would buy me a bag of chocolate biscuits, she knew they were my favourites.

I was very popular with the other children at this time. I felt sorry for them, they all wanted mothers, too. They'd rush over when we were sitting on the lawn and would want to sit near her and touch her, especially the little ones. She always gave them a lolly, but I think it was when she spoke to them or kissed them that they were really happy. That was what they really wanted. She was a very kind person and tried to make a fuss of everyone.

At Christmas, I went and stayed at Morgans'. Although I missed Ivanhoe, I liked June and Dianna, and Mum now had more time for me, because there was less work to do. I was pleased for her in a way, because I was sick of seeing her work so hard.

After tea, she would take me visiting to see Eileen and Nellie, two of her friends who were also servants. They were always happy and laughing and had nice bedrooms, too. They always made a fuss of me, giving me clothes and biscuits and milk.

But after Mum had been at Morgans' about two years, Alice asked her if she would come back to Ivanhoe to work. I wanted her to stay at Morgans', because it was easier for her, but I think Mum still felt a loyalty to the family. It was easy for people to make her feel sorry for them. She was too kind-hearted.

Alice's mother had come to live with them and she was very difficult to look after. I think that's why they wanted Mum back. She had to accept a cut in wages and no annual holidays, but she went anyway. She told me that it was to be permanent and she'd never be leaving there again.

I went to Ivanhoe for Christmas that year, I was about fourteen by then. Judy, June and Dick suddenly seemed a lot older than me. It wasn't the same as our carefree childhood days. Even though we had all loved each other as children, something had changed. We weren't children any more, Judy, June and Dick had begun to get more like their mother. They treated Mum like a servant, now, she wasn't their beloved nanny any more.

June had a friend who was a bit of a snob and this girl was always putting me in my place because I was only the maid's daughter. I'd go and sit in Mum's room and cry. I was suddenly very unsure of my place in the world. I still ate with the family in the dining-room, but I felt like an outsider, especially when Alice would ring a little brass bell and my mother would come in and wait on us.

I suddenly realised that there hadn't been one Christmas dinner when Mum had eaten her meal with us. She'd had hers alone in the kitchen all these years. I never wanted to be in the dining-room again after that, I wanted to be in the kitchen with my mother.

After the summer holidays, Mum took me back to Parkerville, but when I got there, I discovered that Miss Moore had left and I was to have a new House Mother. I felt terrible, I had been living with Miss Moore for nine years and I hadn't even had the opportunity to say goodbye to her.

Why was everything changing? I was really frightened, because my new House Mother had been an enemy of Miss Moore's and I knew she'd take it out on me. Even though Miss Moore had belted me a lot, I was considered one of her pets. I just knew I'd have a bad time.

Also, I was worried that I'd get sent out to work as a domestic and never see my mother again. All the Aboriginal girls were sent out as domestics once they reached fourteen. Only the white kids were trained for anything.

I cried and cried and begged Mum not to leave me there. I had this terrible feeling that if she left me there this time, I'd die. I was so upset I went to the office with Mum to see Sister Dora.

I had to sit on a wooden bench outside and wait while Mum went in. I tried to listen to what they were saying, but they were speaking too softly.

Finally, they called me in, there was an exchange of glances between Miss Button, Sister Dora and Sister Rosemary, then Miss Button said, 'Do you want to leave here, Gladys? Your mother has said she wants to take you with her.' She smiled kindly at me.

'Oh yes', I replied, 'yes please!'. I couldn't believe it, to be with my mother for always, it was too good to be true. I walked over to George Turner to pack.

Pretty soon, the news spread that I was leaving and all the kids crowded round. I handed out keepsakes from my locker. I gave Pat my blue overcoat that was now a bit tight on me, she'd always liked it.

As we set off down the hill, I waved goodbye. I was very excited to think that, at last, Mum and I were going to live at Ivanhoe together. Maybe my childhood dream would come true and I'd be the same as Judy and June. Maybe we'd be one big, happy family, after all. That was what I wanted more than anything.

It wasn't long before my dreams came crashing around my feet. Alice was very cross with Mum for bringing me back. She said I couldn't live at Ivanhoe, I wasn't wanted.

It took a week for Mum to find a family who would take me in. The Hewitts had three boys of their own and often took in older girls. I got on well with the boys and enrolled in Claremont High School. I tried not to think about Ivanhoe. I wasn't allowed to stay there weekends, either. If Mum wanted to see me, she had to visit at the Hewitts'. I felt very hurt by it all.

The Hewitts were very religious, but they had a different kind of religion to me. I'll never forget the first Sunday morning they took us all down to Fremantle. I thought we were going to church, I never realised they intended holding a revivalist meeting on a street corner.

We all stood around in a circle and Mr Hewitt handed me a hymn book. Everyone started singing loudly and raising their hands and shouting, 'Praise the Lord!'. As the meeting got more exuberant, one or two would suddenly leap into the air, shouting, 'Hallelujah brother, Praise the Lord!'.

A lot of people started gathering round and I slowly moved backwards into the crowd, lowering my hymn book as I went. I thought I'd try and pretend I was one of the onlookers.

Unfortunately, Mr Hewitt, who was really quite a sweetie, noticed what I was doing, he grabbed me by the arm and drew me back into the wild circle of worshippers. He whispered in my ear, 'Sing, Glad, sing. Raise your voice to heaven!'

We'd all sing loudly, more people would leap into the air, shouting, 'Hallelujah', then we all had to echo it.

The meeting got more and more frenzied and the minister started shouting out to the onlookers, 'Repent before it's too late!'. All the sinners gathered round seemed quite impressed with the whole proceedings. I suddenly felt a dig in my back and a voice said, 'Now!'. I found myself suddenly yanked from the circle and pulled away. I was amazed when I saw that my rescuer was Warren, the Hewitts' eldest son. We made our way through the entranced crowd and stood against a shop wall.

'I saw you trying to hide before', said Warren. 'Isn't it embarrassing?'

'Yes', I groaned. 'I had no idea it would be like this. I thought we were going to church.'

'We do this every Sunday, you have to be dying to get out of it.'

'Oh, no', I sighed. 'I hope no one I know ever sees me!'.

I had been worrying about starting Claremont High School. I didn't want anybody to find out I'd been in a Home and I was concerned that I wouldn't be able to make friends.

As it turned out, I got along with all the other kids really well, especially Noreen and Doreen, who became my very best friends. Noreen was Scottish and was only in Australia because of the war. It was 1940, and she had been sent out with a lot of other children for safe keeping. She had a terrific sense of humour. I spent a lot of time at her house.

Every lunch hour at school, we had air raid drill. There was a park nearby, with trenches dug in case we were ever bombed. At lunch-time, they'd blow the siren and we all had to run as fast as we could and jump in the trenches. You can imagine the shambles there was, we'd all leap in and fling up sand at each other. It was chaos.

Actually, in a funny sort of way, the war really affected our education. All the young men had joined up and I suppose some of the women had been manpowered, so all our teachers were really old.

I'll never forget Miss Edwards, her fiance had been killed in World War One and she was very sentimental. She loved reading us old romantic novels, especially *Wuthering Heights*. She would sit out the front of the class with tears streaming down her face. Now and then, she'd have to stop completely and blow her nose and try and pull herself together.

During our lunch hour, Noreen, Doreen and I would walk down to the Claremont Shopping Centre. I was always the last back, so I'd call in to the florist and ask if there were any leftover flowers that I could give an old lady who was sick. They always managed to scrounge me up a few and I'd present them to Miss Edwards when I got back to school. 'I'm sorry I'm late, Miss Edwards, but I was buying you these.' And she'd say, 'That's all right, Gladys, you may sit down'. There'd be tears in her eyes.

One day, I was so tired that I went to sleep in school and Miss Edwards noticed. 'I think you'd better sit outside the class for a while, Gladys', she said, 'the fresh air might wake you up'.

I was really scared. I knew that if Mr Simms, the headmaster, came along and saw me sitting there, he'd know I had done something wrong.

I nearly died when I saw the Head coming down the hall. I sat with my head bowed, hoping that he wouldn't notice me. I couldn't bear to think of being caned. It reminded me too much of Parkerville. He stopped when he got to me and said, 'What are you doing out here, girlie?'.

I peered up at him, he was a tall, plumpish man, with small round specs perched on the end of his nose.

'I feel sick', I said, which was the truth.

273

'You poor child', he murmured, 'you shouldn't be sitting out here, come into the office at once'. I followed him down the hall and into his office.

'Now, girlie', he said, 'have you eaten lunch? I know what you young people are like, you get talking and playing and you forget to eat your lunch.'

I thought of all the fabulous biscuits and cakes that the teachers had for morning tea, so I couldn't help replying, 'I haven't eaten anything'.

'I thought so', he said. 'No wonder you feel sick, sit down here.' He sat me down at his desk and then deposited a large glass of milk in front of me, a plate of iced cakes and a huge tin of cream biscuits. 'Eat!' he commanded. I didn't need to be told twice. I bogged in straight away.

'I have to go', he said, 'but when you've finished, you lie down on that old cane lounge, and when the bell goes, you can go home'.

About an hour later, the bell woke me and I got up and left. As I was walking down the hall, Miss Edwards saw me and called, 'Gladys, where did you get to?'.

'Mr Simms took me into his office', I told her.

'Serves you right, Gladys', she said. 'I don't mind you being late, but you must never go to sleep when I'm reading Jane Austen.'

Our chemistry class was always interesting. There weren't many girls doing chemistry, but I liked it.

Doreen had warned me about this class. 'Watch out in Chem', she'd whispered one day as we walked through the door. I didn't realise what she meant, until one day, I stood next to our teacher. He couldn't keep his hands to himself. He loved doing experiments which required him to turn the lights off, and he always chose one of the girls to help him. While you were holding the Bunsen burner, he'd be holding everything else.

He tried it on with Noreen once and she kicked him in the shins. When he found out Noreen and I were friends, he left me alone. I suppose he thought I might follow her example and kick him, too. He preferred girls who were a little more passive.

It was during that year in high school that Mum left Ivanhoe again. I was really angry about that. She'd given up a good job to go back to Alice and now she'd turned around and said that they didn't need her any more and she'd have to find somewhere else to live.

Mum was very hurt, she had pay owing to her which I don't think she ever got. They'd treated me like one of the family in the past, but I was glad now that I didn't belong to them.

One of Mum's friends told her about a job that was going for a cook in the Colourpatch restaurant, it was a little place just opposite the Ocean Beach Hotel, which was an R and R place for American sailors.

Most of the help in the restaurant was voluntary, because they tried to raise money for the armed forces, but the cook's job was a paying one. Mum applied for the job and got it. It was well known around the area what a good cook she was.

Molly Skinner, the author, owned a house just behind the hotel and she said Mum could pay rent and live with her if she wanted to.

Molly was very sympathetic to Aboriginal people and treated them kindly. Mum moved in with her. Molly also said that I could come and stay on weekends. I was very pleased about that, because I had hardly seen Mum for the past few months.

I think Mum would have liked me to live with her full time, but she lacked the confidence to move me away from the Hewitts'. She was frightened that something might go wrong and I'd be taken away. She knew Aboriginal people like her weren't allowed to have families. It was because of that that she tried to keep a low profile.

I loved spending weekends with her, she'd spoil me, and Molly Skinner was always pleased to see me.

Every Saturday afternoon, Mum would give me threepence to go to the pictures with Noreen and Doreen. We had great fun. All the kids from school would be there and we'd yell and scream.

The Colourpatch was really busy on Sundays, so Mum often got me to help out with the waitressing.

The Americans were lovely, they'd leave large tips for me under their plates. All the other waitresses had to hand their tips in, but I was told I was allowed to keep mine. I think it was because Mum was such a good cook. She always gave everyone double helpings and nothing was too much for her. I think she felt sorry for a lot of the servicemen there because some of them were only boys. It was a really happy time for me.

One Sunday night, I arrived back at the Hewitts', to be met with serious faces from the whole family. Mrs Hewitt took Mum into the lounge and I had to sit out in the hall.

'You're in big trouble', Warren whispered. I didn't know what I'd done wrong. Then the youngest Hewitt boy came out and said, 'Gladys, you've sinned!'.

A few minutes later, Mrs Hewitt came out and said, 'Will you please come in, Gladys?'.

I looked at Mum, she was sitting in a chair beside the open fireplace, she looked completely dumbfounded.

'Now, Gladys', said Mrs Hewitt, 'I am going to ask you a question and I want you to answer truthfully. Did you go to the pictures, did you enter that house of sin on Saturday afternoon?' I couldn't think of what to say. 'It's no use trying to deny it', she said. 'One of the ladies from the church saw you.'

That was when I hung my head in shame. I didn't feel sinful, I'd had a great time, but I felt it was expected of me. Mrs Hewitt turned to Mum and said, 'I don't think it will be suitable for Gladys to stay here any longer. I'm trying to turn her into a good Christian and you're letting her sin on Saturday afternoons!'

Mum just looked at me. She'd never heard of pictures being sinful before.

Mrs Hewitt pointed to the corner of the room and said, 'Gladys, I've taken the liberty of packing your suitcases, I think you'd better go now.'

Mum and I went back to Cottesloe. We didn't know what to say to each other, neither one of us could think of a thing. For the first time in our lives, we were together. I don't think Mum knew how to handle it. She was too scared to realise that it had actually happened. She was my mother and I was her daughter and we could be a family now. I think she was afraid to get used to it in case I got taken off her again. She knew Aboriginal people who'd never seen their children again.

Miss Skinner was very happy to have me there.

I finished school at the end of 1943, I was sixteen. All my friends were going on to business college, but I knew that wasn't possible for me.

I spent my time helping Mum in the restaurant. I was put in charge of making up milkshakes in the lolly shop attached to the Colourpatch. I took great pride in my work and people would come from miles to buy a milkshake off me. I experimented with the contents all the time and would put in great dollops of ice-cream. Sometimes, I put in so much the mixer wouldn't turn. They took me off the milkshakes, eventually, I don't think they paid.

After a while, Alice got me a job on trial with a florist in Claremont at six shillings a week. It was a funny set-up in those days. If you were monied people or if you had a name, like Drake-Brockman, it was like 'Open Sesame'. People ran after you, they rushed to serve you. I think it was a hang-up from Victorian England, though there are a lot of people who still do it today.

I was very excited about my job, I used to ride from Cottesloe to Claremont on an old bike.

The other junior who worked there was great. She was as fair as I was dark. She warned me about my new boss. 'She's a bit of an old cow', she said. 'She'll leave money on the floor just to see if you'll pinch it, so watch out.'

Sure enough, I was told to sweep the shop and there, on the black oiled floor, was a two-shilling piece. I gave it to the boss, she feigned surprise and put it in the till. A week later, there was another two-shilling piece on the floor. I handed that in, too, that was when I was told that, from then on, I was on staff and would get ten shillings a week.

Mrs Sales, my boss, was a real martinet. Her husband was a bootmaker and worked at the back of the shop.

He reminded Kathy and me of a little frightened mouse. Sometimes, he'd sneak out and have a cigarette in the old wooden toilet down the back. Mrs Sales disapproved of smoking, so he always made sure she didn't see him go.

One day, she came storming into the shop with an old cigarette butt she'd found. She accused Kathy and I of smoking on her time. She searched our bags for cigarettes. I never smoked, but Kathy did, she always hid hers behind the back door. I suppose it never occurred to our boss that her husband was the culprit, because she'd banned him from smoking. He never questioned her authority about anything else.

Mrs Sales had another florist shop on the corner of Broadway. I used to catch the trolley bus down and take flowers for them to sell. The junior there was called Violet, she was a nice girl and we became friends.

Kathy, Violet and I were all about the same age. We got plenty of attention from the Americans, because they were always going into florist shops to order corsages for their girlfriends. They were very different to Australian men, much more polite.

About a year later, Kathy became engaged to an American sailor, so we'd often go out to the pictures with his friends. I had a great time until they got serious, Americans always wanted to get engaged. For the first time in my life, I felt free. I didn't have to answer for everything I did. Of course, Mum tried to be very strict with me. She was so suspicious, it was all very innocent, but she kept saying I didn't know what the world was like or what men were like. I realise now that she was right. I had had a very protected life. I stopped telling her when I was going out and who I was going out with, it only made her worry.

It wasn't long before I'd become very good friends with one of the customers from the shop. She was an English lady called Lois, her husband had been imprisoned by the Japanese. She was a wonderful person, kind and sincere, but she also liked her beer and always had an American in tow.

It was through Lois that I met a nice Scottish sailor. I went out with him for quite a while, it was a good friendship. For once, Mum approved. She knew how wild the Yanks were, so I suppose she thought I'd be safe with a Scotsman.

Every weekend, the Yanks had a wild brawl down on the seafront and the police were called in. It was almost a regular outing for them. It was difficult during the war, some of the men had been through terrible things, I think they needed to let off steam some way.

I remember, one Sunday, waiting at a bus stop for a bus to my girlfriend's house, when a lady came along. She was catching the same bus as me, so we started to chat.

'You're very beautiful, dear', she said, 'what nationality are you, Indian?'.

'No', I smiled, 'I'm Aboriginal'.

She looked at me in shock. 'You can't be', she said.

'I am.'

'Oh, you poor thing', she said, putting her arm around me, 'what on earth are you going to do?'.

I didn't know what to say. She looked at me with such pity, I felt

278

really embarrassed. I wondered what was wrong with being Aboriginal. I wondered what she expected me to do about it.

I talked to Mum about it and she told me I must never tell anyone what I was. She made me really frightened. I think that was when I started wishing I was something different.

It was harder for Mum than me because she was so broad featured she couldn't pass for anything else. I started noticing that, when she went out, people stared at her, I hadn't realised that before.

The conversation with that lady at the bus stop really confused me. I suddenly felt like a criminal. I couldn't understand why I felt so terrible. Looking back now, I suppose she knew more about how Aboriginal people were treated than I did. She probably knew I had no future, that I'd never be accepted, never be allowed to achieve anything.

I tried for a while after that to talk to Mum and get her to explain things to me, especially about the past and where she'd come from. It was hopeless, we'd been apart too long to get really close. I knew she loved me and I loved her, but, for all my childhood, she had been just a person I saw on holidays. I couldn't confide my worries to her. She just kept saying, 'Terrible things will happen to you if you tell people what you are'. I felt, for her sake as well as my own, I'd better keep quiet. I was really scared of authority. I wasn't sure what could happen to me.

Molly Skinner sold her house, so we had to find somewhere else to live. We managed to rent another place near the Ocean Beach Hotel. It was a nice little weatherboard house.

Mum and I began to disagree a lot more. I had bought myself a few things from my wages and she would give them away to her friends without even asking me. If they said they liked something, she'd say, 'Oh, Glad doesn't want that, she can buy another one, you take it'. People would come and deliberately point out something of mine and she would give it to them straight away, especially if they were white people. I used to think she was trying to impress them. She was trying to buy white friends. It used to really upset me. There were so many things that I didn't understand, then.

Another lady came to help cook at the Colourpatch and I became very good friends with one of her daughters. We went many places together and I often stayed overnight at her house. She had brothers and sisters, I really envied that.

One of her sisters became engaged and I was invited to the engagement party, that was where I met Bill.

It was strange, really, because, all my teenage years, I'd dreamt of this man who I would one day meet and marry, so it was quite a shock to see him at this party. The dreams I'd had about him were always mixed up and recurring. Sometimes, they'd turn into nightmares. My future marriage was to turn out like that, it was to be good and bad, only I didn't know it, then.

As soon as I was introduced to Bill, I knew my carefree days were over. I wasn't ready to settle down and get married, but I knew I didn't have any choice, this was meant to be.

Bill was different from the other men I'd gone out with, he was older, more worldly. I knew he'd been a POW in Germany, but I didn't realise then what a terrible time he'd had.

None of my friends liked Bill and Mum disapproved of him, too. 'He drinks too much', she told me, 'you don't want to marry a drinker'. My friends tried to warn me about him. They said he was wild, sometimes crazy, but I didn't listen.

The day after I'd met Bill, he said, 'You're going to marry me'.

'No, I'm not', I said.

'Yes, you are.'

I was going with someone else at the time, so I thought, well, I might be able to hold him off for a while, but it wasn't to be. We went out for a year before we married. Mum never changed her mind about him. I told him I was Aboriginal, but he said he didn't care. And I don't think he did, then, it was later that he changed.

His parents disapproved of me, they didn't want him marrying a coloured person. At the same time, they were glad to get him off their hands, because they hadn't been able to control him. They were sick of him wrapping trucks around telephone poles.

I managed to get Bill to cut down on his drinking. I hoped it was a change for the better that would last. Mum didn't want to come to the wedding and neither did Bill's family, so we went and got married in a registry office. I was twenty-one. I think Mum had hoped it would all blow over and I'd get interested in someone else. I never told her when I was going to get married, I just went and did it. We'd talked about it before and it had only led to arguments. She had always been very jealous of anyone who took my attention away from her. She wanted me to stay home for the rest of my life and look after her.

After we were married, we lived with Mum. I was very happy. I continued to work at the florist shop. Mrs Sales sold out to a Mrs Richardson and she kept me on because I was good at my job. Richie, as we called her, was a real character, she would lie out the back on a small settee and drink wine all day. She left the running of the shop completely to me. At the end of the day, I'd wake her up and then I would catch the bus home.

Things didn't improve with Bill's family. They were very disappointed that he had actually gone ahead and married me. Bill's mother was very narrow-minded, she used to say things to Bill behind my back. I knew she would never accept me as an equal. I don't know how much Bill's father worried about me being coloured. He was always under the weather. Sometimes, he'd make a big fuss of me because I'd slip him a bit of money. I think he liked anybody who'd give him a few bob.

I knew Bill had had a funny upbringing. I was a real innocent compared to him.

Grandpa Milroy used to travel around putting in petrol bowsers for the Shell Oil Company and Bill's mother was always sending Bill off to the goldfields to haul his father out of the pubs and bring him home. Bill's father gambled away a fortune, and had Bill drinking beer from his early teenage years.

When Bill was fourteen, he had run away from home and got a job up North as a stockman. He told everyone he was sixteen, he could pass for that because he was tall. He loved the life up there and was very upset when his father found him and made him return to Perth.

I found it difficult mixing with Bill's brothers and their friends. I'd been brought up strictly, whereas they lived in a brave new world. It was becoming a permissive society, even then.

Bill was different to his brothers. He had strong ideas and a kind heart. He had religious beliefs. When he was younger, he had wanted to become a priest, his mother was a strict Catholic. Bill had what you'd call a more universal outlook on life, I think that was because he'd seen a lot that other people hadn't. He never talked about his religious beliefs, but I knew they were there, deep inside him. Sometimes, when he talked about the war, I felt that there was a spiritual force that helped him get through. There were many times when he should have died, but didn't. He was meant to come back.

When I found out I was pregnant, I was really excited. Bill was overjoyed, expecting it to be a son, but it was Sally. I couldn't believe that I finally had a family of my own. Mum was really pleased, too. In a strange way, I think it made her feel more secure, she was a grandmother, now.

It wasn't long after that that Bill applied for a tradesman's flat down at Beaconsfield, where he was working as a plumber.

After the war, there was a housing shortage and a lot of these weatherboard clusters had been built, they were mainly tenanted by English people who migrated out here in the hope of a better life. We were pleased to be moving into our own place. The surroundings were very pretty, it had originally been a farm and everyone still called it Mulberry Farm. There was a huge mulberry tree opposite our flat and olive trees dotted all over the place.

When we first moved in, we were always broke, it made a difference, having to pay rent. I had to give up work when I became pregnant. Also, people were always coming around, wanting to borrow money. I felt sorry for them and would give them what I had, but they never paid any of it back. Apparently, this was the norm, but I didn't know. I had to cut down on my lending.

There was plenty of action at Mulberry Farm, domestic fights all the time and some funny things going on. It always gave me a good laugh.

Sally was very sick when she was small, we nearly lost her a couple of times. Sometimes during the night, I'd awake to see the figure of a nun standing next to her cot. It didn't frighten me, I knew she was being watched over, the way I had been when I was a child. I knew that she would never be a strong person, but she wouldn't die young.

Bill began having nightmares again. He'd suffered from them ever since he'd come back from the war. He'd scream and scream at night, I used to feel so sorry for him. Before we married, I had thought that the idea of being a POW was something very heroic and romantic, now I thought differently.

I used to try and get him to talk about his nightmares, it helped him a little, but he'd never go really deeply into what had happened to him. I think there were some things that were too degrading for him to share. I knew there had been one German commandant that had treated him really badly. Bill absolutely hated him, I think if he'd had the opportunity, he would have killed him. Bill would never tell me what had happened. A lot of his nightmares were about this chap. He would dream he couldn't get away.

One time, Bill's mother came around, she said she wanted to ask Bill something. She worked quite a few nights at the trots and she told him that a tall man with an accent had come up to her and said, 'Did you have a son who was a POW during the war in Germany?'.

282

'Yes', she said, 'how did you know?'.

'It's the eyes', he said, 'you have the same eyes. I would recognise those eyes anywhere.' Then, apparently, he disappeared into the crowd.

I'll never forget the look on Bill's face when she asked him who the chap could be. He went as white as a sheet. He knew who it was, but he wouldn't tell us, he just locked himself in his room and wouldn't come out.

There was a real mess after the war, I think a lot of Germans came out to Australia, passing themselves off as different nationalities. This chap was German. I think he was the man Bill hated, I'm sure of it.

It was that episode that precipitated his drinking again. He'd been good since he'd married me, he'd settled down a lot, but now, all he was interested in was forgetting the past in a bottle. He hardly ate, he just drank. Mum had to bring me food from the restaurant, I never had any money. Sometimes, he'd disappear for days and I wouldn't see him. I was worried sick, anything could have happened to him. I knew he had blackouts. I sometimes wondered if he even knew where he'd been all that time.

It got so bad that, in the end, I couldn't stand it, I took Sally and moved back in with Mum. She was pleased to have me there, I think she'd been worried about what Bill might do.

I'd been at Mum's about ten days and I still hadn't seen him. I couldn't help thinking about all the things he'd told me about the war, and I wondered about what he hadn't told me. I started to worry and felt so sad about what they'd done to him. I still loved him. I've never told anyone Bill's war experiences, but perhaps it will help you to understand if I write it down.

Bill fought in the desert with the 2/16th Battalion.

He said he found it so hard to kill other people. I remember him telling me about one time when there were Germans in the sandhills and he could see them, they were outlined like sitting ducks in a shooting gallery. Bill was on the machine gun and the others called to him, 'Shoot you bastard while you've got the chance!'. He said he couldn't, it was too easy. Someone shoved him aside, grabbed the gun and mowed them down. It made him feel sick.

Bill was wounded during a battle for a town and he was placed in the army hospital. That was how he got left behind in the Middle East, because the rest of his battalion was shipped back to fight in New Guinea.

After he recovered, he was placed in the 2/28th and continued to fight in the desert. I remember asking him about the desert, I thought it would be like the beach, but Bill said that the ground was so hard you could only dig shallow trenches.

283

Bill was captured at El Alamein and, along with two thousand other Allied prisoners, was crammed into the holds of the *Nino Bixio*, an Italian freighter. It was very crowded, you couldn't stretch out. If you had somewhere to sit, you were lucky. They were only allowed to have the hatch cover open a little bit to allow access to the latrines. A lot of the men had dysentery, so you can imagine what it was like.

Second day out to sea, they were torpedoed by an Allied submarine.

Bill said he'd been sitting in his usual pose, legs apart, elbows on knees, having a joke with the bloke next to him, when a torpedo whizzed straight through, hit the other side of the hold, exploded and flung everyone back onto him.

When he came to, he was covered in blood and bodies, arms and legs, guts, fingers blown off, he didn't know what belonged to him and what didn't. The whole hold was covered with bits and pieces of human beings. He thought he'd had it. The ship started taking water, some of the men tried to get out through the hole in the side that the torpedo had made, but the swell washed them back in and they were cut to pieces on the torn edges. The steel ladders leading to the top part of the hold had been destroyed, so there was no way out.

Survivors from the top part of the hold threw down ropes and the Captain, who was a big, red-headed Italian, shouted, 'If anyone's alive down there, climb up!'.

By the time Bill got himself out from underneath all the bodies, he realised he was actually still in one piece. He had bits of shrapnel embedded in his arms, legs and chest, but apart from that, he was all right.

He picked up the nearest bloke to him who looked like he might be in one piece and climbed the rope. That turned out to be Frank Potter. Bill said the Captain of the ship did the best he could, he ran round screaming and swearing in Italian, trying to help the wounded.

The next day, an Italian destroyer took them in tow. They beached on the Greek coast and the wounded were taken to shore and laid out along the beach. Bill said there'd been over five hundred men in their hold when they were hit, only seventy survived the torpedo and then a lot of them died on the beach.

Some of the men were terribly wounded, to make matters worse, there was no food or medical supplies. Orderlies were going along the beach, hacking off arms and legs that were only just hanging on. They were using tomahawks and digging out shrapnel with daggers. Bill knew if they tried to dig the shrapnel out of him, he'd die for sure, he was a bleeder and he had a rare blood group.

Those that could walk were marched through the nearest town and put on show like some ruddy great prize. The men spat on them and the women threw their kitchen slops and pots full of excrement onto them.

They stayed in Corinth for a while, and then they were shipped back to Italy and sent to Campo 57.

Bill said the commandant there was a real Fascist, he wasn't like most Italians. He was very hard and liked to see them suffer. He had a sign up which read, *The English are cursed, but more cursed are those Italians who treat them well!*.

The Allies began bombing the area near the camp, that's when Bill escaped. The guards were so frightened they ran off leaving the gates wide open. All the prisoners followed. Bill said to Abercrombe, the bloke that was with him, 'Not down the middle of the road, the Germans will realise we're being bombed and come to round us up. Down in the ditch.'

Sure enough, a few minutes later, along came the Germans and herded everyone back inside. Bill and Abercrombe hid in the ditch till nightfall.

Abercrombe wanted to head south in the hope of meeting up with the Yanks, but Bill talked him into going north to Switzerland. They travelled mainly at night, stealing food and sleeping in the fields.

They eventually came to a small town and hung around the well in the centre of the village, hoping someone friendly would notice them. They knew the Germans were around, but, so far, they hadn't seen any, so they hoped their luck would hold out.

An old bloke came along and looked them over, Bill had picked up a few Italian words, so he told him who they were. The old man fetched the head man, who took them home to his place and gave them some warm food and *vino*.

They thought he was a nice bloke, until he made a pass at them. Bill grabbed him by the collar and told him to put them in touch with the Resistance, or else. He said they'd have to let him make a phone call. Bill listened carefully and realised he was really phoning the Germans. They grabbed him, belted him up, pinched some food and nicked off before the Germans got there.

They kept travelling north, afraid to enter any town after that. Eventually, they were worn out, desperate. They watched another small town for a few days, it seemed all right. They entered and, once again, hung around the well. When a woman came for water, Bill asked her if she could take them to the head man, it turned out it was her husband.

This time they were lucky, these Italians hated the war and the Germans. They took Bill and Abercrombe to a safe farm run by Guiseppe and Maria Bosso and their fourteen-year-old daughter, Edmea. Bill said they were wonderful people, full of guts. They treated him like a son. He learnt to speak Italian fluently and, because he looked like a northern Italian, he sometimes passed himself off as one, drinking *vino* and singing songs with the Germans in the tavern, just like other Italians did. They tried to keep friendly with the Germans; that way, the villagers hoped that when they made their periodical trips through, they would not check too carefully.

During the day, Bill worked in the fields with the other labourers.

When they heard that the farms nearby were being searched for escaped POWs, Bill and Abercrombe would hide out down near a small creek. Sometimes, it was days before it was safe; during this time, they lived on frogs, green snakes and berries, it was far too dangerous for even the Italians to sneak food to them.

Eventually, they'd get word that the coast was clear and the whole village would have a big dance in one of the barns to celebrate the fact that they'd outwitted the Germans again. They'd all laugh and dance and drink too much *vino*.

It was too cold to hide down the creek in winter, so Guiseppe built a big haystack with a room inside. The Germans always stuck their bayonets into every haystack and, if they hit a post, or if there was blood on the end of the bayonet, they'd set fire to the haystack and burn whoever was inside.

One morning, the Bosso family were very upset, because they'd had word that the SS had burnt and slaughtered a whole village for sheltering POWs. The town had a meeting to decide what they were going to do. They all decided to continue hiding Allied prisoners, even if it meant losing the whole village. Bill said he told Guiseppe it was a risk he wouldn't let them take. All the POWs in the village agreed. They all decided to take their chances and move on.

Guiseppe got in touch with the Underground, who said it was no use them trying to join up with the Yanks, it would be better if they headed for Switzerland. They sent two members of the Resistance to guide Bill and Abercrombe over the Swiss Alps. Bill had his twenty-first birthday in the mountains. When they reached the border, the Swiss guards gave them hot chocolate and some warm food. They told them if they crossed into Switzerland, they'd be there for the duration of the war, which could be years, but if they went back and joined up with the Yanks, it might only be a few months, because the Americans were making rapid progress at that stage.

Bill didn't fancy sitting in Switzerland, he had too much spirit for that, so he asked the guides with them to take him and Abercrombe back to Italy. So they took them back over the mountains and then pointed them in the direction where the Yanks were supposed to be advancing. Bill and Abercrombe headed off.

That night, they came to a road and were about to cross, when Bill said, 'Don't, there's something wrong'. There was nothing in sight, but Bill had a premonition it was dangerous. He hid down in the ditch and told Abercrombe to do the same.

Abercrombe was fed up by this stage, so he said, 'Listen ya stupid bastard, there's nothing there, I'm going'. He ran onto the road, but half-way across, a searchlight spotted him and he was gunned down by a machine gun. Bill said he was so shocked he just froze. He knew that he had to move, but he couldn't.

Finally, he forced himself to get going. He walked all night until he came to a large river. He sat down amongst the reeds and pulled out a butt left over from the fags the Swiss guards had given him. He lay down and was half asleep, when he heard the sound of barking dogs coming closer and closer. Germans, he thought. He started to run, a bullet whizzed past his head, missing him by only a few inches. He stopped and turned with his hands in the air.

To his relief, it was only the Italian police. He spoke swiftly and told them he was a labourer on his way to work at a nearby farm. They said, 'You're no labourer, you're a rapist and a murderer. You're wanted in Rome for killing many women.' They showed him a poster with the rapist's picture. Bill said he couldn't believe it, it was his double. He was forced, then, to tell them who he really was, he showed them his dog tags.

'You shouldn't have run', they said, 'we would have let you go. We can't now, because we have to account to the Germans for every bullet we use. If we let you go, they'll know. We have to think of our families, we're sorry.'

Bill was taken and handed over to the SS. They questioned and tortured him for days on end, asking where he had been, who had helped him, where had he hidden. Bill said he would rather have died than tell them a bloody thing. He was like that. He was a very proud man and very stubborn.

Every day, he heard the firing squad in operation, and every day, he wondered if he would be next. They always walked past his cell with their victims, if they turned left past his cell, he knew it was an execution, right and they were transferring the prisoner to somewhere else.

One morning, they came for him. He thought, this is it, I'm going to die. They'd been really brutal to him the day before and got nothing out of him, so he thought they must have decided to give up and shoot him instead.

At the end of the corridor, the guard said, 'You know which way'. Bill turned left and the guard butted him in the back with his rifle, knocking him to the floor. When Bill went to get up, he kicked him hard in the ribs with army boots. Bill rose and felt the guard's rifle hard in his back. 'Turn right! You are being transferred to Germany.'

He was taken to the office, where he was handed over to another guard.

On the way to the train, the guard said, 'Don't try to escape and we'll get along fine'. Bill was surprised that this chap spoke in English. He had boarded the train in the company of this guard and two SS officers.

The German guard gave him a cigarette and said quietly, 'Speak in English, the SS can't understand'. He confided to Bill that he had been educated in England and had fought in the First World War as well. He said he hated the SS, he called them animals. He warned

Bill to watch out for the youngest officer. 'Don't try and escape', he said, 'he'll use any excuse to shoot you'.

This guard was the one who accompanied Bill to the POW camp. Before he handed him over, he gave Bill a heavy overcoat and some good boots.

'Never barter these', he said, 'you won't survive without them'. Bill said he was sorry they hadn't met under different circumstances, he was a really nice bloke.

Bill was taken to Stalag 7A in Moosburg, but was only there a few weeks when they transferred him to Stalag 8C in Sagan. I'm not sure which of the camps he was in was near a Jewish concentration camp, one of them, anyway, because Bill ended up being in several camps on and off. He said it was terrible, being near the Jewish camp, because of the smell and sounds that could be heard day and night. He knew they were people, but they sounded like tortured animals. It was really eerie. He said even though conditions were bad in the POW camps, he hated to think what they were doing to the Jews.

Bill palled up with another bloke who was half Jewish. The Germans treated him badly, they whipped him all the time. Bill tried to stick up for him and they said, 'You want to stick up for a Jew, we'll treat you like a Jew'. It was really bad for him after that.

In the Sagan camp he was in, he had to work in the local coalmines. It was long hours and damp, dangerous work. He developed a bad chest infection, so they said he could do easier work, they sent him to dig potatoes out of the frozen fields. Bill said it was easier down the mines. The only advantage to working in the fields was if you could pinch a potato and use it in camp for bargaining. Bill said they were fed on vegetable soup which was just water. Once a month, the soup had meat in it, a horse's head. The big thing was to get the eyes, otherwise you ended up with a bowl full of wet hair.

Some of the guards at Sagan were really brutal. They loved to burst in in the middle of the night, tell the men to strip and then stand them at attention in the snow. The worse the war went, the meaner they became.

One day, they assembled the men and told them they were going to hand out Red Cross packages. They tipped out Nestles milk, jam, tea, cigarettes all into a pile and then mashed it up together. 'Now', they said, 'you can't complain you didn't get your Red Cross parcels!'. After that, they told the prisoners they had to eat it, it was a big joke to the guards.

One day, towards the end of the war in Europe, they informed the prisoners that they were going to march to another camp. There had been rumours in the camp that the Russians were advancing, so that was probably why they were moving them. They were marched fifty miles to Spremberg, where they thought they would stop, but, instead, they were forced to march another three hundred miles to Duderstadt.

It was very cold and they had to sleep out in the open snow. There was no food, they had to find what they could by the side of the road. Bill said even the German people were starving by then. They stopped near one village and an old German peasant woman ran up to him and shoved a stale piece of black bread into his hand, a guard shot her in the back. Bill said that guard was a real bastard. He was always belting someone and would use any excuse to use his rifle.

On that march, a lot of prisoners died of cold and were just left by the side of the road. I think Bill was really glad that he hadn't traded his heavy overcoat, because he really needed it, then.

When they reached Duderstadt, the conditions were terrible. The camp was infested with lice and there was excrement everywhere. There was only one rough latrine for over a thousand men. Prisoners were dying like flies from dysentery and pneumonia. There was nowhere to put the dead, so they just piled them on top of one another near the gate.

After he'd been there another few days, there was another rumour that the Yanks were close. That scared the Germans and they cut down the torture a bit.

Early one morning, a tank broke down the gates of the camp and a sandy headed Yank popped up and said, 'Any of you guys want some ginger cake and ice-cream?!'.

Bill said the men that had any energy left just cried and cried. The Yanks gave out food, but some of the prisoners had been without for so long that it made them violently ill and they died.

The Yank in charge couldn't believe the state they were all in. He said, 'Is there any one of these German bastards you'd like to kill?'. An English soldier lying on a mat raised his hand. He was so weak he couldn't stand, so two of the Yanks supported him, they held the gun in his hand and helped him point it at the German guard who'd given him a really bad time. 'Help me', the Englishman whispered, and the Yanks pulled the trigger for him. Later that day, the Englishman died. Bill said there was no one there he'd kill, but if he ever met up with a certain SS officer, he would have shot him.

They were all taken by trucks to American transport planes and airlifted to France, where they were given medical treatment before being transferred to England. Bill spent six months in hospital in England before he was fit to sail home.

I thought about everything Bill told me after I had returned to live with my mother. I knew that was just the tip of the iceberg, he hadn't told me the real story.

By the time I'd been with Mum three weeks, he'd sobered himself up and come around to beg me to come back to him. I knew then that if I did, it was for ever, I couldn't leave him again. I had to go back. He had no one. I still loved him. I thought maybe I could help make up for what he'd been through.

It turned out I was wrong. I couldn't heal his mind, it was too damaged, they hadn't broken his spirit or his will to live, but they'd broken his mind. He had a sensitive side to him, they'd destroyed that, degraded him. He couldn't get away from what was inside of him. He couldn't escape from his own memories.

In no time at all, I was pregnant with my second child. They put me into hospital to bring her on, because they said she was going to be too big. I had to sit in hot baths up to my neck and drink schooners of castor oil and cascara. That didn't work, so they fed me some pills and gave me over thirty injections; a week later, I still hadn't had her. Finally, the doctor strapped me up, ruptured the membrane and left me with the nurses.

By the time labour started, I was exhausted. I didn't know how I'd have the strength to give birth. I went into some kind of trance and began speaking in an unknown language, nobody could understand what I was saying. They called the doctor in, and when Jilly was finally born, she shot out and covered him in a gallon of green water.

They took me to the ward, I was really low. I found myself floating in the air, looking down at my body lying on the bed. I could see the matron and doctor working on me, trying to revive me. Suddenly, I was back inside my body and the matron said, 'Thank God, we thought we'd lost you!'. I was advised not to have any more children, or at least to wait three years before another one.

Bill was trying hard to hold himself together, but there were still times when he'd go off on a binge and I wouldn't see him for a few days. On these occasions, Mum would come and stay just to keep me company.

She was doing housework, now, and could work when she pleased. I was glad, because it was easier for her. She was always buying clothes for the kids and dropping in groceries, she knew I had no money.

Bill had a nervous breakdown and they put him in Hollywood Hospital. He couldn't cope with any pressure or responsibility. I used to feel awful when I visited him, it was like all the men in there belonged to a club. Instead of being pleased to see me, he'd make me wait while he finished a game of cards with his mates. I felt like an intruder, they all seemed to be living in some kind of dream world. Bill was sent home, eventually, with a couple of bottles of drugs that were supposed to keep him calm.

By the time Jill was four months old, I was pregnant again. I went to the doctor and he told me I couldn't have the baby, that I had to get rid of it. He sent me home with some tablets to take. I told Mum what he said and she agreed with me that I shouldn't take them. I threw them into the bin.

291

An epidemic of polio hit Mulberry Farm, I caught it. I couldn't move, Mum moved in with us. Bill was working at the time and I needed someone to look after Sally and Jilly. By some miracle, I recovered from the polio.

I went back to the doctor when I was seven months pregnant, he was very cross that I had let the pregnancy continue. I never told him I'd had polio as well, I could imagine what he'd say. I gave birth to a son that November, it was an easy birth.

When Billy was born, I saw a golden angel hovering over me and I heard beautiful music. The angel was very happy that Billy had come into the world. Of course, Bill was overjoyed that he had a son at last.

Bill applied for a State Housing home in Manning. Mum was living with us permanently, now. I really needed her help with three little ones so close together and Bill the way he was. When Billy was six months old, we moved to Manning. It was nothing but bush, then.

There was a large swamp at the back of us, there was nothing the kids loved better than an excursion down the swamp, it was alive with wildlife, turtles, frogs, gilgies, grey cranes. It reminded me of the bush from my own childhood days. I encouraged the children to take an interest in the wildlife. It was good for them to learn about nature and how important it is to our lives.

We'd only been in Manning a month, when Mum began to complain about all the Aborigines living in the swamp. 'Did you hear that music last night?' she said. 'They been having corroborees every night, I think I'll go down there and tell them all off.'

I often sat and listened to it with her after that. I've never been to a corroboree, but that music had always been inside of me. When I was little, I was told Aboriginal music was heathen music. I thought it was beautiful music; whenever I heard it, it was like a message, like I was being supported, protected.

One night, I told Mum that there were no Aborigines in the swamp. She'd been complaining she couldn't sleep and she was sick of those blackfellas having a party every night. I don't think she believed me. 'You heard the music, Glad', she said, 'there's a big mob of them down there'.

'There's no one down there', I told her, 'it's a spiritual thing'. After that, we just accepted it. She'd sit out and listen to it and then go to bed. We didn't hear it every night, but it was there on and off right up until Bill died. Then it stopped.

Mum heard this other thing, too, she said there was a crocodile in the swamp. We only heard that noise at night. She'd say to the kids to be careful when they went down the swamp, to watch out for the crocodile. Sally and Jilly were buggers for nicking off whenever they could. I remember Mum saying to Sally, 'Aren't you scared of meeting that crocodile?'. I couldn't help laughing, because I knew that was why Sally kept going down there, she wanted to meet him.

Bill seemed to pull himself together when we first went to the Manning house. I began to hope for a better future for us all. He managed to get a good job and cut down on his drinking. His nearest watering hole was the Raffles Hotel, he'd go there for a few beers after work and then come home. I knew he was worried about us being on our own, because we had no street lights, then.

On the weekends, he worked for the Italian market gardeners in Spearwood. He loved mixing with them and speaking Italian. He had never forgotten the kindness of the Bossos during the war. He'd come home, loaded up with fruit and vegetables and bottles of *vino*. He often did jobs for them free of charge. I think he felt indebted to all Italian people because they'd been so good to him.

Pretty soon, there were other houses going up around us. A widow with three children moved in at the back of us. Grace was such a nice person and Mum often had a chat and a cup of tea with her.

One morning, Bill was sitting on the bus going to work, when the chap next to him said, 'You look a bloody sight better than the last time I saw you!'.

Bill said, 'Do I know you?'.

'You only saved my life, you bastard', the man replied. It was Frank Potter, one of the men Bill had dragged up from the hold. It turned out he and his wife lived only a few streets away. They saw a lot of each other after that.

Bill began having nightmares again. It seemed that things would just start going right for us and then the whole circle would start all over again.

Things started getting really bad, we were so desperate, we'd gone through Mum's savings and Bill had hocked everything we had of value and spent the money on drink. The doctors increased his dosages of pills and other medicines, but, combined with the alcohol, it only made him worse. There were times he'd mistake me for a German SS officer; when he looked at me, his eyes were glazed, it was like he wasn't really seeing me at all. One night, he nearly strangled me. He was screaming 'SS, SS', and had his hands around my throat.

There were times when it was like something had taken him over, that was when I really got frightened, because I didn't know what was going to happen. He'd yell and scream and tell us all to get out the house or he'd kill us. Mum and I would run with the children to Grace's house. She was good to us, she knew we had nowhere else to go. Sometimes, we'd sleep the night there, other times, I'd sneak to the back fence and listen to see if he was still shouting. Generally, once he went to sleep, he was all right, we'd go back home, then. A few times when we spent the night at Grace's, I'd hear his voice calling

293

me, 'Gla-ad, Gla-ad . . .', in a really quiet way, as if to indicate that he wouldn't hurt me if I came to him. I never went outside on those occasions, I knew he'd kill me. It scared me so much because the voice wasn't really his, it was like he'd suddenly turned into a stranger.

When we returned in the morning, Bill would have no idea of what had happened. When I told him, he'd get really scared and commit himself to Hollywood again. He told me he thought, one day, he might really kill us all and he couldn't bear that thought, because we loved him and he loved us.

One winter, just after Bill had come out of hospital, it was really cold. Sally had been sick with croup, the river had flooded and water covered over half of our backyard. There were no drains, so it just lay there, the house was damp right through, even though we had fires going day and night. Several of the houses near us were evacuated and the people given alternative accommodation. Even Grace at the back moved in with her mother, she was sick of seeing the fungus grow on her walls.

'We've got to get blankets for the children', I told Bill. 'Doesn't the Canteen's Trust Fund give money to ex-servicemen in dire circumstances?'

We had no money for blankets, so we usually all ended up in the double bed, it meant we were warm, but no one got any sleep. Mum managed to get us some hot water bottles, but it wasn't enough.

Bill was very proud, he hated asking for help. Finally, he relented and said he would write to them. We waited eagerly for their reply, when it came, it was short and sweet, they said we weren't desperate enough.

I was really disgusted, it was the same old story. It had taken years before the Repatriation Department would even give Bill a partial pension, because they considered him a malingerer.

No one understood in those days, if you'd lost an arm and a leg, you had no worries, but if there was something wrong with your mind, you were a malingerer. When I think about that, it makes me feel sorry for the Vietnam veterans now, they are fighting the same attitudes.

Bill became very bitter after the Trust Fund refused us, it made him feel as though everyone was looking down on him, as though he was complaining about nothing. I felt then that the war hadn't been worth it.

By the time Billy was just over two years old, I became pregnant again. It was a really bad time to have another child. I lay in bed at night, unable to sleep. I'd prayed and prayed and I'd gotten no answers. My usual capacity for overcoming my problems seemed to have deserted me. I knew I would have to give up my part-time job and I wondered how on earth we'd put food on the table. Bill had been in hospital on and off for months. He seemed happy with his weekend passes to come home, that way, he had no worry. He was drifting deeper and deeper into the protection of the hospital. I was too scared to approach anyone for help. I never complained about Bill's drinking, I felt it was a family thing and I shouldn't talk about it to others.

One night, I was at my lowest ebb, I'd been praying and I just fell onto the bed, exhausted. When I opened my eyes some time later, there was a light in the room. At the centre of the light stood three men, behind them, the yellow sands of the desert dotted with small white buildings. The men were dressed in long robes and their heads were covered. The middle one was the spokesman, he was dressed likewise, except for a type of sleeveless robe in the colours of dark grey, black, yellow or white. He told me that was the colour of my line and that it reached back to the olden days. He said that a great leader would be born into my house. I suddenly felt very happy. It was like I had a special secret. I slept soundly after that, and, when I awoke, I felt really alive and well.

I never told Mum about my vision, I knew it would worry her, even though she had them herself from time to time. I was a changed person after that. I knew I had the strength to face anything.

I left work when my clothes started becoming too tight. I didn't worry any more; somehow, we seemed to be managing, I just looked forward to the birth of the baby.

I think I always worried unconsciously about dying and leaving the children. I knew my mother wouldn't be allowed to keep them, they'd be taken off her and she probably wouldn't be allowed to see them ever again. I knew that would destroy her, she didn't have the strength to rebuild her life again. Bill's parents wouldn't take them, not that I wanted them to, they'd be unhappy with them, so it would probably mean an orphanage or maybe the children would be separated and adopted out. I couldn't bear that to happen to the most wonderful gifts God had given me, so the assurance of my vision had lain that ghost to rest.

Bill came out of hospital when I was about seven months pregnant, he'd been in there a long time. This time, he really tried to help himself. I hoped that he would stay on his feet a bit longer this time and he did. He started to work again and was looking forward to the baby.

I began having a lot of pain and eventually went into hospital, it was different from the pain I'd experienced with the others, it was a lot more acute. Bill drove me to the maternity hospital and left me. He was as white as a sheet. It was funny, really, he got morning sickness with the boys and I had it with the girls, so he knew it would be a son.

As he drove away, he said, 'Don't die!'.

It was about nine o'clock at night and it was a small private hospital, not like the large ones I'd had the others in. A neighbour had recommended it, she said the Matron had delivered hundreds of babies and was better than any doctor.

There was no one at the front of the hospital, but I could see a light glowing towards the end of a long passage that stretched from the front to the back. I walked towards it, I was in agony. At the end of the corridor, the door was wide open, it was a bedroom, and there was Matron, lying on a large double bed with her huge Alsatian dog asleep beside her. She had a fag protruding from the corner of her mouth and she was reading the paper. I felt embarrassed, I didn't know what to do. I knocked shyly.

'Who are you?' she said. The dog suddenly leapt up and started growling at me. 'Shut up!' Matron said and whacked him with her paper. She got out of bed and pulled a floral housecoat over her nightie. 'I'm Mrs Milroy', I gasped, the pain was getting really bad.

'How long have you been like this?' she said as she led me to a small examining room. 'Hoist yourself up there', she commanded, pointing to a flat sheet-covered table. 'I want to have a look at you.' She examined me and then said, 'You poor thing, no wonder you're in pain, it's a breech. I'll call your doctor.'

My doctor arrived, but said he could do nothing, it was all up to me.

I didn't know such pain existed. I pushed and groaned, sweat was pouring off me, I lost a lot of blood. I was convinced my whole insides were going to spill out onto the table. I became exhausted and just lay there.

My doctor just stood in the corner and watched me. He never said one word of encouragement or held my hand. I remembered then that he was a strict Catholic. I thought, he's waiting for me to die, they always give the children priority over the mother.

I heard the Matron call him a bastard, then she patted me hard around the face and said, 'Come on, you lazy bitch, don't stop bloody pushing. I'm not going to let you go now!' I was sure I was going to die. She grabbed me and started screaming, trying to get through to me. 'You lazy bitch', she yelled, 'you bloody well start pushing, you're not giving up now just because of that bastard in the corner. You can do it, come on, I haven't lost one yet.'

The screaming got through and I tried again, but it was no use.

Then, something made me glance to the side of the room. The most beautiful angel I'd ever seen was standing there. I felt the feathers, they were so soft and white. The face looked at me with love, smiled and said, 'It's Sally's birthday'. I repeated to myself, 'It's Sally's birthday'. I didn't know I'd been in the room all night and it was now morning.

I felt a renewed strength, I pushed and David was born. 'Thank God', the Matron said, and I knew that was true.

I'd lost so much blood, it was all over the place. I knew I'd have to have a transfusion.

I heard a strange noise and realised it was Matron's cats meowing at the door, they were probably asking for their breakfast. Matron opened the door and shooed them away. She returned a few minutes later with her husband, Clarrie, who was clad in an old pair of striped cotton pyjamas.

'The stretcher won't fit through the door', she explained to me. 'Clarrie'll lift you through the door and then onto the stretcher.' I felt really weak, but I almost laughed. The whole hospital suddenly struck me as really funny.

I was woken late in the afternoon by a lass with a cup of tea. I asked to see my baby, he was beautiful. I nursed him for a couple of days, but then they had to take him to PMH for observation. They were worried about him. Even though I knew he would be all right, I felt very unhappy. It seemed awful being separated from him so soon.

Bill came to visit me and was very distressed that I'd had a bad time and upset that they'd taken David to the children's hospital. He always blamed himself when things went wrong, I knew he'd started drinking again, not heavily, just enough to relieve the pressure of the situation while I was in hospital.

It was terrible being there on my own, all the other mothers had their babies. I had nothing to do except be milked like a cow for the baby's food supply, which was taken by taxi to PMH.

I decided I'd offer to help Elsie, the middle-aged cook, she was always complaining she had too much work to do. She was a strange person; for some reason, she seemed to have trouble with the elastic in her over-sized bloomers, they hung down below her dress and she was always hoisting them up.

For breakfast, Elsie gave us Weeties, toast and jam and a cup of tea. I was starving, I knew I needed more food than that if I was going to recover. I had jaundice and I looked as yellow as a daffodil.

'I want eggs for breakfast', I told her one morning.

'Can't have 'em', she said. 'If I give you eggs, they'll all be yelling for eggs.'

'But you've got plenty of eggs', I said. 'Down the back, there's eggs lying all over the ground where the chooks have dropped them. Look, I'll cook them myself, you won't have to do it.'

'All right', she said 'but don't let the others see you with them'.

I walked out into the back garden of the hospital. Clarrie was still asleep on his old iron bed, he loved sleeping outdoors. All the chooks were perched along his body, I tried to move quietly so as not to wake him. He must have sensed someone was there, because he suddenly leapt up and threw his grey blanket off, the chooks leapt into the air, squawking and carrying on. 'Sorry, Clarrie', I said. 'I'm just getting some eggs.' He grunted, pulled the rug back over himself and went back to sleep.

I couldn't help laughing. I cooked myself up a big batch of eggs with lots of toast and a steaming hot cup of tea, then I walked back into the ward and said, 'Look what I'm having for breakfast'. It was on after that, all the other mothers wanted eggs, too. Elsie was very cross with me.

We never had ladies who came around and cleaned the wards, Matron said they cost too much money. She let Bob, her Alsatian dog, patrol the wards, instead. Any papers or books left on the floor were quickly whisked away by his large mouth and taken out the back.

He never touched your slippers, so I think he knew what his duties were. He kept the cats out, too. Elsie was always encouraging the cats in. She fed them bits of our dinner while she was cooking it. They jumped all over the kitchen table trying to see what Elsie was cooking, she'd toss them bits and pieces from her pots.

As soon as Bob smelt dinner cooking, he'd tear into the kitchen, because he knew Elsie would have the cats in there. We waited for it every night, Elsie would start swearing and hitting Bob, the cats would shriek and claw and knock all sorts of china over in the ensuing fight. The whole fracas only lasted a few minutes. Once the cats were outside again, Bob would come and stand at the top of the ward and growl, as if daring us to drop one thing on his nice clean floor.

When Saturday morning came around, Elsie told us all there'd be no dinner until three o'clock in the afternoon.

'But we'll be starving by then', I said.

'You can have a late morning tea', she informed us and left. I followed her into the kitchen. 'What's going on?' I asked. 'Why will lunch be so late?'

'Betting day', she said, 'we'll all be too busy picking our horses to bother with you lot. No babies born here on Saturdays.'

Sure enough, the wireless blared away all morning, Clarrie's old yellow Chev flashed back and forth past the window on its way to the SP bookie at Como Hotel. At three o'clock, Elsie served us lunch. She really outdid herself. It was a big roast dinner with a wonderful pudding and a large cream sponge for afternoon tea. Elsie told us she had had a good win.

I was still very yellow, so Matron decided I needed a blood transfusion. She hired a nurse to come and sit with me and I lay reading while the blood dripped slowly into my vein.

Suddenly, I began to feel really ill. I looked at the nurse and said, 'I think I'm going to die'. She stuck a thermometer in my mouth. When she pulled it out, she said, 'Good God, one hundred and four!'.

She pulled the tubes from my arm and blood spurted out all over the sheets. 'I'm sorry', she said. 'Guess you were incompatible with that lot!'

The next day, they brought David back from PMH. It was wonderful to be able to cuddle and feed him like the other mothers. After a couple of days, I was well enough to go home, besides, I was missing the children and I knew Mum would have a lot to cope with.

When David was very small, Mum's brother Arthur and his wife, Adeline, and their children popped in to visit us. It was the first time I had seen Arthur in years and years. Mum and I were terribly excited.

Bill was lying down at the time, I went in and asked him to come out and meet them. 'Come and meet Arthur and his family', I said, 'you'll like them'.

'I don't want to meet them', he said. 'I don't want to know them.'

I was really hurt, I knew if they had been white, he would have come out straight away. Bill was a strange man, he wasn't prejudiced against other racial groups, just Aboriginals.

He never liked us having our people to the house. We had to cut ourselves off. I think it was his upbringing. A friend called Jean White used to come and stay with us; sometimes, he never minded her, because she was very light. Jean could pass for anything.

Bill had spent a lot of his childhood in country towns, I think that moulded his attitudes to Aboriginal people. Down South, Aboriginals were really looked down on. Bill would have been brought up with that.

Bill went back into hospital and I began my regular visits to him again. I always took Sally, she was the eldest, and sometimes, I'd take Billy and Jill as well.

Each time I visited him, I noticed some familiar faces missing, as well as new ones that had been admitted.

I always sensed when someone had taken their own life, there was a depression about the ward and not the usual cheery greeting for the kids. Bill would be silent. I never stayed long on those days. Bill didn't want visitors, then, neither did the other men, they just all wanted to be there with each other. I think probably many of them had also thought of taking their own lives. I felt very sad on these occasions and very uncertain. The kids knew there was something wrong, but they didn't understand.

Also, the doctors used to experiment with various drugs and treatments, and this would also result in marked emotional and personality changes. They'd ask the men to volunteer for new forms of therapy. Bill had shock treatment quite a lot and all sorts of other things done to him, but nothing helped.

I suppose many people must wonder why on earth I didn't just take the kids and leave. Well, I nearly did, on several occasions, but Bill always threatened me. He said if I left him, he'd make sure the children were taken off me. He said, 'Nobody will let someone like you bring up kids and you know it. I'm the one that'll get custody, I'll give them to my parents.'

I knew what he meant. I always had a sinking feeling in my stomach when he said that. Aboriginal women weren't allowed to keep children fathered by a white man. He was right, I couldn't take the chance of losing them, I had to stay and try and cope somehow. They were all I had.

One year, Bill was in hospital for nearly twelve months. That was the year I began attending spiritualist meetings.

Mrs Davies was in charge of these meetings, she was a wonderful person, very good and kind. I liked her as soon as I met her and she took to me, too. She told me I had a wonderful aura and that I could help people if I wanted to.

I used to do healing with the hands. Sometimes, a person would be healed mentally, sometimes spiritually, sometimes physically. I would feel a power come into me, it would build up in my hands and then flow from me to whoever I touched. The power comes from God, it's a very positive thing. It's pure love, love for people. I love people, I'm interested in all kinds of people. I think that's why God gave me that gift, He loves people, too.

I gave it up after a while, because it left me too exhausted, and, although I wanted to help others, I had my own family to think of. Also, some wealthy women used to come to these meetings and they'd make a big deal out of me, offer me presents and money, I hated that, it was so superficial. It's wrong to accept money for doing something like that.

In April 1959, my daughter Helen was born.

Even though he was sick at the time, Bill managed to drive me to hospital. He looked so ill, it made me sad. I told him not to visit me, just to ring, I knew it'd be too much for him, otherwise. He started crying, he felt useless, like he was no good to any of us. That bloody war, I thought. I kissed his cheek and patted his hand. I tried to convey the message that I understood, that I didn't blame him. I knew Helen would be my last child.

New year's eve, 1960, was one I've never forgotten. I awoke suddenly, feeling frightened. There was a light in the corner of the bedroom, it was the spirit of Christ. I'd never seen Him in the spirit form before, His arms were outstretched as though He'd come for someone. I screamed and told Him to go away, I knew I was looking at death. I knew I wouldn't have Bill much longer, that was what He'd come to tell me. I was too scared to sleep at night after that, wondering when it was going to happen.

One night in October, ten months later, Bill came into the lounge-room where I was sitting by myself. I found I needed small moments alone to renew my strength and I only usually got these times after the children were well and truly asleep.

'I feel odd, Glad', he said. 'I can't get warm. I feel as though I'm not really here, it's like I'm fading away.' I jumped up and felt him, he was cold. I felt his spirit had left his body.

I knew then he was going to die. God was preparing me by giving us this time alone together.

Bill sat down and we talked into the early hours of the morning. It was strange, it was suddenly as though he was his old self, as though he'd been released from something. We talked about the children and we laughed. Bill said he hadn't felt so good in a long time. He said he knew tomorrow would be a new beginning for all of us.

In the morning, I wondered whether I should ring his mother and tell her Bill was going to die. I decided not to, I knew she'd think I was crazy. I couldn't tell anyone.

Bill was in such a good mood at breakfast that he kept Billy home from school, so he and David and Billy could all have a game of footy together.

I left for work.

A neighbour rang me at twelve that day to tell me Bill had died. I was shocked. I went home immediately, but couldn't pull myself together, I walked around in a daze. If it hadn't been for Mrs Mainwaring, a neighbour, I don't know what I would have done. She told the children about their father. I don't know if they understood or not. It's hard enough for an adult to understand death.

Later that night, I went out to Bill's room. It seemed so empty. I noticed suddenly that his bottle of medicine was empty, I felt sick. I knew deep down he'd never take his own life, but it still worried me. I'd had it drummed into me at Parkerville that such people went straight to hell. I didn't want him to go to hell, I started to cry, I felt so depressed.

I begged God to tell me where he'd gone, I had to know. I just couldn't go on, not knowing. I closed my eyes. When I opened them again, I was surrounded by light. I could see Bill standing in a garden near a tree, he looked confused. Then, I saw Jesus, in a long, white robe, beckon to him. There were other people there, sitting on the lawn, all of them listening to what Jesus said. He spoke to Bill and suddenly Bill wasn't lost any more, he was happy. He joined the others on the lawn. When that vision finished, I was surrounded by a glow of pure love, I was so happy. I knew Bill was all right.

If it hadn't been for that vision, I'd never have coped with Bill's funeral. Bill's mother didn't attend, she disagreed with the cremation, even though it was what Bill had always said he wanted.

Every time a friend came and spoke to me at the funeral, they'd give me a small sip of brandy. The undertaker kept giving me sips of brandy, too. I felt as though I was floating, I didn't normally drink. Someone pressed some smelling salts into my hand, I sniffed them and nearly passed out, they were very strong. When I got home, Mum put me to bed. The following morning, I had a splitting headache.

A fortnight after Bill's death, I went back to work. I had a lot of bills to pay.

We were given a Legatee who was a real godsend. He was able to get my insurance policy paid out and that covered a lot of our debts. I applied for a war pension and was granted it. Actually, if I hadn't been so desperate, I would have refused it. I felt the whole department had been so mean to Bill. They'd done nothing for him while he was alive. Why did someone have to die before they recognised the seriousness of the problem?

Although I still grieved for Bill, I felt as though a load had been lifted from my shoulders. I was much more relaxed, I didn't have to worry about money and the children could make as much noise as they liked. I let them run, screaming, through the house day and night, I felt they needed it. I often had them all in bed with me, poor little kids, they needed all the love they could get.

They had a lot to cope with, the kids at school were asking questions and the teachers were talking about them. Sally had told me she'd overheard two of the teachers talking and it had made her angry. 'Who do they think they are?' she asked me. 'We don't want their pity. Don't they understand it's better he's gone?' She'd been close to her father, but she also knew what he was like. In some ways, they were similar, they were both rebels.

Bill had only been dead a short time when a Welfare lady came out to visit us. I was really frightened because I thought, if she realised we were Aboriginal, she might have the children taken away. We only had two bedrooms and a sleepout and there were five children, as well as Mum and me.

This woman turned out to be a real bitch. She asked me all sorts of questions and walked through our house with her nose in the air like a real snob. She asked where we all slept, and when I told her Helen slept with me, she was absolutely furious. She said, 'You are to get that child out of your bed, we will not stand for that. You work something else out, the children aren't to be in the same room as you. I'll come back and check to make sure you've got another bed.'

I never told her we often all slept together, or that I was still breast-feeding Helen. I just agreed with everything she said. I didn't want her to have any excuse to take the children off me.

304

It was after the visit from the Welfare lady that Mum and I decided we would definitely never tell the children they were Aboriginal. We were both convinced they would have a bad time, otherwise. Also, if word got out, another Welfare person might come and take them away. That would have killed us both.

Mum said she didn't want the children growing up with people looking down on them. I understood what she meant. Aboriginals were treated the lowest of the low. It was like they were the one race on earth that had nothing to offer.

When I was little, Mum had always pinched my nose and said, 'Pull your nose, Gladdie, pull it hard. You don't want to end up with a big nose like mine.' She was always pulling the kids' noses, too. She wanted them to grow up to look like white people.

I suppose, looking back now, it seems awful that we deprived them of that heritage, but we thought we were doing the right thing at the time. With Bill gone, we now had some hope of a future and I knew he would want the children to get on in the world.

I took on any job that was going, I wasn't afraid to work. Sometimes, I had four jobs on the go. I forced myself to learn how to drive, even though I was petrified of the thought of actually going on the road. I knew I would need that independence and it meant I could take the children on outings. They hadn't had much up until then.

After I'd managed to pay off all the extra debts, our lives really began to change. I never had to worry about where the next meal was coming from, now, and I could buy the kids lollies and fruit, sometimes, we even went to the pictures.

I also found that, now we were on our own, I worried less about Mum. She would always have a home with me, and there was enough money for all of us to get by on. Best of all, she had her own family now. All her life, she'd had to mother other people's children, now she had her own flesh and blood. I hoped that would make up for some of her past.

When the opportunity to buy my own florist business came up, I grabbed it. I had always wanted to be my own boss. My old friend Lois gave me a loan, she knew I would pay her back. I soon had that shop on its feet and doing twice as well as when the previous owners had it. It gave me a new independence and something to be proud

305

of. Also, it gave us the extra money we needed to get us through the children's teenage years.

I'm very proud of my children and the way they turned out.

I feel embarrassed now, to think that, once, I wanted to be white. As a child, I even hoped a white family would adopt me, a rich one, of course. I've changed since those days.

I'm still a coward, when a stranger asks me what nationality I am, I sometimes say a Heinz variety. I feel bad when I do that. It's because there are still times when I'm scared inside, scared to say who I really am.

But, at least, I've made a start. And I hope my children will feel proud of the spiritual background from which they've sprung. If we all keep saying we're proud to be Aboriginal, then maybe other Australians will see that we are a people to be proud of. I suppose every mother wants her children to achieve greatness, or, at least, one of them. All I want my children to do is to pass their Aboriginal heritage on.

I suppose, in hundreds of years' time, there won't be any black Aboriginals left. Our colour dies out; as we mix with other races, we'll lose some of the physical characteristics that distinguish us now. I like to think that, no matter what we become, our spiritual tie with the land and the other unique qualities we possess will somehow weave their way through to future generations of Australians. I mean, this is our land, after all, surely we've got something to offer.

It hasn't been an easy task, baring my soul. I'd rather have kept hidden things which have now seen the light of day. But, like everything else in my life, I knew I had to do it. I find I'm embarrassed sometimes by what I have told, but I know I cannot retract what has been written, it's no longer mine.

The only way I can explain it is by one of my favourite rules, which I haven't always followed. Let me pass this way but once and do what good I can, I shall not pass this way again. Maybe someone else is walking a road that's like mine.

Chapter Thirty

SOMETHING SERIOUS

It took several months to work through Mum's story and, during that time, many tears were shed. We became very close.

Although she'd finally shared her story with me, she still couldn't bring herself to tell my brothers and sisters. Consequently, I found myself communicating it to them in bits and pieces as it seemed appropriate. It was, and still is, upsetting for us all. We'd lived in a cocoon of sorts for so long that we all found it difficult to come to terms with the experiences Mum had been through.

By the beginning of June 1983, Nan's health wasn't too good.

'You've got to take her to the doctor', I told Mum one day. 'She's not well.'

'You know how she hates doctors.'

'But what if it's something serious? You'll just have to force her to go.'

Mum took Nan to see our local doctor a few days later. They sent Nan for a chest X-ray, which revealed that one of her lungs had collapsed.

When Mum phoned through the news to me, I said gently, 'I think you should prepare yourself, Mum. I'm not trying to make a big deal out of this, but I think it will be serious.'

'You mean you think she might die?'

'Yes.'

'You don't know what you're talking about, Sally! It's only a collapsed lung, they can fix that!'

'But they have to find out what caused the collapse, don't they?'

'Well . . . yes. She has to go into hospital in two days' time for tests.'

The night before Nan was due to go into hospital, she stayed at my place. Mum had arranged weeks before to babysit some of her other grandchildren and it was an arrangement she couldn't break.

I made Nan a cup of tea and we sat in the lounge-room to talk.

'I'd like you to listen to a story, Nan, it's only a couple of pages.

307

Is it okay if I read it to you?'

'Oooh, yes. I like a good story.'

'You tell me if you like it.'

'All right.'

I read her the section on Arthur's boxing days. When I stopped, she said, 'That's a wonderful story, a really good one. I did enjoy it, where did you get such a story from?'

'This is what I've been writing, Nan', I grinned. 'That's Arthur's story.'

'No! I can't believe it! That's Arthur's story?'

'Yep!'

'I didn't know he had a good story like that. You got to keep that story safe. Read me some more.'

I read a little more, and then we began to talk about the old days and life on Corunna Downs Station. For some reason, Nan was keen to talk. As she went on and on, her breath began to come in shorter and shorter gasps. Her words tumbled out one over the other, as if her tongue couldn't say them quickly enough.

When I could see that she was very tired, I said, 'Would you like to lie down for a while now?'.

'Yes, I think I will', she sighed. 'I feel tired, now.'

Our lounge suite was a real oldie, it was low to the floor, so I had to haul Nan up.

'You got to get me a better seat', she complained.

'I know, I'll bring one over from Mum's.'

I took Nan into my bedroom and she climbed into the double bed.

'Gladdie won't be here till late', she muttered.

'You can sleep till she comes. Do you want another cuppa?'

'No thanks. I think I'll just lie here.'

'Okay. I'm going to put the kids to bed. If you want anything, sing out.'

After I'd settled the children down, I walked quietly past Nan's bedroom door. I expected her to be asleep, but she wasn't.

'Sally', she called. 'Come here.'

'What is it?'

'I want to tell you more about the station', she smiled. I nearly stopped her, she could hardly breathe, but how could I tell her not to talk when it had taken a lifetime for her to get to this point?

I listened quietly as she spoke about wild ducks and birds, the blue hills and all the fruit that grew along the creek. Her eyes had a faraway look and her face was very soft. I kept smiling at her because she was smiling at me, but, inside, I wanted to cry. I'd seen that look before, on Arthur's face. I knew she was going to die. Nan finally settled down and closed her eyes. I tucked her in again.

'Hmmmn, this is a really good rug', she said sleepily. 'Where did you get such a rug?'

'Mum gave it to me', I muttered. And, turning off her light, I walked back into the kitchen.

'She's going to die, Paul', I said sadly.

'Aah, you're just worried because she's going into hospital tomorrow', he replied in that pragmatic way of his. 'Once she's had her lung fixed and the cataracts taken off her eyes, she'll be fine.'

'It's more than that. I've seen that look before, on Arthur's face. They become all soft. They start to talk about things they've hidden for years.'

Mum arrived a couple of hours later to take Nan home. She helped Nan down our front verandah steps, but, half-way down, Nan stopped, then she turned and said, 'Kiss me, Sally, you might not see me again'. I kissed her cheek.

I walked with them to the car, the air was cold and damp. Usually, I waved goodbye from the porch, but tonight, I felt compelled to walk with Nan as far as possible.

As Mum started up the engine, Nan unwound her window and handed me a black and red vinyl pencil case.

'Keep this', she said.

'What are you giving Sally?' Mum asked.

'Nothing. Just something for the kids.' There was a twinkle in her eye. I knew there was money inside.

When I visited Nan in hospital the following evening, she was very bright. Mum had been there on and off all day.

'Hi, Nan', I said as I walked up to her bed. 'How are they treating you?'

'The nurses are lovely. And that old lady next to me, she's gone now, but she ordered my tea and showed me where the toilet was.'

'Aah, you've been spoilt!'

'She was a lovely old lady, she's gone home, now, what a lovely person she was', Nan grimaced. She always did that when she spoke about how lovely someone was.

'How's the tucker?'

'Very good', she replied, as if surprised. 'They gave me meat and casserole and a soup and a lovely caramel sweet.' Pausing in her description, she turned to Mum and said, 'Gladdie, do you remember I used to make a sweet like that?'.

'Yes, that's right', Mum replied. She looked tired.

'One of the good old recipes, eh?' I commented.

'Yes, and very nice.'

'Well, I'm glad they're treating you right, Nan. I brought some more of Arthur's story to read. Do you want to listen, or are you too tired?'

'Read it!'

'You sure you're not too tired?'

'No.' She folded her hands in her lap and leaned back against the pillows, waiting for me to begin. It was a long chapter, so I only read her half. As I read, Nan oohed and aahed in the appropriate places.

'I'll read you the rest tomorrow night', I said.

'That's a good idea.'

'You look tired, do you want to sleep now?'

'I'd better. They're putting that thing down my throat tomorrow.'

'I know, that's why you need a good sleep, you want to be strong for tomorrow.'

'You won't feel anything', Mum reassured her. 'They give you some medicine so you don't feel it go down.'

'Yes, you told me before.'

'I'll see you tomorrow, Nan', I said. 'I've still got that pencil case you gave me.'

She smiled. 'Those old papers in it will come in handy', she chuckled. Nan was speaking in code. She never liked Mum to know how much money she'd given anyone.

We had to wait a day for the results of the bronchoscopy. I decided to spend the day at Jill's because it was near the hospital, and I wanted to be on the spot when we got the news.

We were fortunate, Mum's dream had been fulfilled and our sister Helen was doing her residency at the hospital, so she was able to get the results for us straight away. We had a doctor in the family at last.

Mum and I were sitting at the kitchen table having some lunch when Jill came back from answering the front door.

'I think you should prepare yourself', she said to Mum. 'Helen's just come home in tears, she's in her room. You'd better go and see her.'

Mum and I rushed into Helen's room. Jill took all the children into the lounge-room and involved them in a game of snakes and ladders.

Helen sat on the edge of her bed, crying. When she saw us, she murmured, 'She's got a tumour. I suspected it all along, but I guess I was hoping it was something else.'

'Is it malignant?' Mum asked.

'Well, at her age and with her history of heavy smoking, of course it'll be malignant!' said Helen crossly. She was very upset.

Mum began to cry. I couldn't find any tissues, so I passed her a towel.

'How long?' I asked.

'They haven't completed the tests, yet. We won't know until tomorrow afternoon. Depends on if it's a slow-growing tumour or a fast-growing one, but as she's already symptomatic, it must be pretty large.'

I told the news to Jill, then made a cup of tea for Mum and Helen.

Mum gulped hers down and then went into Jill's room to cry on her own.

I left her for half an hour, then went in to find her still sprawled across the bed, crying her heart out.

'She's expecting me this afternoon', Mum sobbed when she saw me. 'I told her I'd go down.'

'Would you like me to go?'

'Are you sure you'll be all right?'

'I'll be all right.'

'You go then. I'll probably be okay by tonight, I'll see her then. Would Helen like to go with you.'

'I'll ask her.'

It took us only five minutes to reach the hospital. As we mounted the stairs that led to Nan's ward, Helen began to cry again.

'You going to be okay?' I asked.

'I'll be all right', she murmured.

When we reached Nan's bed, she was lying on her back in a little short hospital gown. She was very hot, and, under the oxygen mask, her breathing was laboured.

The doctor was there. When he saw Helen, he said, 'We think when we put the bronchoscope down that some of the bacteria may have spilled over into her bloodstream, the danger is septicaemia'.

Helen held Nan's hand, we both sat down beside her bed. Nan seemed to be slipping in and out of consciousness. It was too much for Helen, tears began to flow silently down her cheeks. She reached for a tissue, and just as she was wiping her face, Nan opened her eyes and said, 'What's wrong, Helen?'.

'Nothing', she replied, and looked away. Nan looked straight at me. I looked back. I was only confirming what she already knew inside.

We stayed for a few hours and left when Nan was asleep.

The rest of the results came through the following afternoon and Mum was called to the hospital to discuss them. I visited again that night. To my surprise, I found Nan sitting up in bed, eating tea. She looked much better.

'Gosh, that looks like a good meal', I said as I walked up to her bed. It seemed such a silly thing to say, somehow. She was dying, oughtn't I to say something much more profound?

'It's lovely, Sally', Nan smiled. 'There's so much here I can't eat it all.'

I glanced at Mum, she looked like she was holding together. Nan ignored both of us and went on eating. I looked from one to the other. Silence.

Something was going on. No one was saying anything. Finally, I said, 'So, what's happening?'. Nan began to eat a little faster.

Mum said defensively, 'She's coming home for the weekend, then she's coming back on Monday to start radiotherapy'.

Mum could tell by the look on my face I didn't approve. She looked down at her feet.

'How do you feel about that, Nan?' I asked.

'Ooh, you know me, Sally. I'm frightened, I'd rather do without it.' She shrugged her shoulders and looked at Mum. It was a gesture of confusion.

'You'll be able to breathe better if you have it', said Mum firmly.

'Why does she have to have it?' I asked.

'Oh, Sally', said Mum crossly, 'she's only scared because it's an unknown quantity. The doctors said it will help.'

And people always think doctors know best, I thought angrily.

'What do you think, Nan?' I asked her. She shook her head. 'Do you know what they do to you?'

'No'.

I was sure the doctor must have told her, but I tried to explain as simply as possible about the machine and the rays and the benefits that it could have.

When I'd finished, Mum said, 'She should at least try it, Sally'.

'Do you want to try it, Nan?' I asked.

'I'm frightened of it, Sally. Glad told the doctors my legs are weak. I can't get round. I don't know. Helen says I should have it. She's a doctor, I suppose she should know.'

'Well, Nan', I sighed, 'if that's what you want, then try it once. But if you don't like it, you tell 'em so, you stick up for yourself. If you don't like it, you tell them, no more!'

'I don't think I should try it at all', she replied.

I agreed with her whole-heartedly, but I could see Mum was under pressure from all sides and I didn't want to make it harder for her, so I said nothing.

'Try it once', Mum encouraged. 'Then, if you don't like it, I won't make you have any more.'

'Promise?'

'Promise.'

After that, we laughed and talked and joked for over an hour about old times. We laughed about the way Nan hid money under the mattress and the times she'd tried to feed Curly at the wrong end. We talked about the cool drink man and how, if the lawnmower man didn't come soon, the grass would be so high we wouldn't be able to see the house.

Finally, Mum said, 'Well, we'd better go now. It's getting late.'

'Are you going too, Sally?' Nan asked. She gave me one of her looks, I knew she wanted to talk to me alone.

'I have to go now, Nan', I told her, 'but I promise you that we are going to have a good talk over the weekend'.

That evening, Mum and I had a talk. We were both feeling very emotional, it was difficult for either of us to be rational about anything. Our main difference of opinion was whether Nan should have treatment or not. I was totally against it because I felt Nan was more afraid of hospitals than dying. Mum felt it could be a good thing, because the doctors had said it could give Nan another six months, though they couldn't guarantee this.

I was also feeling very angry because no one had told Nan the complete truth about radiotherapy. She was under the impression it had no side-effects and that a nurse would hold her hand the whole time she was under the machine. Neither of these was true. It just confirmed the opinion Nan had inculcated in me over the years about doctors in general.

In desperation, I finally said to Mum, 'Do you know what Nan said to Margaret back in February?' Margaret was my mother-in-law.

'What?'

'She told her she knew she didn't have long to live. You see, she's been living with dying for a long time, now. It's the hospital she's frightened of.'

'How do you know she said that?'

'Margaret told me on the phone last night.'

Mum was taken aback at this revelation. 'I'm just trying to do the right thing', she sighed weakly.

'I know you are, but don't you see; it's Nan's business what happens to her body and no one else's. Let her do what she wants, not what we think is right.'

Nan was due to come out of hospital the following morning. As Helen was finishing her shift at ten o'clock, she said she would pick up Nan from her ward and bring her down to Jill's house. Mum was going to pick her up from there at eleven and come to my place for lunch.

By one o'clock in the afternoon, they still hadn't arrived. I began to worry, I wondered if Nan had suddenly taken a turn for the worse.

They finally arrived around one thirty. They both looked upset. Nan came in slowly and quietly, she sat down in the lounge-room and just looked at the floor. For some reason, a picture suddenly flashed through my mind of one of our old dogs just after he'd been hurt. I must be going crazy, I thought, shaking my head.

I went into the kitchen to put the kettle on and Mum followed me out.

'What's happened?' I whispered. 'Nan looks awful.'

'You won't believe it', Mum replied. 'It's terrible. I'm so upset.' I glanced at Mum, she was wearing the same look as Nan.

'What on earth has happened?' I asked forcefully. I knew something was terribly wrong.

Mum wiped a tear from her eye and said softly, 'You know Helen was supposed to pick her up from the ward at ten?'.

'Yes.'

'Well, when she went to the ward, Nan wasn't there.'

'You telling Sally what happened?' a croaky voice suddenly interrupted from the lounge-room.

'Yes dear', Mum replied.

'Come in the lounge and talk', I said. 'I think Nan wants us to talk in there.' I sat down opposite Mum and Nan and waited for them to tell me the story.

'What happened, Nan?' I asked, after we'd all sat in silence for a few seconds.

'It was terrible, Sally', she said. 'I'm never goin' back there. They treat you like an animal.'

I sat patiently while Nan wiped her mouth and her eyes with a large men's handkerchief. Then, I said, 'Didn't Helen pick you up?'.

'Oh yes, she came. I wasn't there! I had been there, I was all dressed, waitin' for her to come and get me when this man came in. He told me to hop in the wheelchair. "What for?" I said, "I'm goin' home!"'. "You have to see the doctor for a minute", he said.'

'Where did he take you?'

'Oh, to some room. I had to take all my clothes off, there wasn't even a nurse there, and they didn't even give me one of those hospital dresses to put on. They made me lie down on the bed, and then this man and that man started thumping my chest. It hurt real bad.'

'Was your doctor there?'

'No! They was all strangers, strange men comin' in one after the other, all thumping me round the chest. I had to lie there with nothing on, nothing to cover me!'

'You promised me you'd tell them no more medical students!' I growled at Mum.

'I did! I did! These weren't medical students, they were registrars!'

'They was all strangers', Nan interrupted. 'Strangers, Sally! There I am with nothin' to cover me. I felt 'shamed.'

'The bastards', I said angrily. 'Why on earth didn't you yell at them to stop, Nan?'

'I did! I begged them to stop, but, even though I was sobbing, they wouldn't leave me alone. I was hurtin' real bad. My chest feels so sore. There was one bloke with a beard and big hands, he really hurt me. He said he couldn't stop, because he had to find out what was wrong with me.'

'Bulldust! They told you what you had yesterday!'

'They cruel, Sally, real cruel. I said to one of them, "You just doin' this to me cause I'm black, aren't you?". He said, "Oooh, you mustn't think that. We're trying to help you." They wasn't tryin' to help me. They was only doin' that cause I'm black! That's what it was, Sal, it was my colour!'

I wanted to cry. She was so hurt. I was so angry I wanted to cry and scream and beat all those doctors up.

'That's why we're so late', Mum said. 'Poor Nan could hardly walk when Helen brought her down to Jill's.'

'Why did they do it, do you know?'

'Helen said she thinks it was a practice exam for the registrars. Apparently, they give them mock exams and they always choose patients with good medical signs. Doesn't that make you sick?'

'A practice exam, by God! The bastards, who do they think they are?'

'They shouldn't have done that to me, should they, Sally?'

314

'No, they shouldn't, Nan. You're right, you were treated like an animal. They should be ashamed of themselves. They wouldn't want someone treating them like that. Have you complained, Mum?'

'No.'

'Why not? God, they need a bomb put under them and I'm just the one to do it!'

'You're not to go down there, Sally', Mum said crossly. 'I know what you're like, you're a terrible stirrer, you'll get down there and you'll lose your temper. You'll make it hard for Helen, she has to work there.'

'No one's going to treat my grandmother like that!'

'I bet they don't do that to white people', Nan said.

'What are you doing?' Mum asked as I walked to the phone.

'I'm ringing the bastards up! This is only the beginning. By the time I get through with them, they won't know what hit them!'

'No, you're not!' Mum shouted as she leapt from her chair. She tore the phone from my hands and slammed it back down. 'I've never asked much of you', she said tearfully, 'but I'm asking this, leave it alone. For your sister's sake, let her finish her course. I will make sure that Helen complains and tells them what we think, but you are not to do it, Sally, I'm frightened of what you might say.'

My blood was boiling. 'But this is so inhumane. It should be on TV and in the papers! How many other old people have had the same experience? No one wants to rock the boat just because they're doctors. They're not God! That's how they keep their power, you know, they stick together like glue and count on the apathy of the silent majority!'

'I agree, Sally, I really do, but I'm thinking of Helen. She was very upset when she brought Nan home. It's her place to complain, not yours!'

I groaned out loud. When it came to issues like this, I was a person of action. Doing nothing was like Mum asking me to cut off my right arm. I glanced down at Nan, she was looking a little better. 'Nan', I sighed, 'you decide, what do you think I should do?'.

She thought seriously for a while and then she said slowly, 'They was wrong in treatin' me like an animal. They was brutes. I feel rotten inside about this, Sal, real rotten, but I think Glad is right. It's not Helen's fault, you shouldn't make it hard for her. She's the one workin' there, let her complain.'

'You sure that's what you want?'

'Yes. I'm not goin' back there, Sal. I'm not havin' that treatment. You don't know what they might do to me.'

'Well praise the Lord for that!' I said. 'You're better off without them, Nan.'

'Too right!'

'Doctors give you the shits, don't they?'

Nan chuckled. 'Ooh, don't make me laugh, Sally, it hurts my chest.'

Chapter Thirty-One

GOOD NEWS

The following Monday, Mum arrived early with Nan. We had decided that it was best if Nan stayed with us each day during the week while Mum was at work.

Nan brought her black bag laden with biscuits and lollies for the kids.

'I've got a surprise for you, Nan', I said. 'Paul and I cleaned out the sleepout.'

'What have you done with all that rubbish?'

'It wasn't rubbish! It's down in the shed. We've put a bed in there for you and a table, that way, you can have an afternoon sleep without the kids disturbing you.'

'Can I see it?'

'Yeah, come and look.'

'Ooh, doesn't it look nice!' she smiled as she peered through the bedroom doorway. 'Who'd have thought all that rubbish was covering up a nice room like this?'

'You've got the louvres, so you'll get plenty of fresh air if you want.'

'Yes, louvres are good. That's why I like the sleepout at Glad's place.'

When Mum came to pick Nan up that afternoon, she said, 'Well, had a good day?'.

'A lovely quiet day, Gladdie.'

'You ready to go home, then.'

Nan looked from me to Mum. 'I think I'll stay a few more days.'

Mum was aghast, 'You can't be here all the time, Sally's got a baby to look after. She can't have you as well.'

'I don't mind, Mum. She can stay.'

'It's settled, then', said Nan.

I took Mum out to show her the sleepout. Nan had already put her black bag in there.

'Are you sure this isn't going to be too much for you?'

'Naah, she's okay. And even if it is, won't be for long.'

'The doctors couldn't say exactly how long, could be six months,

316

nine months.'

'No, Mum, I think she'll go well before Christmas.'

'I don't like it when you talk like that. It's like you want her to die.'

'I suppose I do, in a way, but only because I think it's what she wants.'

'No one wants to die.'

'Maybe you get to the stage where you're happy to go.'

'You haven't talked like this to Nan, have you?'

'No.'

We walked back into the lounge-room.

'What do you think?' asked Nan.

'Very nice', replied Mum. 'When do you want me to pick you up?'

'Oh, make it Wednesday, that all right, Sally?'

'Yep. Whenever you like.'

When Mum came back on Wednesday, Nan told her she wasn't going home.

'This isn't your home', Mum argued, 'this is Sally's house. The dogs are missing you, and the cats.'

'Oh, they'll be all right.'

'Sally, tell her she has to come.'

'She can stay here if she wants to.'

'Now Nan . . . ', Mum began.

'Look, Gladdie', Nan interrupted. 'I wheel the baby when he's crying and I've done a bit of raking in the garden. Sally can't do it all. I'll stay here till the end of the week and then I'll come home for the weekend.'

I walked Mum to her car. 'Don't worry about her, Mum', I said, 'she's having a good time'.

'I can see that. What does she do all day?'

'Oh, nothing much. Just potters around the house. Eats like a horse. Has snacks during the night. I have to make her up a bowl of Weetbix and leave it out for her. In the morning, it's always gone.'

'She's always been a big eater.'

'She told me to tell you to bring her cane chair over.'

'She'll be moving in permanently if you're not careful.'

Nan kept her word and went home for the weekend. On Sunday, Mum rang.

'Hi, Mum, what's up? Nan not worse, is she?'

'No, she's as bright as a button. Look, I feel silly about this, but she's been on at me all weekend. I told her she could have a couple of days at your place and a couple at Jilly's, but she says she can't have her own room at Jill's. And she won't go to Ruth and David's for the same reason.'

'What does she want to do?' I laughed.

'She wants to know if she can live with you during the week and

317

come home to me on weekends.'

'Yeah, that's fine', I replied. 'I bet she's been giving you a hell of a time.'

'Well, you know what she's like.'

I heard a voice in the background and then Mum saying, 'Yes, it's all right, you can live with Sally'.

'You know, Mum', I said, 'I think she likes being here so she can complain about you'.

Over the next few weeks, our lives fell into a pattern that tended to revolve around Nan and the baby. Amber and Blaze loved having Nan live with us. Not only did they have an unlimited supply of goodies which were doled out generously, but they also had a captive audience before which they could perform all the television advertisements they had learnt by heart.

Every night, Amber read Nan a bedtime story. The stories were about Aboriginal children in the Western Desert. Nan loved to listen to them, and when Amber was finished reading, she'd tell about some of the things she'd done as a child.

Blaze was particularly horrified one night when she told him how tasty witchetty grubs were. 'Hmmn', she said, 'you gobble them up. They good tucker, real good tucker.' Blaze returned to me in the kitchen with a rather green look on his face.

'Did ya hear what she said?' he asked.

'I heard.'

'Have you ever eaten them, Mum?'

'No. But when you were a baby, you used to eat snails.'

'Aw yuk! Don't tell me any more!'

'All right', I laughed. A few minutes later, Blaze returned to the kitchen and whispered, 'Don't tell Nan about the snails. She might give me them instead of lollies.'

Nan and the children became very close. The three of them spent hours closeted away in her room. Even though Blaze was only five, he treated Nan like a real lady, worrying over where she was going to sit and whether she was warm enough. Whenever I wanted Blaze, I knew where to look, on the end of Nan's bed.

'Blazey', I said to him one day, 'Nan's tired. She's supposed to be having her afternoon sleep and you're in here talking.'

'She's all right, Mum', he answered confidently, 'aren't you, Nan? I'm telling her stories.'

'Do you want me to take him out?'

'Naah, he's good. 'Minds me of Bill when he was little. Leave him here.'

One afternoon, after his usual session with Nan, he strolled into the kitchen and garbled out a set of instructions in what, to me, sounded like a foreign language.

'What was that?'

'That's what Nan taught me', he said, smiling. He was obviously very proud of himself. 'You know how we speak English, well she doesn't. That's what she speaks.'

'I see. And what does it mean?'

'It means get me a drink! I'm still waiting, you know.'

I laughed and poured him out a drink of cordial. He gulped it down so quickly half of it went over his jumper. 'Gotta go now, Mum. That was just a practice. She's gunna teach me more.'

Then, one afternoon, just after we'd finished lunch, Nan said, 'You still doin' that book?'.

'Yep.'

'I dunno if it will do any good.'

'Maybe it won't', I sighed, 'but it's better than nothing'.

'Arthur's story was real good.'

'Yours could be like that.'

'Oooh, no, I got secrets, Sally. I don't want anyone to know.'

'Everything can't be a secret.'

'You dunno what a secret is.'

'I don't like secrets. Not when they're the sort of secrets you could use to help your own people.'

'It wouldn't make no difference.'

'That's what everyone says. No one will talk. Don't you see, Nan, someone's got to tell. Otherwise, things will stay the same, they won't get any better.'

'Course they won't talk, Sally. They frightened. You don't know what it was like. You're too young.'

'I'm not too young to understand. If you'd just tell me a little.'

'That's just it, you dunno what you're doin' writin' this book. Bad things might happen to you. If I tell you some things, next thing, you'll be tellin' everyone, I know what you're like.'

'You don't have to worry about me. I can take care of myself.'

Nan paused and looked at me shrewdly. She was quiet for a minute or so, then she added, 'Maybe I will tell you some things'.

'Really?' I couldn't believe it.

'I don't want to tell you everything.'

'You don't have to. I'll settle for anything, Nan, anything.' I was desperate.

'I can keep my secrets?'

'Yeah.'

'All right. I tell you some things, but that's all.'

'You want to start now?'

'Aah', she sighed, 'I'm tired now. Tomorrow.'

'Okay.'

When Blaze came home from pre-school that afternoon, the first thing he said to Nan was, 'C'mon, Nan, let's go to your room'.

Nan laughed. 'You just after more lollies', she said.

'No I'm not, Nan, honest. I want to tell you what I said for news.'

'Well, can't I hear your news, too?' I asked.

'Okay. I stood out the front, you know, Mum? I said, "I've got some good news this morning. I'd like you all to know I got a bit of blackfella in me." '

Nan burst out laughing and so did I.

'Why are you laughing?'

'We're not, darling, we're not', I smiled. 'That was good news. What did the kids say.'

'Ah, nothin', but later on, Stewart wanted to know which bit, and I didn't know what to say.'

That night, Mum made her usual phone call to check on how Nan was going.

'She's fine', I said. 'And I've got good news.'

'What?'

'She's agreed to talk.'

'You're joking.'

'Nope. She's going to start tomorrow. Mind you, she says she's still going to keep her secrets, but anything's better than nothing.'

'You know, I think it was because we had an argument over the weekend.'

'What did you argue about?'

'Oh, the same old thing, the past. I told her she never realised what a lonely little girl I was. I asked her to tell me about my grandmother and she said, "You don't want to know about her, she was black!".'

'What did you say?'

'I said I didn't care what colour she was. I never knew anything about her till Arthur started talking. I've always wanted a family and she deprived me of even knowing I had a grandmother.'

'You reckon she's been thinking about that, eh?'

'I dunno if she's been thinking about that or not. I started to cry, you see, couldn't stop. That upset her. Maybe she's been thinking about that.'

'Could be. Did you ask about your sister again?'

'Yes, of course I did, but she always gets so upset when I ask about that.'

'She didn't tell you anything, then?'

'Not a damn thing. You will tell me what she says, won't you?'

'Of course.'

The following morning, I set up my recorder and, after a cup of tea, we sat down to talk.

'What do you want me to say?' Nan asked.

'Anything. Just tell me what you want to. Maybe you could start with Corunna Downs.'

'Righto.' I waited patiently as Nan sat staring at the recorder. 'You sure that thing's on, I can't hear it.'

'You only hear it when I play something back.'

'Oh. You sure you'll get my voice on it?' I burst out laughing. 'What you laughin' at?'

'You! A few weeks ago, you were threatening to hide this recorder and now you're worried you won't get on it.'

Nan looked a little sheepish. 'Ah well, that's the way of it!' she chuckled.

DAISY CORUNNA'S STORY

(1900 — 1983)

My name is Daisy Corunna, I'm Arthur's sister. My Aboriginal name is Talahue. I can't tell you when I was born, but I feel old. My mother had me on Corunna Downs Station, just out of Marble Bar. She said I was born under a big, old gum tree and the midwife was called Diana. Course, that must have been her whitefella name. All the natives had whitefella and tribal names. I don't know what her tribal name was. When I was comin' into the world, a big mob of kids stood round waitin' for to get a look at me. I bet they got a fright.

I was happy up North. I had my mother and there was Old Fanny, my grandmother. Gladdie 'minds me of Old Fanny, she's got the same crooked smile. They both got round faces like the moon, too. I 'member Old Fanny always wore a handkerchief on her head with little knots tied all the way around. Sometimes, my granddaughter Helen 'minds me of her, too. They both short and giggly with skinny legs. Aah, she was good for a laugh, Old Fanny.

She loved panning for tin. All the old people panned for tin. You could see it lyin' in the dirt, heavy and dark, like black marbles. Old Fanny said I had good eyes, sometimes she took me with her for luck. We traded the tin for sugar or flour. They never gave us money.

Old Fanny went pink-eye* to Hillside one day. I never saw her again. They tell me she died on Hillside, maybe she knew she was going to die. She was a good old grandmother.

On the station, I went under the name Daisy Brockman. It wasn't till I was older that I took the name Corunna. Now, some people say my father wasn't Howden Drake-Brockman, they say he was this man from Malta. What can I say? I never heard 'bout this man from Malta before. I think that's a big joke.

Aah, you see, that's the trouble with us blackfellas, we don't know who we belong to, no one'll own up. I got to be careful what I say. You can't put no lies in a book.

Course, I had another father, he wasn't my real father like, but he looked after us just the same. Chinaman was his name. He was very tall and strong. The people respected him. They were scared of him.

---

* *pink-eye* — term used by Aboriginal people of north-west Australia, similar to the more widely known term *walkabout*. A period of wandering as a nomad, often as undertaken by Aborigines who feel the need to leave the place where they are in contact with white society, and return for spiritul replenishment to their traditional way of life. Can also simply mean a holiday, usually without leave.

He was Arthur's Aboriginal father, too. He was a powerful man.

My poor mother lost a lot of babies. I had two sisters that lived, Lily and Rosie. They were, what do they call it? Full blood, yes. I was the light one of the family, the little one with blonde hair. Of course, there was Arthur, but they took him away when I was just a baby.

I 'member Old Pompee, he was the old boy that looked after the vegetable garden, he told me my mother cried and cried when they took Arthur. She kept callin' to him like. Callin' to him to come back. The people thought Arthur was gettin' educated so he could run the station some day. They thought it'd be good to have a blackfella runnin' the station. They was all wrong. My poor old mother never saw him again.

Rosie and I was close. Lily was older than me. I spent a lot of time with Rosie. I was very sad when she died. She was only young. My mother nursed her, did everything for her, but we lost her. Good old Rosie, you know I been thinkin' 'bout her lately. She was what you call a good sport.

I'll tell you a story about our white man's names. My mother was in Hedland with the three of us when an English nursing sister saw her near the well. She said, 'Have you got names for your three little girls?'.

Mum said, 'No'.

She said, 'Well, I'll give you names, real beautiful ones. We'll call this one Lily, this one Rosie and this little one Daisy.' I was the short one of the family. We didn't mind being called that, we thought we were pretty flowers.

I haven't told you about my brother Albert, yet. He was light, too. He used to tease me. He'd chase me, then he'd hide behind a big bush and jump out and pretend he was the devil-devil. Oooh, he was naughty to me. They took Albert when they took Arthur, but Albert got sick and came back to the station. He was a good worker. He liked playing with me. He called me his little sister.

They was a good mob on Corunna. A real good mob. I been thinkin' 'bout all of them lately. There was Peter Linck, the well-sinker. I think he was German, he lived at the outcamp. He had Rosie, not my sister Rosie, another one. Then there was Fred Stream, by jingoes, there was a few kids that belonged to him. He had Sarah, her children were really fair, white blackfellas, really.

Aah, that colour business is a funny thing. Our colour goes away. You mix us with the white man, and pretty soon, you got no blackfellas left. Some of these whitefellas you see walkin' around, they really black underneath. You see, you never can tell. I'm old now, and look at me, look at the skin on my arms and legs, just look! It's goin' white. I used to be a lot darker than I am now. I don't know what's happened. Maybe it's the white blood takin' over, or the medicine they gave me in hospital, I don't know.

The big house on Corunna was built by the natives. They all worked together, building this and building that. If it wasn't for the natives, nothing would get done. They made the station, Drake-Brockmans didn't do it on their own.

At the back of the homestead was a big, deep hole with whitewash in it. It was thick and greasy, you could cut it with a knife. Us kids used to mix the whitewash with water and make it like a paint. Then we'd put it all over us and play corroborees. Every Saturday afternoon, we played corroboree. We mixed the red sand with water and painted that on, too. By the time we finished, you didn't know what colour we were.

I 'member the kitchen on Corunna. There was a tiny little window where the blackfellas had to line up for tucker. My mother never liked doin' that. We got a bit of tea, flour and meat, that was all. They always rang a bell when they was ready for us to come. Why do white people like ringin' bells so much?

Every morning, they woke us up with a bell. It was only 'bout five o'clock, could have been earlier. We all slept down in the camp, a good way from the main house. Every morning, someone would light a lamp, walk down into the gully and ring a bell. When I was very little, I used to get frightened. I thought it was the devil-devil come to get me.

There was a tennis court on Corunna. Can you 'magine that? I think they thought they were royalty, puttin' in a tennis court. That's an Englishman's game. They painted it with whitewash, but it didn't stay white for long, I can tell you. I had a go at hitting the ball, once. I gave up after that, it was a silly game.

I saw plenty of willy-willies up there and cyclones, too. By jingoes, a cyclone is a terrible thing! When one was coming, my mother hid me. I wasn't allowed to move. She was worried I might get killed. Get taken away by the wind. I was only small. I 'member one time we hid in the kitchen, when my mother wasn't looking, I sneaked up to the window and peeked out. You should have seen it! There was men's hats, spinifex, empty tanks, everything blowin' everywhere. It's a funny thing, but those old tanks always ended up settlin' on the tennis court.

There was a food store on Corunna. It had tin walls, tin roof and a tiny window near the top covered with flywire. You wouldn't believe the food they had in there, sacks of apricots, potatoes, tobacco, everything. It makes my mouth water just thinkin' about it. When it was siesta time, the other kids used to lift me up and poke me through the window. I'd drop down inside as quiet as a mouse when the cat's after him. Then I'd pick up food and throw it out the window. If they heard someone coming, they'd cough, then run away. I'd hide behind the sacks of potatoes and wait for them to come back for me. I had a good feed on those days.

The people were really hungry sometimes, poor things. They didn't get enough, you see. And they worked hard. You had to work hard, if you didn't do it, then they call the police in to make you work hard. When things was like that, one of the men would put me through the window again. I suppose I should feel bad about stealin' that food. Hunger is a terrible thing.

Aah, you see, the native is different to the white man. He wouldn't let a dog go without his tea.

Of course, the men all wanted their tobacco as well. The white man called it Nigger Twist. It was a twist like a licorice, only thicker. It's terrible, when you think about it, callin' something like that Nigger Twist. I mean, we all called it that because we thought that was its name.

Sometimes, we'd pinch the eggs the chooks lay in the hay shed. Aah, that old hay shed, it's kept a lot of secrets. Now there was plenty of stockmen up North, then, and they all wanted girls. We'd be hearin' all this noise in the hay shed, the hay'd be goin' up and down, the hens'd be cluckin', the roosters crowin'. Then, by and by, out would come a stockman and one of the girls. They'd be all covered in hay. 'We just bin lookin' for eggs', they'd say.

There was a government ration we used to get now and then. It was a blanket, we all called it a flag blanket, it had the crown of Queen Victoria on it. Can you imagine that? We used to laugh about that. You see, we was wrappin' ourselves in royalty.

Then there was a mirror and a comb, a cake of soap and a couple of big spotted handkerchiefs. Sometimes, the men were lucky and got a shirt, the women never got anything.

I 'member my mother showin' me a picture of a white woman, she was all fancied up in a long, white dress. 'Ooh, Daisy', she said, 'if only I could have a dress like that'. All the native women wanted to look like the white women, with fancy hairdos and fancy dresses.

Later, my mother learnt how to sew, she was very clever. She could draw anything, she loved drawing. She drew pictures in the sand for me all the time. Beautiful pictures. Maybe that's where you get it from, Sally.

We were cunning when we were kids. There was a big water trough on Corunna, it was used for the animals, even the camels had a drink from it. Mrs Stone always warned us not to muck around in the trough. We'd wait till she was sleeping, then we'd sneak down to the garden and dive in the trough. It was slimy and there was a lot of goona* in the water, but we didn't care. I 'member holding my breath and swimming under the water. I looked up and I could see the faces

* *goona* — faeces.

of all the animals lookin' down at me as if to say, 'What are you doin'
in our water, child?'.

They had a good cook on Corunna for a while, Mrs Quigley. She
was a white woman, a good woman. I think Nell and Mrs Stone, the
housekeeper, were a bit jealous of her. Nell was Howden's first white
wife. They were real fuddy-duddies and didn't like her talkin' to anyone.

The cook had a little girl called Queenie and it was my job to look
out for her. We were 'bout the same age, ooh, we had good times!
We'd laugh and giggle at anythin'. We were giggling gerties, that's
what Queenie's mother used to call us.

I taught Queenie all about the bush. We'd go out after a big rain.
Sometimes, the rain was so heavy up North, it hurt when it hit you.
That's the kind of rain you get in the wet. One day, the place would
be desert, the next day, green everywhere. Green and gold, beautiful,
really. I'd take Queenie out into the bush and we'd watch a little seed
grow. 'Look now', I'd say to Queenie, 'it's getting bigger'. By the time
we finished lookin', that seed'd be half an inch long.

In the evenings, I liked to sit and watch the kangaroos and other
animals come down and drink at the trough. The crows and the birds
would have a drink, too, and do a bit of goona. I just liked to sit
and watch them all. Course, you know, Corunna has blue hills all round
it. They always looked soft that time of night. Sometimes, my mother
would sit and watch, too. We knew how to count our blessings, then.

I was a hard worker on Corunna. I been a hard worker all my life.
When I was little, I picked the grubs off the caulies and cabbages at
the back of the garden. I got a boiled sweet for that. Now the blackfellas
weren't allowed to pick any vegetables from the garden. You got a
whipping if you were caught. Old Pompee, he used to sneak us tomatoes.
And so he should have, he was eatin' them himself.

We all loved the orphaned lambs. We were their mother and their
father. We fed them with a bottle with a turkey feather stuck in it.
There was one lamb I fed, dear little thing she was, she was blind.
She kept bumpin' into the fence and the other lambs. Poor thing.
I was so upset I told cook about it and she told me this story.

'You know, Daisy, when I was a young child in Sydney, I had very
bad eyesight. One day, an old lady came to visit us and she asked
my mother if she could have a go at curing me. Mother said yes. They
sat down and put a single grain of sugar in each eye. Ooh, it hurt!
I cried and cried, but pretty soon, I could see. I'll give you some sugar,
you try that with your lamb.'

I did what she said, and pretty soon, that lamb's eyes were watering
all over the place. Next thing I knew, it was runnin' around like all
the other lambs, not bumpin' into anything. She was a wise woman,
that cook.

Aah, we played silly games when we were kids. I always played with
Rosie and Topsy. That Topsy, she was one of a kind, I tell you. One

day, Mrs Stone gave her a cake of soap and told her to take a bath. You know what she did? She threw the soap back and said, 'I'm not takin' no bath!'. Can you 'magine cheekin' a white woman like that? Aah, she was great fun, old Topsy.

There was a creek that cut across Corunna in the wet. We loved swimming in it and catching fish. They were like sardines, we threw them on the hot ashes and then gobbled them up. They were nice, but you had to be careful of the bones.

All sorts of wild fruit grew along the creek. There was a prickly tree with fruit like an orange, but with lots of big seeds in it. You could suck the seeds. Then there was another one shaped like a banana, that was full of seeds, too. You ate the flesh and spat out the seeds. There wasn't much food in that one, just juice. There was another prickly tree that had yellow flowers like a wattle, wild beans grew off that tree. When they swelled up, we picked them and threw them in the ashes. They were good.

The best one of all was like a gooseberry bush. Aah, if you could find a patch of that, no one saw you, you just stayed there and ate. You could smell those ones a good way away, they smell like a ripe rockmelon. We'd sniff and say, 'Aah, something ripe in there, somewhere'. We'd lift up all the bushes looking for them, they were only tiny. When we found them, we'd say, 'Hmmmn, mingimullas, good old mingimullas'. I never tasted fruit like those mingimullas. They had soft green leaves like a flannel, ooh, they were good to eat.

There was another tree we used to get gum from to chew. It grew on little white sticks. We'd collect it and keep it in a tin. It went hard, like boiled lollies. You know, jubes always 'mind me of that gum. Perhaps that's why I like jubes.

Rosie and I were naughty. We'd pinch wild ducks' eggs and break up their nests. And we'd dig holes to get lizards' eggs. We could tell where the lizards had covered up their eggs. We'd dig them all out, get the eggs and bust them. Those poor creatures. They never harmed us and there we were, breakin' up their eggs. We're all God's creatures, after all.

Rosie and I used to catch birds, too. We'd get a bit of wire netting and make a cage, then we'd take it down the creek and throw wheat around. We kept the cage a little bit lifted up and we tied a long bit of string to the wood underneath.

You should have seen all the cockies, they loved wheat. When there was a big mob of them, we'd pull the string, down would come the cage and we would have them trapped. Trouble was, we couldn't do anything with them, they kept biting us. In the end, we let them go. We did silly things in those days.

When I got older, my jobs on Corunna changed. They started me working at the main house, sweeping the verandahs, emptying the toilets, scrubbing the tables and pots and pans and the floor. In those days, you scrubbed everything. In the mornings, I had to clean the hurricane lamps, then help in the kitchen.

There were always poisonous snakes hiding in the dark corners of the kitchen. You couldn't see them, but you could hear them. Sssss, ssssss, ssssss, they went. Just like that. We cornered them and killed them with sticks. There were a lot of snakes on Corunna.

Once I was working up the main house, I wasn't allowed down in the camp. If I had've known that, I'd have stayed where I was. I couldn't sleep with my mother now and I wasn't allowed to play with all my old friends.

That was the worst thing about working at the main house, not seeing my mother every day. I knew she missed me. She would walk up from the camp and call, 'Daisy, Daisy', just like that. I couldn't talk to her, I had too much work to do. It was hard for me, then. I had to sneak away just to see my own family and friends. They were camp natives, I was a house native.

Now, I had to sleep on the homestead verandah. Some nights, it was real cold, one blanket was too thin. On nights like that, the natives used to bring wool from the shearing shed and lay that beneath them.

I didn't mind sleeping on the verandah in summer because I slept near the old cooler. It was as big as a fireplace, they kept butter and milk in it. I'd wait till everyone was asleep, then I'd sneak into the cooler and pinch some butter. I loved it, but I was never allowed to have any.

Seems like I was always getting into trouble over food. I'm like a lamb that's never been fed. I 'member once, Nell asked me to take an apple pie to the house further out on the station. Nell's real name was Eleanor, but everyone called her Nell. Anyway, I kept walkin' and walkin' and smellin' that pie. Ooh, it smelled good. I couldn't stand it any longer, I hid in a gully and dug out a bit of pie with my fingers. It was beautiful. I squashed the pie together and tried to make out like it was all there. Hmmmnnn, that was good tucker, I said to myself as I walked on.

When I gave the pie to Mrs Stone, I had to give her a note that Nell had sent as well. If I had have known what was in that note, I'd have thrown it away. It said, if any part of this pie is missing, send the note back and I will punish her.

Mrs Stone looked at the note, then she looked at the pie, then she said, 'Give this note back when you go'. I did. And, sure enough, I got whipped with the bullocks cane again.

Nell was a cruel woman, she had a hard heart. When she wasn't whippin' us girls with the bullocks cane for not workin' hard enough, she was hittin' us over the head. She didn't like natives. If one of us was in her way and we didn't move real quick, she'd give us a real hard thump over the head, just like that. Ooh, it hurt! White people are great ones for thumpin' you on the head, aren't they? We was only kids.

Aah, but they were good old days, then. I never seen days like that ever again. When they took me from the station, I never seen days like that ever again.

They told my mother I was goin' to get educated. They told all the people I was goin' to school. I thought it'd be good, goin' to school. I thought I'd be somebody real important. My mother wanted me to learn to read and write like white people. Then she wanted me to come back and teach her. There was a lot of the older people interested in learnin' how to read and write, then.

Why did they tell my mother that lie? Why do white people tell so many lies? I got nothin' out of their promises. My mother wouldn't have let me go just to work. God will make them pay for their lies. He's got people like that under the whip. They should have told my mother the truth. She thought I was coming back.

When I left, I was cryin', all the people were cryin', my mother was cryin' and beatin' her head. Lily was cryin'. I called, 'Mum, Mum, Mum!'. She said, 'Don't forget me, Talahue!'.

They all thought I was coming back. I thought I'd only be gone a little while. I could hear their wailing for miles and miles. 'Talahue! Talahue!' They were singin' out my name, over and over. I couldn't stop cryin'. I kept callin', 'Mum! Mum!'

I must have been 'bout fourteen or fifteen when they took me from Corunna. First day in Perth, I had to tidy the garden, pick up leaves and sweep the verandahs. Later on, I used an old scythe to cut the grass. All the time, I kept wonderin' when they were goin' to send me to school. I saw some white kids goin' to school, but not me. I never asked them why they didn't send me, I was too 'shamed.

Funny how I was the only half-caste they took with them from Corunna. Drake-Brockmans left the others and took me. Maybe Howden took me 'cause I was his daughter, I don't know. I kept thinkin' of my poor old mother and how she thought I was gettin' educated. I wanted to tell her what had happened. I wanted to tell her all I was doin' was workin'. I wasn't gettin' no education. How could I tell her, I couldn't write. And I had no one to write for me.

It wasn't the first time I'd been in Perth. I'd been there before with the first wife, Nell. Now I was with the second wife, Alice. Nell had died. When I'd been there before, I'd had to look after Jack and Betty, they were the children. I was only a kid myself. I was 'bout ten and Jack was 'bout six, I can't remember how old Betty was. We was all kids, but I had to do the work.

Aah, she was a hard woman. She was hard on her own kids, too. She bossed Howden around. He didn't step out of line with Nell around. She was a suspicious type of woman. I don't think many people liked her. When I was in Perth with her, she didn't even give me a place to sleep. I had to find my own place. There was a big, empty trunk on the verandah of the house we were stayin' in, I climbed in there at night. At least, it kept me out of the wind.

You see, I went to Perth with Nell, and I came back. My mother would be thinkin' I'd come back this time, too. She'd be thinkin' it was like before, but it wasn't. They just wanted me to work.

We moved into Ivanhoe, a big house on the banks of the Swan River in Claremont. I was lookin' after children again, there was Jack and Betty, Judy, June and Dick. I was supposed to be their nanny. You know, like they have in England. I had to play with them, dress them, feed them and put them to bed at night. I had other chores to do as well. I never blamed the children, it wasn't their fault I had to work so hard. I felt sorry for them.

At night, I used to lie in bed and think 'bout my people. I could see their campfire and their faces. I could see my mother's face and

Lily's. I really missed them. I cried myself to sleep every night. Sometimes, in my dreams, I'd hear them wailing, 'Talahue! Talahue!', and I'd wake up, calling 'Mum! Mum!' You see, I needed my people, they made me feel important. I belonged to them. I thought 'bout the animals, too. The kangaroos and birds. And, of course, there was Lily, I wondered if she had a new boyfriend. I missed her, I missed all of them.

Alice kept tellin' me, 'We're family now, Daisy'.

Thing is, they wasn't my family. Oh, I knew the children loved me, but they wasn't my family. They were white, they'd grow up and go to school one day. I was black, I was a servant. How can they be your family?

The only friend I had then was Queenie's mother, Mrs Quigley. She was housekeeping for the Cruikshanks in Claremont. I used to sneak over and visit her whenever I could. She understood the North, she knew how hard it was for me. She never said much, but I knew she understood. I never stayed with her long, I was worried they'd notice I was missing. And, of course, you had times in those days when you had to be in. The blackfella couldn't live his own life, then.

Aah, Queenie's mother was a kind woman. She told a real good story. Sometimes, she'd tell me something funny to cheer me up.

I did all the work at Ivanhoe. The cleaning, the washing, the ironing. There wasn't nothing I didn't do. From when I got up in the morning till when I went to sleep at night, I worked. That's all I did really, work and sleep.

By jingoes, washing was hard work in those days. The old laundry was about twenty yards from the house and the troughs were always filled with dirty washing. They'd throw everything down from the balcony onto the grass, I'd collect it up, take it to the laundry and wash it. Sometimes, I thought I'd never finish stokin' up that copper, washin' this and washin' that. Course, everything was starched in those days. Sheets, pillowcases, serviettes, tablecloths, they was all starched. I even had to iron the sheets. Isn't that silly, you only goin' to lay on them.

The house had to be spotless. I scrubbed, dusted and polished. There was the floors, the staircase, the ballroom. It all had to be done.

Soon, I was the cook, too. Mind you, I was a good cook. I didn't cook no rubbish. Aah, white people, they got some funny tastes. Fussy, fussy, aaah, they fussy. I 'member I had to serve the toast on a silver tray. I had to crush the edges of each triangle with a knife. Course, you never left the crusts on sandwiches, that was bad manners. Funny, isn't it? I mean, it's all bread, after all.

I had my dinner in the kitchen. I never ate with the family. When they rang the bell, I knew they wanted me. After dinner, I'd clear up, wash up, dry up and put it all away. Then, next morning, it'd start all over again. You see, it's no use them sayin' I was one of the family, 'cause I wasn't. I was their servant.

I 'member they used to have real fancy morning and afternoon teas.

334

The family would sit on the lawn under a big, shady umbrella. I'd bring out the food and serve them. You know, I saw a picture like that on television. It was in England, they were all sittin' outside in their fancy clothes with servants waitin' on them. I thought, well fancy that, that's what I used to do. They must have that silly business in quite a few countries.

I 'member the beautiful cups and saucers. They were very fine, you thought they'd break with you just lookin' at them. Ooh, I loved them. Some of them were so fine, they were like a seashell, you could see through them. I only ever had a tin mug. I promised myself one day I would have a nice cup and saucer. That's why, whenever my grandchildren said, 'What do you want for your birthday?', I always told them a cup and saucer.

In those days, the Drake-Brockmans were real upper class. They had money and people listened to them. Aah, the parties they had. I never seen such parties. The ladies' dresses were pretty and fancy. I always thought of my mother when I saw their dresses. How she would have loved one.

I never liked Perth much, then. I was too scared. I was shy, too. I couldn't talk to strangers. People looked at you funny 'cause you were black. I kept my eyes down. Maybe some of those white people thought the cat got my tongue, I don't know. I'm not sayin' they was all bad. Some of them was nice. You get nice people anywhere. Trouble is, you get the other ones as well. 'Cause you're black, they treat you like dirt. You see, in those days, we was owned, like a cow or a horse. I even heard some people say we not the same as whites. That's not true, we all God's children.

Course, when the white people wanted something, they didn't pretend you wasn't there, they 'spected you to come runnin' quick smart. That's all I did sometimes, run in and out. Someone was always ringin' that damn bell.

I'm 'shamed of myself, now. I feel 'shamed for some of the things I done. I wanted to be white, you see. I'd lie in bed at night and think if God could make me white, it'd be the best thing. Then I could get on in the world, make somethin' of myself. Fancy, me thinkin' that. What was wrong with my own people?

In those days, it was considered a privilege for a white man to want you, but if you had children, you weren't allowed to keep them. You was only allowed to keep the black ones. They took the white ones off you 'cause you weren't considered fit to raise a child with white blood.

I tell you, it made a wedge between the people. Some of the black men felt real low, and some of the native girls with a bit of white in them wouldn't look at a black man. There I was, stuck in the middle. Too black for the whites and too white for the blacks.

I 'member when more native girls came into Perth as servants, they all looked to Nellie and me. Nellie worked for the Courthope family, they were good to her. The other native girls thought we were better than them because we had some white in us.

It was a big thing if you could get a white man to marry you. A lot of native people who were light passed themselves off as white, then. You couldn't blame them, it was very hard to live as a native. One of my friends married a Slav. I think that's how you call it. He was a foreigner, anyway. She came to say goodbye to me and Nellie. We was all cryin'. She'd promised her husband never to talk or mix

336

with any natives again. We didn't blame her, we understood. He wouldn't have married her, otherwise.

Nellie was from Lyndon Station, she was the daughter of the station manager, Mr Hack, but he never owned her. The Courthope family got her from Mogumber to be a servant in their house. Nellie was lucky, because she got treated kindly. She worked very hard like me, but they was good to her. She had a lovely room.

Aah, she was a laugh, that Nellie. She always wanted to be white. All those baths in that hydrogen peroxide and dyin' her hair red. Sometimes, she'd forget to take those baths and then she'd go black again.

You know, I been thinkin' a lot 'bout this. People mustn't say the blackfella has never done anythin' good for this country. I knew this black woman, Tillie, she was a servant and she joined the Salvation Army. She led a real good life, helpin' her own people when she could. She made me feel bad for not goin' to church on Sunday night when she could take me. I didn't like church. People there didn't understand what it was like for the natives.

I 'member the minister at Christ Church started up a sewing circle for all the native servants. We had to go down there and he'd give us a talk, then we'd sew. One time, he went on and on, tellin' us how we must save ourselves for marriage. It was very embarrassing, we couldn't look at him. Most of us had already been taken by white men. We felt really 'shamed.

One day, we were sittin' in the garden sewing when boys from Christ Church Grammar School came past. They laughed at us and called us awful names. Then, they threw pebbles at us. I never went back there, I was too 'shamed to say why.

Now Sal, this is just between you and me. I don't want Amber hearin' this, she's too young. You watch out for her after I'm gone. She's goin' to be very beautiful. All the men'll want her. Some men can't be trusted. They just mongrels. They get you down on the floor and they won't let you get up. Don't ever let a man do that to you. You watch out for Amber. You don't want her bein' treated like a black woman.

We had no protection when we was in service. I know a lot of native servants had kids to white men because they was forced. Makes you want to cry to think how black women have been treated in this country. It's a terrible thing. They'll pay one day for what they've done.

Aah, white people make you laugh the way they beat the native to teach him not to steal. What about their own kids? I seen white kids do worse than that and no one touches them. They say, he's sowin' his oats or that kid got the devil in him, but they not belted. Poor old blackfella do the same thing, they say you niggers don't know right from wrong and they whip you! I tell you, this is a white man's world.

The only one I had in Perth was Arthur. Now if I had've been livin' with my big brother Arthur, he'd have protected me. He was a strong man. I 'member I was standin' in the kitchen cooking when I heard this knock. I turned around and there's this big native lookin' through the flywire.

'Is that you, Daisy?' he said.

'Who are you?' I asked.

'Aah, you not Daisy', he said. 'She had real fair hair. Come on Mrs, you tell me where Daisy is.'

'What you want her for?' I wasn't gunna let him in the door.

'That's for me to know and you to find out', he said. Aah, I thought, he's got tickets on himself.

'You listen here', I growled at him. 'We don't like strange blackfellas hangin' round here. You better get goin' before the mistress comes home. She'll take a stick to you.' I was tryin' to frighten him, he was a big man.

'Don't you go gettin' uppity with me, Mrs', he said. 'Thinkin' you're better just 'cause you work for white people. I got every right to be lookin' for my little sister Daisy. I want her to know she's got a brother who's gettin' on in the world.'

I couldn't believe it. Can you 'magine that? This big, ugly blackfella was my brother.

'You Arthur?'

'Now how did you come by my name, Mrs?'

'You cheeky devil', I said, 'I'm your sister Daisy'. He just stood there. 'Well, come in', I said. I didn't want him out there clutterin' up the verandah.

'What did you dye your hair for?' he asked. 'You was the only one of us with blonde hair.'

'Don't be stupid. This is the colour of my hair!'

Cheeky devil, he pulled my hair. Maybe he 'spected the colour to come off. Maybe he thought I put boot polish on my hair, I don't know. 'By gee, you a devil!' I told him. I should have known he was my brother, I was fightin' with him, wasn't I?

It wasn't so bad after that. Arthur would come and take me out. Sometimes, he even took me in a car. Can you 'magine that? All us natives drivin' round Perth in a real car? Aah, he thought he was somebody, that Arthur. All the girls wanted him, then. He was the only blackfella they knew with a bit of money in his pocket. He was nice to them all, wasn't he cunning?

We always went to see the horses. We loved horses. One time, he took me to the Show. By gee, he was tough. He'd take on anyone. I said to him, 'Don't you get into no fights when you're out with me. It's not proper. I'll give you what for if you get silly.' You see, he loved showin' off, lived for it.

If he wouldn't settle down, I'd say, 'You just a silly old blackfella'.

He'd settle down quick smart after that. He didn't want any of those girls thinkin' he was old.

One day, he said to me, 'Daisy, don't talk to me like that when we out. I'm your brother, you got to show me some respect.' Hmmph, the way he carried on you'd think he was a white man.

When he didn't come, I missed him. We always had a good laugh together. Sometimes, he was too busy puttin' crops in to bother with me. He was a hard worker, he did it all on his own.

When he couldn't come to see me, he'd write. I felt real important, gettin' a letter with my name on it. Trouble was, I couldn't read. I couldn't have nothin' private 'cause I always had to get someone to read it for me.

Aah, he was a clever man. We had fights all the time, but I was proud of that man.

I hadn't seen Arthur for a long time when I had Gladdie.

Before I had Gladdie, I was carryin' another child, but I wasn't allowed to keep it. That was the way of it, then. They took our children one way or another. I never told anyone I was carryin' Gladdie.

Now how this all came about, that's my business, I'll only tell a little. Everyone knew who the father was, but they all pretended they didn't know. Aah, they knew, they knew. You didn't talk 'bout things, then. You hid the truth.

Alice bought me a cane pram to wheel Gladdie in. She gave Gladdie a doll. I kept Gladdie with me in my room.

Howden died not long after she was born. When I came home from hospital, he said, 'Bring her here, let me hold her'. He wanted to nurse Gladdie before he died.

After he died, I never had time for anything. I had Gladdie and the other children to look after. There were times when Gladdie ate so much she 'minded me of the little baby pigs runnin' round the station.

It was hard for me with her. Sometimes, she'd be cryin', cryin', and I couldn't go to her. I had too much work to do.

When Arthur saw her, he thought she was beautiful. I think he was jealous, he wanted her to belong to him.

Strange, isn't it, at one time, I was goin' to live with Arthur. It was before I had Gladdie, they said they didn't want me any more. Then, they changed their minds. Arthur told me he had a real nice whitefella for me to marry. After Gladdie was born, Arthur wanted us both to go with him. I wasn't allowed to go anywhere. I had to have permission and they wouldn't let me go. I knew Arthur would be good to Gladdie, she had him by the heart-strings. When it came to little ones, that Arthur was tender-hearted.

When Gladdie was 'bout three years old, they took her from me. I'd been 'spectin' it. Alice told me Gladdie needed an education, so they put her in Parkerville Children's Home. What could I do? I was too frightened to say anythin'. I wanted to keep her with me, she was all I had, but they didn't want her there. Alice said she cost too much to feed, said I was ungrateful. She was wantin' me to give up my own flesh and blood and still be grateful. Aren't black people allowed to have feelin's?

I cried and cried when Alice took her away. Gladdie was too young

340

to understand, she thought she was comin' back. She thought it was a picnic she was goin' on. I ran down to the wild bamboo near the river and I hid and cried and cried and cried. How can a mother lose a child like that? How could she do that to me? I thought of my poor old mother then, they took her Arthur from her, and then they took me. She was broken-hearted, God bless her.

When Gladdie was in Parkerville, I tried to get up there as often as I could, but it was a long way and I had no money. When I did get paid, Alice was always takin' money out that she said I owed her. It was a hard life. I always got Gladdie something nice to eat when I went up. She loved food, I think she gets that from me.

Parkerville wasn't a bad place, there was plenty of kids for her to play with and there was bush everywhere. I knew she'd love the bush. I used to take her for a bit of a walk, show her the birds and animals like. She was always real glad to see me. I knew she didn't want to stay there, but what could I do? It wasn't like I had a place of my own. It wasn't like I had any say over my own life.

It was during the thirties that they told Gladdie I might die. My cousin Helen Bunda was real sick. They asked me to give blood for her. I said yes. She belonged to me, I had to give blood, but I was real scared.

You never know what doctors are goin' to do to you. The silly buggers, they lost the first lot of blood they took, so they took some more. I was so weak I couldn't lift my head. I was that weak. I think I turned white with all the blood they took from me.

Helen died and I heard the doctors say, 'Doesn't matter, she was only a native'. Then, they looked at me and the nurse said, 'I think this one's going, too'. You see, they treat you just like an animal. Alice came and got me, she was very cross. She took me back to Ivanhoe and nursed me. She was a good bush nurse.

They brought Gladdie down from Parkerville to say goodbye to me. She looked real frightened when she saw me. I tricked all of them, I didn't die, after all. Pretty soon, I was up and doin' all the work again. That's the last time I give blood.

Helen had been a good old cousin. She was mean, though. She'd walk five miles to save a ha'penny. She was good with her hands. No one could sew the way she could. She'd had a hard life, work, work, work. They'd sent her to Moore River. I don't know if you ever heard of it, terrible place. She had three kids there and was made to leave them there and go back to service. I think all those kids died. It was a terrible place. No one wanted to go to Moore River, no fear. Poor old Bunda. I knew how she felt, it was the same with all of us.

When she died, I thought her things would come to me, I was her family. Turned out I got nothin', not a penny. The white family that she was workin' for got it all. They said she made a will leavin' it

341

to them. Bunda didn't know nothin' 'bout will-makin'. I don't think she could even write much. That family even come and asked me to give back the brooch she'd given me. The cheek of it. Bunda belonged to me, she'd given it me before she died and they come and asked for it back. 'That brooch doesn't belong to you now, Daisy', they said, 'it's ours now, you got to hand it over'. I felt very bitter 'bout that. Right inside my heart, I felt bitter.

Arthur finally got married in the thirties and I lost track of him. The Depression was on and I knew he'd be havin' trouble makin' ends meet. It was just as well Gladdie and I hadn't gone with him. We'd be only two more mouths to feed. He worked real hard, did anythin' to put food on the table. I think he lost his farm in the Depression. Those white people at Mucka, they were always after his farm. Funny, isn't it, the white man's had land rights for years, and we not allowed to have any. Aah, this is a funny world.

Couple of times, Arthur saw Gladdie at Parkerville. He had a real soft spot for her. Then he got too busy with his own family to see her. I think she missed him. She loved visitors.

The thirties was hard for everyone. You never threw anythin' away, there was always someone who could use it. It broke my heart to see men standin' round for food. Not just black men, white ones, too. If I knew someone who was hungry, I'd give them food. I gave away some of my clothes and shoes, whatever I could find. You can't be rotten to people when they in trouble, that's not the blackfella's way.

When Gladdie was 'bout fourteen, she left Parkerville. She'd been with me for holidays at Ivanhoe, and when I took her back, she didn't want to stay. You see, she found out she was havin' this new House Mother and she was a cruel woman. Gladdie was real frightened. I said to them, 'Can she come with me, she's almost grown up, now'.

They asked Gladdie if she wanted to leave Parkerville and she said, 'Too right!'. She didn't want to be stayin' with a cruel woman.

I took her back to Ivanhoe with me. I thought she could stay in my room, but, after two days, Alice said, 'Look Daisy, you can't keep her here. You'll have to find somewhere else for her to go.' I was real upset 'bout that.

They'd told me to leave before, reckoned they couldn't afford me. I had to go and work for Mrs Morgan. Then, a few years later, Alice begged me to come back. She said it was for good. That Ivanhoe was my home. I thought it would be Gladdie's, too. Aah, you see, promises, promises. The promises of a wealthy family are worth nothin'.

I found a family to take Gladdie in. They was religious people and they often took girls in. I knew they'd be good to her. She was real upset, she couldn't understand why they didn't want her at Ivanhoe.

One day, the Hewitts, that was their name, they said they couldn't trust Gladdie no more. 'She's been goin' to the pictures', they said. 'Pictures are a sin.' They said they didn't want her bein' a bad influence on the other kids. They packed her bags and said I had to take her.

I was livin' in my own place by then. Alice had kicked me out again. Aah, I was silly to believe her. She owed me back wages, got me to work for nothing, then kicked me out. I was just used up. I been workin' for that family all those years, right since I was a little child, and that's how I get treated. I left a good job to go back to Ivanhoe. I was silly. I should have known. When they didn't want Gladdie stayin' there, I should have known.

I reckon they wasted their money, it was all that high livin'. Everyone thought they was real important. Hmmph, I never seen any of their money. Howden, he promised Arthur and me money. He said he'd leave us some. Haa, that's how you get treated by rich people, real rotten. I think they get greedy, they live for the money. All Alice ever gave me was a couple of odds and ends and an old broom. After all those years, that was all I got. I hear now when you leave a job, you get a gold watch. That's better than a broom.

I 'member there was this beautiful picture of Fremantle that Alice had. She was sendin' a lot of stuff to auction houses, then. You see, they was goin' to live in Sydney. I asked if I could have that picture, but they said it was goin' to auction. There was some other pictures I asked for, but they made a big bonfire and burnt them. God will make them pay, they was religious pictures.

I thought, well, I got wages now, I'll buy my own things. Some people you're better off without.

My new job was a cook in a restaurant. All the soldiers and sailors loved to come in, because we served good tucker and I gave them plenty. I never cook rubbish. By gee, they could eat. They all wanted second helpings. I felt sorry for them. Some of them were only kids. Goin' to war like that, it's not right.

I shared a house with a good woman. She liked Gladdie, she was good to her. Gladdie and I was livin' together for the first time. She was makin' new friends and so was I. Pretty soon, I was goin' to the trots and other places. I really loved the horses. I'm like Arthur, I got a tender spot for all God's creatures.

Gladdie left school and Alice got her a job as a florist. They didn't want to take her, because she was a native. They were pleased they took her in the end, because everyone loved Gladdie.

Now you'd be thinkin' that, after all those years apart, we'd get on real good. Well, we didn't. Gladdie liked to do things her way and I liked to do things my way. We was fightin' and fightin'. By jingoes, we had some rows.

Gladdie was silly in those days, always wantin' to know her future. She didn't know what she was meddlin' with. You leave the spirits alone. You mess with them, you get burnt. She had her palm read, her tea leaves read, I don't know what she didn't get read. I never went with her to any of these fortune tellers. They give you a funny feeling inside. Blackfellas know all 'bout spirits. We brought up with them. That's where the white man's stupid. He only believes what he can see. He needs to get educated. He's only livin' half a life.

Gladdie didn't like some of my friends and I didn't like some of hers. Now maybe she was right 'bout some of my friends and maybe she wasn't, but I think it's true that you don't get many real true friends in this life. There's not many that'll stand by you in trouble. They the rare ones. Gladdie was always tellin' me I was too suspicious. She said I didn't trust her. Maybe I didn't. Maybe it was the men I didn't trust. Gladdie was innocent. She knew nothin' 'bout life. She didn't know what could happen.

One day, she just went off and got married. She was only twenty-one. I s'pose she didn't tell me because she knew I didn't like Bill. He was a drinker. I never liked men who were drinkers. What was she goin' and gettin' married for, anyway? She should have been home, lookin' after her mother.

Well, there's no use cryin' over spilt milk. What's done is done. They got a State Housing place in Mulberry Farm, that's near Beaconsfield. It wasn't a bad little place. I used to visit them, take them a bit of meat. There were some poor families there. Sometimes, I gave them meat, too. I don't 'member anyone sayin' thank you. Still, you can't let people go hungry.

Pretty soon, I was havin' grandchildren. You was the first, Sally, but you was so sick. Jilly wasn't like you, she was real healthy and she wasn't naughty. We never had to play with Jilly in the middle of the night.

I felt real sorry for Gladdie. She didn't realise how bad Bill was when she married him. He kept disappearing. She was worried sick. She never knew where he was. It was the grog, you see. The grog got the better of him. I'm not sayin' he was a bad man. He had a hard time during the war.

When Gladdie was carrying Billy, she got polio. There wasn't one family in Mulberry Farm that wasn't touched with polio. It was a terrible thing. I was worried you kids might get sick, too. That's when I moved in. Gladdie couldn't walk, she was stuck in bed. There was no one to look after you and Jilly. Bill didn't like me there. He was jealous. He wanted Gladdie to himself. What could she do? She needed someone to mind the kids. He was no good around the house.

Now, I tell you something, Sal, this is a sacred thing, so I better speak quiet. I helped your mother with that polio. You see, our family's always had powers that way. I don't want to say no more. Some things I'm tellin' you 'cause I won't be here much longer. That's something you should know.

Gladdie and Bill was offered a house in Manning. It was made from bricks and bigger than the one we was livin' in. Billy was a baby, then, and Gladdie was over the polio. I liked the new place. There was bush everywhere. You couldn't see nothin' but bush, and it was near the river. Aah, the birds and the wildlife, it was wonderful. Trouble was, it stank at night. We was near the swamp. That night air was bad for you, Sally. It made you sick. You should have been up North, you're no good in the cold.

Now, this is something I've told no one. You mightn't believe me. 'Member when we first moved there? Couple of nights, you came out on the back verandah and found Gladdie and me sittin' there, 'member we made you go away? You was always in the wrong place at the wrong time. Well, we was listenin' to music. It was the blackfellas playin' their didgeridoos and singin' and laughin' down in the swamp. Your mother could hear it. I said to her one night, 'I'm goin' down there and tell those natives off. Who do they think they are, wakin' all the white people up.' That's when Gladdie told me. She said, 'Don't go

346

down there, Mum, there's no one there, only bush'. You see, we was hearin' the people from long ago. Our people who used to live here before the white man came. Funny, they stopped playin' after your father died. I think now they was protectin' us. Fancy, eh? Those dear, old people. You see, the blackfella knows all 'bout spirits.

It was hard for us with Bill. He couldn't get away from the grog. We had no money. Grog's a curse. I'm glad you didn't marry a drinkin' man. I 'member when Bill used to see all those little red devils sittin' on the end of his bed. He kept beggin' me to take them away. I don't think he should have been takin' that medicine and drinkin' too. It made him worse. Aah, doctors don't know nothin'. They kept sendin' him home. He needed help. Gladdie and I couldn't help him.

There was rows all the time with Bill. You know all 'bout that, so I'll say no more. Just between you and me, Bill's parents didn't like natives. They said things 'bout Gladdie behind her back. They said she wasn't good enough for Bill. They blamed her for his troubles. It wasn't her fault, she was doin' the best she could.

'Member we used to keep you kids out the way? We didn't want to upset him. Any little thing upset him. We was frightened of what he might do.

I never told anyone this, but you was close to your father, you knew what he was like. I never even told your mother. I just kept it to myself. When Gladdie wasn't around, Bill used to call me a bloody nigger. I know he had a bad time in the war, but he shouldn't have called me that. No one should call anyone a bloody nigger. I kept quiet 'bout that 'cause I didn't want to cause trouble, but it hurt me real bad to hear him say that.

I was glad when he got real sick. It meant he couldn't touch Gladdie no more.

We was lucky we had those old people protectin' us. Bill could have killed us all.

One time, he asked me to hide the axe. It was the voices he used to hear. They kept tellin' him to kill us all, even you little ones. Bill said to me, 'Dais, hide the axe tonight. They want me to kill you all again and I'm afraid I'll do it.'

He wasn't a bad man, he was just very sick. Sometimes, he'd put himself in hospital. Sometimes, he'd keep himself awake all night, just pacing up and down, up and down. He really had to fight hard not to kill us. You see, there was a part of him that was real good.

When he died, I'd been expectin' it. I had that feelin' inside he might be goin' soon. I think Gladdie knew, too. We didn't talk 'bout it. You didn't talk 'bout things like that.

Course, you know little David found the body. Poor little bloke, he was only 'bout two, then. He thought Bill was asleep, he kept tryin' to wake him up.

David and you are a lot alike, Sal. He wasn't naughty like you, mind, but you both got a feel for the spiritual side of things. I 'member you played on your own a lot. Course, you wasn't on your own, was you? The angels was with you. Your mother was like that, and me, too, I s'pose. You see, you never know what's gunna get passed down. Our people was strong in the spirit.

I think Bill knew he was goin' to die. He made his peace. He knew where he was goin'. 'Member he played footy with Billy and David? Aah, it was a sad time. If it hadn't been for the grog and the war, he'd have been a different man. A good man.

Bill's parents were mongrels after he died. They didn't help Gladdie. They wasn't interested in you kids. We had no money, nothin' left to sell. We didn't know what we was goin' to do, we was desperate. Gladdie wrote to the Drake-Brockmans in Sydney to see if they could give us a loan. They said they was broke, too.

Lois was good to your mother, then. She gave us some money. Frank Potter was good to us. Turned out his heart was as big as his belly.

We was worried 'bout you kids, then. We thought the government might come and get you. They didn't like people like us rearin' kids with white blood in them. Seems like no one took account of the black blood. You belonged to us, Bill's family didn't want you. You kids loved the bush, you got things passed down to you from Gladdie and me. Things that you only got 'cause we was black.

I tried to stay out the way after Bill died. Gladdie could pass for anythin'. You only had to look at me to see I was a native. We had to be careful. 'Tell them they're Indian', I told her. 'You don't want them havin' a bad time.'

Your mother got work, and pretty soon, we had food on the table, good food. Bill drank money and we ate it.

There was men interested in Gladdie, she was a beautiful woman. She didn't want no one. All she wanted was you kids. Good men are rare in this world.

Well, Sal, that's all I'm gunna tell ya. My brain's no good, it's gone rotten. I don't want to talk no more. I got my secrets, I'll take them to the grave. Some things, I can't talk 'bout. Not even to you, my granddaughter. They for me to know. They not for you or your mother to know.

I'm glad I won't be here in body when you finish that book. I'm glad I'm goin'. You a stirrer, you gunna have a lot of talkin' to do. I can't stick up for myself, you see. It's better you do it. Look out for your mother, she's like me.

Aah, you've always been naughty. I'm not frightened for you any more, Sal, you'll be protected. I think maybe this is a good thing you're doin'. I didn't want you to do it, mind. But I think, now, maybe it's a good thing. Could be it's time to tell. Time to tell what it's been like in this country.

I want you grandchildren to make something of yourselves. You all got brains. One of you could be like Mr Hawke, Prime Minister, one day. I hope you'll never be 'shamed of me. When you see them old fellas sittin' in the dirt, remember that was me, once.

Aah, I'm tired of this world, now. I want to get on to the next one. I'm afraid I'll go before I'm ready, can you understand that? God's got a spot up there for me, I dunno what it's like, but it's a spot. Probably a bit of bush, eh? What do you think? Old Arthur'll be waitin' for me. We can have a good old fight. I bet he's causin' trouble up there.

I feel real tired, now, Sal, the fight's gone out o' me. I got no strength left.

Now you asked me 'bout the future. That's a hard question. I got no education, how can I answer a question like that? You think I'm a fortune teller, eh?

But I'll tell you what I'm wonderin'. I'm wonderin' if they'll give the blackfellas land. If it's one thing I've learnt in this world it's this, you can't trust the government. They'll give the blackfellas the dirt and the mining companies'll get the gold. That's the way of it.

I don't like this word Land Rights, people are gettin' upset 'bout it. I dunno what this word means. I've heard it on the news.

You know what I think? The government and the white man must own up to their mistakes. There's been a lot of coverin' up. Maybe they want us all to die off so no one'll talk. No use you goin' on at me, Sal, you can't blame us old ones for not wantin' to talk. We too scared.

Well, I'm hopin' things will change one day. At least, we not owned any more. I was owned by the Drake-Brockmans and the government and anyone who wanted to pay five shillings a year to Mr Neville to have me. Not much, is it? I know it's hard for you, Sal, hard for you to understand. You different to me. I been scared all my life, too scared to speak out. Maybe if you'd have had my life, you'd be scared, too.

Aah, I can't really say what will happen. I s'pose it don't concern me no more.

As for my people, some of them are naughty, they drink too much. Grog's a curse, I've seen what it can do. They got to give it up. They got to show the white man what they made of.

Do you think we'll get some respect? I like to think the black man will get treated same as the white man one day. Be good, wouldn't it? By gee, it'd be good.

Chapter Thirty-Two

THE BIRD CALL

When Nan finished telling me her story, I was filled with conflicting emotions. I was happy for her because she felt she'd achieved something. It meant so much to be able to talk and to be believed. But I was sad for myself and my mother. Sad for all the things Nan felt she couldn't share.

Although, there was one thing I had learnt; that had quite surprised me. Nan's voice had changed as she reminisced. She could speak perfect English when she wanted to, and usually did, only occasionally dropping the beginning or ending of a word. But in talking about the past, her language had changed. It was like she was back there, reliving everything. It made me realise that at one stage in her life it must have been difficult for her to speak English, and therefore to express herself.

But this, too, only made me even more aware of how much we still didn't know. My mind went over and over her story; every word, every look. I knew there were great dark depths there, and I knew I would never plumb them.

I felt, for Mum's sake, I should make one last effort to find out about her sister. So a few nights later, when Nan and I were on our own, I said, 'There's something I want to ask you. I know you won't like it, but I have to ask. It's up to you whether you tell me anything or not.'

Nan grunted. 'Ooh, those questions, eh? Well, ask away.'

'Okay. Has Mum got a sister somewhere?'

She looked away quickly. There was silence, then, after a few seconds, a long, deep sigh.

When she finally turned to face me, her cheeks were wet. 'Don't you understand, yet', she said softly, 'there are some things I just can't talk 'bout'. Her hand touched her chest in that characteristic gesture that meant her heart was hurting. It wasn't her flesh and blood heart. It was the heart of her spirit. With that, she heaved herself up and went out to her room.

I went to bed with a face full of tears and a mind full of guilt. I was so insensitive, sometimes. I should have known better.

The early morning brought some peace. I would never ask her another thing about the past. And I had hope. She hadn't extinguished my small shred of hope. Why, she'd even admitted that she was pregnant before she had Mum. That was such a big thing. For the moment, it would have to be enough. I stretched and shouted towards the ceiling, 'I'm not giving up, God. Not in a million years. If she's alive, I'll find her, and I expect you to help!'

One night later that week, Nan called me out to her room.

'What on earth are you doing?' I laughed when I found her with both arms raised in the air and her head completely covered by the men's singlet she was wearing.

'I'm stuck', she muttered, 'get me out'. I pulled the singlet off and helped her undress. It had become a difficult task for her, lately. Her arthritis was worse and cataracts now almost completely obscured her vision.

'Can you give me a rub?' she asked. 'The Vaseline's over there.' I picked up the jar, dobbed a big, greasy lump of it onto her back and began to rub. Nan loved Vaseline. Good for keeping your body cool and moist, she always told me. She had a lot of theories like that. I continued to massage her in silence for a few minutes.

'Ooh, that's good, Sally', she murmured after a while. As I continued to rub, she let out a deep sigh and then said slowly, 'You know, Sal . . . all my life, I been treated rotten, real rotten. Nobody's cared if I've looked pretty. I been treated like a beast. Just like a beast of the field. And now, here I am . . . old. Just a dirty old blackfella.'

I don't know how long it was before I answered her. My heart felt cut in half. I could actually see a beast in a field. A work animal, nothing more.

'You're not to talk about yourself like that', I finally replied in a controlled voice. 'You're my grandmother and I won't have you talk like that. The whole family loves you. We'd do anything for you.'

There was no reply. How hollow my words sounded. How empty and limited. Would anything I said ever help? I hoped that she sensed how deeply I felt. Words were unnecessary for that.

When I finished rubbing, I helped her into her nightclothes. This was no mean feat, there were so many. It was well into winter, now, and Nan was anxious about the cold. I pulled a clean men's singlet over her head, then a fleecy nightgown and a bedjacket. While she pulled a South Fremantle football beanie down over her head, I covered her feet with two pairs of woollen socks. After that, she wound two long scarves around her neck.

'Are you sure you'll be warm enough?' I asked sarcastically.

'I think you better help me into that cardigan', she answered after a second's thought, 'better safe than sorry'.

Once that was on, I pulled back the rugs and she rolled in on top of her sheepskin. As I passed her a hot water bottle, she said, 'Do you know what I did? I put a wool rug under my sheet, it'll keep out the draught.'

'Good', I smiled as I tucked her in. 'Do you want me to turn your heater on?' Often, she had it going all night.

'I'll do without it, takes the oxygen out of the air.'

'Okay. Remember when we were kids and you used to put all that newspaper between your sheets to keep warm?' Nan chuckled. 'We heard you every time you rolled over', I laughed.

'That's a good old standby, newspaper. Don't you ever forget it.'

'I won't.'

'Leave the light on tonight, it might help me sleep.'

'You usually have it off.'

'I know, but I can't sleep with it off, so I might as well try with it on.'

I had half closed the door when she suddenly murmured, 'Aah, Sal, you're too good to me, too good . . .'

'You're my grandmother', I replied quietly, 'how do you expect me to treat you?'.

She never answered. Her eyes were closed.

I went straight to bed myself after that. I curled up and pretended I was in God's womb. I felt so hurt. I wanted to contain the deep emotions that were threatening to swamp me. For the first time in my life, the darkness comforted me. I lay there in a tight little ball, thinking about Nan. I wondered why she couldn't sleep. I knew it wasn't her illness. It was a thing of the spirit. She was probably thinking back over her life. Pictures from the past were probably running through her mind. I prayed one of them wasn't a beast in a field.

When Nan was getting ready to go home that weekend, she said, 'You'll keep what I told you safe, won't you?'.

'Of course I will.'

'You liked it?'

'I thought it was real good.'

'You see, Arthur's not the only one with a good story.'

'He sure isn't!'

'I'll be back on Monday, bring you some goodies. Here', she squeezed my hand, 'buy the kids something'.

'You've got to stop giving me money', I protested.

'Come on, Nan', Mum called from the front porch, 'the dogs'll be hungry for their tea'.

'I'm coming', Nan replied crossly. Then, turning to me, she whispered, 'She's never worried about the dogs' tea before, Sally'.

353

'Well, she hasn't got you to feed them, now.'

'Do her good to do a bit of work for a change', Nan chuckled. She loved being in a position of power over Mum. Whenever Mum growled at her or tried to hurry her along, she would say, 'You speak to me like that again, Gladdie, and I'll move in with Sally for good. Then you'll be sorry.' Poor Mum couldn't win.

The weekend passed quickly. When Nan hadn't arrived at my place by ten o'clock Monday morning, I began to worry. The phone rang and I rushed to answer it.

'Sally?' It was Mum.

'What's wrong?'

'She's taken a sudden turn for the worse. The doctor says she can't be moved.'

'Is she conscious?'

'At the moment, she's slipping in and out.'

'I'm coming over.'

'Jill's coming, too.'

'Good.' I hung up. It'd come so suddenly. She'd been living with me for over six weeks. She hadn't seemed like someone who was dying.

From then on, Nan was confined to bed. Jill, Mum and I took four-hourly shifts so she was never alone. Bill and David came when they could. Bill was a great help with the lifting. And when Helen was off duty, she also came and sat with Nan.

Poor Helen, Nan would go on and on about how useless doctors were. It was a sensitive area. No one had the courage to disagree with her.

One night, Jill and I sat watching Nan sleep. Jill whispered, 'Doesn't seem fair, does it?'.

'How do you mean?'

'Well, we're only just coming to terms with everything, finding ourselves, what we really are. And now, she's dying. She's our link with the past and she's going.' I couldn't look at Jill. She sighed, 'With her gone, we could pass for anything. Greek, Italian, Indian . . . what a joke. We wouldn't want to, now. It's too important. It'd be like she never existed. Like her life meant nothing, not even to her own family.'

'We're all really changing. I know we don't talk about it, but it's there.'

'When this is over', Jill said, 'I'm going to stand up and be counted'.

I felt very close to Jill, just then. We both stayed there quietly watching as Nan peacefully slept. It was a promise. A promise from our spirits to hers. We would never forget.

I got sick after that. Mum and Jill reckoned it was emotional, it probably was. I was so sick I couldn't get out of bed without fainting. Paul's mother moved in to look after me and the children. I was very angry with myself for being sick. I felt I should be with the rest of my family. They were all struggling on.

The atmosphere had been electric over the past week. We were all physically exhausted. Some days, we walked around not saying anything, other days, we joked about nothing at all, every now and then, we fought. We all knew something more than Nan's body was dying. She was a symbol. Part of us was going, too. We couldn't explain it. It was just a time none of us understood.

Things finally came to a head and Mum asked Ruth, my brother David's wife, if she would mind doing the nightshift. Ruth was a trained nursing aide and had nursed many people with terminal illnesses. She was only too pleased to help. She'd wanted to all along, but knew we were all very sensitive, so had refrained from intruding.

It was Ruth, more than anyone, who understood Nan's fear of going before she was ready. They had little talks about it, during which Ruth would reassure her. Nan and Ruth had conflicted in the past, they were both stubborn, but as Ruth nursed her so tenderly, she came to mean a great deal to Nan.

When I was a little better, I began visiting Nan again. It was lovely to hear her say, 'Where's my nursie, is she still here? What would I do without her, Sally, she's so good to me.' It made me want to cry when she talked like that. I felt it was a victory that Nan could accept the love that Ruth offered. I felt so proud of Ruth. I hoped that, one day, I could do something special for her.

By the time Nan had been bedridden well over a week, I began to worry she might have a slow, lingering death. I knew she was concerned she might lose her mental faculties before dying. She'd always made me promise that if I noticed she was going a bit funny, I'd tell her.

One night, I confided my fears to Ruth.

'The doctors told us that, in the case of lung cancer, it could go to the brain. I suppose the longer it takes, the more likely it is to happen. Nan would hate that.'

'Do you think we should pray?' Ruth suggested.

'I pray every night.'

'No, I mean with her. It might help her to let go.'

'It might be a good idea, we'd have to ask her, couldn't force anything on her.'

We moved close to Nan's bedside and clasped her hands.

'Nan', Ruth said quietly, 'can you hear me?'. Nan nodded. 'Sally wants to talk to you, Nan.'

I squeezed her hand and then said gently, 'Nan, we were wondering if you would like us to pray for you. We would ask God to take you quickly if you like. You know how Ruth's told you you won't go before you're ready? Well, that's true. We won't pray unless you want us to. It's up to you.'

Tears slowly slid from under her closed eyelids. She lay quietly for a few minutes, then squeezed both our hands and said firmly, 'Do it. Please do it.'

I looked at Ruth. 'You do it', she said.

We bowed our heads. What was I going to say? I tightened my grip on Nan's hand, cleared my throat and said, 'God . . . you know this is about Nan. We really love her and we know you do, too. She's tired of this world, now, she's ready to go. We know you've got a good place up there. A big, old gum tree where she can sit and play her mouth organ. Arthur's waiting for her and the others. Please show your mercy and take Nan quickly?' When I finished, I couldn't see for tears in my eyes. Ruth was crying, too.

Nan squeezed both our hands and then gently let go. Within a few minutes, she was asleep.

The Silver Chain sister visited that afternoon. As I saw her to the door, she said, 'Your grandmother's changed. I think she's decided to die.'

'She has', I agreed. 'It won't be long, now.'

She grasped my arm and looked at me with pity in her eyes. 'You're wrong, dear', she said, 'I've seen this happen before, many, many times. They give up the will to live, but they don't die, because their bodies just won't let them. She has a very strong heart and a good pulse. It could be weeks.'

'That won't happen with her', I replied confidently. 'She'll be gone soon.'

The sister shrugged her shoulders sympathetically. 'Don't count on it, dear, you'll only be disappointed. There'd be a chance if her pulse was weak, but it's not. I think you should face up to the fact that this could go on for quite a while.'

The following morning, my phone rang very early.

'Hello', I said as I lifted the receiver.

'I heard the bird call.' It was Jill's voice.

'What bird call?'

'This morning, about five o'clock. I heard it, Sally. It was a weird sound, like a bird call, only it wasn't. It was something spiritual, something out of this world. I think she'll be going soon.'

After breakfast, I hurried over. There was an air of excitement about the place. The heaviness that we'd all been living under seemed to have suddenly lifted.

Mum was mystified about the bird call. I think she felt a little left out. Jill couldn't understand why Mum hadn't heard it, it'd been so loud and gone on and on.

When I walked into Nan's room, I couldn't believe my eyes, she didn't look sick any more. Her face was bright and she was propped up in bed, smiling. Something had definitely happened, but none of us knew what. Even Mum and Jill were happier and bustling around like their old selves.

356

'Nan, you look really good', I said in surprise.

'Feel good, Sal.'

I just stood there, smiling. She seemed so contented. Almost like she had a secret. I was desperate to ask her about the call, but I didn't know where to begin. I sat by the bed and patted her hand.

Just then, Mum popped in. 'Doesn't she look well, Sally', she said happily. 'Look at her face, it looks different.'

'Sure does.'

'Get me some toast, Gladdie', Nan said cheekily, 'I'm hungry'. Mum rushed out with tears in her eyes.

'Nan', I said slowly as she looked at me, 'about that call, you weren't frightened when you heard it, were you?'.

'Ooh, no', she scoffed, 'it was the Aboriginal bird, Sally. God sent him to tell me I'm going home soon. Home to my own land and my own people. I got a good spot up there, they all waitin' for me.'

A lump formed in my throat so big I couldn't speak, let alone swallow. Finally, I murmured, 'That's great, Nan . . .'.

Mum popped back in with tea and toast. ' 'Bout time', Nan chuckled. She ate a little and then lay back. 'Think I'll sleep, now', she sighed. We tiptoed out.

'Tell me about the call again', I said to Jill.

Jill's face was a mixture of fear, amazement and triumph as she described to Mum and I what happened.

'Wish I'd heard it', sighed Mum.

'Me too', I said enviously.

Later, I whispered to Mum, 'You know, Jill must be very special to have heard that call'. Mum agreed. We both wondered what Jill's future held.

Nan had a very peaceful day that day. A happy day. The intense feeling that had surrounded our house for so long was gone, replaced by an overwhelming sense of calm.

At five-thirty the following morning, Ruth rang for an ambulance. Nan had insisted on it.

As they wheeled her out, she grasped Mum's hand one last time. There was an unspoken message in her eyes as she whispered, 'Leave my light burning for a few days'.

They placed her in the ambulance and Ruth climbed in beside her. Mum stood silently watching, accepting Nan's choice. Knowing that this was her final sacrifice. She wanted our old family home free of death.

My phone rang at seven that same morning.

'Sally? It's Ruth. Nan died twenty minutes ago. It was very peaceful.'

'Thanks', I whispered.

I slowly replaced the receiver. I felt stiff. I couldn't move. Tears suddenly flooded my cheeks. For some reason, Jill's words from the previous day began echoing inside of me. I heard the bird call, I heard the bird call. Around and around.

'Oh, Nan', I cried with sudden certainty, 'I heard it, too. In my heart, I heard it.'